P9-DFI-250

Teen Titans

CHANGING OF THE GUARD

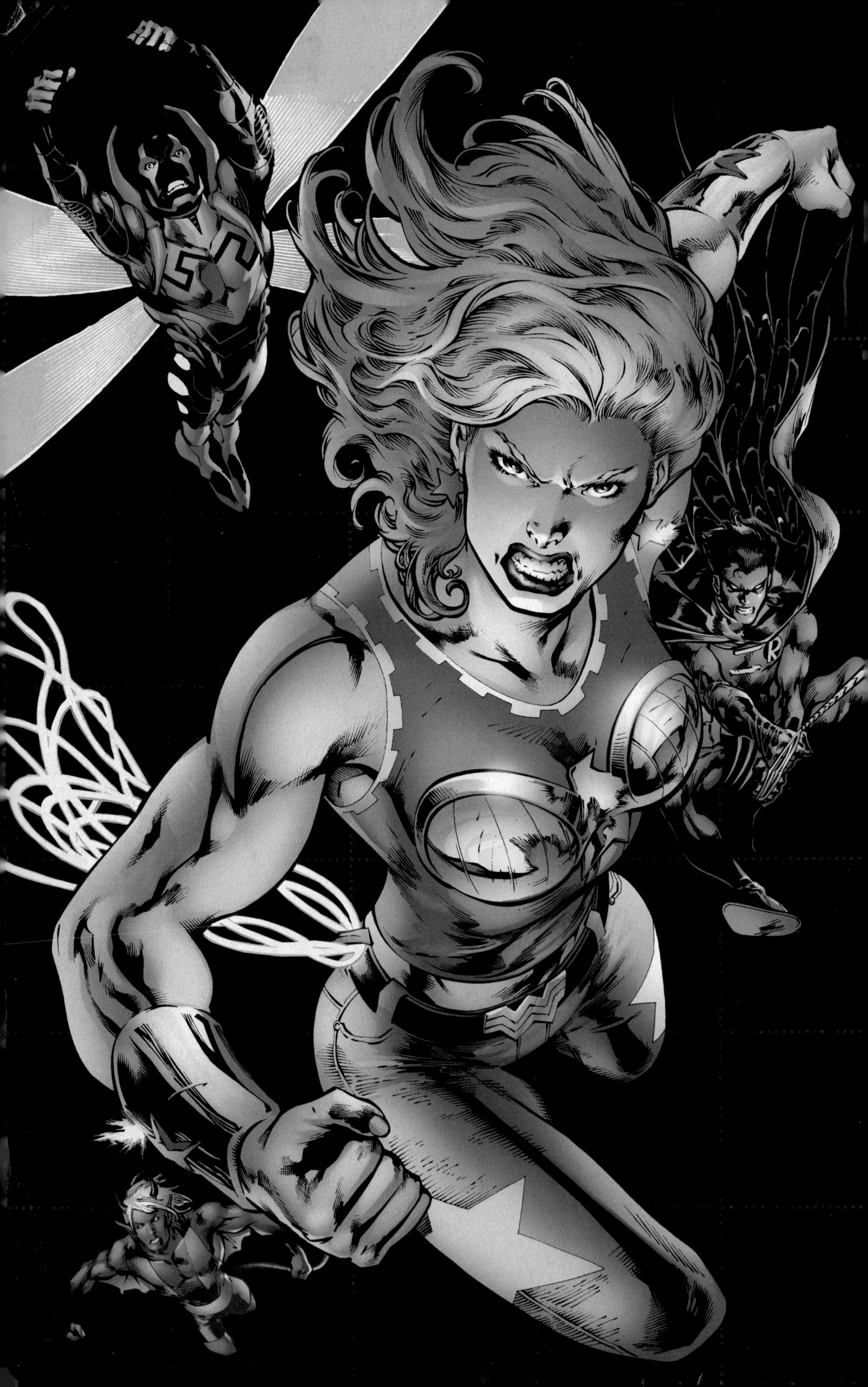

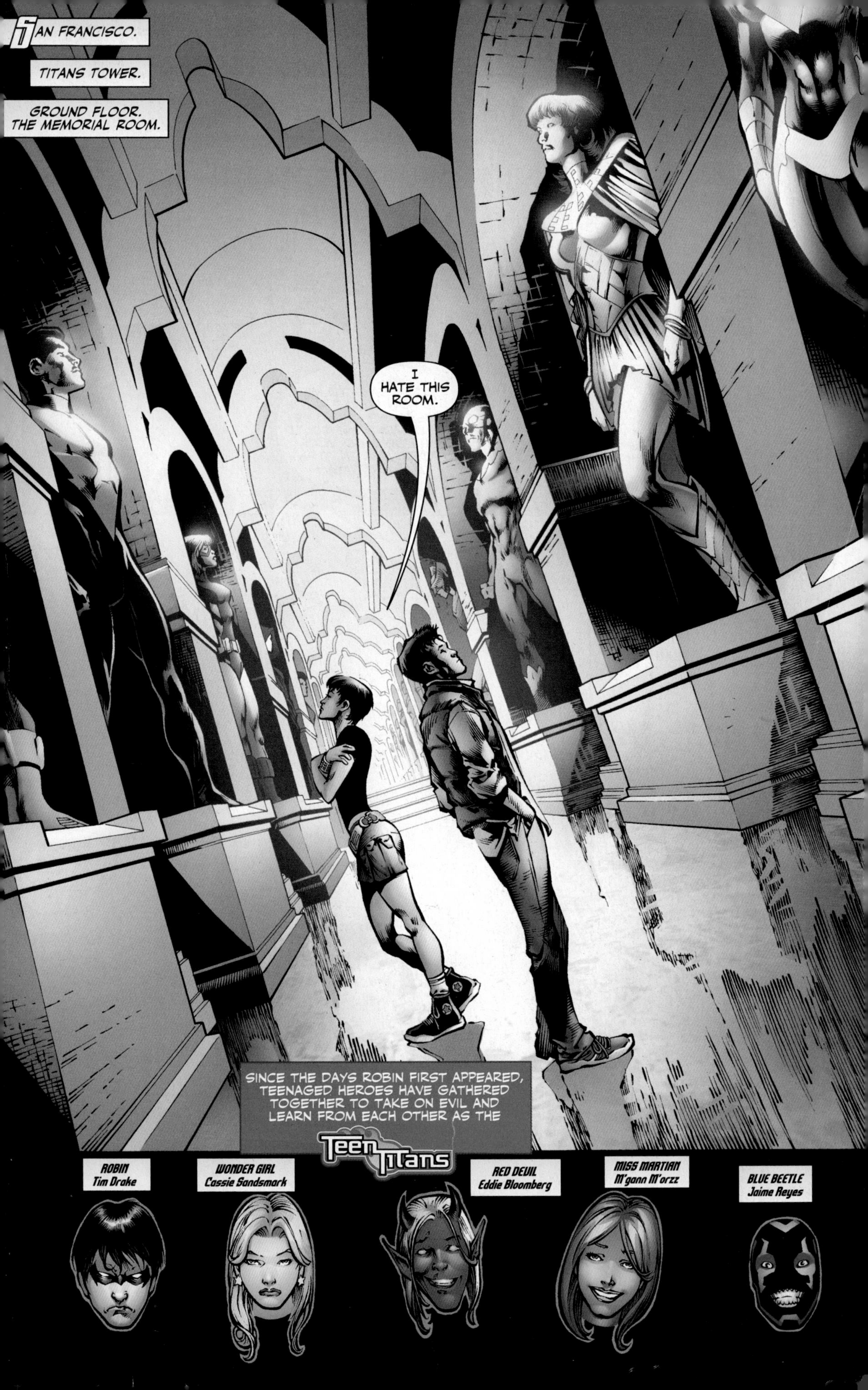
SAN FRANCISCO.
TITANS TOWER.
GROUND FLOOR. THE MEMORIAL ROOM.
I HATE THIS ROOM.
SINCE THE DAYS ROBIN FIRST APPEARED, TEENAGED HEROES HAVE GATHERED TOGETHER TO TAKE ON EVIL AND LEARN FROM EACH OTHER AS THE
TEEN TITANS
ROBIN Tim Drake
WONDER GIRL Cassie Sandsmark
RED DEVIL Eddie Bloomberg
MISS MARTIAN M'gann M'orzz
BLUE BEETLE Jaime Reyes

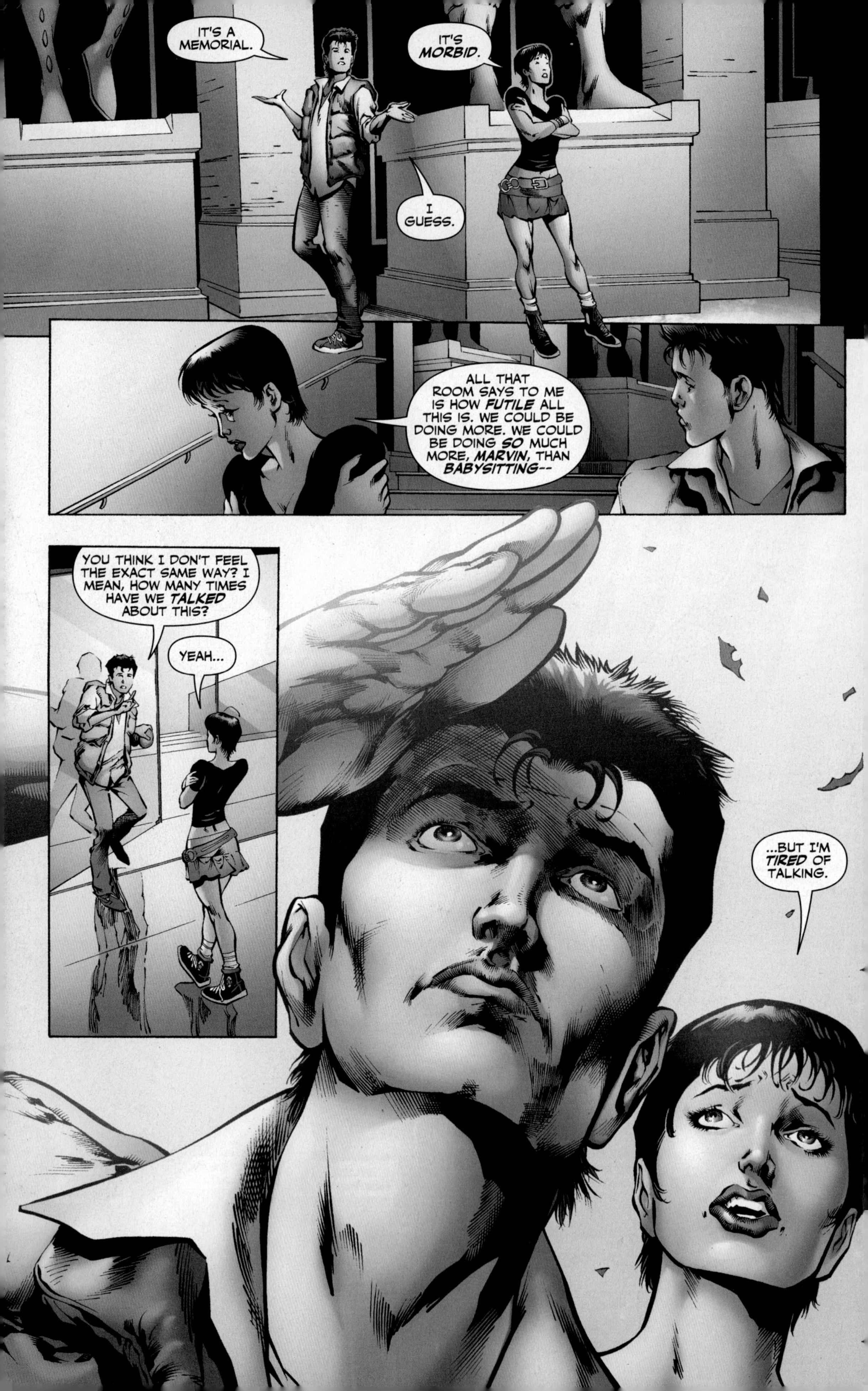
IT'S A MEMORIAL.
IT'S MORBID.
I GUESS.
ALL THAT ROOM SAYS TO ME IS HOW FUTILE ALL THIS IS. WE COULD BE DOING MORE. WE COULD BE DOING SO MUCH MORE, MARVIN, THAN BABYSITTING--
YOU THINK I DON'T FEEL THE EXACT SAME WAY? I MEAN, HOW MANY TIMES HAVE WE TALKED ABOUT THIS?
YEAH...
...BUT I'M TIRED OF TALKING.

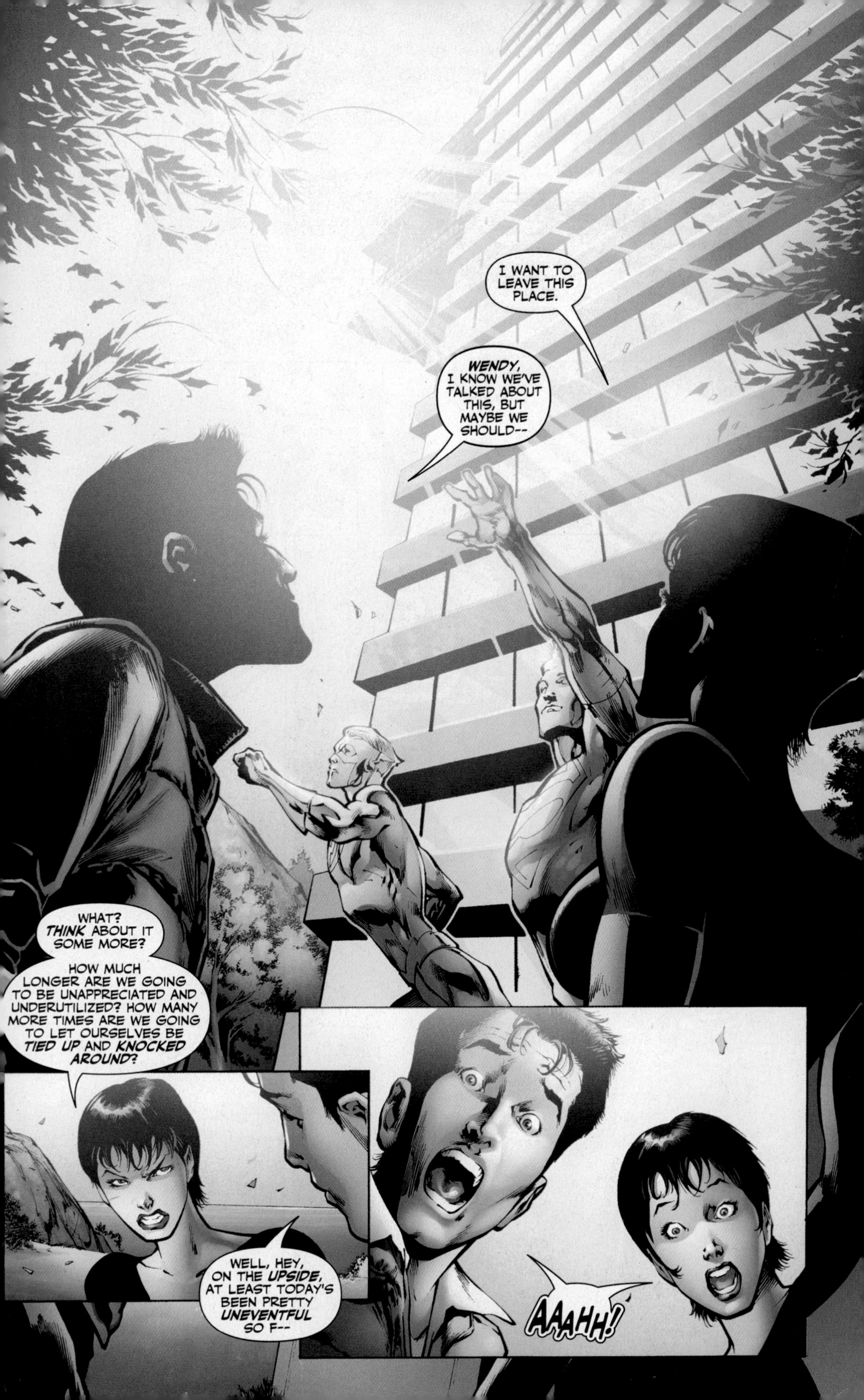
I WANT TO LEAVE THIS PLACE.
WENDY, I KNOW WE'VE TALKED ABOUT THIS, BUT MAYBE WE SHOULD--
WHAT? THINK ABOUT IT SOME MORE?
HOW MUCH LONGER ARE WE GOING TO BE UNAPPRECIATED AND UNDERUTILIZED? HOW MANY MORE TIMES ARE WE GOING TO LET OURSELVES BE TIED UP AND KNOCKED AROUND?
WELL, HEY, ON THE UPSIDE, AT LEAST TODAY'S BEEN PRETTY UNEVENTFUL SO F--
AAAHH!

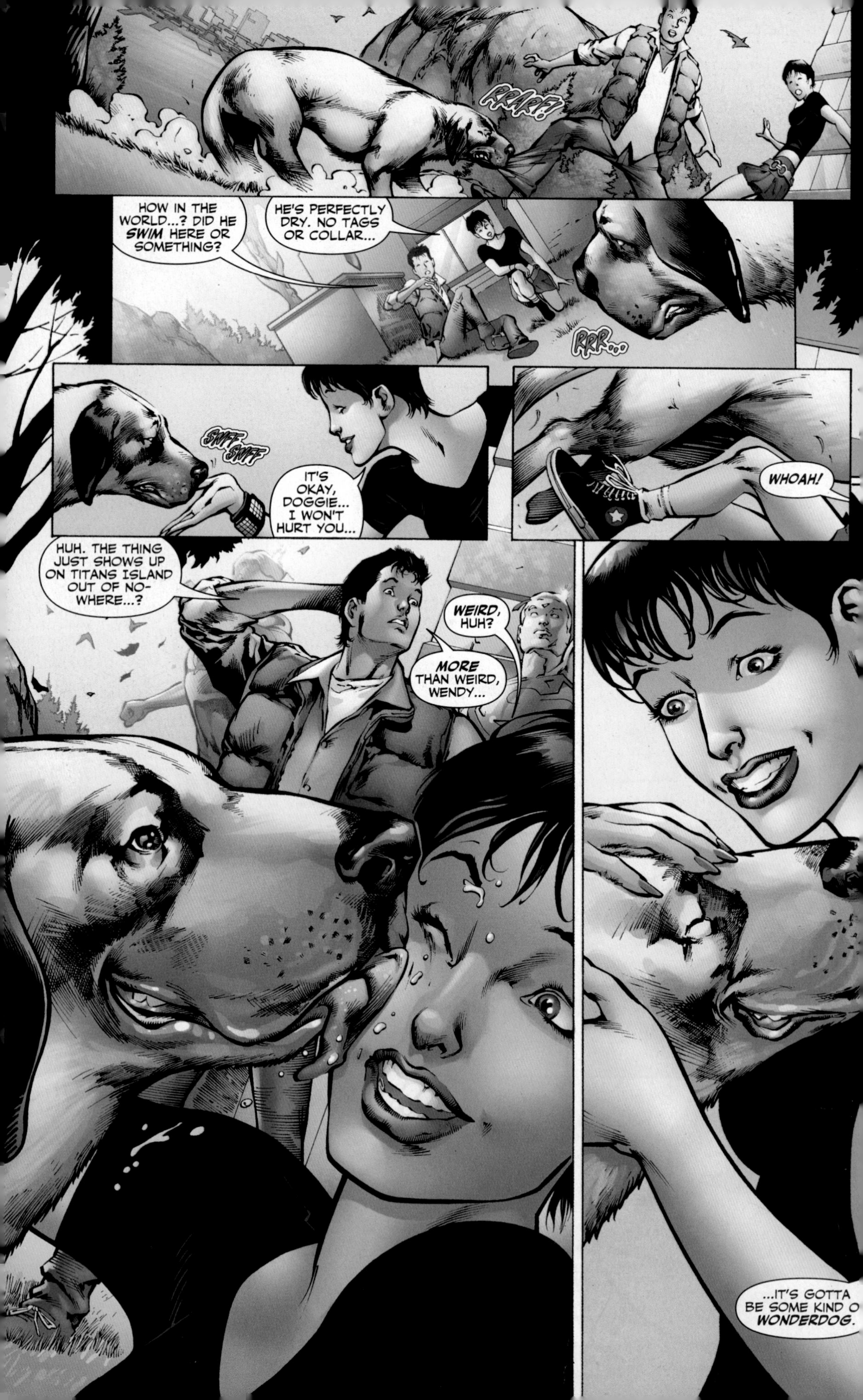
RRARF!
HOW IN THE WORLD...? DID HE SWIM HERE OR SOMETHING?
HE'S PERFECTLY DRY. NO TAGS OR COLLAR...
RRR...
SNFF SNFF
IT'S OKAY, DOGGIE... I WON'T HURT YOU...
WHOAH!
HUH. THE THING JUST SHOWS UP ON TITANS ISLAND OUT OF NO-WHERE...?
WEIRD, HUH?
MORE THAN WEIRD, WENDY...
...IT'S GOTTA BE SOME KIND O WONDERDOG.

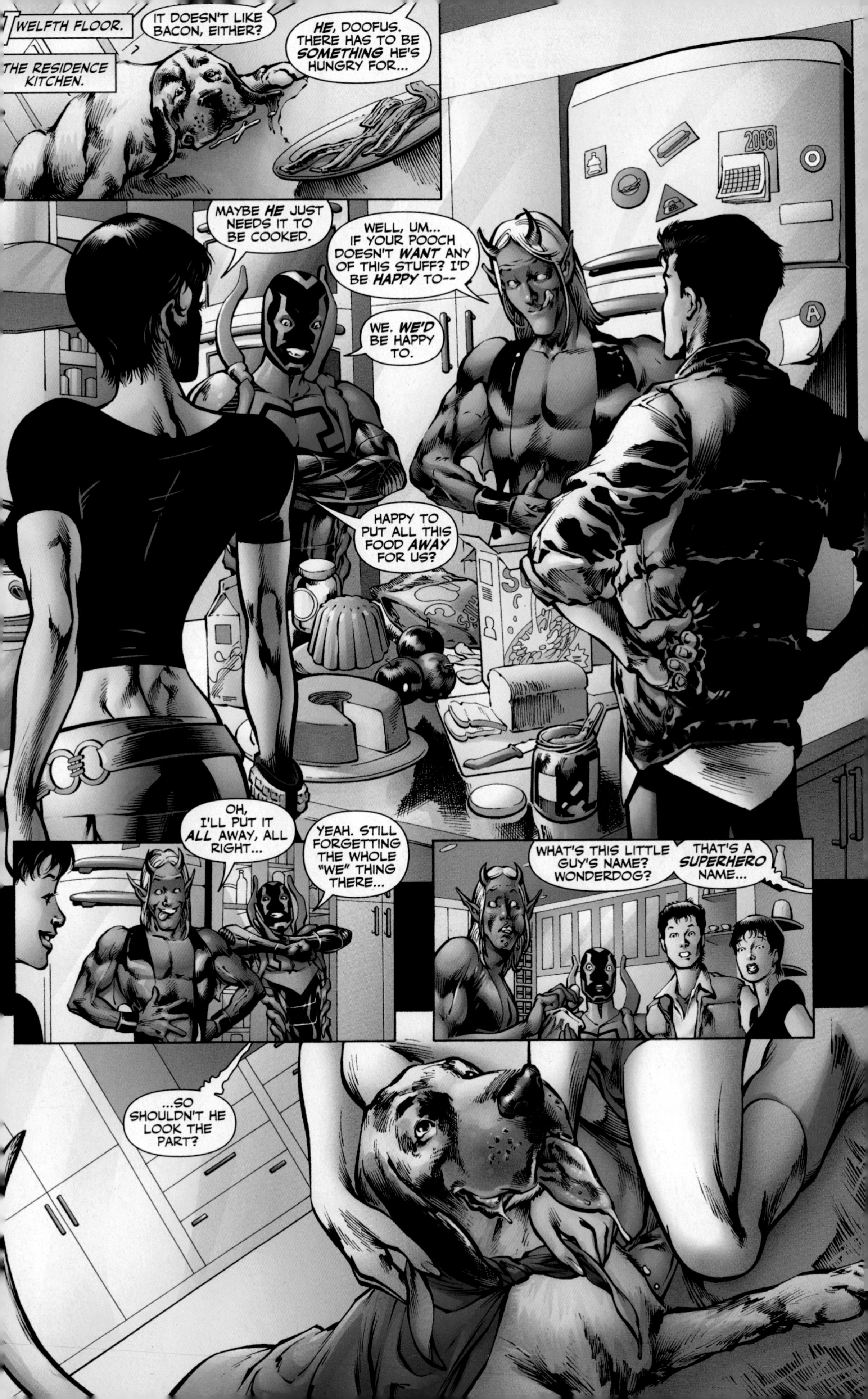
TWELFTH FLOOR.
THE RESIDENCE KITCHEN.
IT DOESN'T LIKE BACON, EITHER?
HE, DOOFUS. THERE HAS TO BE SOMETHING HE'S HUNGRY FOR...
MAYBE HE JUST NEEDS IT TO BE COOKED.
WELL, UM... IF YOUR POOCH DOESN'T WANT ANY OF THIS STUFF? I'D BE HAPPY TO--
WE. WE'D BE HAPPY TO.
HAPPY TO PUT ALL THIS FOOD AWAY FOR US?
OH, I'LL PUT IT ALL AWAY, ALL RIGHT...
YEAH. STILL FORGETTING THE WHOLE "WE" THING THERE...
WHAT'S THIS LITTLE GUY'S NAME? WONDERDOG?
THAT'S A SUPERHERO NAME...
...SO SHOULDN'T HE LOOK THE PART?

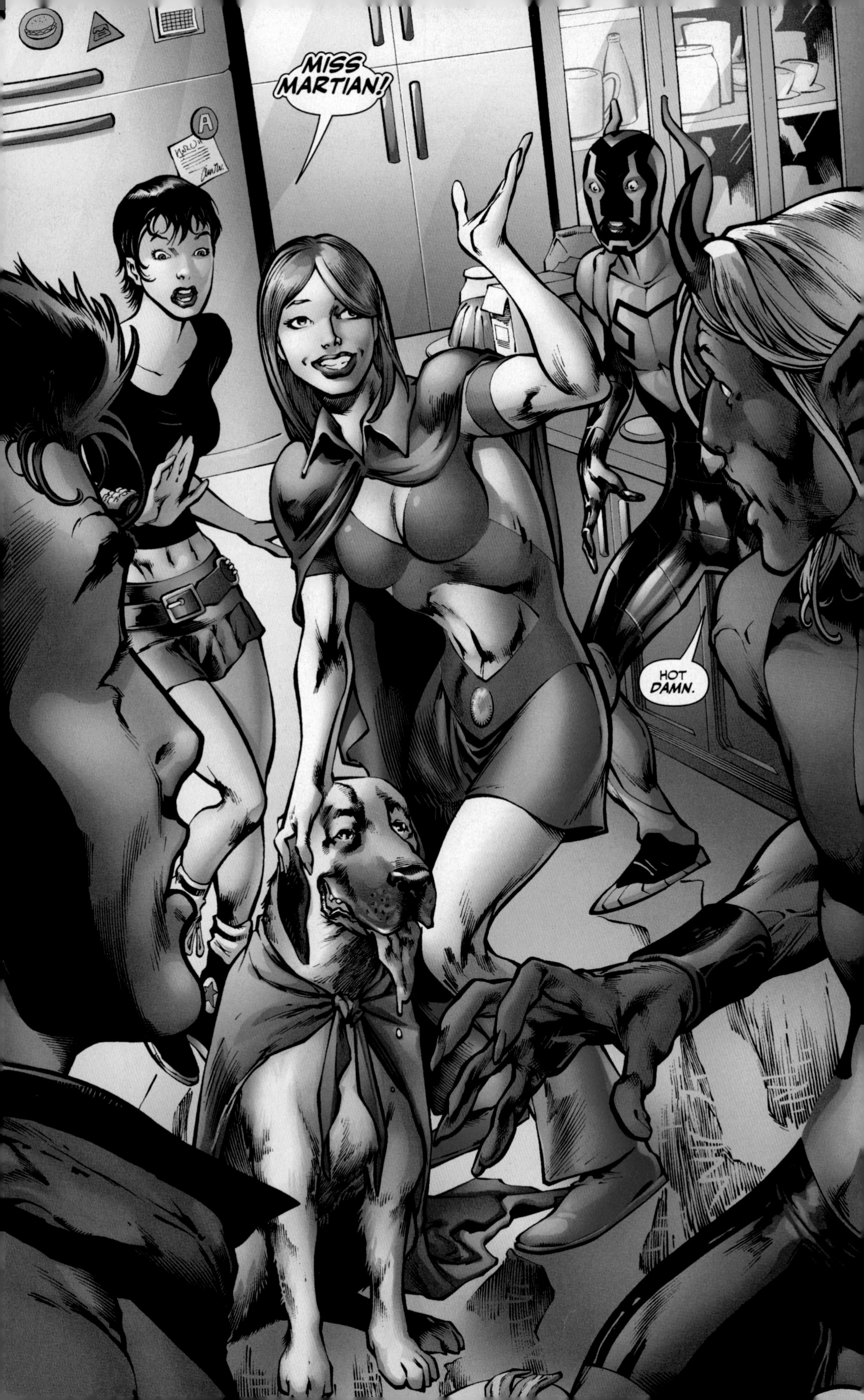
MISS MARTIAN!
HOT DAMN.

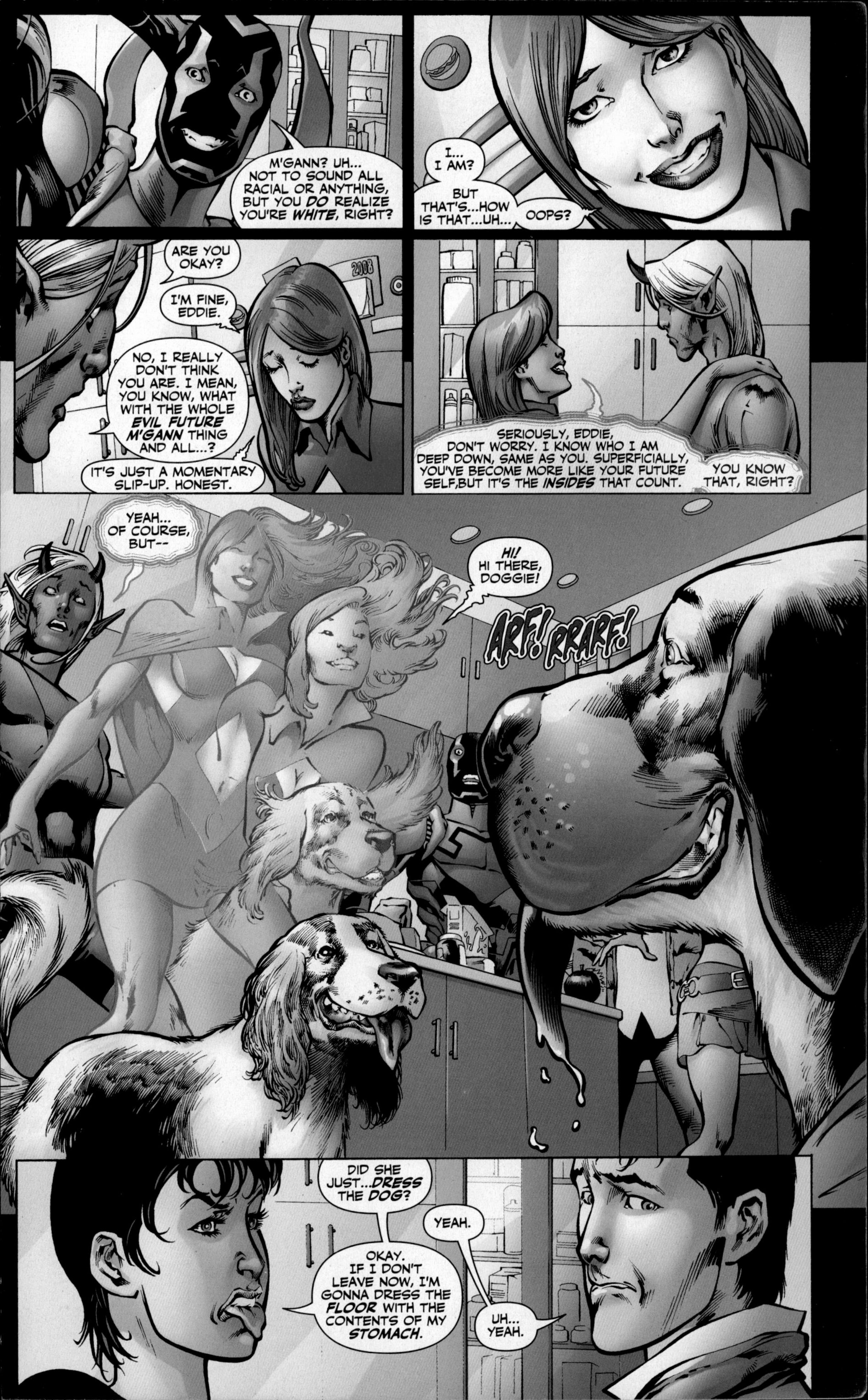
M'GANN? UH... NOT TO SOUND ALL RACIAL OR ANYTHING, BUT YOU DO REALIZE YOU'RE WHITE, RIGHT?
I... I AM?
BUT THAT'S...HOW IS THAT...UH...
OOPS?
ARE YOU OKAY?
I'M FINE, EDDIE.
NO, I REALLY DON'T THINK YOU ARE. I MEAN, YOU KNOW, WHAT WITH THE WHOLE EVIL FUTURE M'GANN THING AND ALL...?
IT'S JUST A MOMENTARY SLIP-UP. HONEST.
SERIOUSLY, EDDIE, DON'T WORRY. I KNOW WHO I AM DEEP DOWN, SAME AS YOU. SUPERFICIALLY, YOU'VE BECOME MORE LIKE YOUR FUTURE SELF,BUT IT'S THE INSIDES THAT COUNT.
YOU KNOW THAT, RIGHT?
YEAH... OF COURSE, BUT--
HI! HI THERE, DOGGIE!
ARF! RRARF!
DID SHE JUST...DRESS THE DOG?
YEAH.
OKAY. IF I DON'T LEAVE NOW, I'M GONNA DRESS THE FLOOR WITH THE CONTENTS OF MY STOMACH.
UH... YEAH.

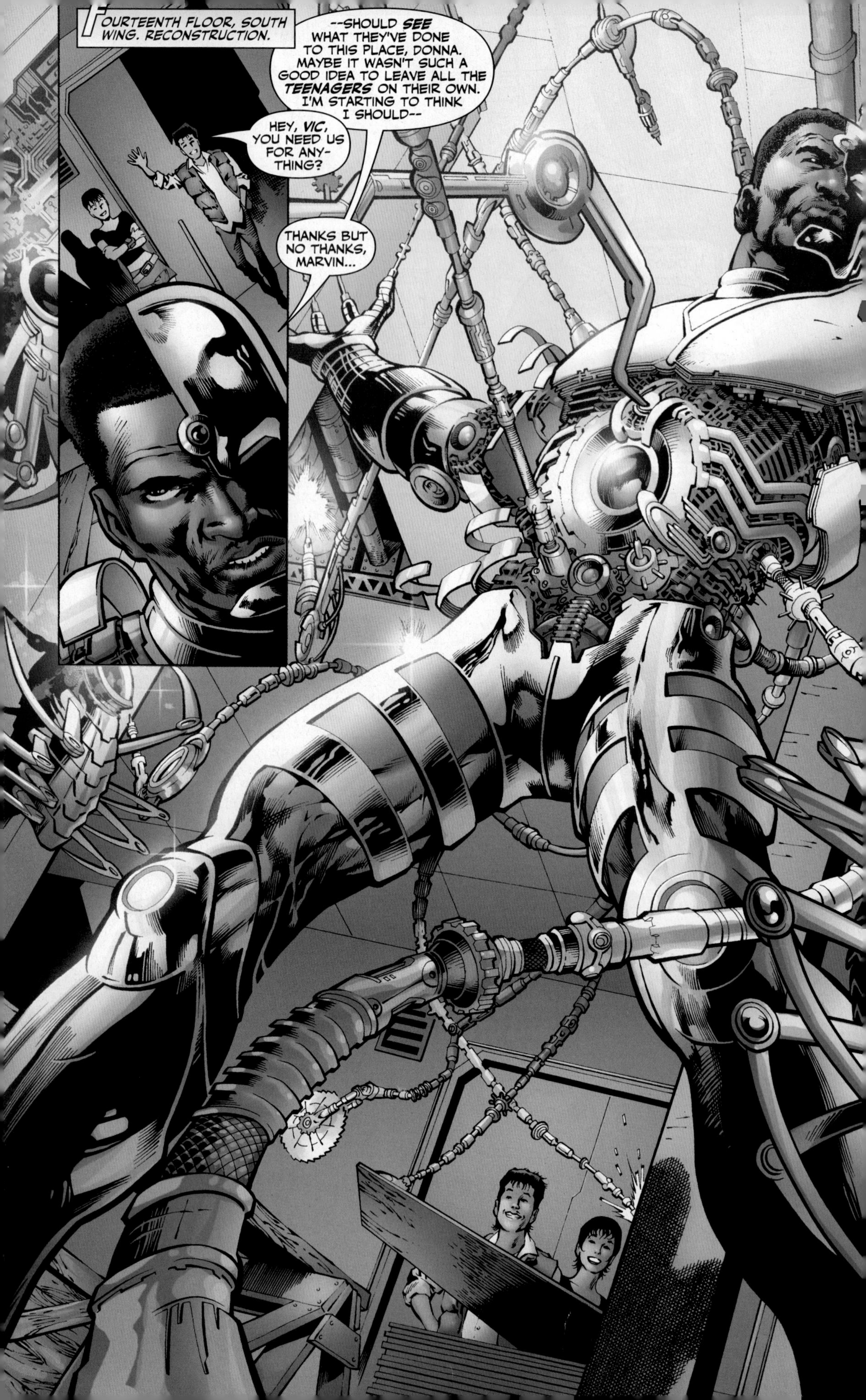
FOURTEENTH FLOOR, SOUTH WING. RECONSTRUCTION.
--SHOULD SEE WHAT THEY'VE DONE TO THIS PLACE, DONNA. MAYBE IT WASN'T SUCH A GOOD IDEA TO LEAVE ALL THE TEENAGERS ON THEIR OWN. I'M STARTING TO THINK I SHOULD--
HEY, VIC, YOU NEED US FOR ANY-THING?
THANKS BUT NO THANKS, MARVIN...

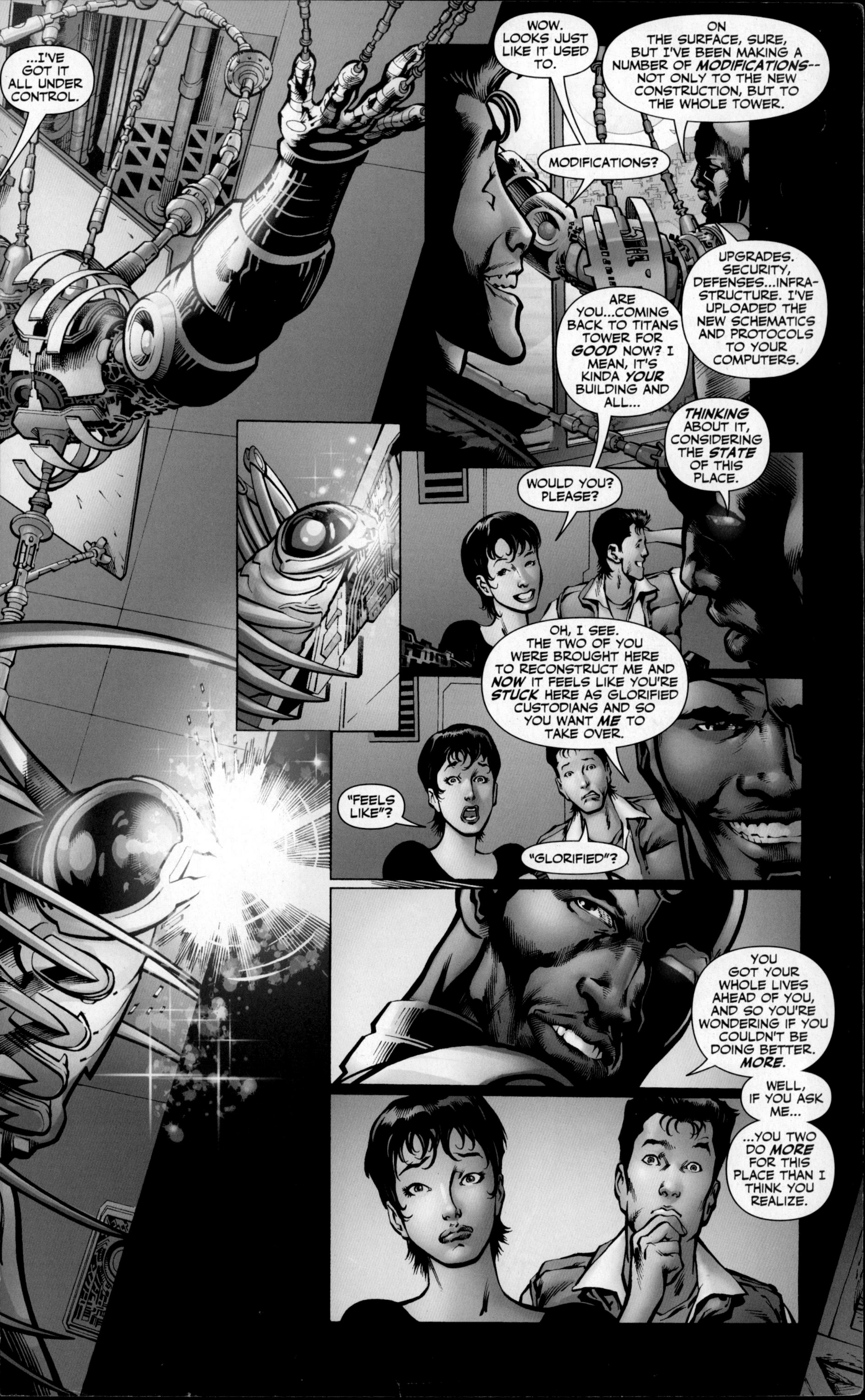
...I'VE GOT IT ALL UNDER CONTROL.
WOW. LOOKS JUST LIKE IT USED TO.
ON THE SURFACE, SURE, BUT I'VE BEEN MAKING A NUMBER OF MODIFICATIONS-- NOT ONLY TO THE NEW CONSTRUCTION, BUT TO THE WHOLE TOWER.
MODIFICATIONS?
UPGRADES. SECURITY, DEFENSES...INFRA-STRUCTURE. I'VE UPLOADED THE NEW SCHEMATICS AND PROTOCOLS TO YOUR COMPUTERS.
ARE YOU...COMING BACK TO TITANS TOWER FOR GOOD NOW? I MEAN, IT'S KINDA YOUR BUILDING AND ALL...
THINKING ABOUT IT, CONSIDERING THE STATE OF THIS PLACE.
WOULD YOU? PLEASE?
OH, I SEE. THE TWO OF YOU WERE BROUGHT HERE TO RECONSTRUCT ME AND NOW IT FEELS LIKE YOU'RE STUCK HERE AS GLORIFIED CUSTODIANS AND SO YOU WANT ME TO TAKE OVER.
"FEELS LIKE"?
"GLORIFIED"?
YOU GOT YOUR WHOLE LIVES AHEAD OF YOU, AND SO YOU'RE WONDERING IF YOU COULDN'T BE DOING BETTER. MORE.
WELL, IF YOU ASK ME...
...YOU TWO DO MORE FOR THIS PLACE THAN I THINK YOU REALIZE.

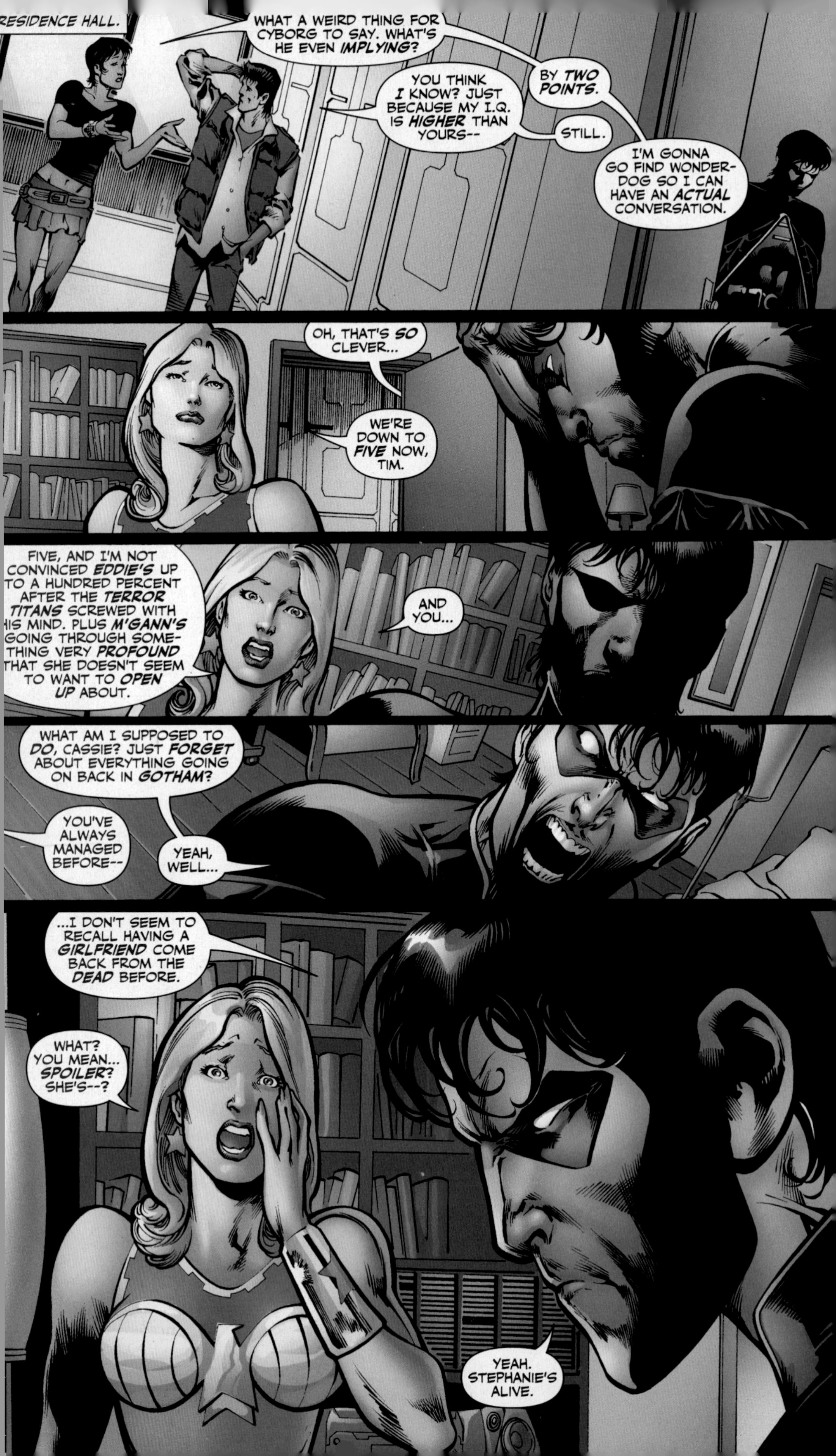

RESIDENCE HALL.
WHAT A WEIRD THING FOR CYBORG TO SAY. WHAT'S HE EVEN IMPLYING?
YOU THINK I KNOW? JUST BECAUSE MY I.Q. IS HIGHER THAN YOURS--
BY TWO POINTS.
STILL.
I'M GONNA GO FIND WONDER-DOG SO I CAN HAVE AN ACTUAL CONVERSATION.
OH, THAT'S SO CLEVER...
WE'RE DOWN TO FIVE NOW, TIM.
FIVE, AND I'M NOT CONVINCED EDDIE'S UP TO A HUNDRED PERCENT AFTER THE TERROR TITANS SCREWED WITH HIS MIND. PLUS M'GANN'S GOING THROUGH SOME-THING VERY PROFOUND THAT SHE DOESN'T SEEM TO WANT TO OPEN UP ABOUT.
AND YOU...
WHAT AM I SUPPOSED TO DO, CASSIE? JUST FORGET ABOUT EVERYTHING GOING ON BACK IN GOTHAM?
YOU'VE ALWAYS MANAGED BEFORE--
YEAH, WELL...
...I DON'T SEEM TO RECALL HAVING A GIRLFRIEND COME BACK FROM THE DEAD BEFORE.
WHAT? YOU MEAN... SPOILER? SHE'S--?
YEAH. STEPHANIE'S ALIVE.

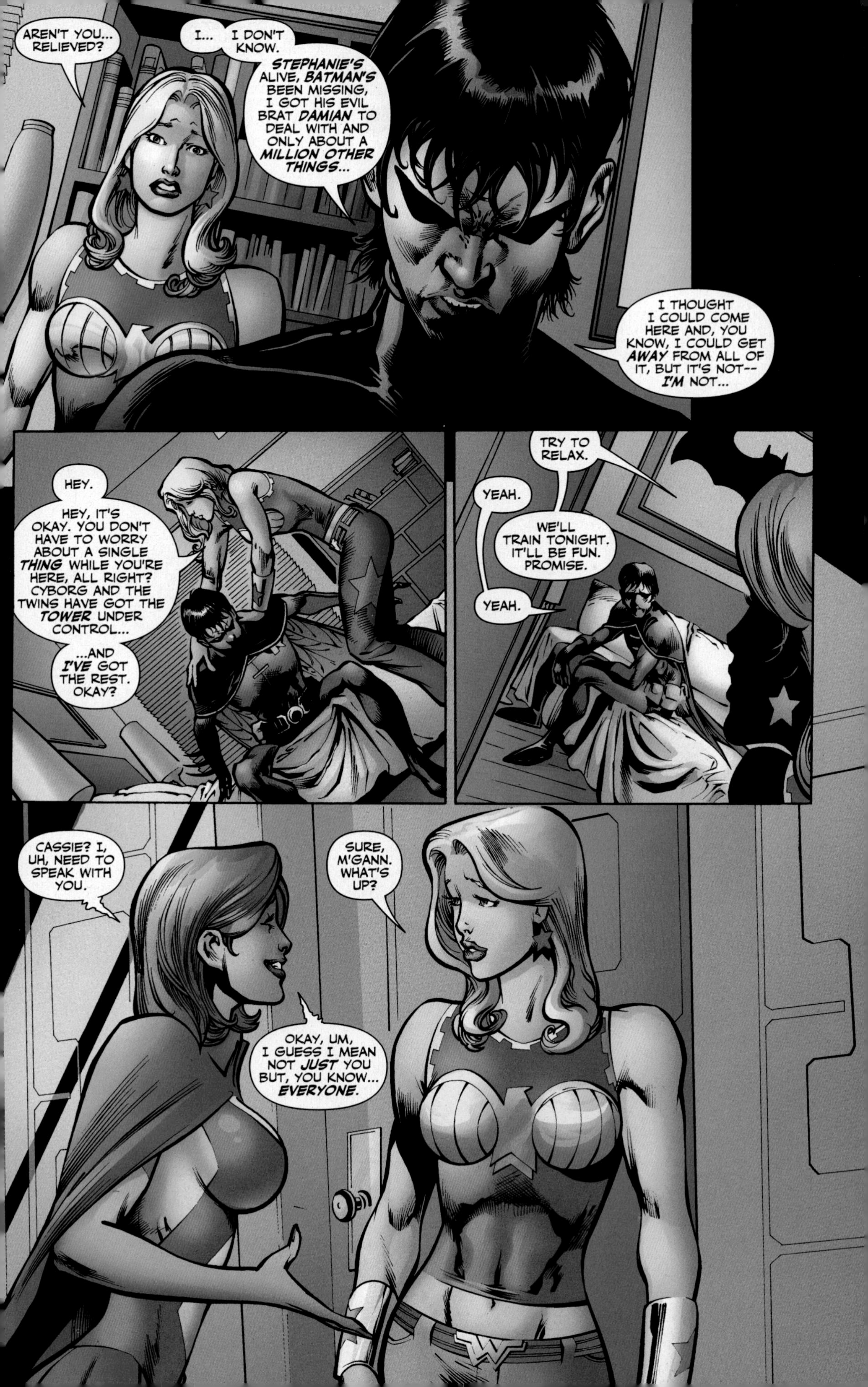

AREN'T YOU... RELIEVED?
I... I DON'T KNOW.
STEPHANIE'S ALIVE, BATMAN'S BEEN MISSING, I GOT HIS EVIL BRAT DAMIAN TO DEAL WITH AND ONLY ABOUT A MILLION OTHER THINGS...
I THOUGHT I COULD COME HERE AND, YOU KNOW, I COULD GET AWAY FROM ALL OF IT, BUT IT'S NOT-- I'M NOT...
HEY.
HEY, IT'S OKAY. YOU DON'T HAVE TO WORRY ABOUT A SINGLE THING WHILE YOU'RE HERE, ALL RIGHT? CYBORG AND THE TWINS HAVE GOT THE TOWER UNDER CONTROL...
...AND I'VE GOT THE REST. OKAY?
TRY TO RELAX.
YEAH.
WE'LL TRAIN TONIGHT. IT'LL BE FUN. PROMISE.
YEAH.
CASSIE? I, UH, NEED TO SPEAK WITH YOU.
SURE, M'GANN. WHAT'S UP?
OKAY, UM, I GUESS I MEAN NOT JUST YOU BUT, YOU KNOW... EVERYONE.

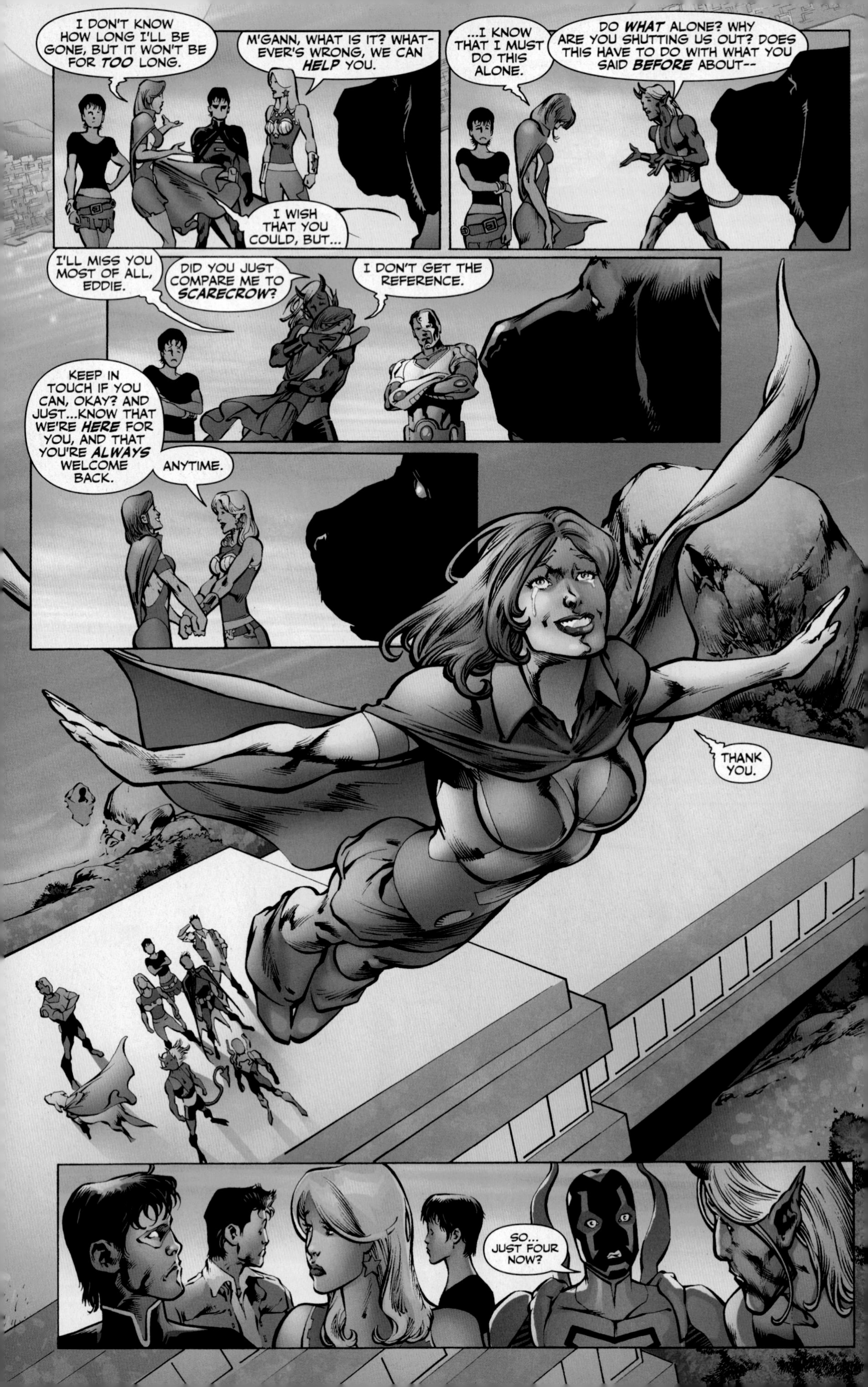
I DON'T KNOW HOW LONG I'LL BE GONE, BUT IT WON'T BE FOR TOO LONG.
M'GANN, WHAT IS IT? WHAT-EVER'S WRONG, WE CAN HELP YOU.
I WISH THAT YOU COULD, BUT...
...I KNOW THAT I MUST DO THIS ALONE.
DO WHAT ALONE? WHY ARE YOU SHUTTING US OUT? DOES THIS HAVE TO DO WITH WHAT YOU SAID BEFORE ABOUT--
I'LL MISS YOU MOST OF ALL, EDDIE.
DID YOU JUST COMPARE ME TO SCARECROW?
I DON'T GET THE REFERENCE.
KEEP IN TOUCH IF YOU CAN, OKAY? AND JUST...KNOW THAT WE'RE HERE FOR YOU, AND THAT YOU'RE ALWAYS WELCOME BACK.
ANYTIME.
THANK YOU.
SO... JUST FOUR NOW?

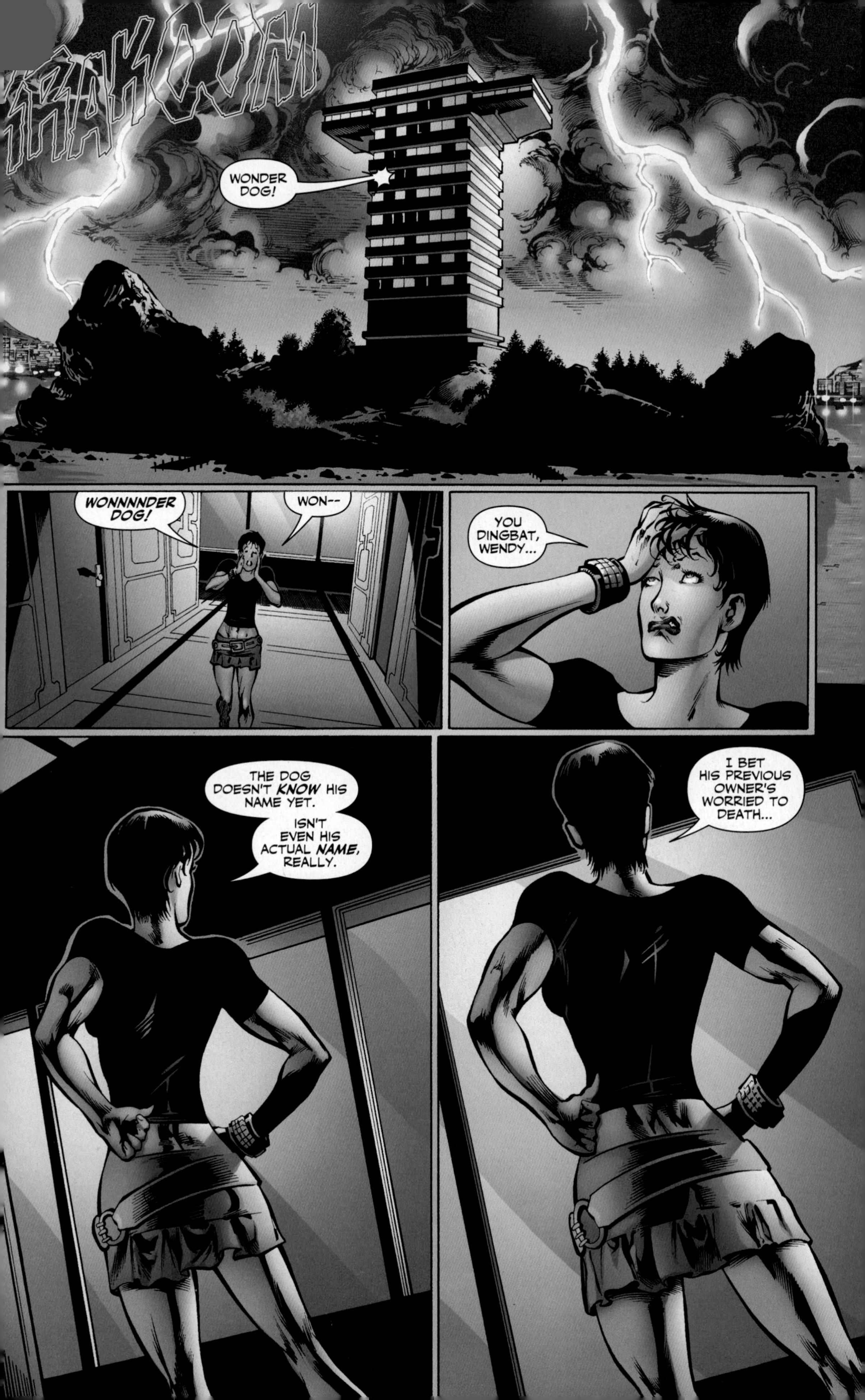
WONDER DOG!
WONNNNDER DOG!
WON--
YOU DINGBAT, WENDY...
THE DOG DOESN'T KNOW HIS NAME YET.
ISN'T EVEN HIS ACTUAL NAME, REALLY.
I BET HIS PREVIOUS OWNER'S WORRIED TO DEATH...

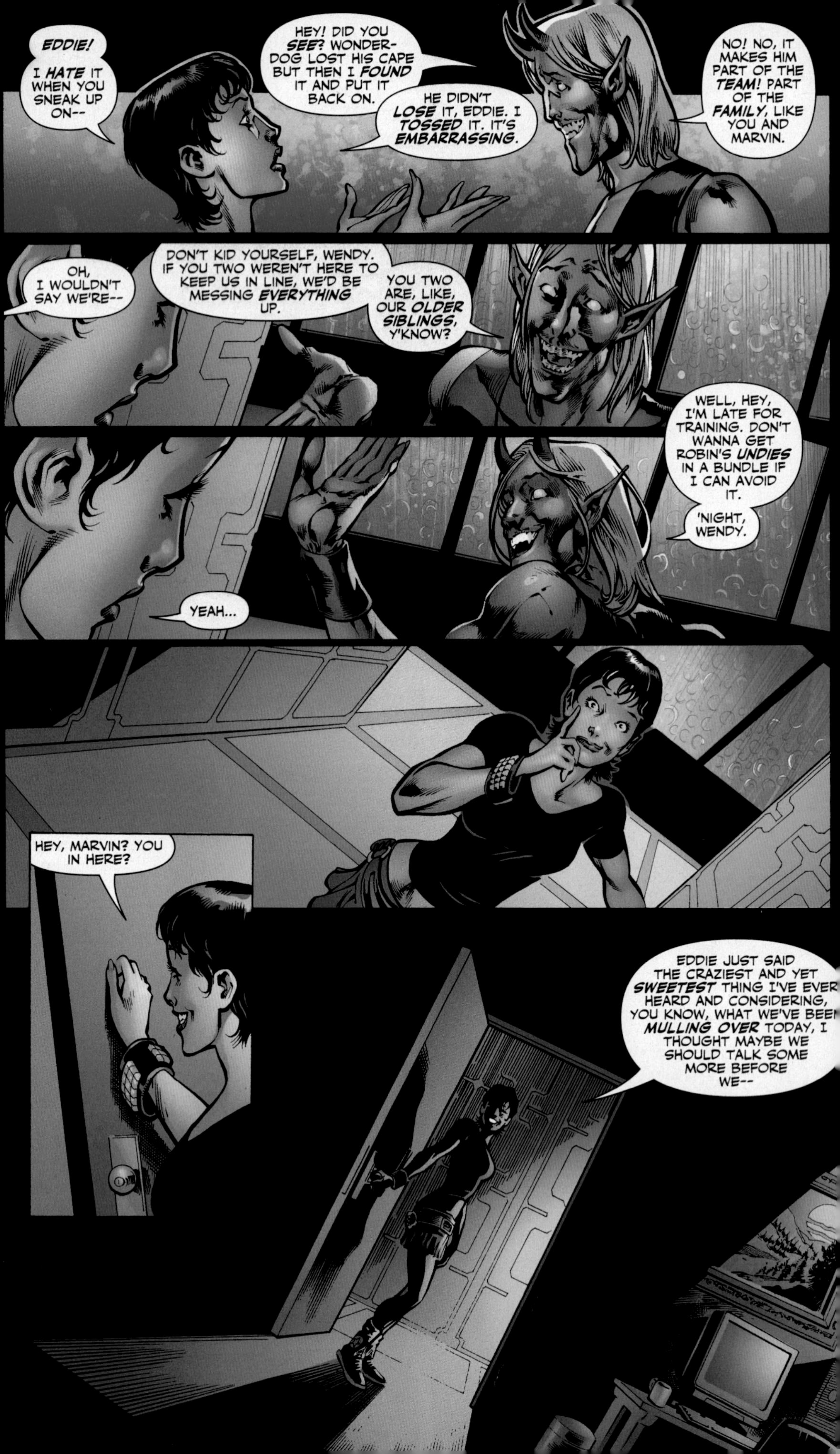
EDDIE! I HATE IT WHEN YOU SNEAK UP ON--
HEY! DID YOU SEE? WONDER-DOG LOST HIS CAPE BUT THEN I FOUND IT AND PUT IT BACK ON.
HE DIDN'T LOSE IT, EDDIE. I TOSSED IT. IT'S EMBARRASSING.
NO! NO, IT MAKES HIM PART OF THE TEAM! PART OF THE FAMILY, LIKE YOU AND MARVIN.
OH, I WOULDN'T SAY WE'RE--
DON'T KID YOURSELF, WENDY. IF YOU TWO WEREN'T HERE TO KEEP US IN LINE, WE'D BE MESSING EVERYTHING UP.
YOU TWO ARE, LIKE, OUR OLDER SIBLINGS, Y'KNOW?
WELL, HEY, I'M LATE FOR TRAINING. DON'T WANNA GET ROBIN'S UNDIES IN A BUNDLE IF I CAN AVOID IT.
'NIGHT, WENDY.
YEAH...
HEY, MARVIN? YOU IN HERE?
EDDIE JUST SAID THE CRAZIEST AND YET SWEETEST THING I'VE EVER HEARD AND CONSIDERING, YOU KNOW, WHAT WE'VE BEEN MULLING OVER TODAY, I THOUGHT MAYBE WE SHOULD TALK SOME MORE BEFORE WE--

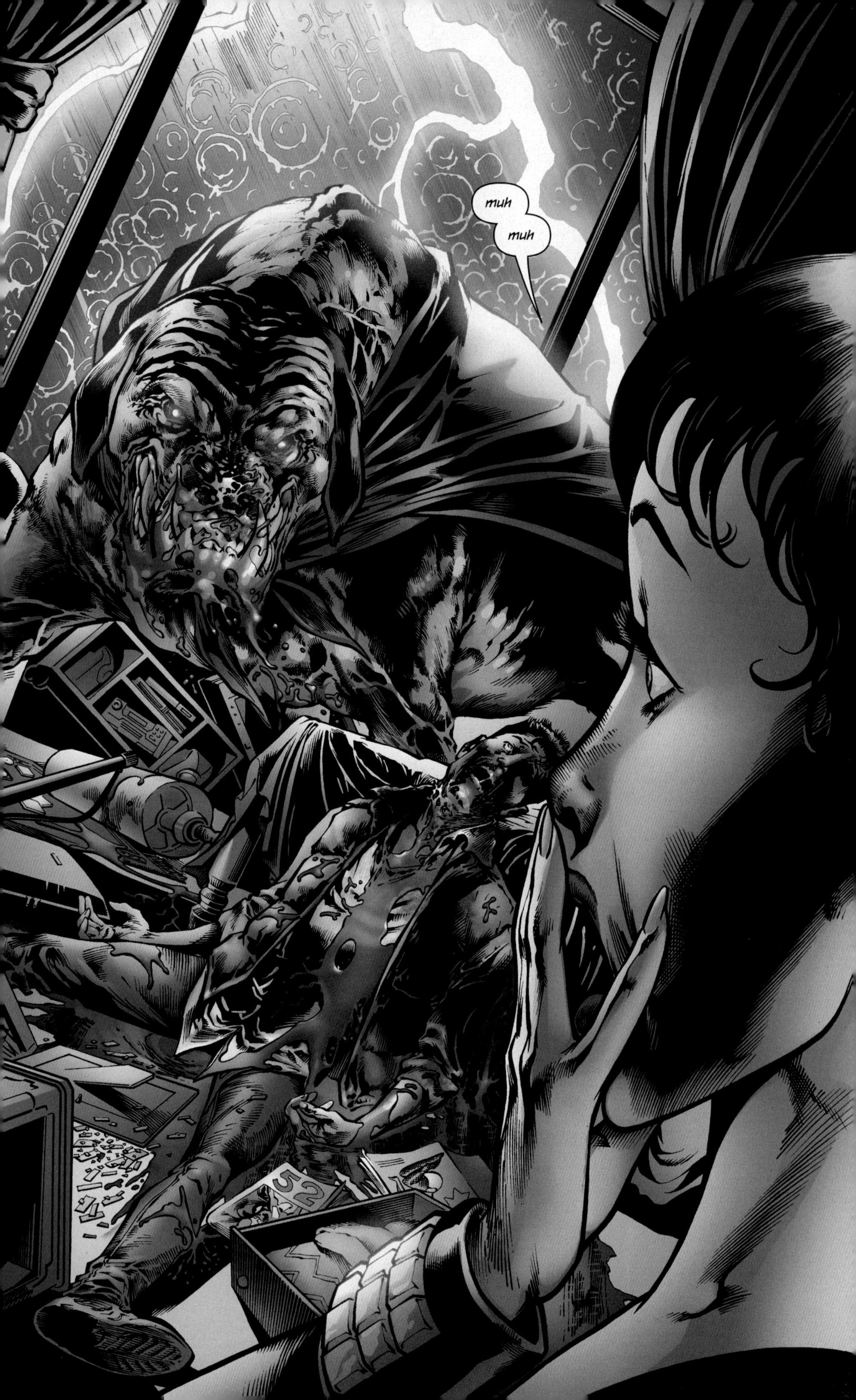
muh
muh

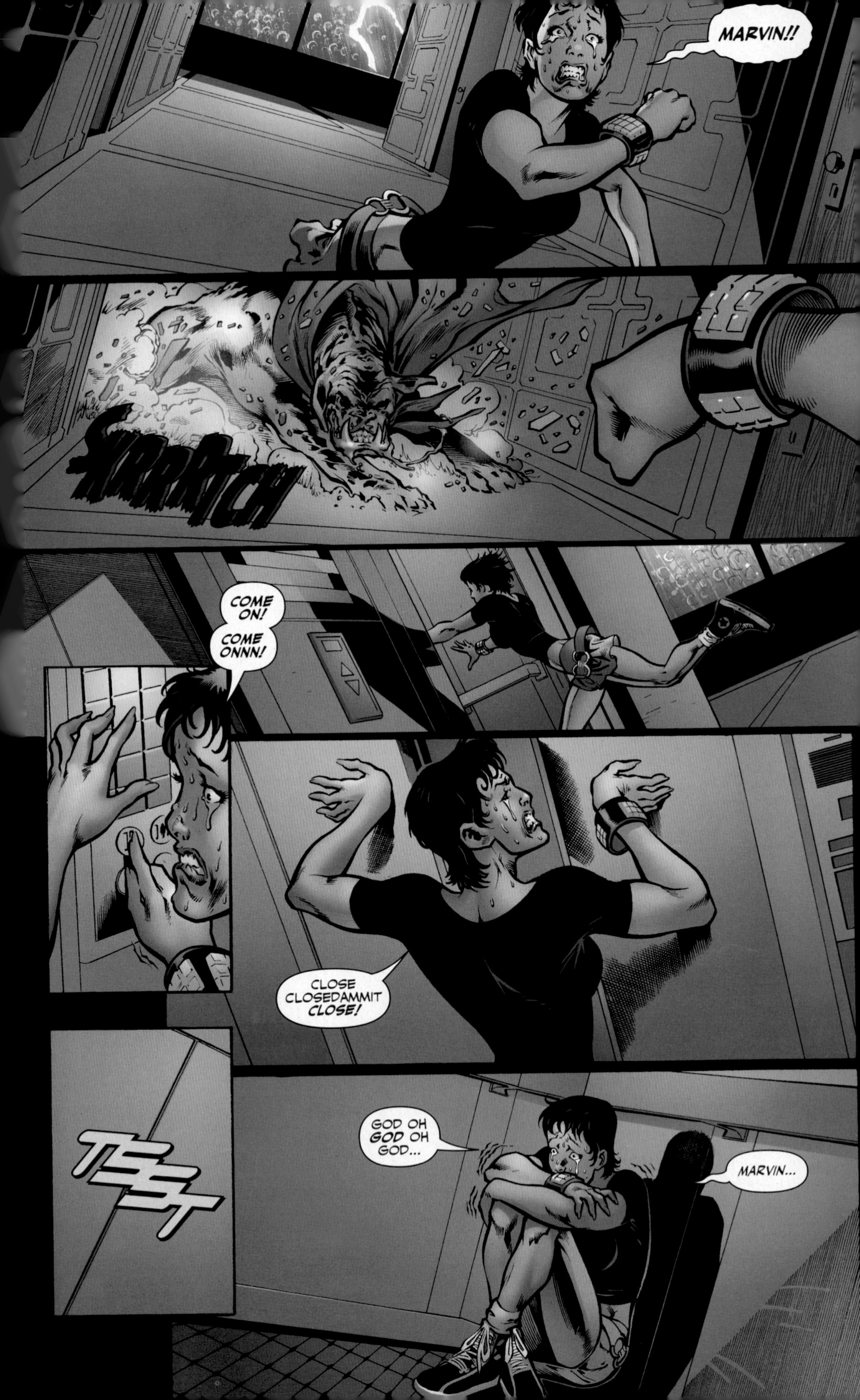
MARVIN!!
SKRRRTCH
COME ON!
COME ONNN!
CLOSE CLOSEDAMMIT CLOSE!
TSSST
GOD OH GOD OH GOD...
MARVIN...

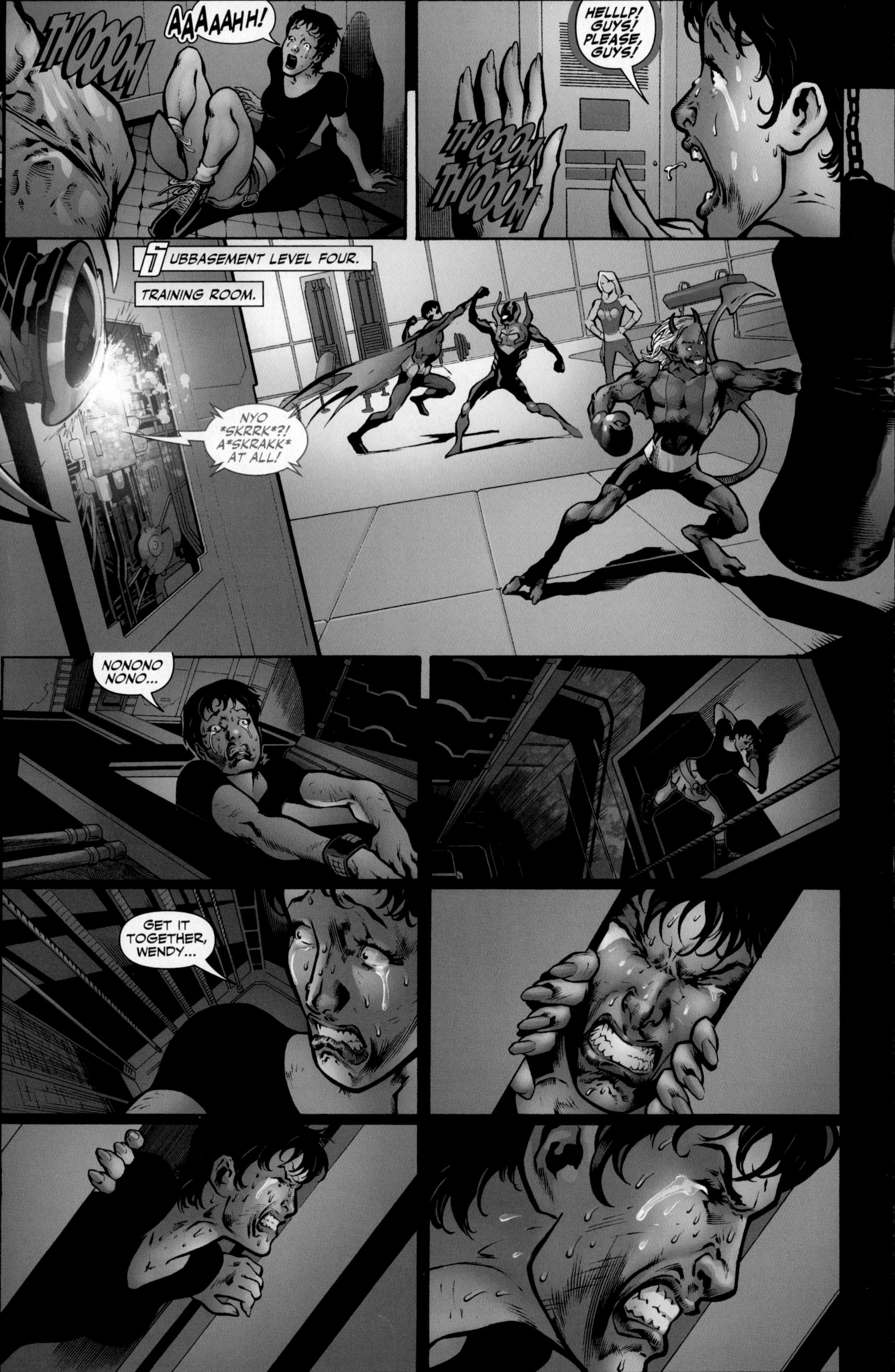
THOOOM
AAAAAHH!
HELLLP! GUYS! PLEASE, GUYS!
THOOOM THOOOM
SUBBASEMENT LEVEL FOUR.
TRAINING ROOM.
NYO *SKRRK*?! A*SKRAKK* AT ALL!
NONONO NONO...
GET IT TOGETHER, WENDY...

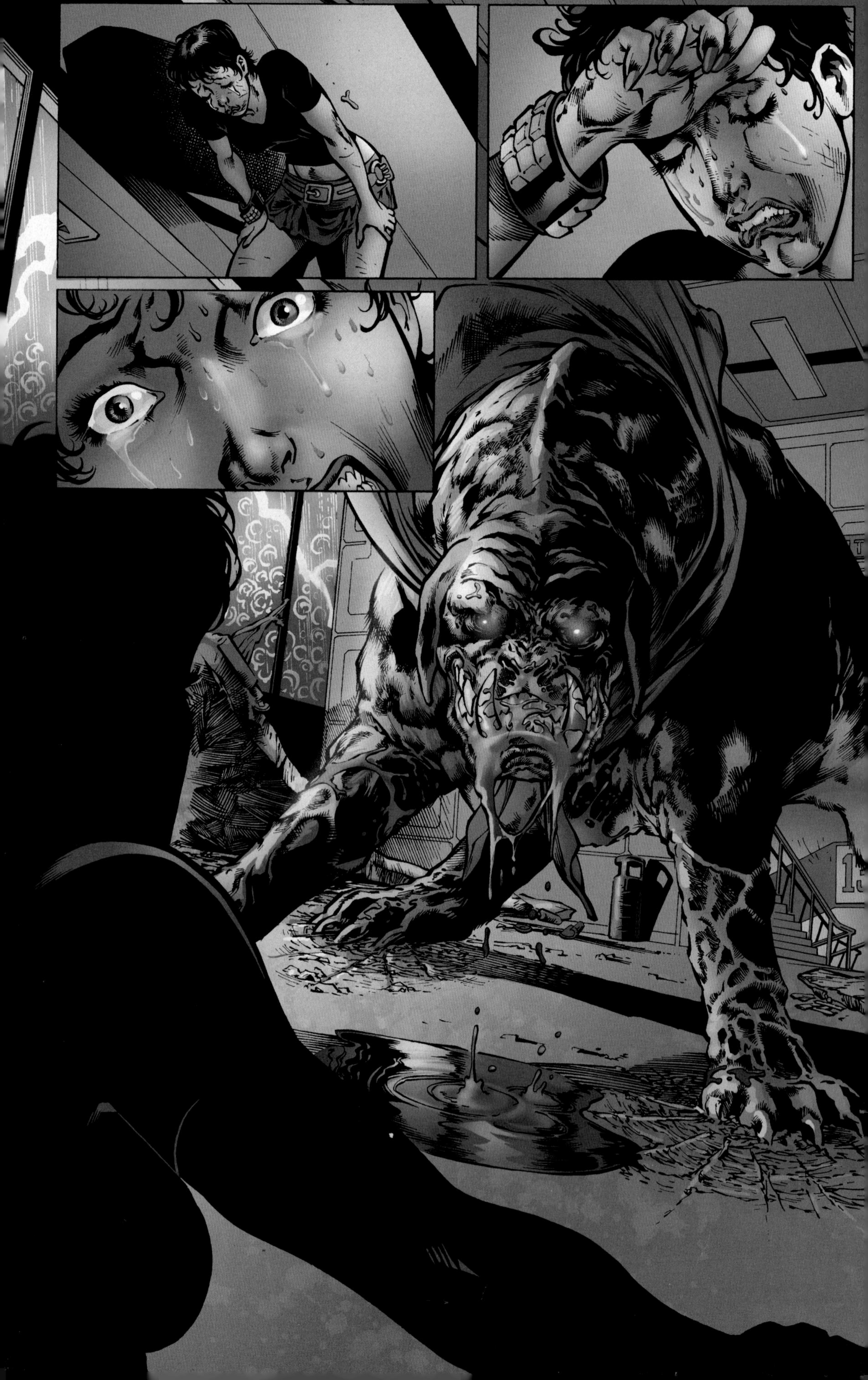

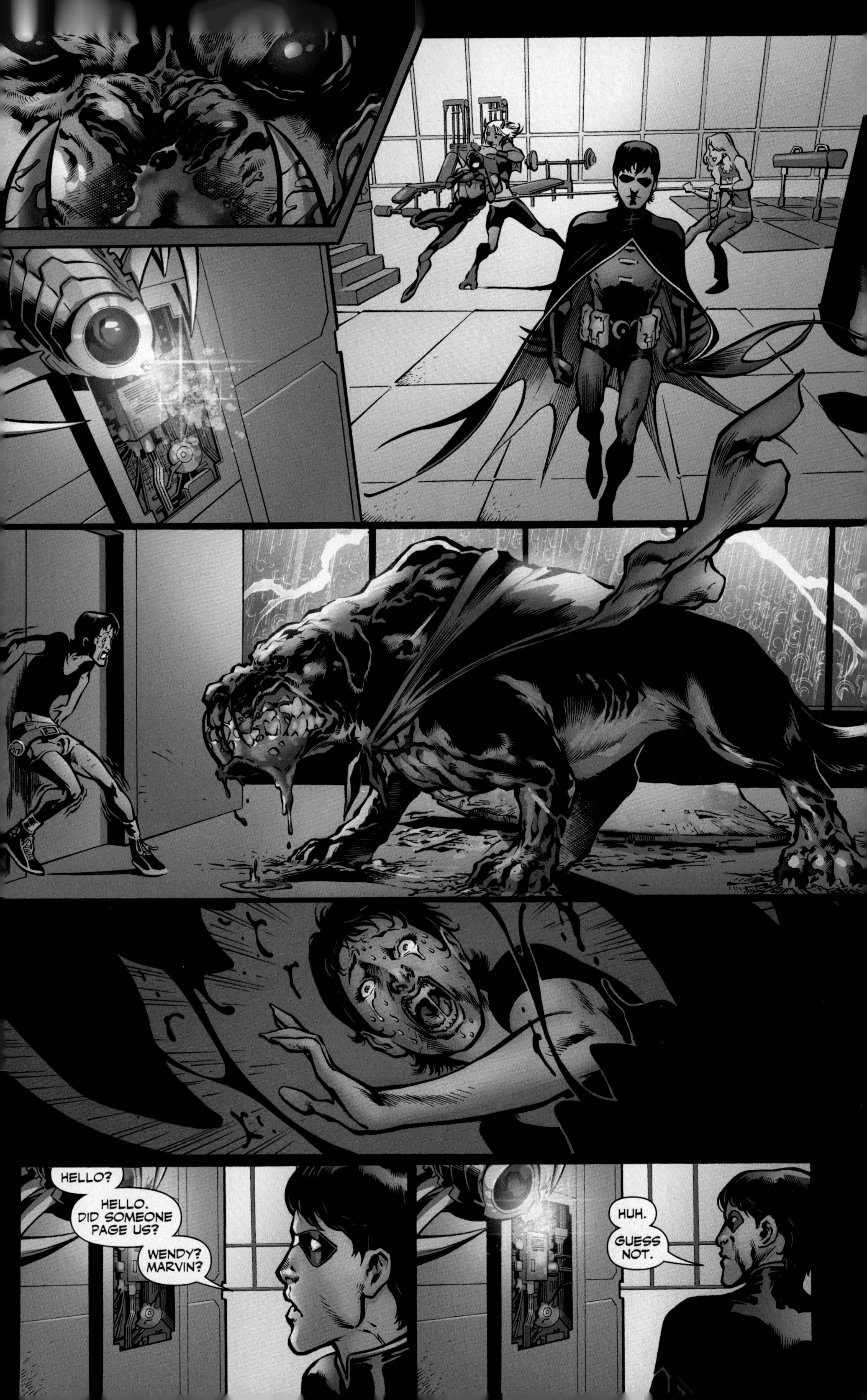
HELLO?
HELLO. DID SOMEONE PAGE US?
WENDY? MARVIN?
HUH. GUESS NOT.

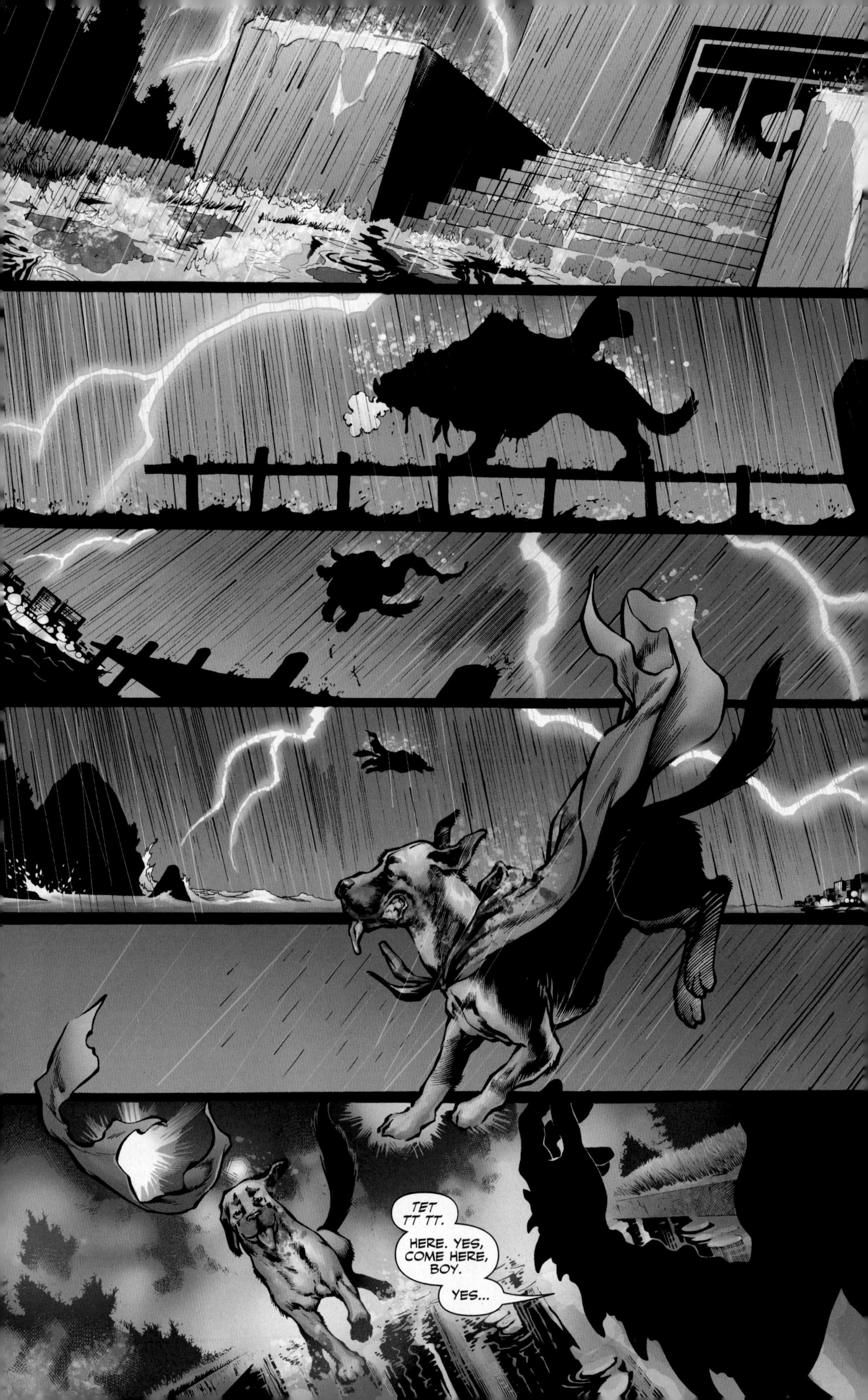
TET
TT TT.
HERE. YES, COME HERE, BOY.
YES...

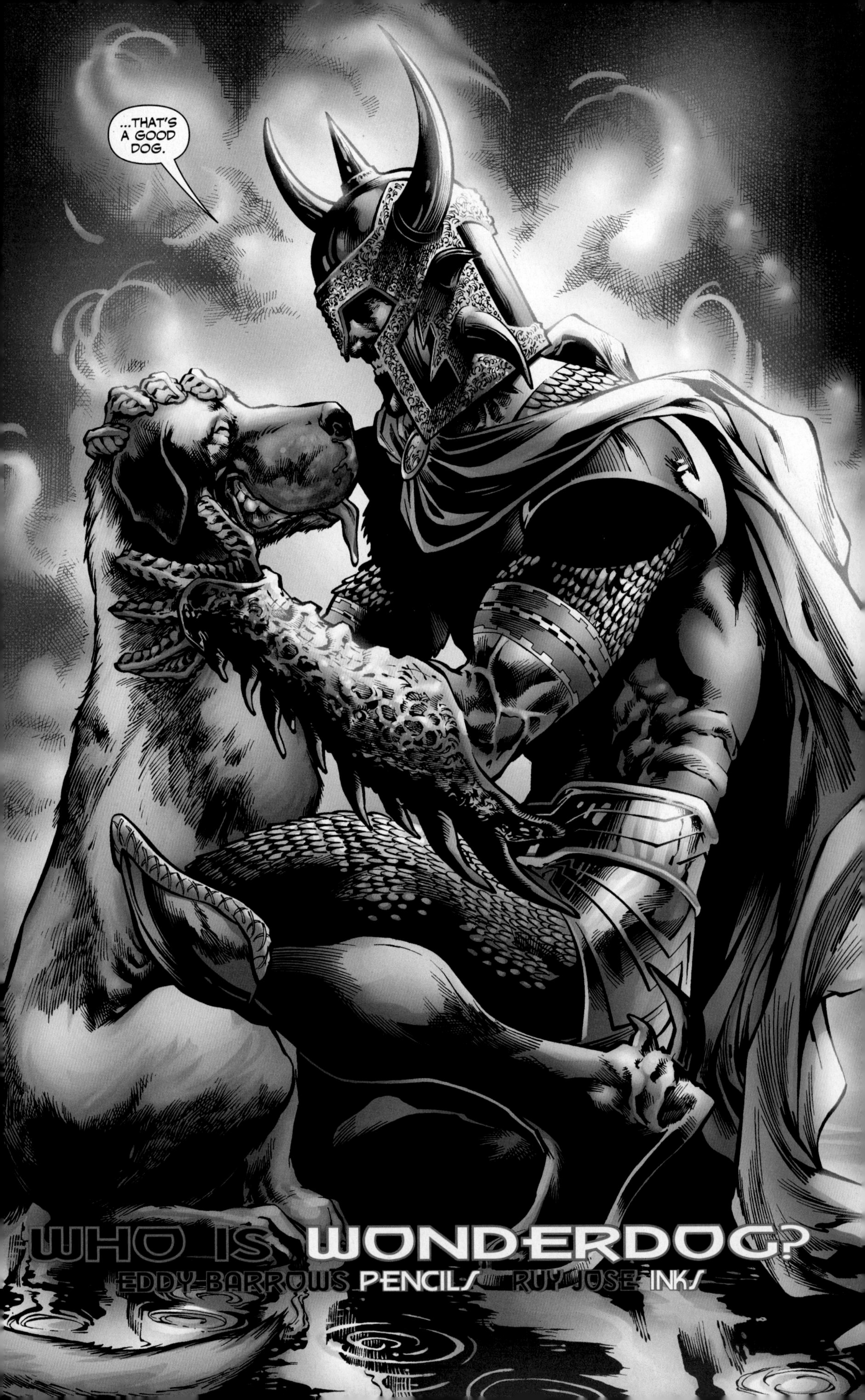
...THAT'S A GOOD DOG.
WHO IS WONDERDOG?
EDDY BARROWS PENCILS RUY JOSE INKS

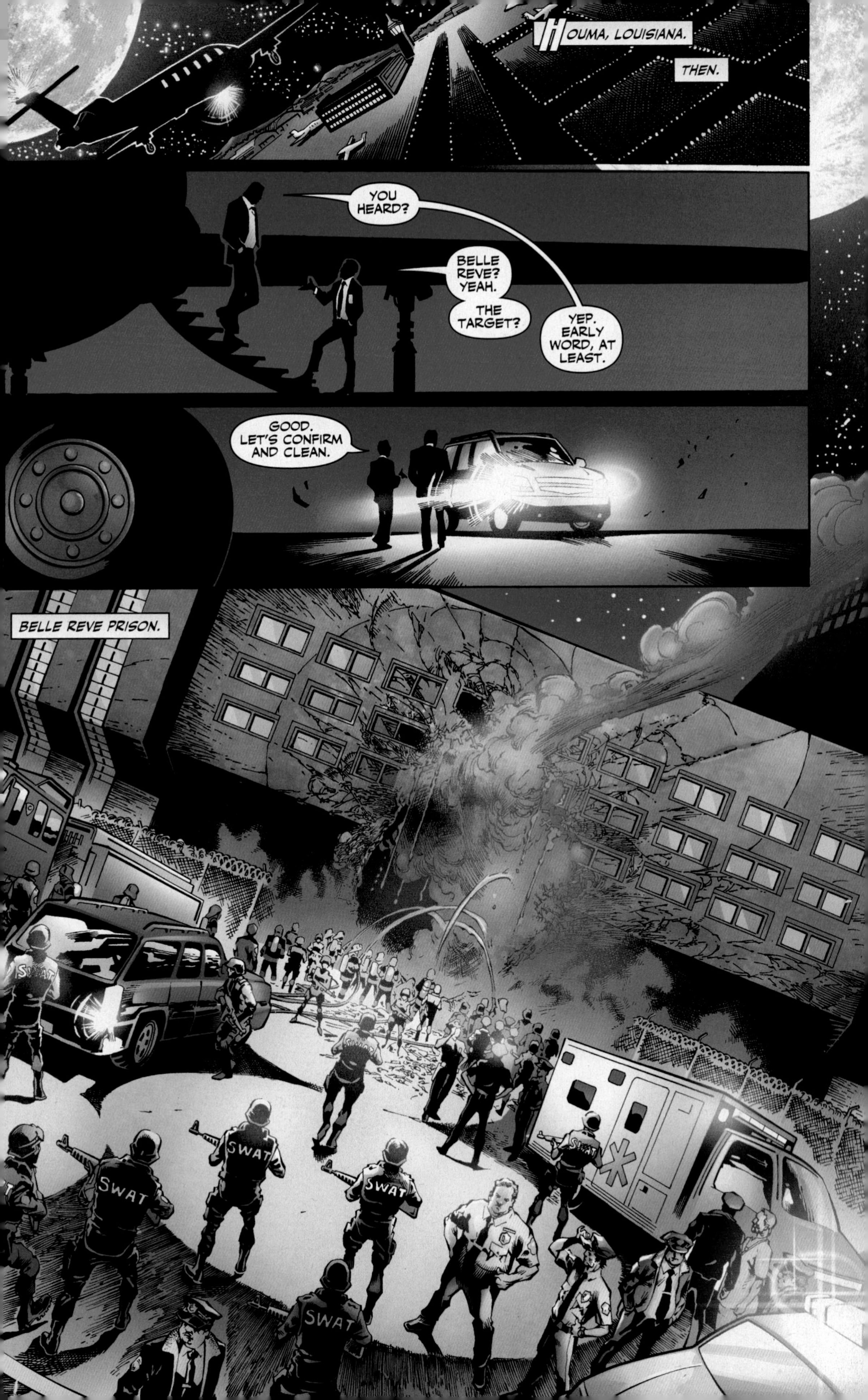
HOUMA, LOUISIANA.
THEN.
YOU HEARD?
BELLE REVE? YEAH.
THE TARGET?
YEP. EARLY WORD, AT LEAST.
GOOD. LET'S CONFIRM AND CLEAN.
BELLE REVE PRISON.
SWAT
SWAT
SWAT
SWAT
SWAT
SWAT
SWAT

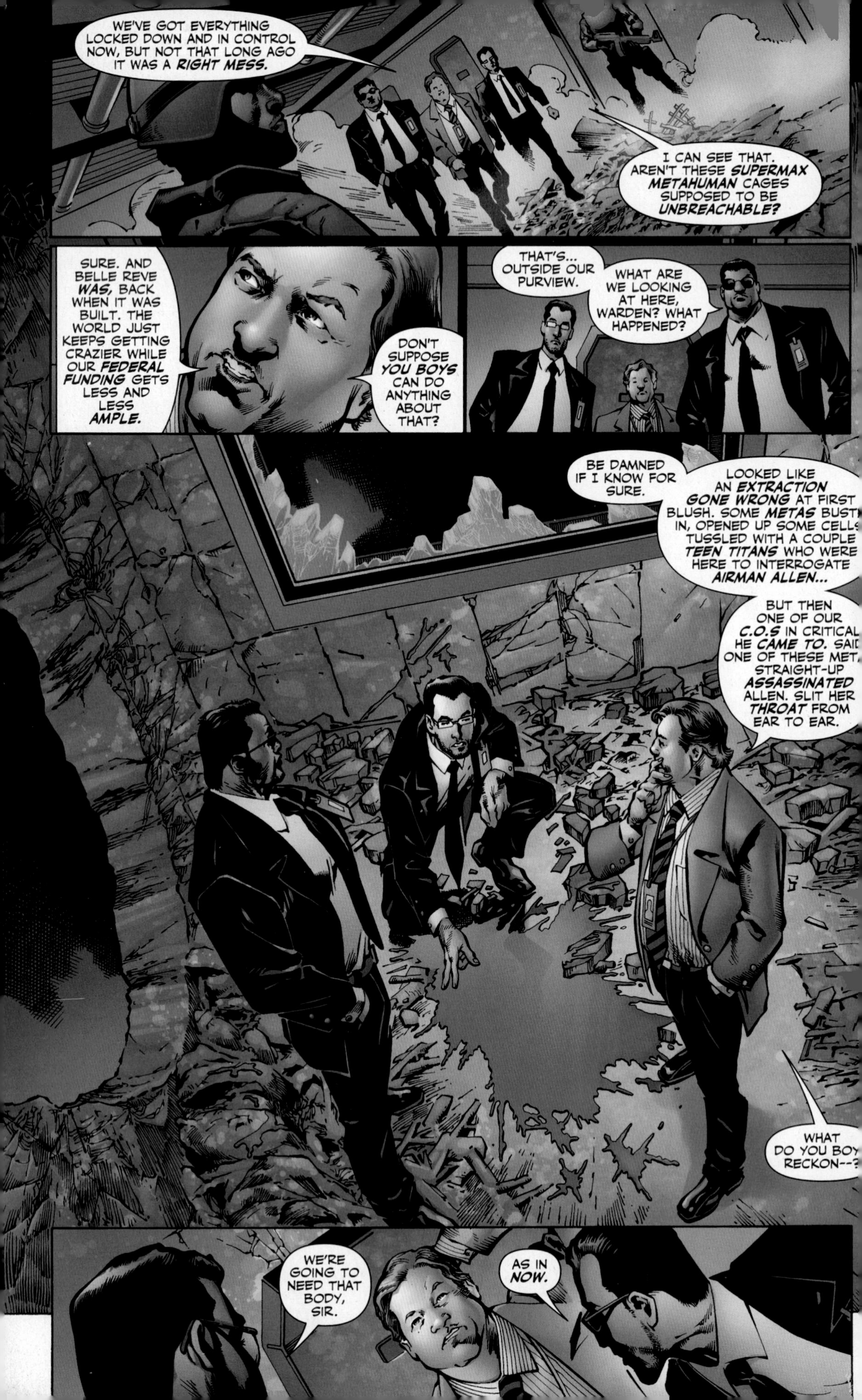
WE'VE GOT EVERYTHING LOCKED DOWN AND IN CONTROL NOW, BUT NOT THAT LONG AGO IT WAS A RIGHT MESS.
I CAN SEE THAT. AREN'T THESE SUPERMAX METAHUMAN CAGES SUPPOSED TO BE UNBREACHABLE?
SURE. AND BELLE REVE WAS, BACK WHEN IT WAS BUILT. THE WORLD JUST KEEPS GETTING CRAZIER WHILE OUR FEDERAL FUNDING GETS LESS AND LESS AMPLE.
DON'T SUPPOSE YOU BOYS CAN DO ANYTHING ABOUT THAT?
THAT'S... OUTSIDE OUR PURVIEW.
WHAT ARE WE LOOKING AT HERE, WARDEN? WHAT HAPPENED?
BE DAMNED IF I KNOW FOR SURE.
LOOKED LIKE AN EXTRACTION GONE WRONG AT FIRST BLUSH. SOME METAS BUST IN, OPENED UP SOME CELLS TUSSLED WITH A COUPLE TEEN TITANS WHO WERE HERE TO INTERROGATE AIRMAN ALLEN...
BUT THEN ONE OF OUR C.O.S IN CRITICAL HE CAME TO. SAID ONE OF THESE MET STRAIGHT-UP ASSASSINATED ALLEN. SLIT HER THROAT FROM EAR TO EAR.
WHAT DO YOU BOY RECKON--?
WE'RE GOING TO NEED THAT BODY, SIR.
AS IN NOW.

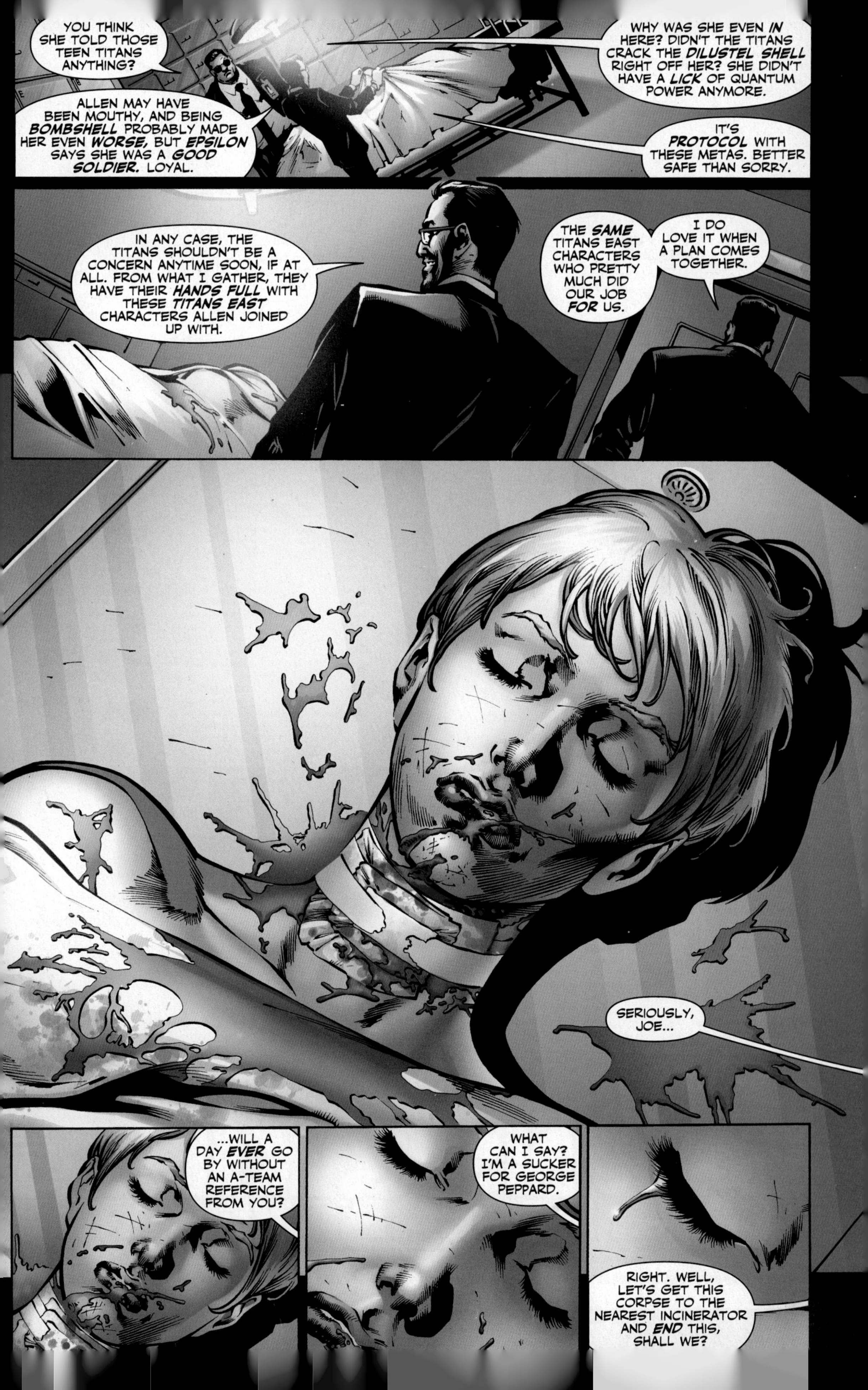
YOU THINK SHE TOLD THOSE TEEN TITANS ANYTHING?
ALLEN MAY HAVE BEEN MOUTHY, AND BEING BOMBSHELL PROBABLY MADE HER EVEN WORSE, BUT EPSILON SAYS SHE WAS A GOOD SOLDIER. LOYAL.
WHY WAS SHE EVEN IN HERE? DIDN'T THE TITANS CRACK THE DILUSTEL SHELL RIGHT OFF HER? SHE DIDN'T HAVE A LICK OF QUANTUM POWER ANYMORE.
IT'S PROTOCOL WITH THESE METAS. BETTER SAFE THAN SORRY.
IN ANY CASE, THE TITANS SHOULDN'T BE A CONCERN ANYTIME SOON, IF AT ALL. FROM WHAT I GATHER, THEY HAVE THEIR HANDS FULL WITH THESE TITANS EAST CHARACTERS ALLEN JOINED UP WITH.
THE SAME TITANS EAST CHARACTERS WHO PRETTY MUCH DID OUR JOB FOR US.
I DO LOVE IT WHEN A PLAN COMES TOGETHER.
SERIOUSLY, JOE...
...WILL A DAY EVER GO BY WITHOUT AN A-TEAM REFERENCE FROM YOU?
WHAT CAN I SAY? I'M A SUCKER FOR GEORGE PEPPARD.
RIGHT. WELL, LET'S GET THIS CORPSE TO THE NEAREST INCINERATOR AND END THIS, SHALL WE?

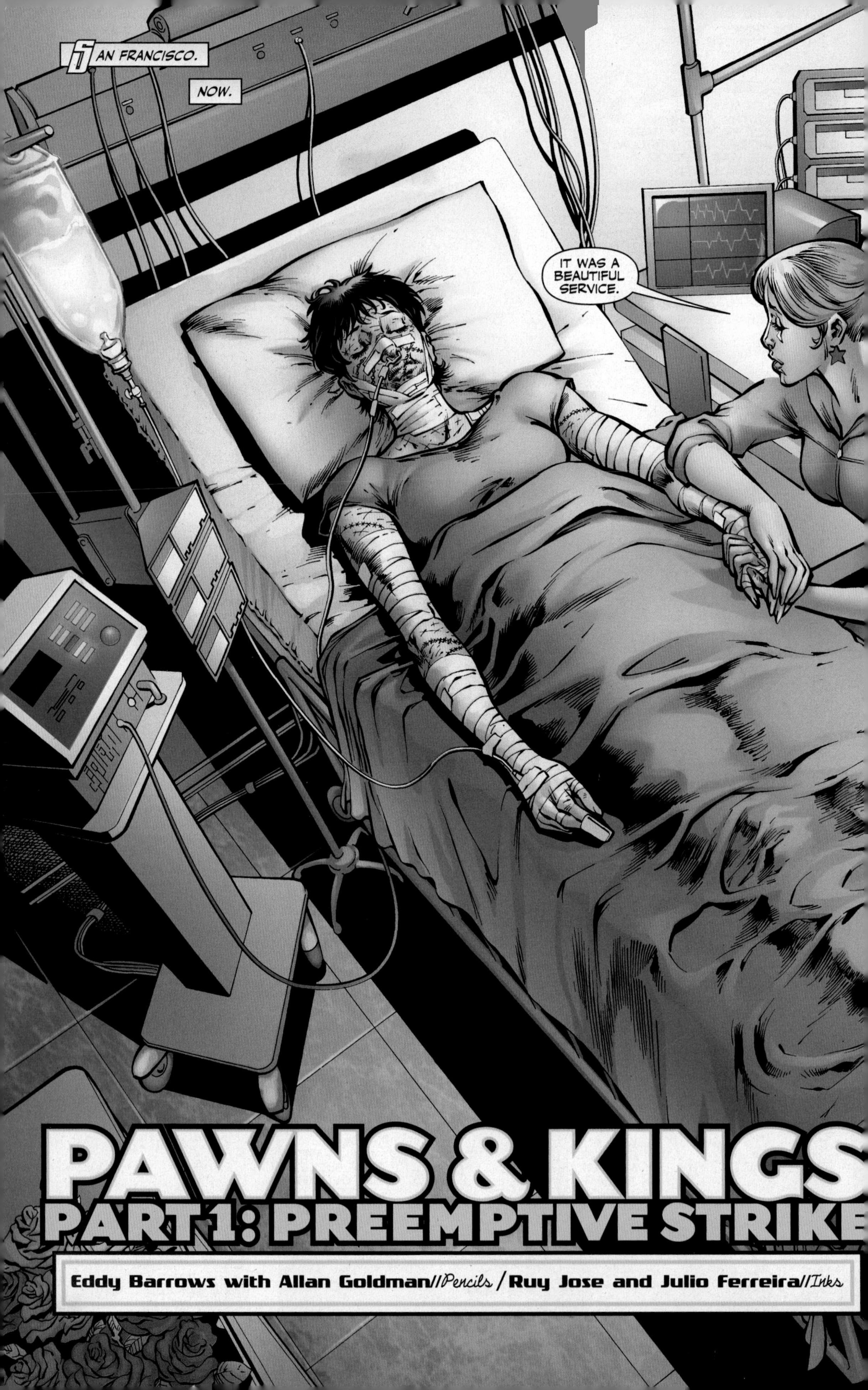
SAN FRANCISCO.
NOW.
IT WAS A BEAUTIFUL SERVICE.
PAWNS & KINGS
PART 1: PREEMPTIVE STRIKE
Eddy Barrows with Allan Goldman//Pencils / Ruy Jose and Julio Ferreira//Inks

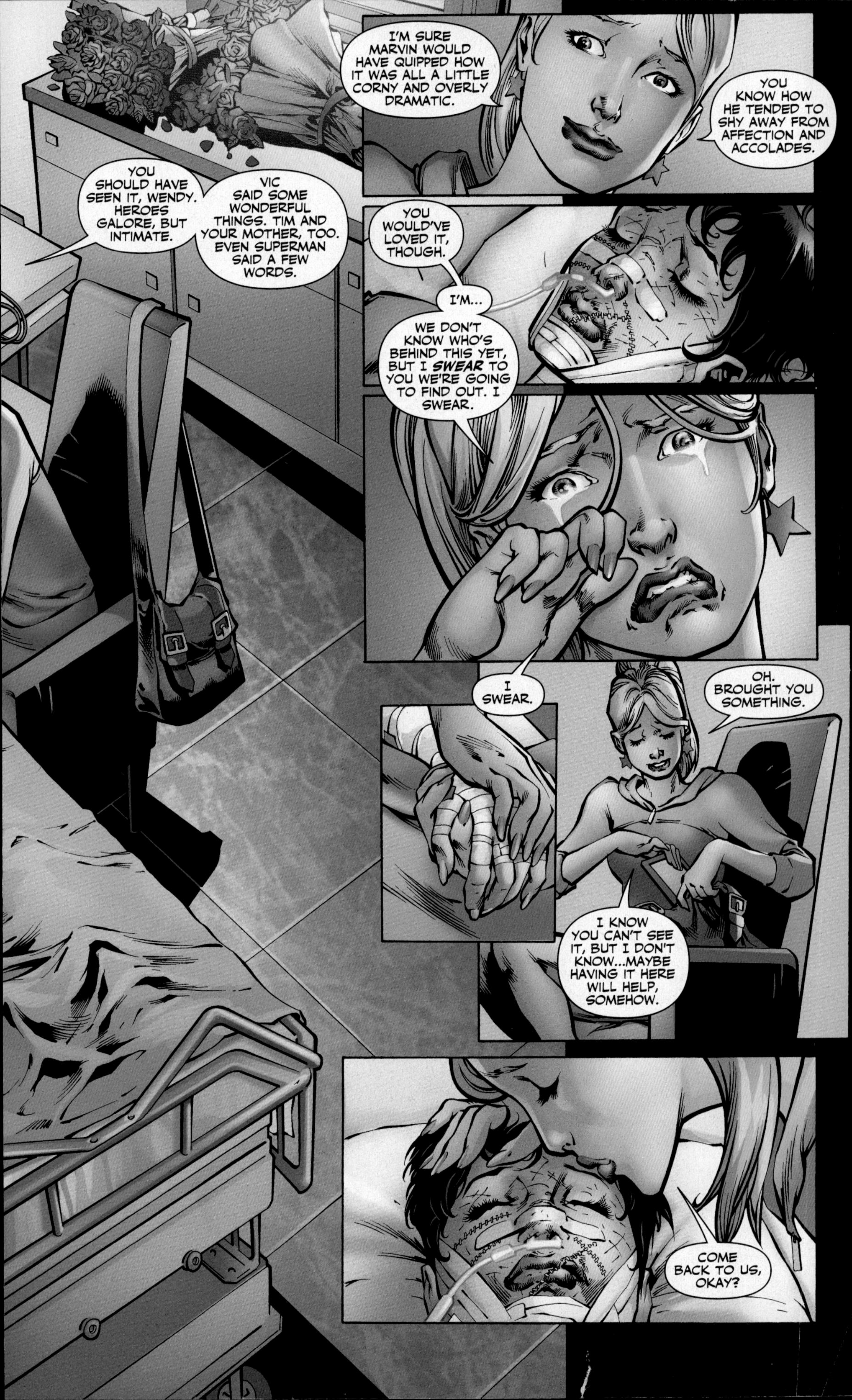
I'M SURE MARVIN WOULD HAVE QUIPPED HOW IT WAS ALL A LITTLE CORNY AND OVERLY DRAMATIC.
YOU KNOW HOW HE TENDED TO SHY AWAY FROM AFFECTION AND ACCOLADES.
YOU SHOULD HAVE SEEN IT, WENDY. HEROES GALORE, BUT INTIMATE.
VIC SAID SOME WONDERFUL THINGS. TIM AND YOUR MOTHER, TOO. EVEN SUPERMAN SAID A FEW WORDS.
YOU WOULD'VE LOVED IT, THOUGH.
I'M...
WE DON'T KNOW WHO'S BEHIND THIS YET, BUT I *SWEAR* TO YOU WE'RE GOING TO FIND OUT. I SWEAR.
I SWEAR.
OH. BROUGHT YOU SOMETHING.
I KNOW YOU CAN'T SEE IT, BUT I DON'T KNOW...MAYBE HAVING IT HERE WILL HELP, SOMEHOW.
COME BACK TO US, OKAY?

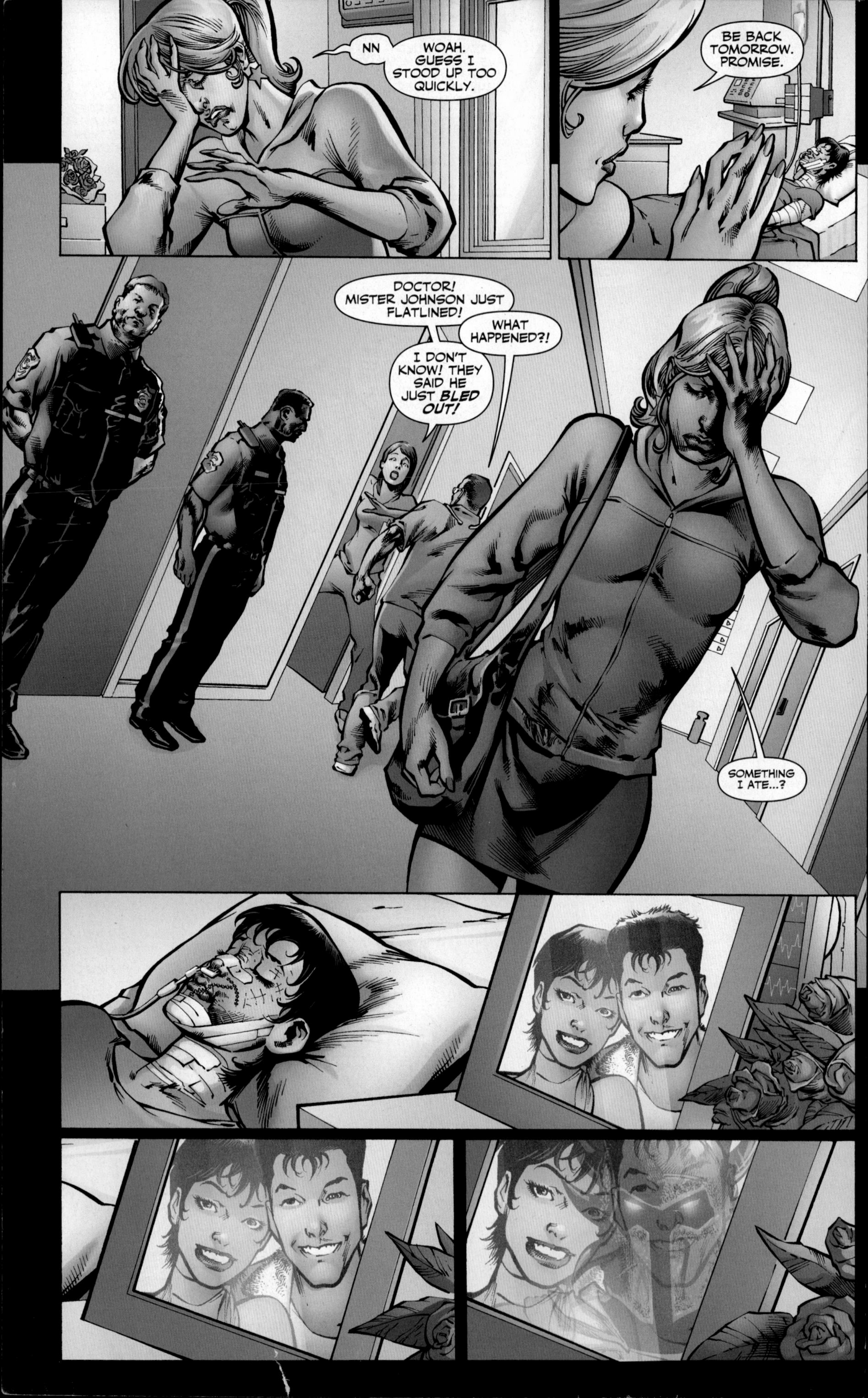
NN
WOAH. GUESS I STOOD UP TOO QUICKLY.
BE BACK TOMORROW. PROMISE.
DOCTOR! MISTER JOHNSON JUST FLATLINED!
WHAT HAPPENED?!
I DON'T KNOW! THEY SAID HE JUST BLED OUT!
SOMETHING I ATE...?

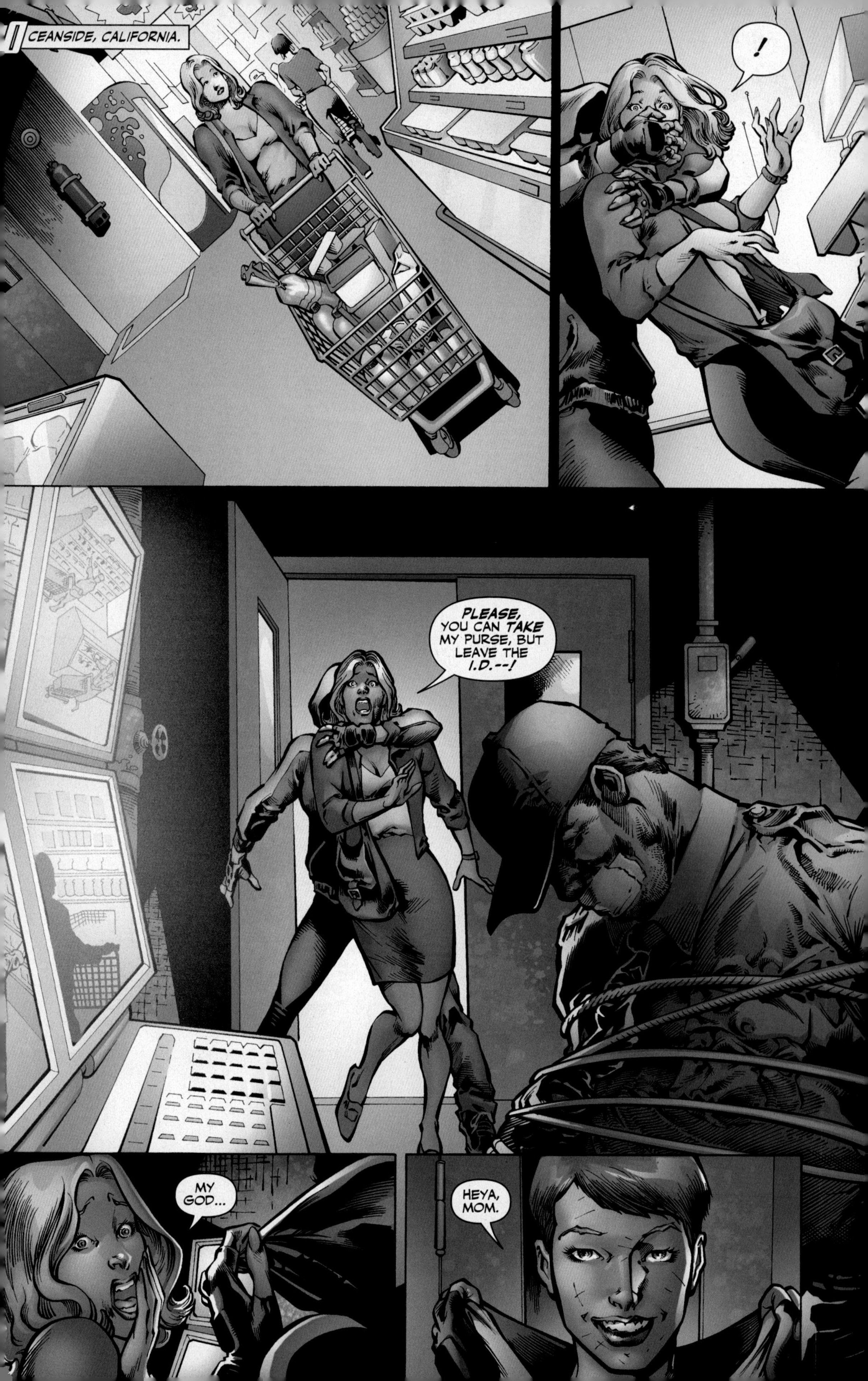
OCEANSIDE, CALIFORNIA.
!
PLEASE, YOU CAN TAKE MY PURSE, BUT LEAVE THE I.D.--!
MY GOD...
HEYA, MOM.

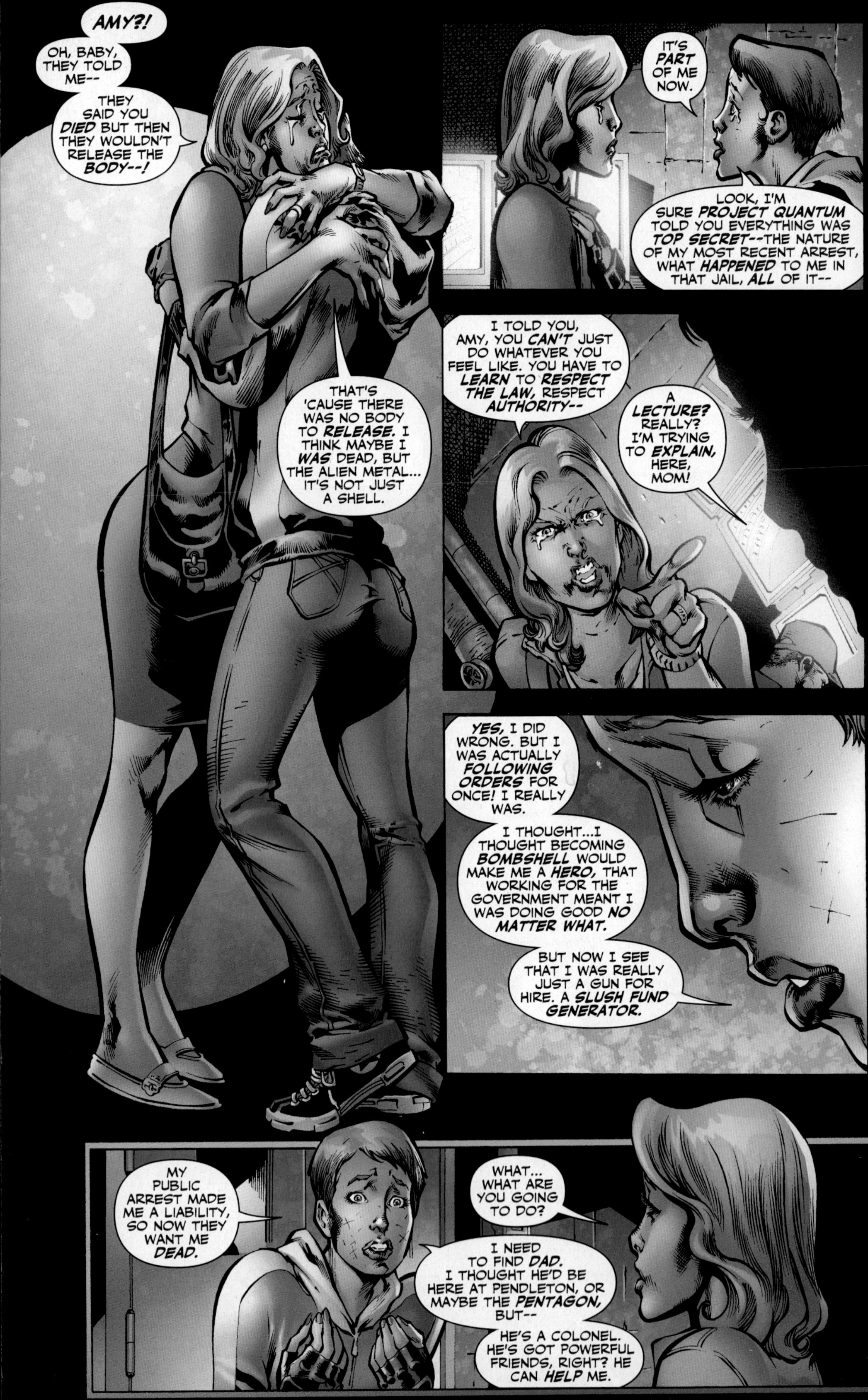
AMY?!
OH, BABY, THEY TOLD ME--
THEY SAID YOU DIED BUT THEN THEY WOULDN'T RELEASE THE BODY--!
THAT'S 'CAUSE THERE WAS NO BODY TO RELEASE. I THINK MAYBE I WAS DEAD, BUT THE ALIEN METAL... IT'S NOT JUST A SHELL.
IT'S PART OF ME NOW.
LOOK, I'M SURE PROJECT QUANTUM TOLD YOU EVERYTHING WAS TOP SECRET--THE NATURE OF MY MOST RECENT ARREST, WHAT HAPPENED TO ME IN THAT JAIL, ALL OF IT--
I TOLD YOU, AMY, YOU CAN'T JUST DO WHATEVER YOU FEEL LIKE. YOU HAVE TO LEARN TO RESPECT THE LAW, RESPECT AUTHORITY--
A LECTURE? REALLY? I'M TRYING TO EXPLAIN, HERE, MOM!
YES, I DID WRONG. BUT I WAS ACTUALLY FOLLOWING ORDERS FOR ONCE! I REALLY WAS.
I THOUGHT...I THOUGHT BECOMING BOMBSHELL WOULD MAKE ME A HERO, THAT WORKING FOR THE GOVERNMENT MEANT I WAS DOING GOOD NO MATTER WHAT.
BUT NOW I SEE THAT I WAS REALLY JUST A GUN FOR HIRE. A SLUSH FUND GENERATOR.
MY PUBLIC ARREST MADE ME A LIABILITY, SO NOW THEY WANT ME DEAD.
WHAT... WHAT ARE YOU GOING TO DO?
I NEED TO FIND DAD. I THOUGHT HE'D BE HERE AT PENDLETON, OR MAYBE THE PENTAGON, BUT--
HE'S A COLONEL. HE'S GOT POWERFUL FRIENDS, RIGHT? HE CAN HELP ME.

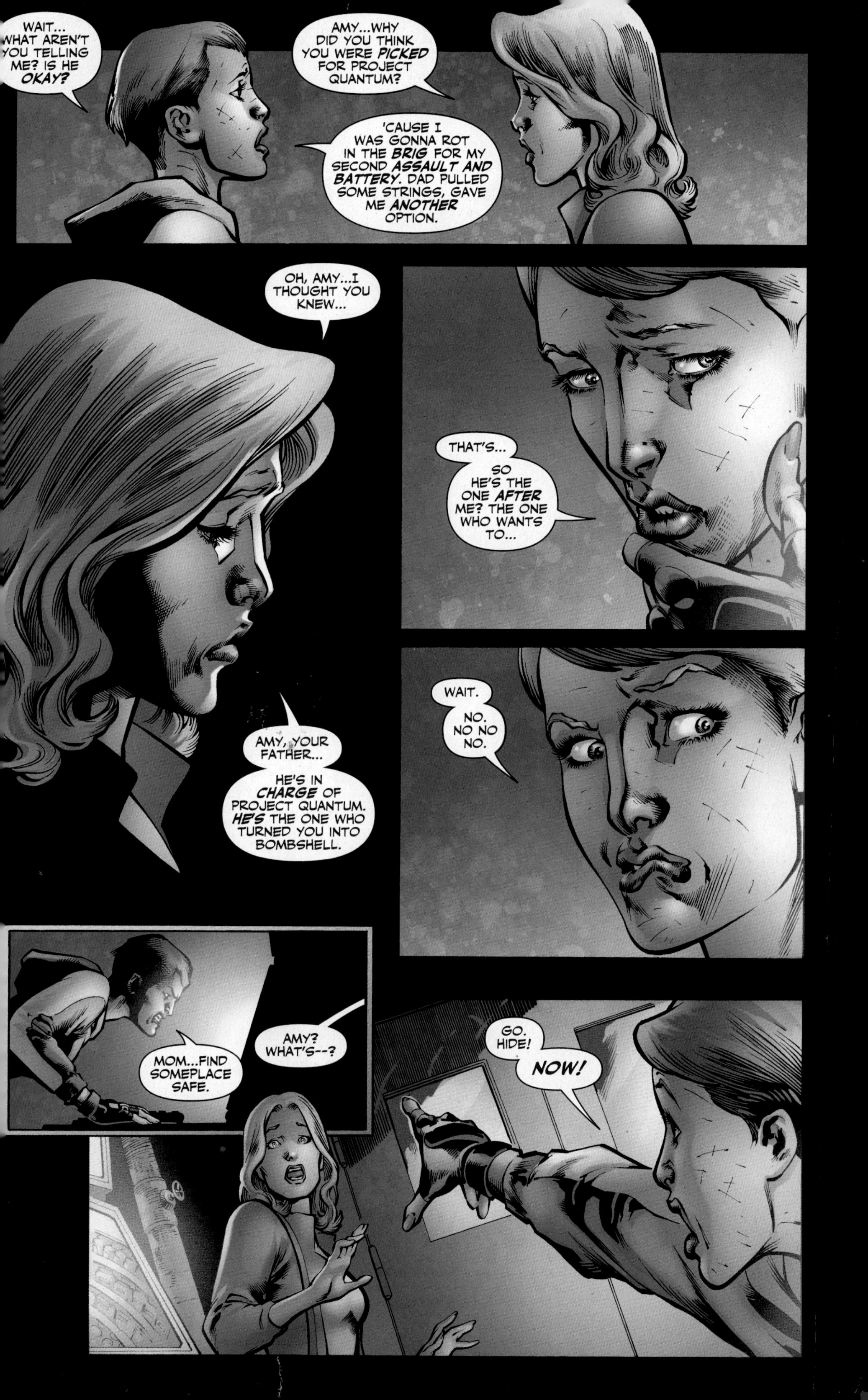
WAIT... WHAT AREN'T YOU TELLING ME? IS HE OKAY?
AMY...WHY DID YOU THINK YOU WERE PICKED FOR PROJECT QUANTUM?
'CAUSE I WAS GONNA ROT IN THE BRIG FOR MY SECOND ASSAULT AND BATTERY. DAD PULLED SOME STRINGS, GAVE ME ANOTHER OPTION.
OH, AMY...I THOUGHT YOU KNEW...
THAT'S...
SO HE'S THE ONE AFTER ME? THE ONE WHO WANTS TO...
AMY, YOUR FATHER...
HE'S IN CHARGE OF PROJECT QUANTUM. HE'S THE ONE WHO TURNED YOU INTO BOMBSHELL.
WAIT.
NO. NO NO NO.
MOM...FIND SOMEPLACE SAFE.
AMY? WHAT'S--?
GO. HIDE!
NOW!

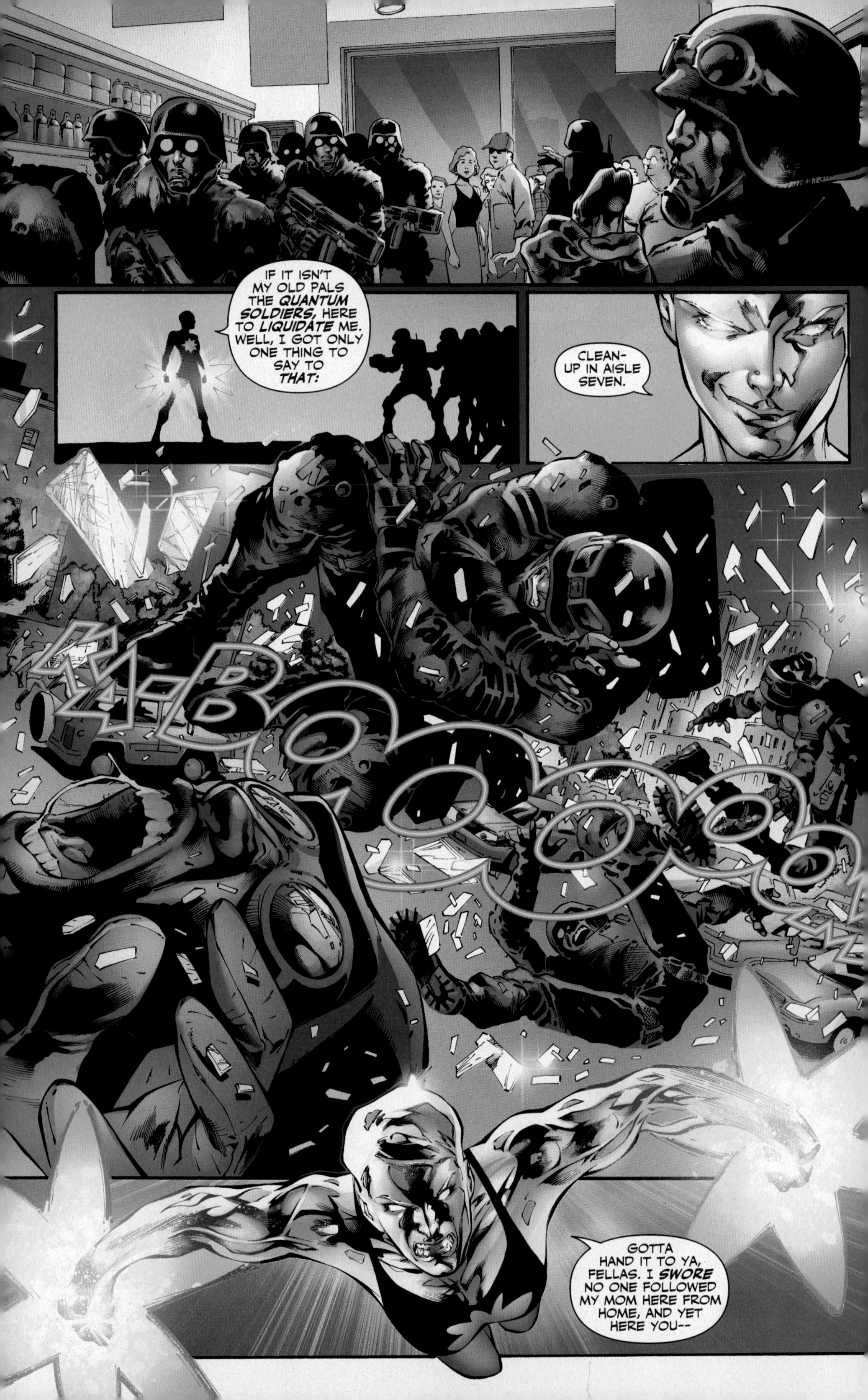
IF IT ISN'T MY OLD PALS THE QUANTUM SOLDIERS, HERE TO LIQUIDATE ME. WELL, I GOT ONLY ONE THING TO SAY TO THAT:
CLEAN-UP IN AISLE SEVEN.
KA-BOOOOOM
GOTTA HAND IT TO YA, FELLAS. I SWORE NO ONE FOLLOWED MY MOM HERE FROM HOME, AND YET HERE YOU--

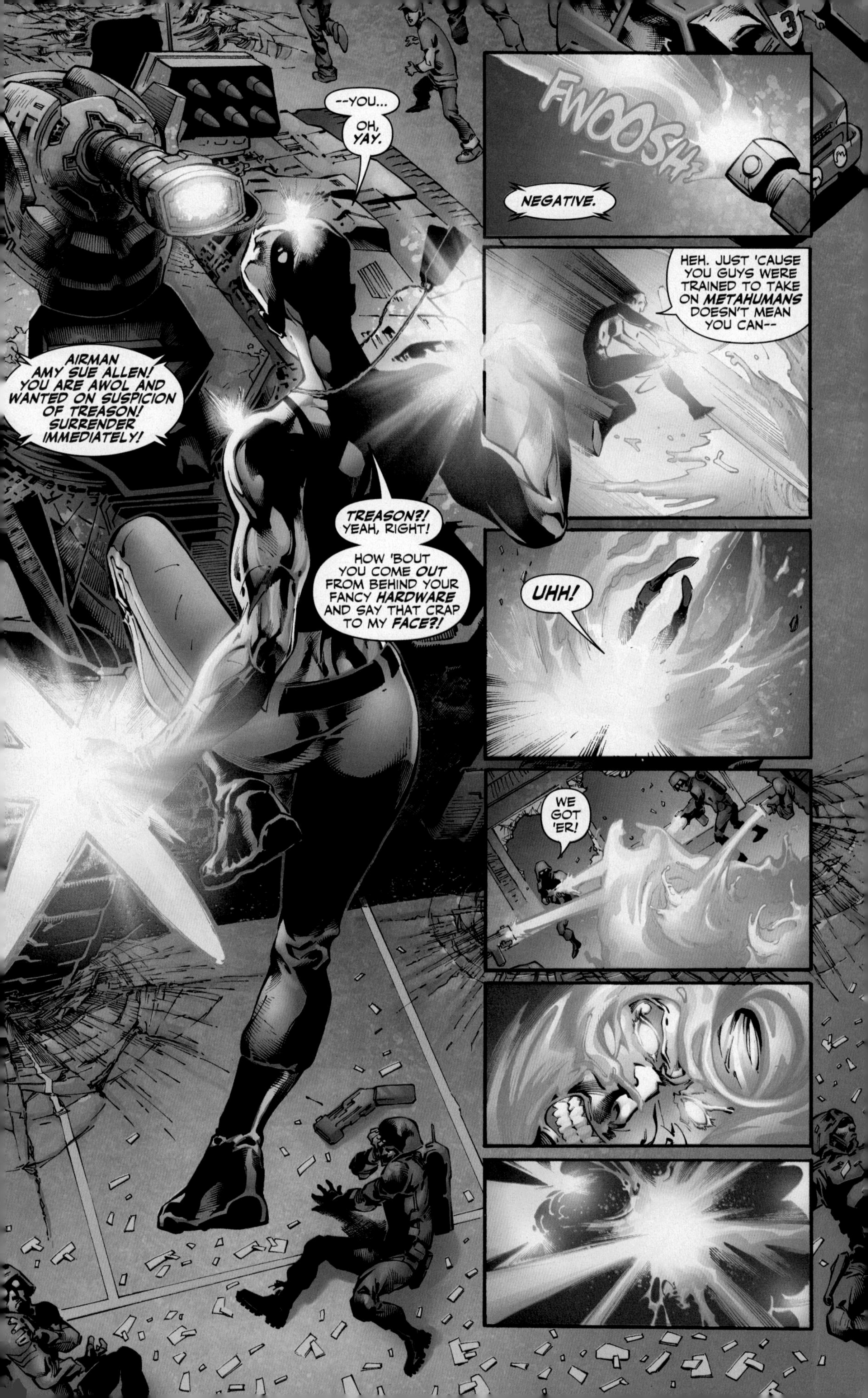
--YOU... OH, YAY.
AIRMAN AMY SUE ALLEN! YOU ARE AWOL AND WANTED ON SUSPICION OF TREASON! SURRENDER IMMEDIATELY!
TREASON?! YEAH, RIGHT!
HOW 'BOUT YOU COME OUT FROM BEHIND YOUR FANCY HARDWARE AND SAY THAT CRAP TO MY FACE?!
FWOOSH
NEGATIVE.
HEH. JUST 'CAUSE YOU GUYS WERE TRAINED TO TAKE ON METAHUMANS DOESN'T MEAN YOU CAN--
UHH!
WE GOT 'ER!

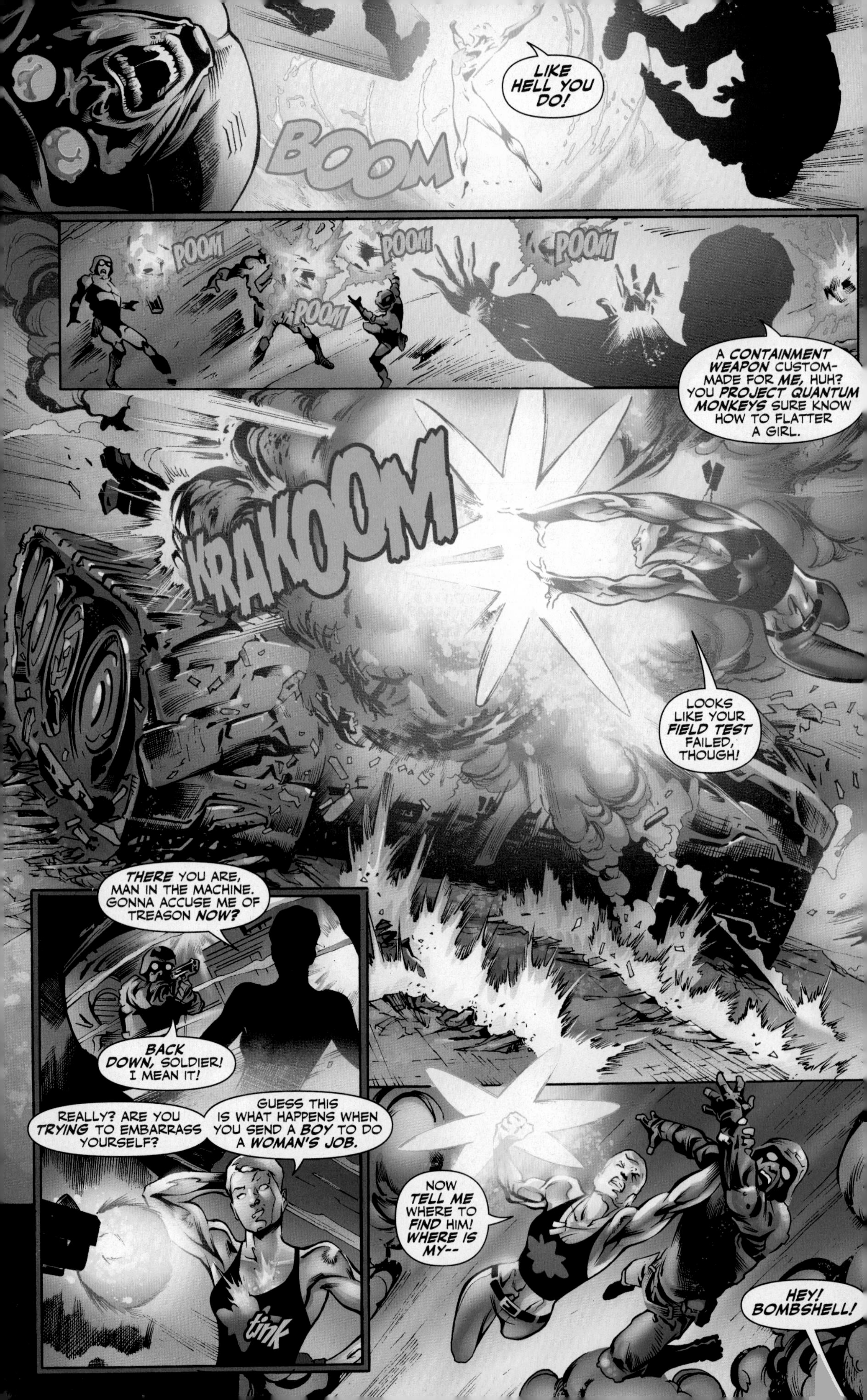
LIKE HELL YOU DO!
BOOM
POOM
POOM
POOM
POOM
A CONTAINMENT WEAPON CUSTOM-MADE FOR ME, HUH? YOU PROJECT QUANTUM MONKEYS SURE KNOW HOW TO FLATTER A GIRL.
KRAKOOM
LOOKS LIKE YOUR FIELD TEST FAILED, THOUGH!
THERE YOU ARE, MAN IN THE MACHINE. GONNA ACCUSE ME OF TREASON NOW?
BACK DOWN, SOLDIER! I MEAN IT!
REALLY? ARE YOU TRYING TO EMBARRASS YOURSELF?
GUESS THIS IS WHAT HAPPENS WHEN YOU SEND A BOY TO DO A WOMAN'S JOB.
tink
NOW TELL ME WHERE TO FIND HIM! WHERE IS MY--
HEY! BOMBSHELL!

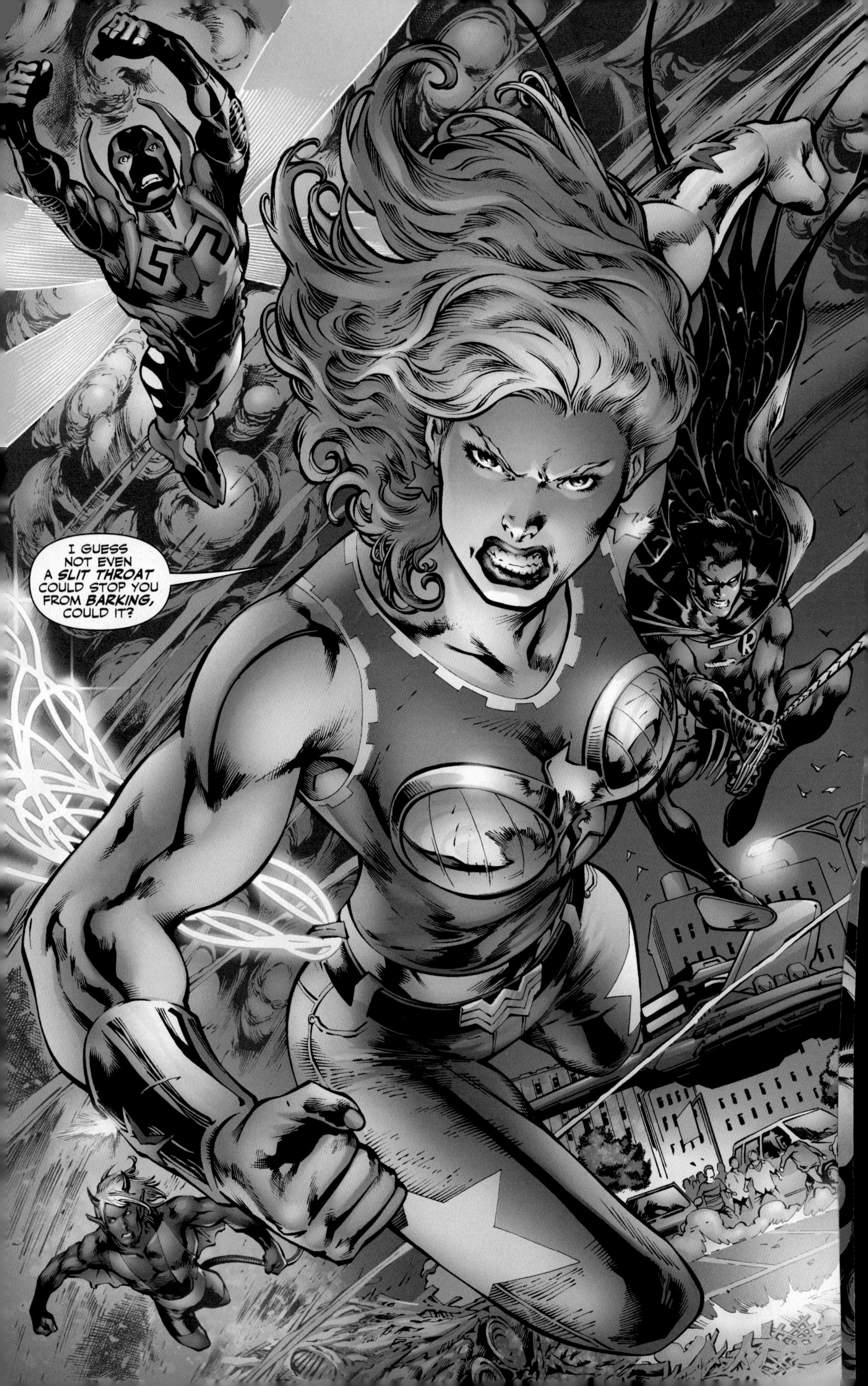
I GUESS NOT EVEN A SLIT THROAT COULD STOP YOU FROM BARKING, COULD IT?

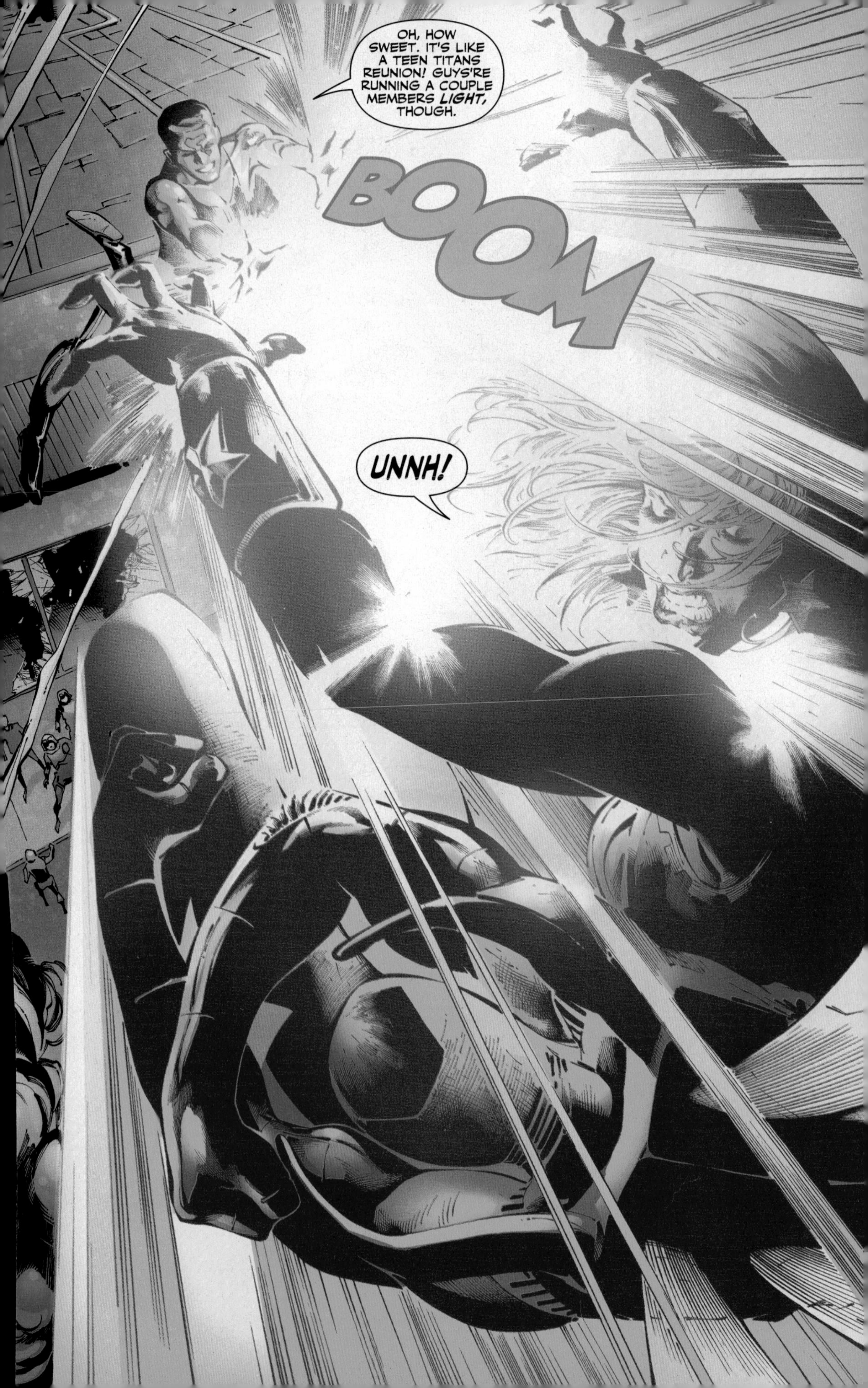
OH, HOW SWEET. IT'S LIKE A TEEN TITANS REUNION! GUYS'RE RUNNING A COUPLE MEMBERS LIGHT, THOUGH.
BOOM
UNNH!

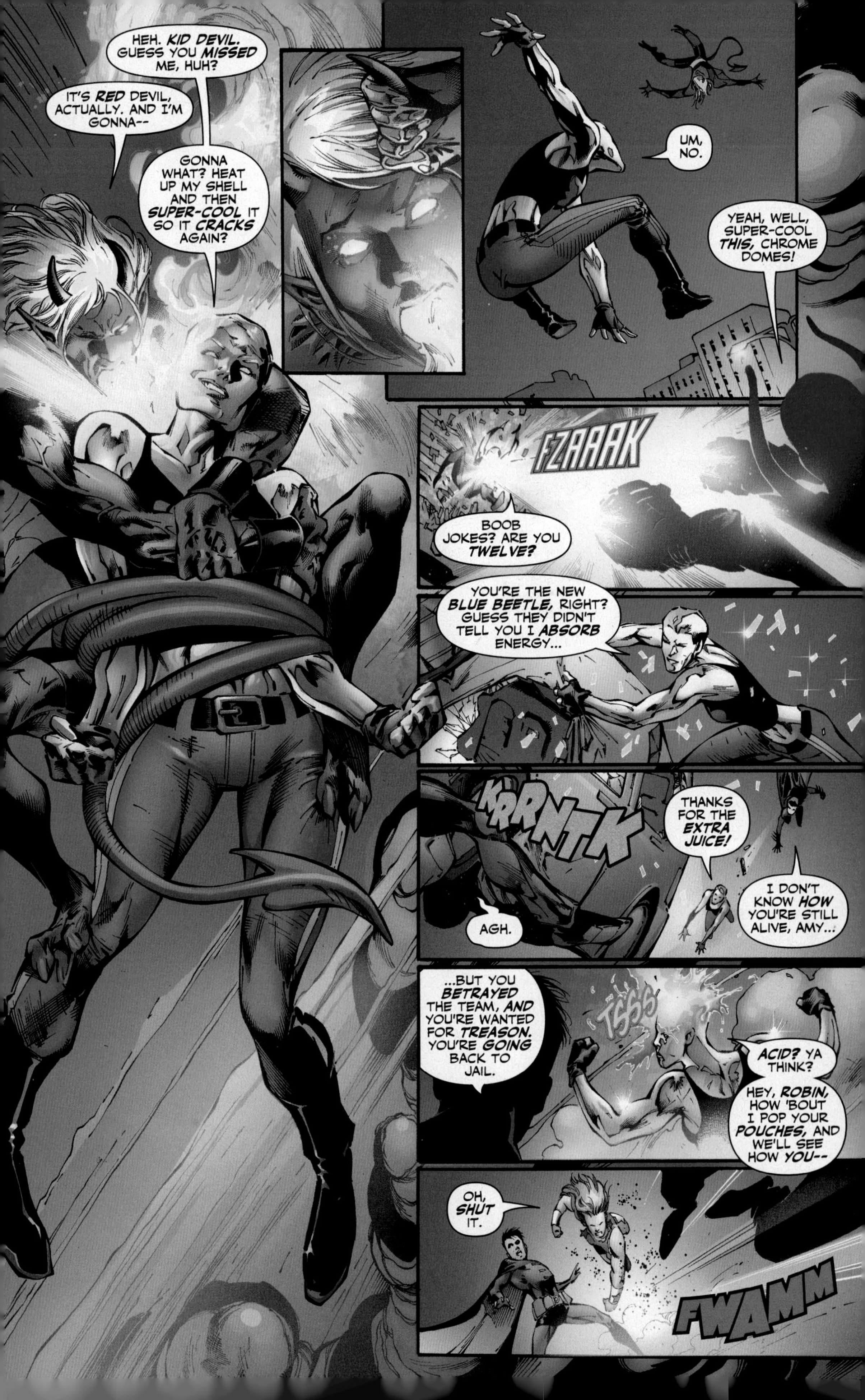
HEH. KID DEVIL. GUESS YOU MISSED ME, HUH?
IT'S RED DEVIL, ACTUALLY. AND I'M GONNA--
GONNA WHAT? HEAT UP MY SHELL AND THEN SUPER-COOL IT SO IT CRACKS AGAIN?
UM, NO.
YEAH, WELL, SUPER-COOL THIS, CHROME DOMES!
FZAAAK
BOOB JOKES? ARE YOU TWELVE?
YOU'RE THE NEW BLUE BEETLE, RIGHT? GUESS THEY DIDN'T TELL YOU I ABSORB ENERGY...
KRRNTK
THANKS FOR THE EXTRA JUICE!
AGH.
I DON'T KNOW HOW YOU'RE STILL ALIVE, AMY...
...BUT YOU BETRAYED THE TEAM, AND YOU'RE WANTED FOR TREASON. YOU'RE GOING BACK TO JAIL.
TSSS
ACID? YA THINK?
HEY, ROBIN, HOW 'BOUT I POP YOUR POUCHES, AND WE'LL SEE HOW YOU--
OH, SHUT IT.
FWAMM

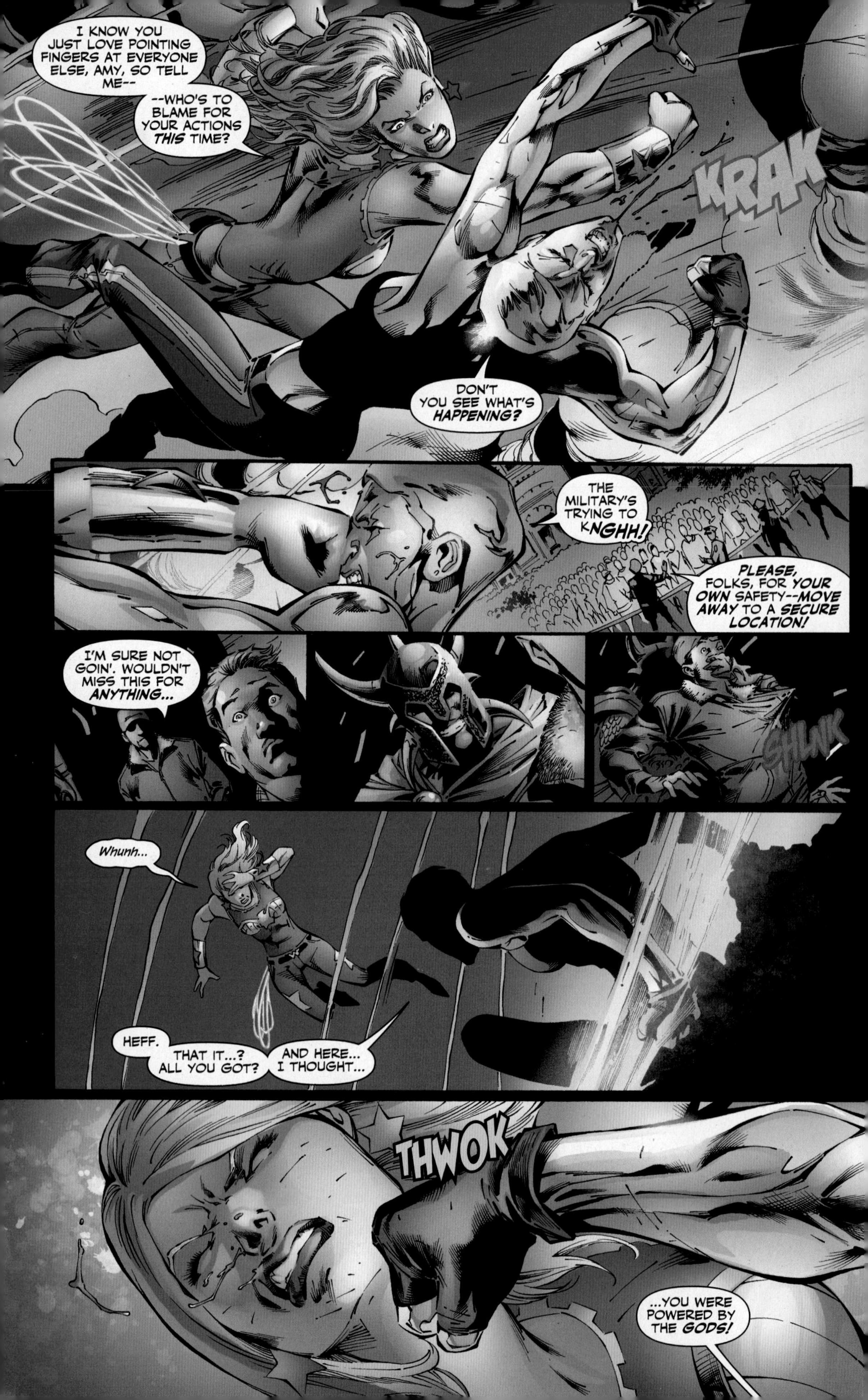
I KNOW YOU JUST LOVE POINTING FINGERS AT EVERYONE ELSE, AMY, SO TELL ME--
--WHO'S TO BLAME FOR YOUR ACTIONS *THIS* TIME?
KRAK
DON'T YOU SEE WHAT'S *HAPPENING?*
THE MILITARY'S TRYING TO K*NGHH!*
PLEASE, FOLKS, FOR *YOUR OWN* SAFETY--*MOVE AWAY* TO A *SECURE LOCATION!*
I'M SURE NOT GOIN'. WOULDN'T MISS THIS FOR *ANYTHING...*
SHUNK
Whunh...
HEFF.
THAT IT...? ALL YOU GOT?
AND HERE... I THOUGHT...
THWOK
...YOU WERE POWERED BY THE *GODS!*

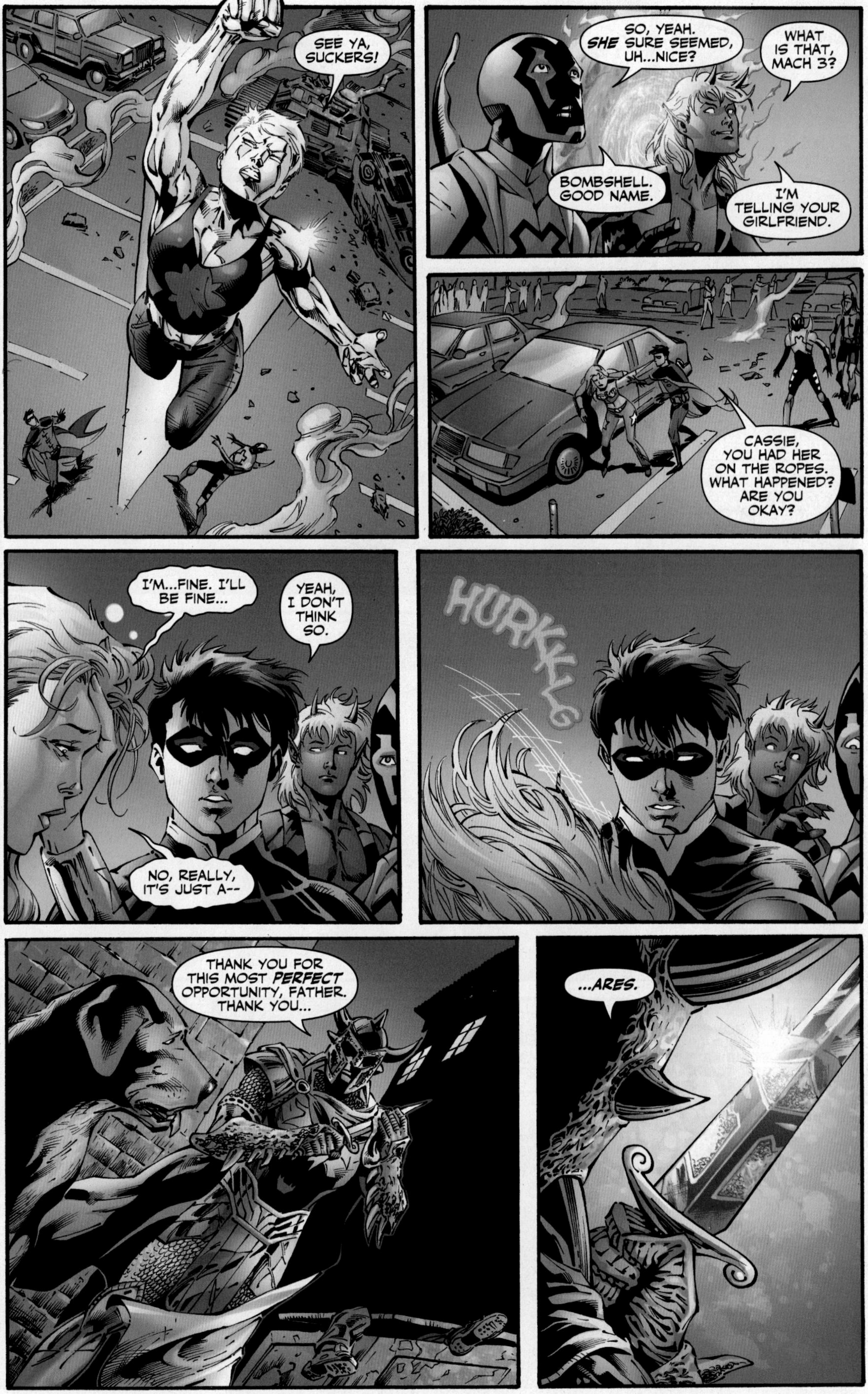

SEE YA, SUCKERS!
SO, YEAH. SHE SURE SEEMED, UH...NICE?
WHAT IS THAT, MACH 3?
BOMBSHELL. GOOD NAME.
I'M TELLING YOUR GIRLFRIEND.
CASSIE, YOU HAD HER ON THE ROPES. WHAT HAPPENED? ARE YOU OKAY?
I'M...FINE. I'LL BE FINE...
YEAH, I DON'T THINK SO.
NO, REALLY, IT'S JUST A--
HURKKLG
THANK YOU FOR THIS MOST PERFECT OPPORTUNITY, FATHER. THANK YOU...
...ARES.

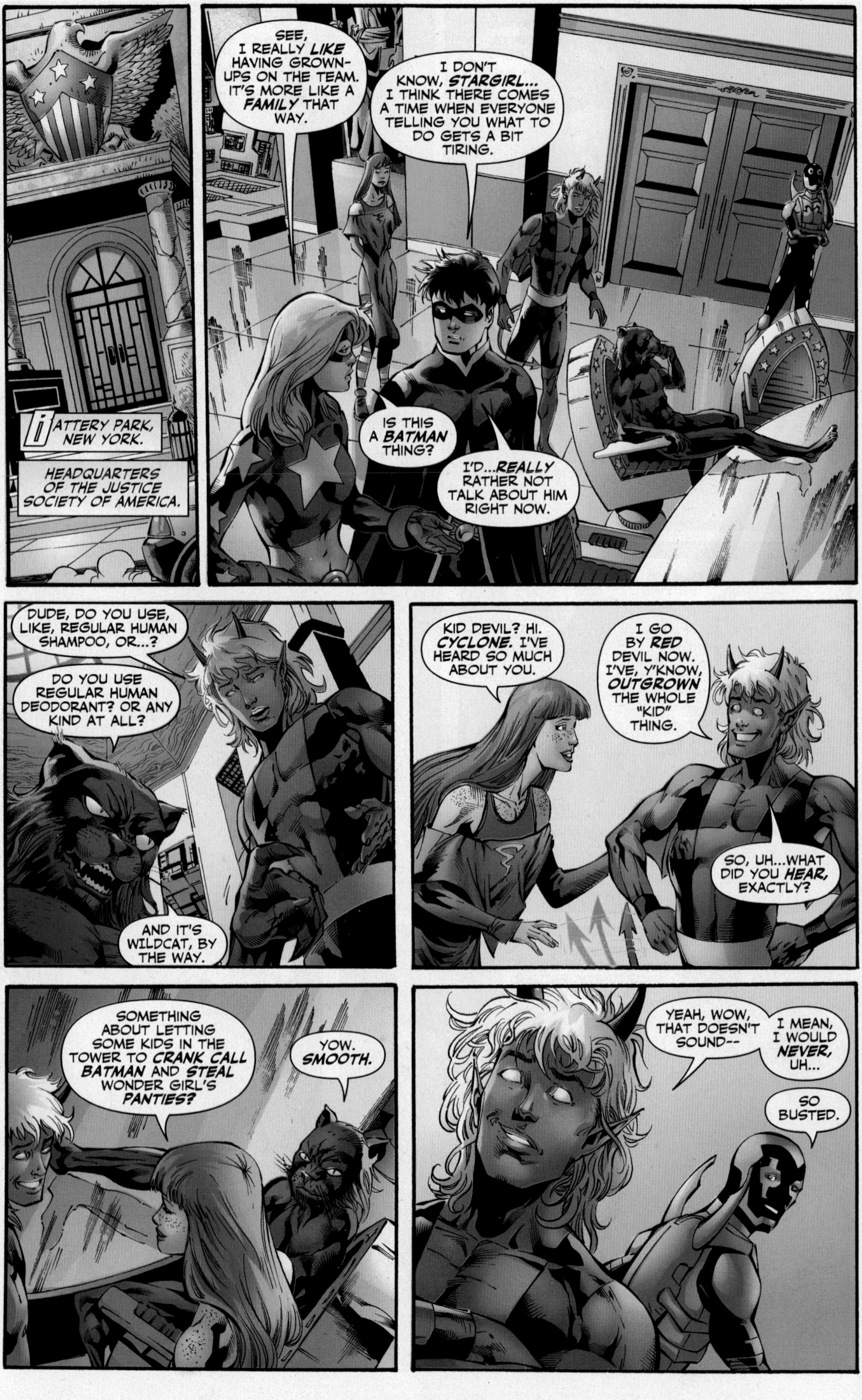
BATTERY PARK, NEW YORK.
HEADQUARTERS OF THE JUSTICE SOCIETY OF AMERICA.
SEE, I REALLY LIKE HAVING GROWN-UPS ON THE TEAM. IT'S MORE LIKE A FAMILY THAT WAY.
I DON'T KNOW, STARGIRL... I THINK THERE COMES A TIME WHEN EVERYONE TELLING YOU WHAT TO DO GETS A BIT TIRING.
IS THIS A BATMAN THING?
I'D...REALLY RATHER NOT TALK ABOUT HIM RIGHT NOW.
DUDE, DO YOU USE, LIKE, REGULAR HUMAN SHAMPOO, OR...?
DO YOU USE REGULAR HUMAN DEODORANT? OR ANY KIND AT ALL?
AND IT'S WILDCAT, BY THE WAY.
KID DEVIL? HI. CYCLONE. I'VE HEARD SO MUCH ABOUT YOU.
I GO BY RED DEVIL NOW. I'VE, Y'KNOW, OUTGROWN THE WHOLE "KID" THING.
SO, UH...WHAT DID YOU HEAR, EXACTLY?
SOMETHING ABOUT LETTING SOME KIDS IN THE TOWER TO CRANK CALL BATMAN AND STEAL WONDER GIRL'S PANTIES?
YOW. SMOOTH.
YEAH, WOW, THAT DOESN'T SOUND--
I MEAN, I WOULD NEVER, UH...
SO BUSTED.

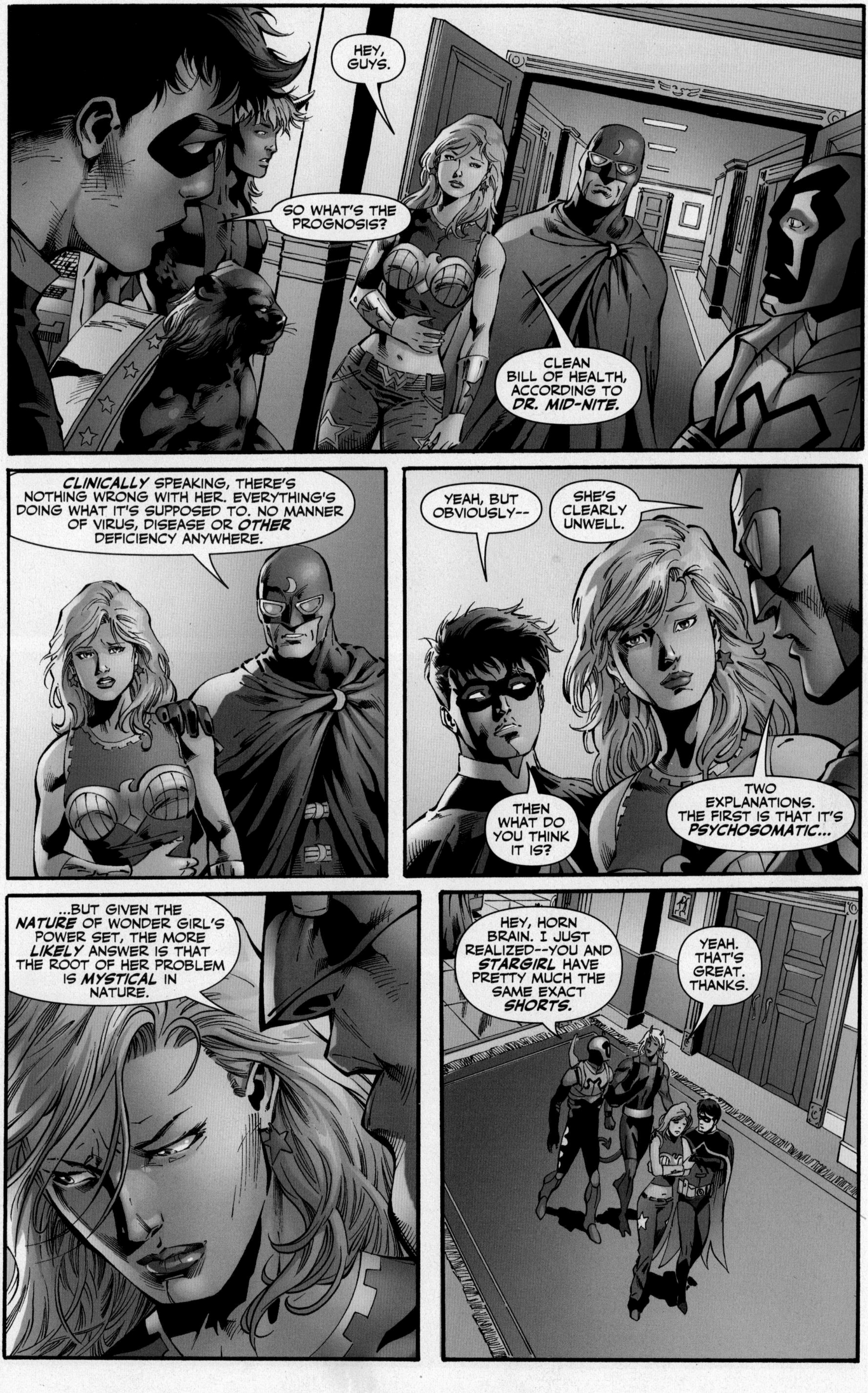
HEY, GUYS.
SO WHAT'S THE PROGNOSIS?
CLEAN BILL OF HEALTH, ACCORDING TO DR. MID-NITE.
CLINICALLY SPEAKING, THERE'S NOTHING WRONG WITH HER. EVERYTHING'S DOING WHAT IT'S SUPPOSED TO. NO MANNER OF VIRUS, DISEASE OR OTHER DEFICIENCY ANYWHERE.
YEAH, BUT OBVIOUSLY--
SHE'S CLEARLY UNWELL.
THEN WHAT DO YOU THINK IT IS?
TWO EXPLANATIONS. THE FIRST IS THAT IT'S PSYCHOSOMATIC...
...BUT GIVEN THE NATURE OF WONDER GIRL'S POWER SET, THE MORE LIKELY ANSWER IS THAT THE ROOT OF HER PROBLEM IS MYSTICAL IN NATURE.
HEY, HORN BRAIN. I JUST REALIZED--YOU AND STARGIRL HAVE PRETTY MUCH THE SAME EXACT SHORTS.
YEAH. THAT'S GREAT. THANKS.

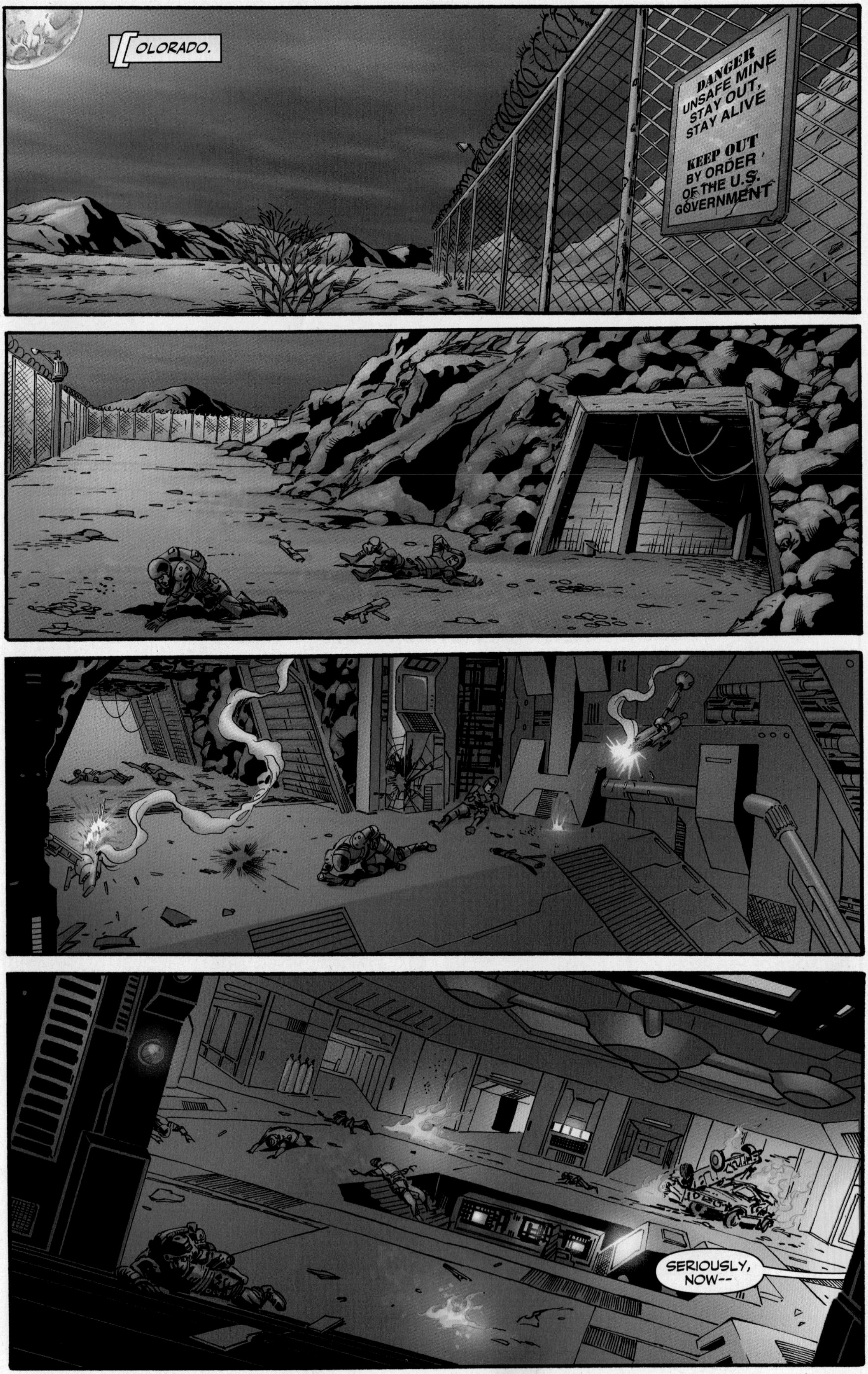
COLORADO.
DANGER
UNSAFE MINE
STAY OUT,
STAY ALIVE
KEEP OUT
BY ORDER
OF THE U.S.
GOVERNMENT
SERIOUSLY, NOW--

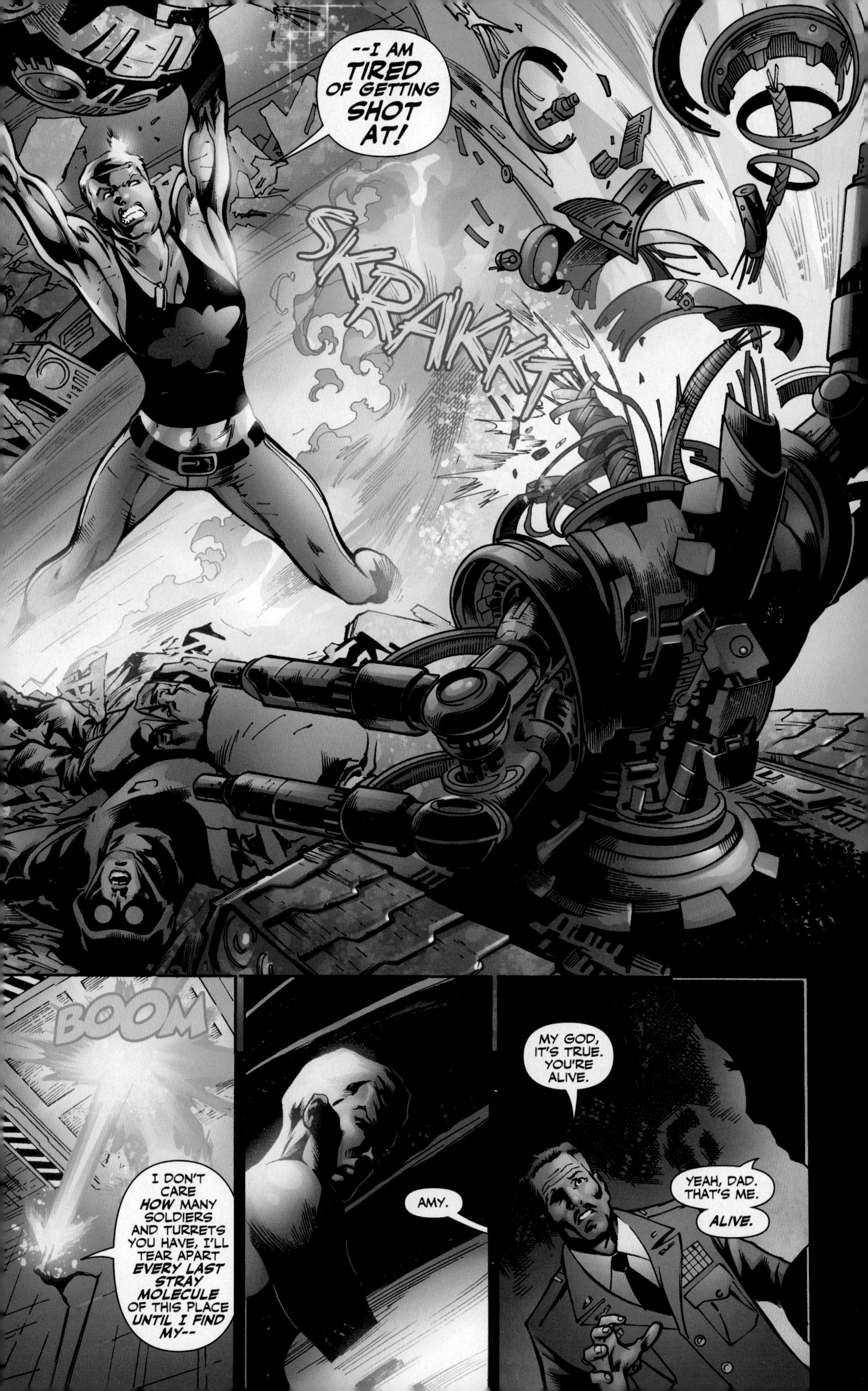
--I AM TIRED OF GETTING SHOT AT!
SKRAKKKT
BOOM
I DON'T CARE HOW MANY SOLDIERS AND TURRETS YOU HAVE, I'LL TEAR APART EVERY LAST STRAY MOLECULE OF THIS PLACE UNTIL I FIND MY--
AMY.
MY GOD, IT'S TRUE. YOU'RE ALIVE.
YEAH, DAD. THAT'S ME.
ALIVE.

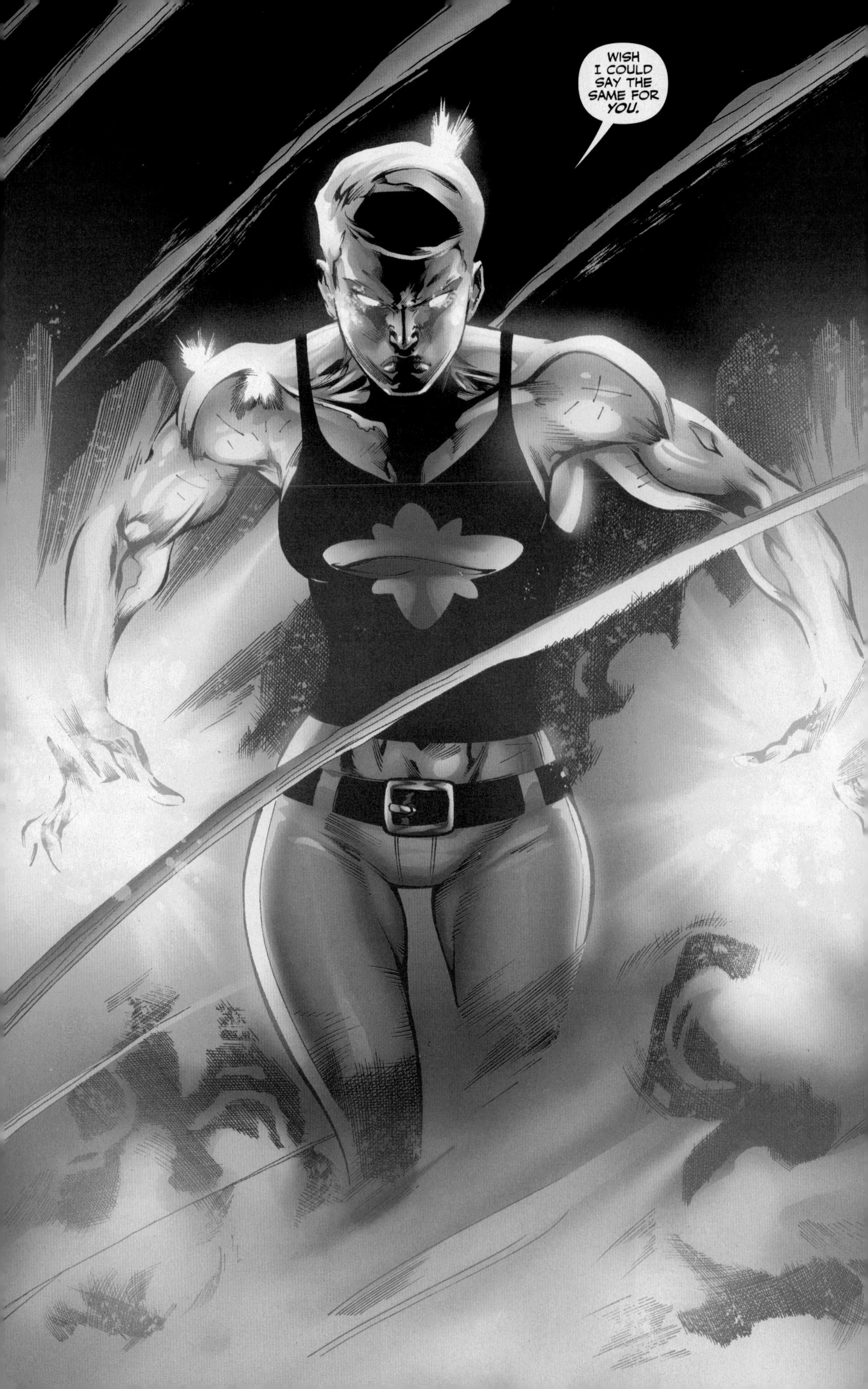
WISH I COULD SAY THE SAME FOR YOU.

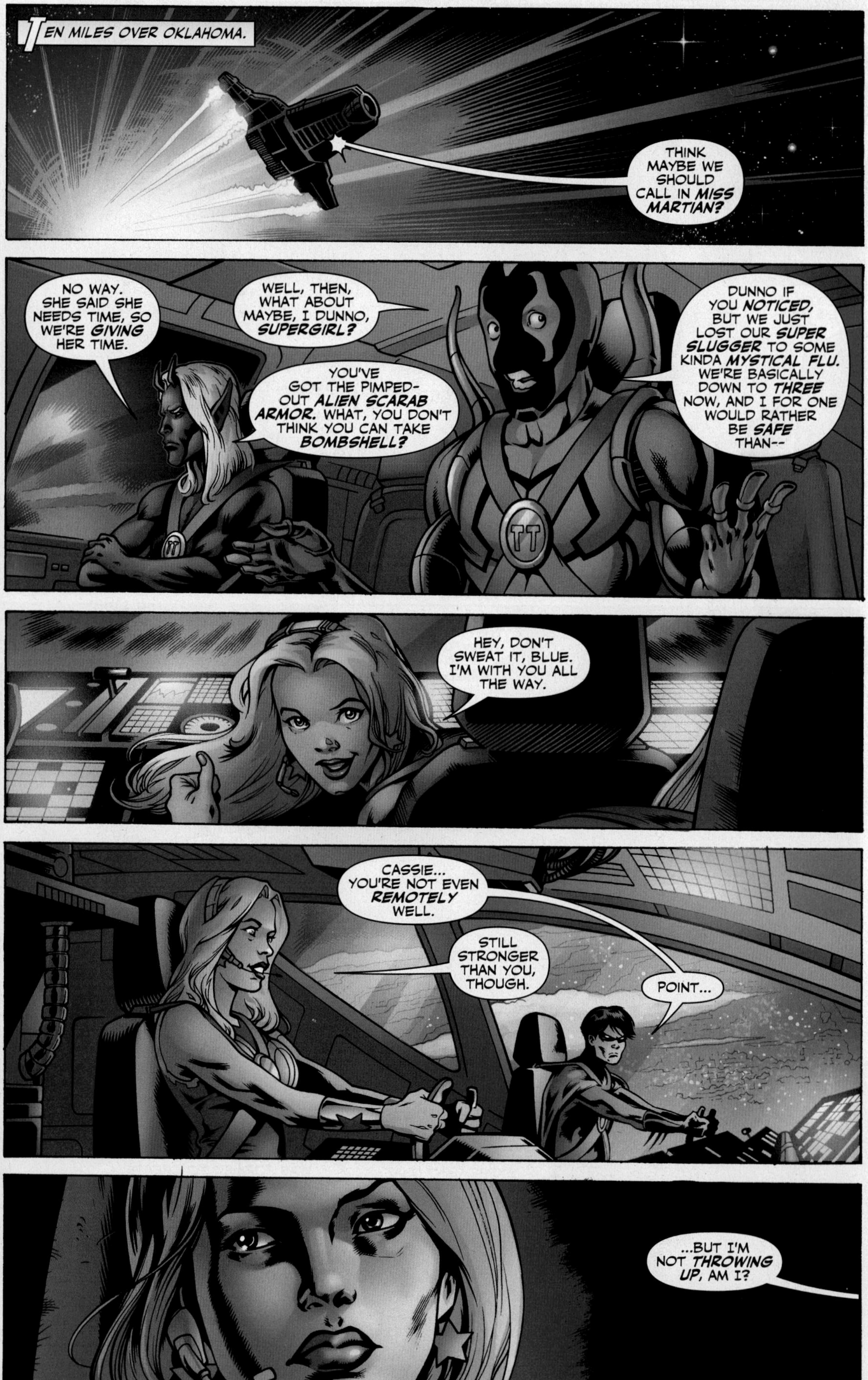
TEN MILES OVER OKLAHOMA.
THINK MAYBE WE SHOULD CALL IN MISS MARTIAN?
NO WAY. SHE SAID SHE NEEDS TIME, SO WE'RE GIVING HER TIME.
WELL, THEN, WHAT ABOUT MAYBE, I DUNNO, SUPERGIRL?
YOU'VE GOT THE PIMPED-OUT ALIEN SCARAB ARMOR. WHAT, YOU DON'T THINK YOU CAN TAKE BOMBSHELL?
DUNNO IF YOU NOTICED, BUT WE JUST LOST OUR SUPER SLUGGER TO SOME KINDA MYSTICAL FLU. WE'RE BASICALLY DOWN TO THREE NOW, AND I FOR ONE WOULD RATHER BE SAFE THAN--
HEY, DON'T SWEAT IT, BLUE. I'M WITH YOU ALL THE WAY.
CASSIE... YOU'RE NOT EVEN REMOTELY WELL.
STILL STRONGER THAN YOU, THOUGH.
POINT...
...BUT I'M NOT THROWING UP, AM I?

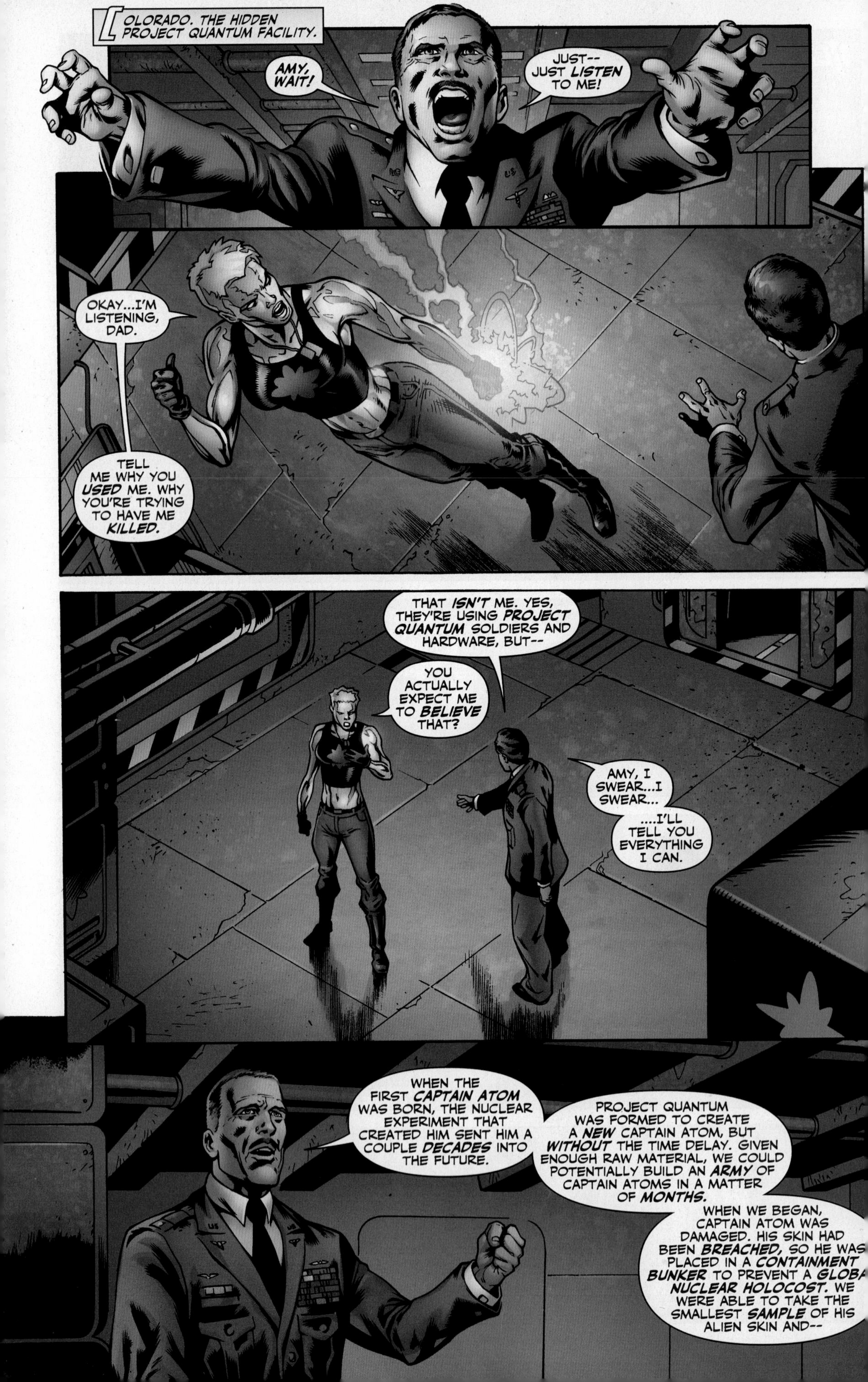
COLORADO. THE HIDDEN PROJECT QUANTUM FACILITY.
AMY, WAIT!
JUST-- JUST LISTEN TO ME!
OKAY...I'M LISTENING, DAD.
TELL ME WHY YOU USED ME. WHY YOU'RE TRYING TO HAVE ME KILLED.
THAT ISN'T ME. YES, THEY'RE USING PROJECT QUANTUM SOLDIERS AND HARDWARE, BUT--
YOU ACTUALLY EXPECT ME TO BELIEVE THAT?
AMY, I SWEAR...I SWEAR...
....I'LL TELL YOU EVERYTHING I CAN.
WHEN THE FIRST CAPTAIN ATOM WAS BORN, THE NUCLEAR EXPERIMENT THAT CREATED HIM SENT HIM A COUPLE DECADES INTO THE FUTURE.
PROJECT QUANTUM WAS FORMED TO CREATE A NEW CAPTAIN ATOM, BUT WITHOUT THE TIME DELAY. GIVEN ENOUGH RAW MATERIAL, WE COULD POTENTIALLY BUILD AN ARMY OF CAPTAIN ATOMS IN A MATTER OF MONTHS.
WHEN WE BEGAN, CAPTAIN ATOM WAS DAMAGED. HIS SKIN HAD BEEN BREACHED, SO HE WAS PLACED IN A CONTAINMENT BUNKER TO PREVENT A GLOBA NUCLEAR HOLOCOST. WE WERE ABLE TO TAKE THE SMALLEST SAMPLE OF HIS ALIEN SKIN AND--

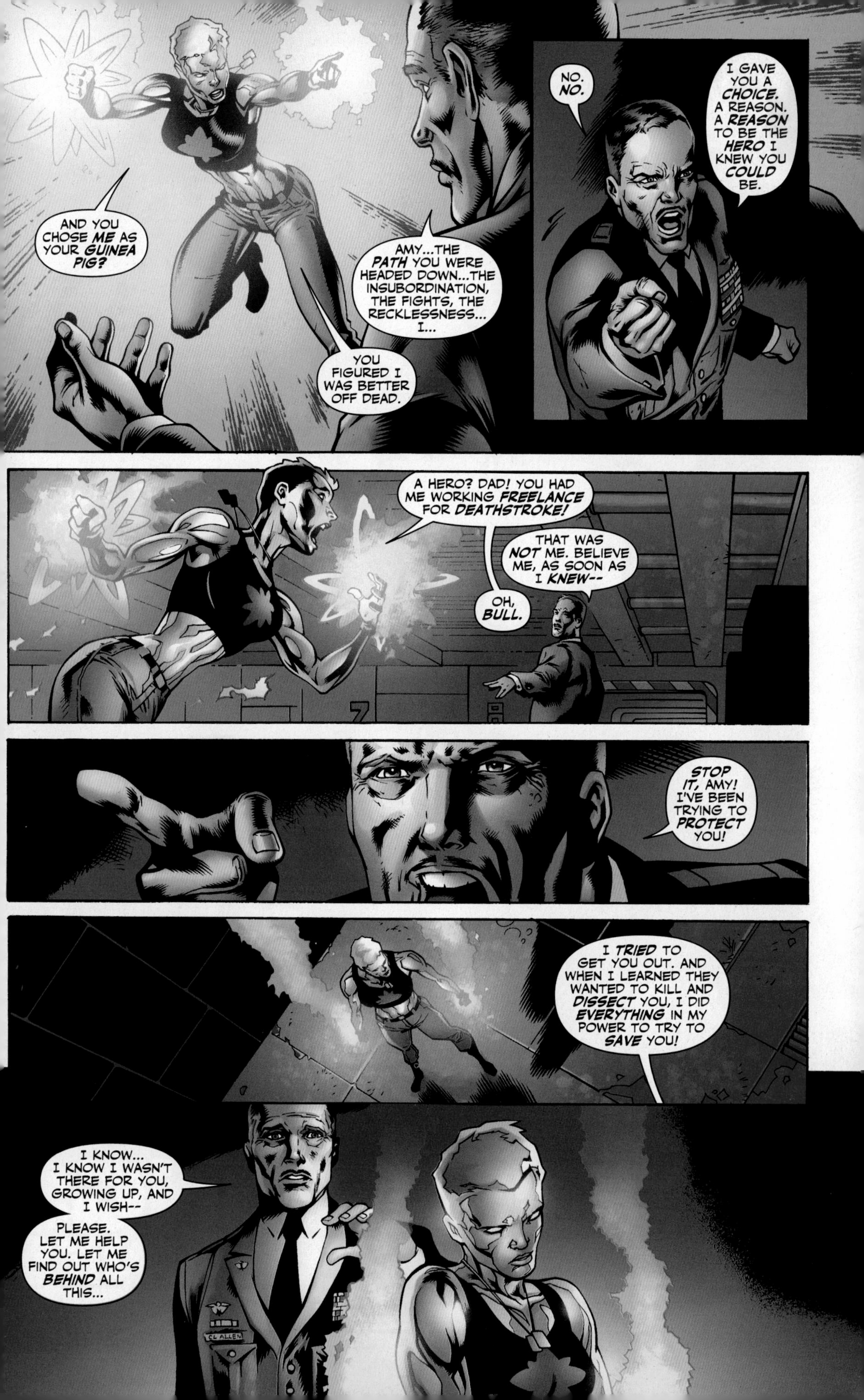
AND YOU CHOSE ME AS YOUR GUINEA PIG?
AMY...THE PATH YOU WERE HEADED DOWN...THE INSUBORDINATION, THE FIGHTS, THE RECKLESSNESS... I...
YOU FIGURED I WAS BETTER OFF DEAD.
NO. NO.
I GAVE YOU A CHOICE. A REASON. A REASON TO BE THE HERO I KNEW YOU COULD BE.
A HERO? DAD! YOU HAD ME WORKING FREELANCE FOR DEATHSTROKE!
THAT WAS NOT ME. BELIEVE ME, AS SOON AS I KNEW--
OH, BULL.
STOP IT, AMY! I'VE BEEN TRYING TO PROTECT YOU!
I TRIED TO GET YOU OUT. AND WHEN I LEARNED THEY WANTED TO KILL AND DISSECT YOU, I DID EVERYTHING IN MY POWER TO TRY TO SAVE YOU!
I KNOW... I KNOW I WASN'T THERE FOR YOU, GROWING UP, AND I WISH--
PLEASE. LET ME HELP YOU. LET ME FIND OUT WHO'S BEHIND ALL THIS...
CL ALLEN

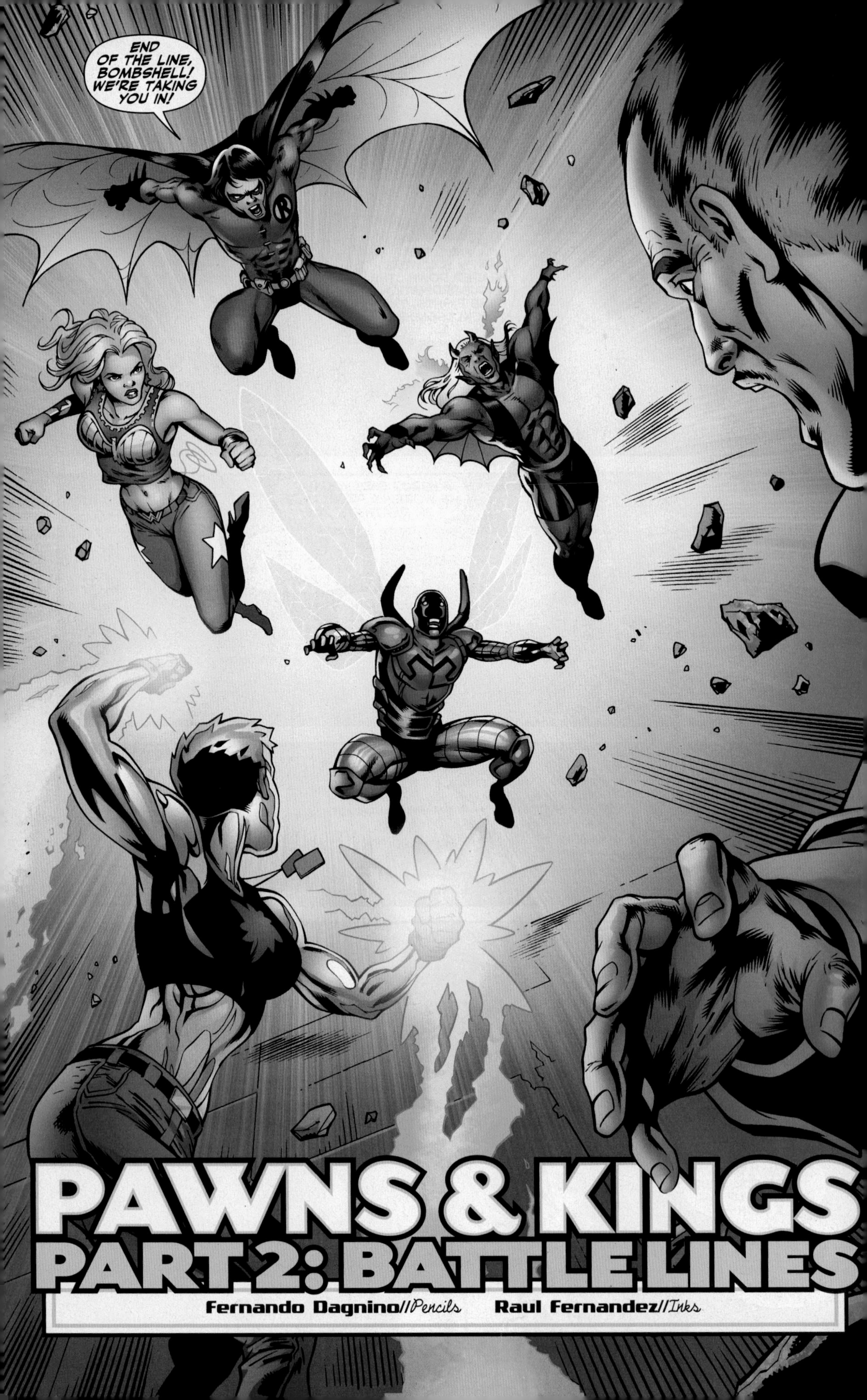
END OF THE LINE, BOMBSHELL! WE'RE TAKING YOU IN!
PAWNS & KINGS
PART 2: BATTLE LINES
Fernando Dagnino//Pencils Raul Fernandez//Inks

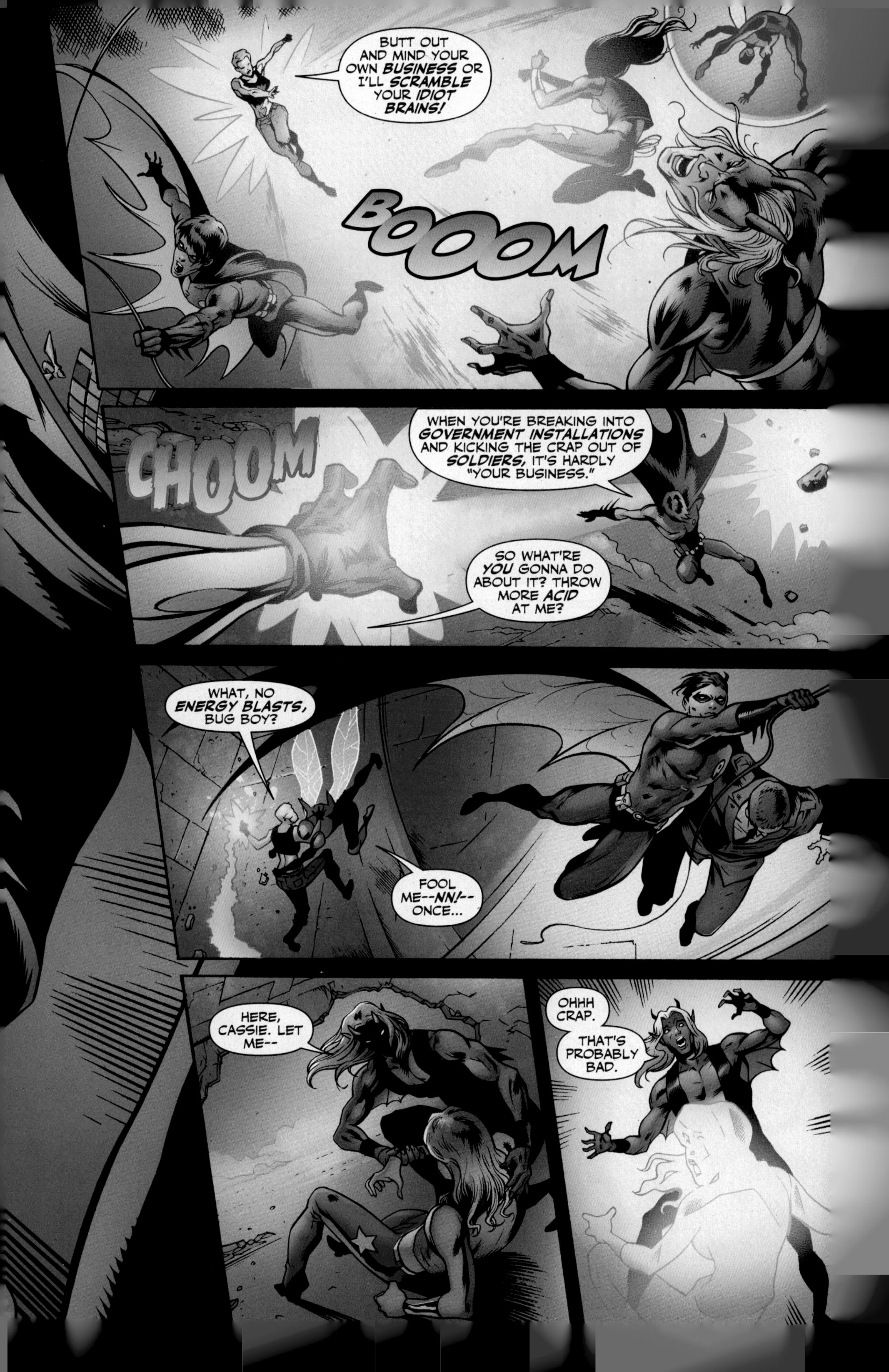

BUTT OUT AND MIND YOUR OWN BUSINESS OR I'LL SCRAMBLE YOUR IDIOT BRAINS!
BOOOOM
CHOOM
WHEN YOU'RE BREAKING INTO GOVERNMENT INSTALLATIONS AND KICKING THE CRAP OUT OF SOLDIERS, IT'S HARDLY "YOUR BUSINESS."
SO WHAT'RE YOU GONNA DO ABOUT IT? THROW MORE ACID AT ME?
WHAT, NO ENERGY BLASTS, BUG BOY?
FOOL ME--NN!-- ONCE...
HERE, CASSIE. LET ME--
OHHH CRAP.
THAT'S PROBABLY BAD.

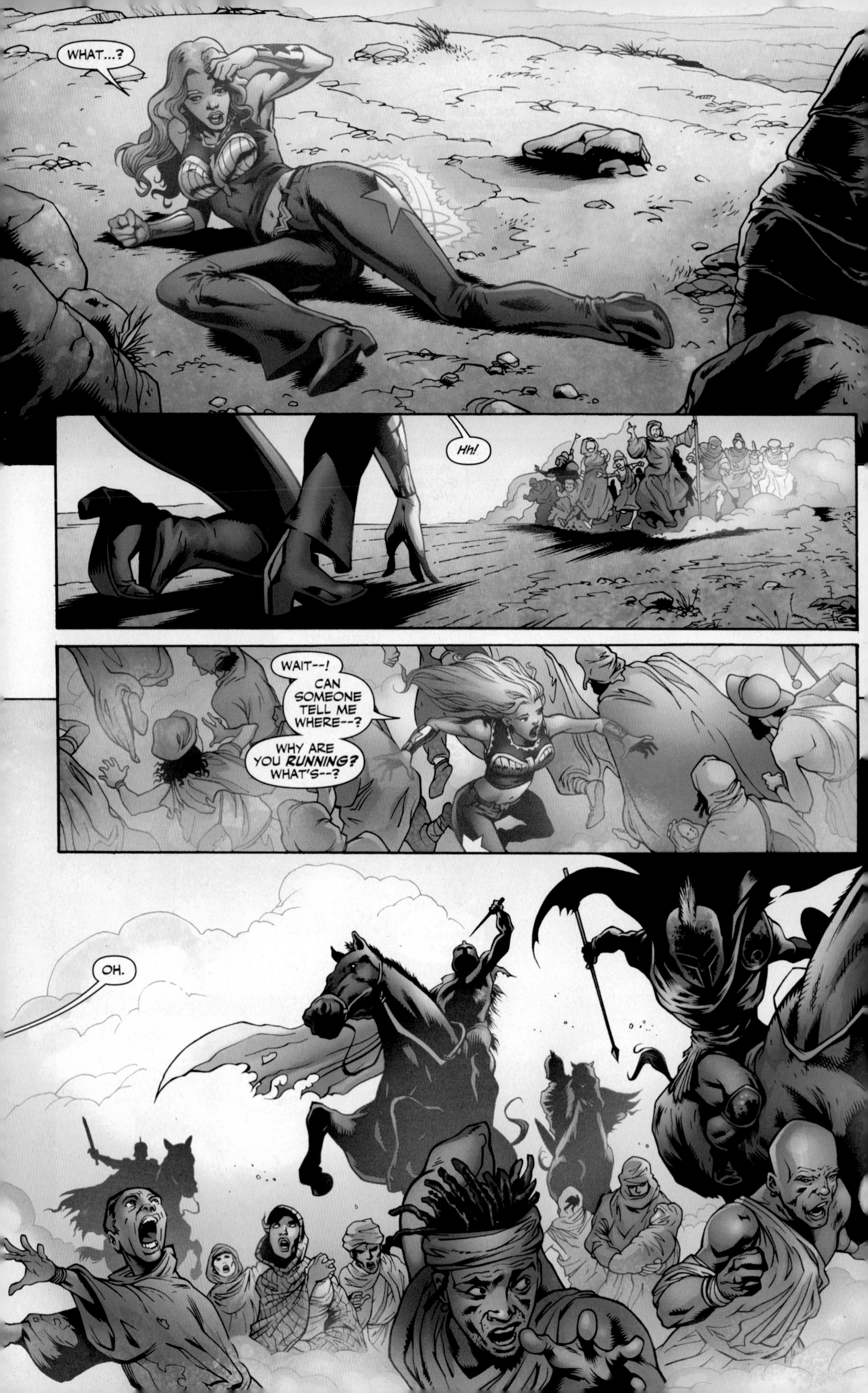
WHAT...?
Hh!
WAIT--!
CAN SOMEONE TELL ME WHERE--?
WHY ARE YOU *RUNNING?* WHAT'S--?
OH.

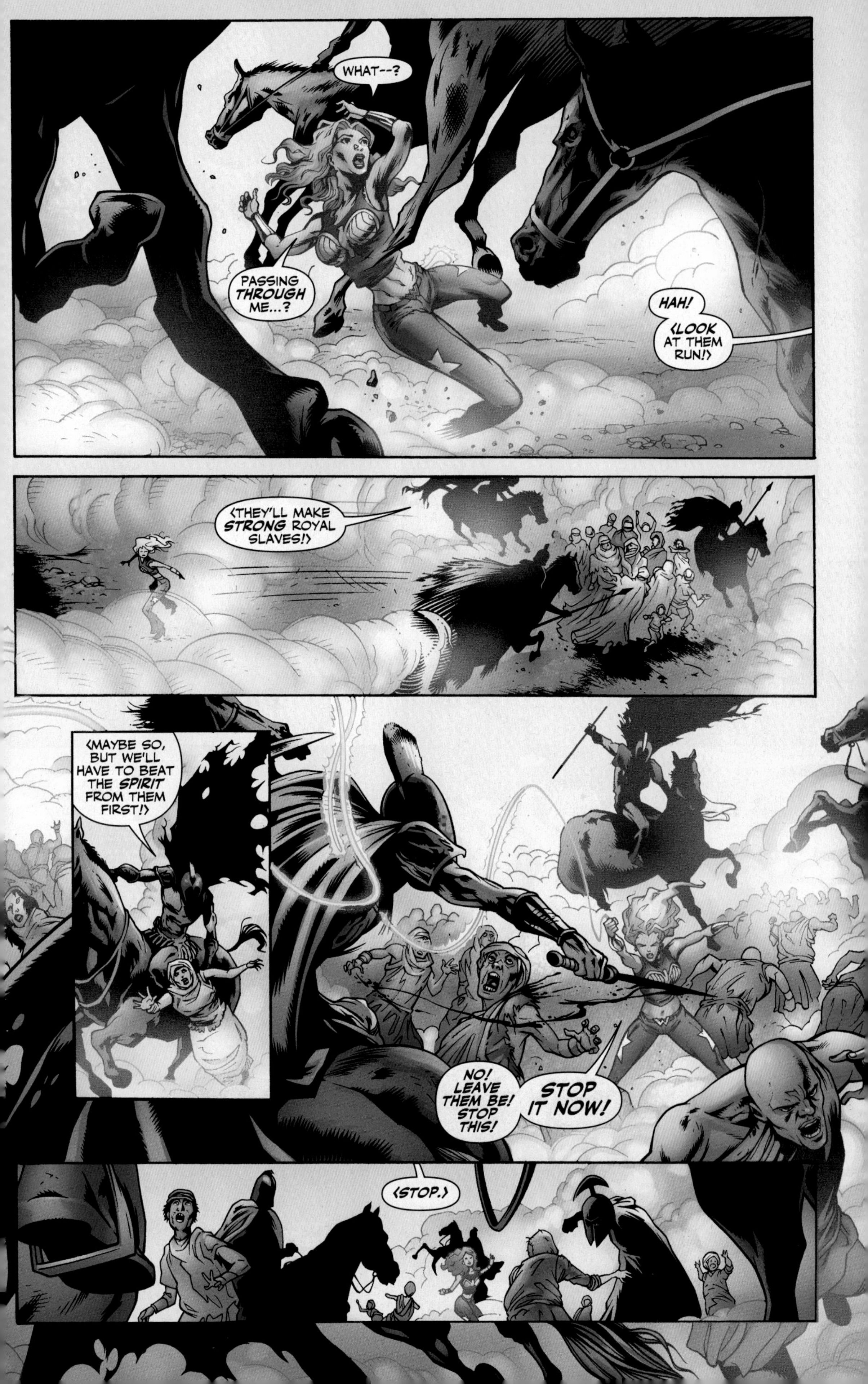

WHAT--?
PASSING THROUGH ME...?
HAH!
‹LOOK AT THEM RUN!›
‹THEY'LL MAKE STRONG ROYAL SLAVES!›
‹MAYBE SO, BUT WE'LL HAVE TO BEAT THE SPIRIT FROM THEM FIRST!›
NO! LEAVE THEM BE! STOP THIS!
STOP IT NOW!
‹STOP.›

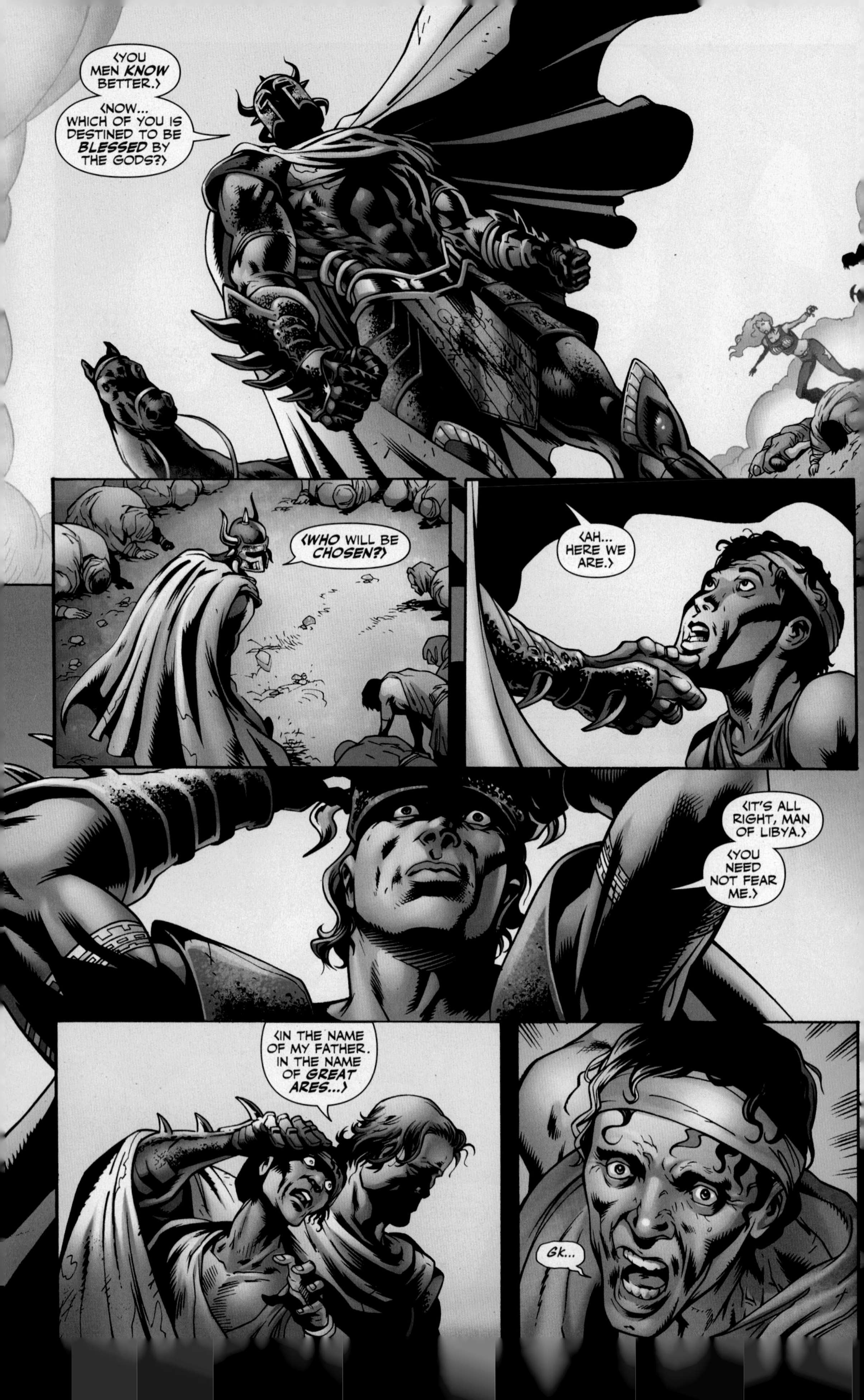

‹YOU MEN KNOW BETTER.›
‹NOW... WHICH OF YOU IS DESTINED TO BE BLESSED BY THE GODS?›
‹WHO WILL BE CHOSEN?›
‹AH... HERE WE ARE.›
‹IT'S ALL RIGHT, MAN OF LIBYA.›
‹YOU NEED NOT FEAR ME.›
‹IN THE NAME OF MY FATHER. IN THE NAME OF GREAT ARES...›
GK...

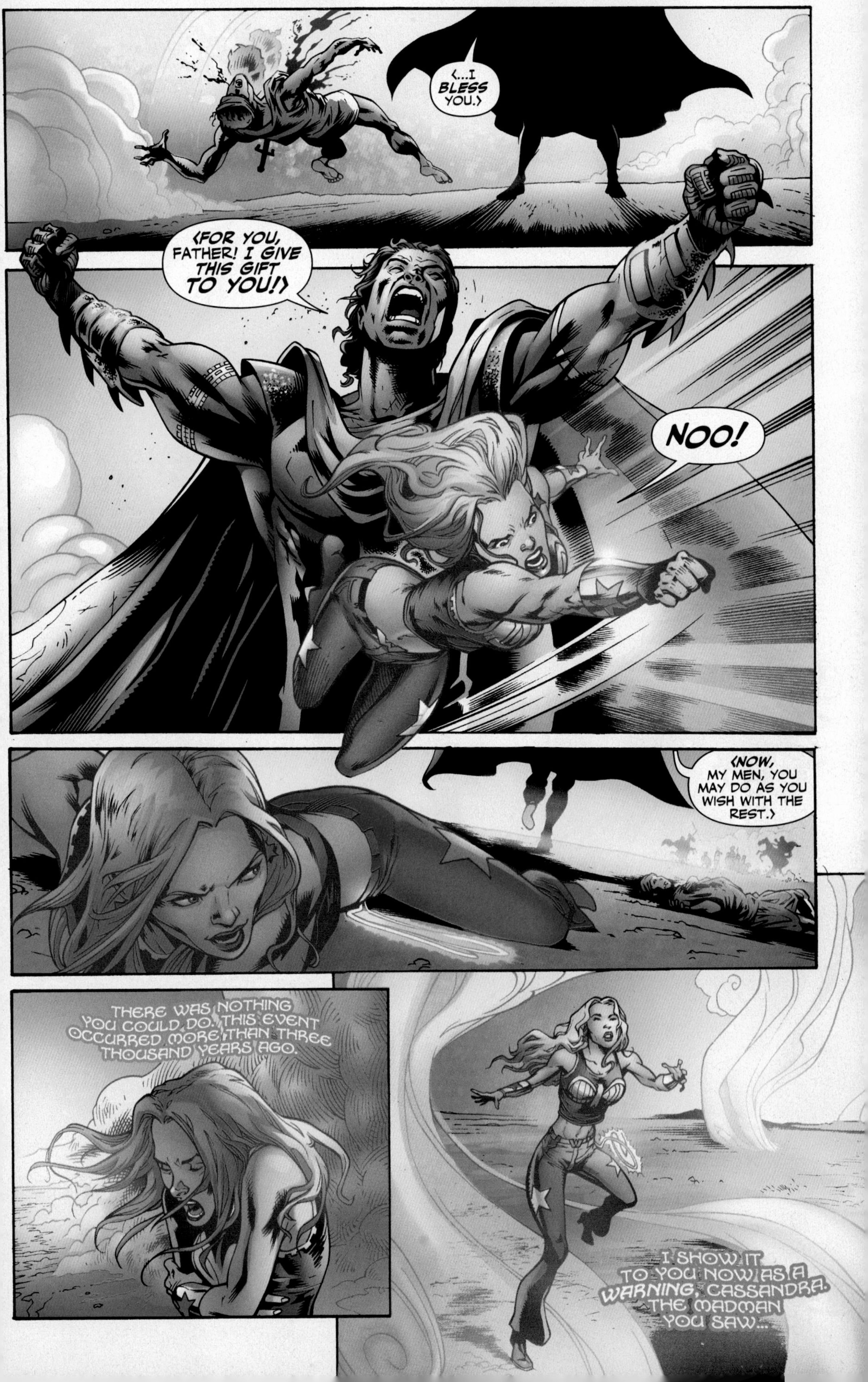
<...I BLESS YOU.>
<FOR YOU, FATHER! I GIVE THIS GIFT TO YOU!>
NOO!
<NOW, MY MEN, YOU MAY DO AS YOU WISH WITH THE REST.>
THERE WAS NOTHING YOU COULD DO. THIS EVENT OCCURRED MORE THAN THREE THOUSAND YEARS AGO.
I SHOW IT TO YOU NOW AS A WARNING, CASSANDRA. THE MADMAN YOU SAW...

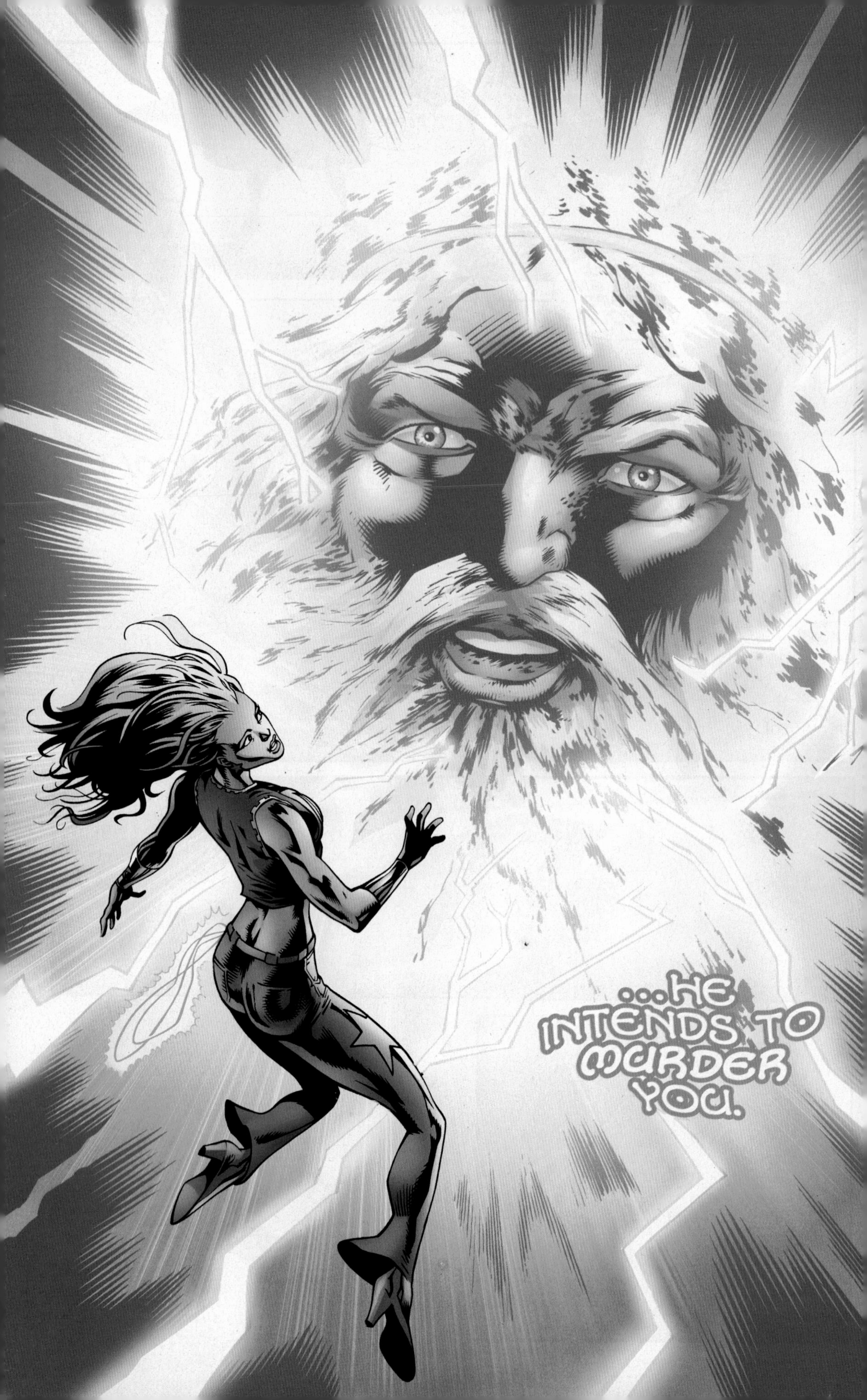
...HE INTENDS TO MURDER YOU.

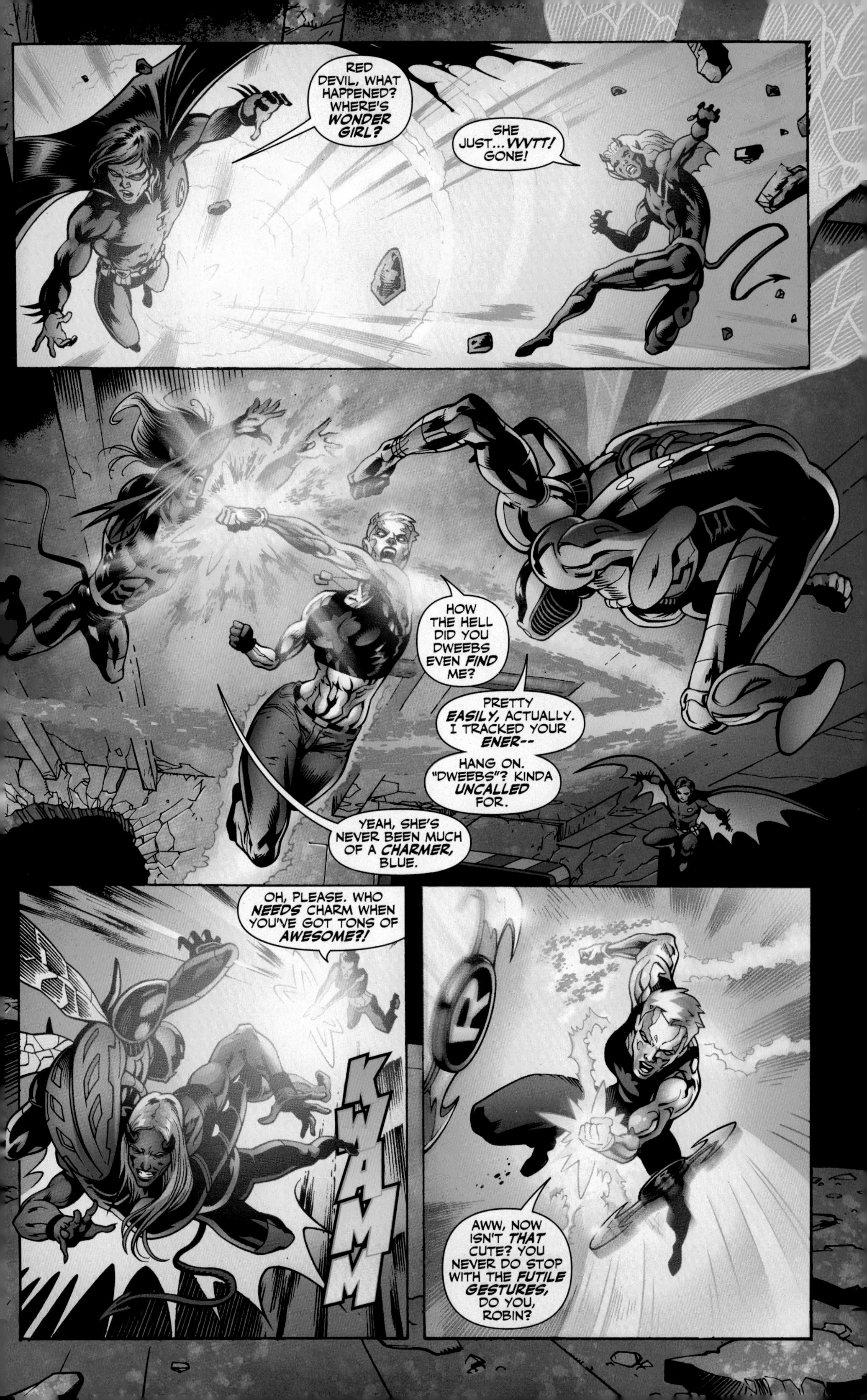

RED DEVIL, WHAT HAPPENED? WHERE'S WONDER GIRL?
SHE JUST...VVVTT! GONE!
HOW THE HELL DID YOU DWEEBS EVEN FIND ME?
PRETTY EASILY, ACTUALLY. I TRACKED YOUR ENER--
HANG ON. "DWEEBS"? KINDA UNCALLED FOR.
YEAH, SHE'S NEVER BEEN MUCH OF A CHARMER, BLUE.
OH, PLEASE. WHO NEEDS CHARM WHEN YOU'VE GOT TONS OF AWESOME?!
KWAMM
AWW, NOW ISN'T THAT CUTE? YOU NEVER DO STOP WITH THE FUTILE GESTURES, DO YOU, ROBIN?

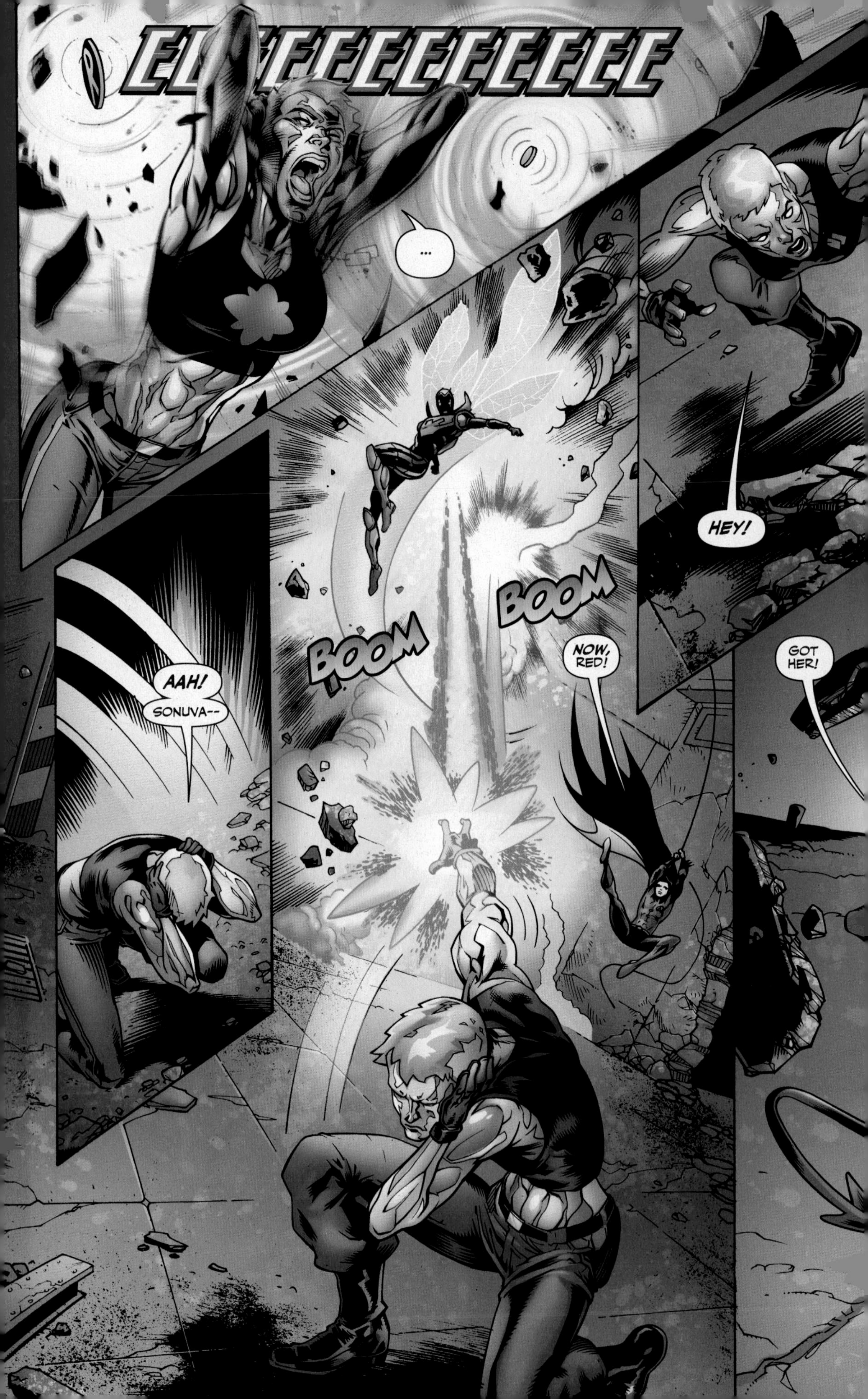
EEEEEEEEEEEEE
...
HEY!
BOOM
BOOM
AAH!
SONUVA--
NOW, RED!
GOT HER!

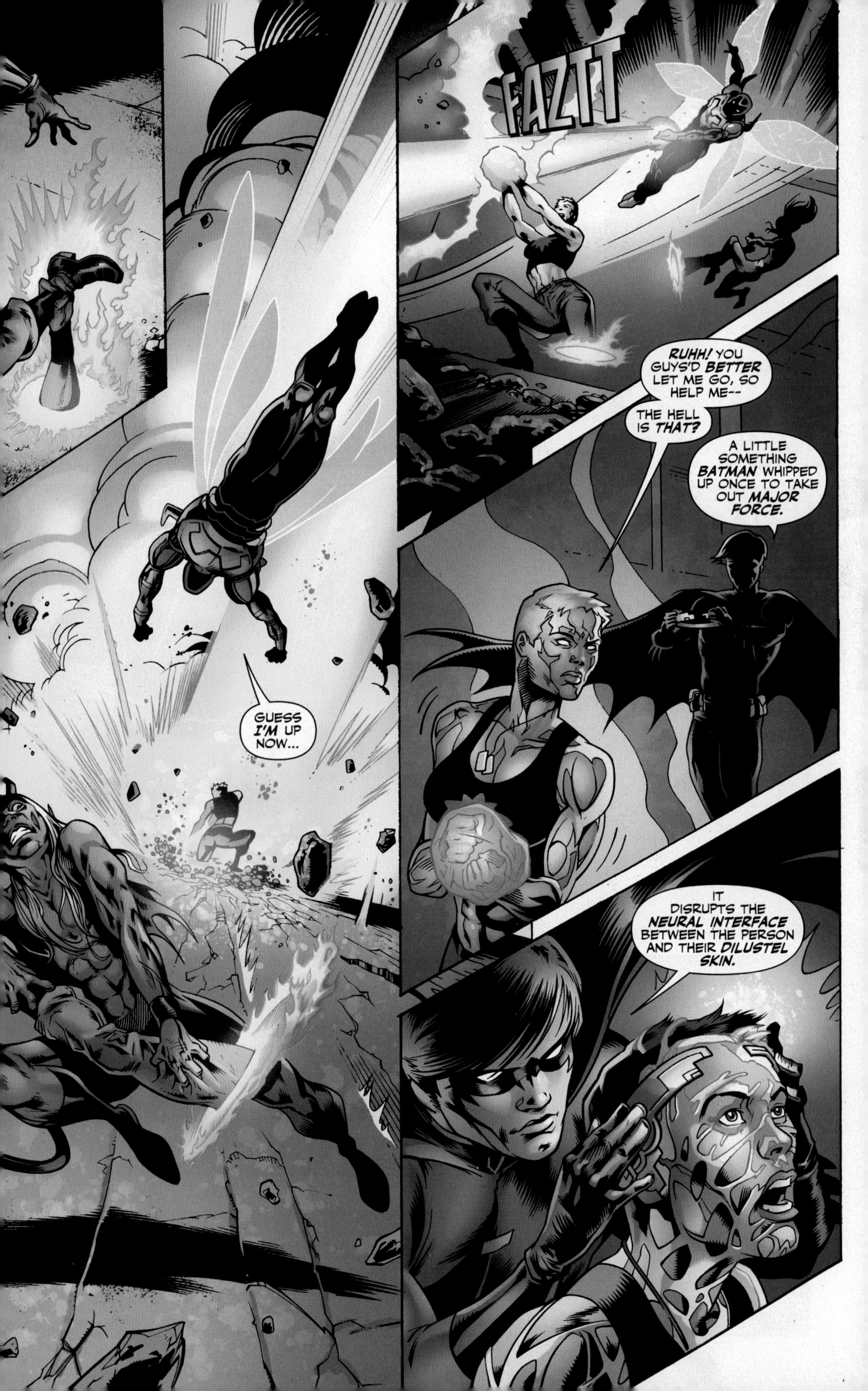
GUESS I'M UP NOW...
FAZTT
RUHH! YOU GUYS'D BETTER LET ME GO, SO HELP ME--
THE HELL IS THAT?
A LITTLE SOMETHING BATMAN WHIPPED UP ONCE TO TAKE OUT MAJOR FORCE.
IT DISRUPTS THE NEURAL INTERFACE BETWEEN THE PERSON AND THEIR DILUSTEL SKIN.

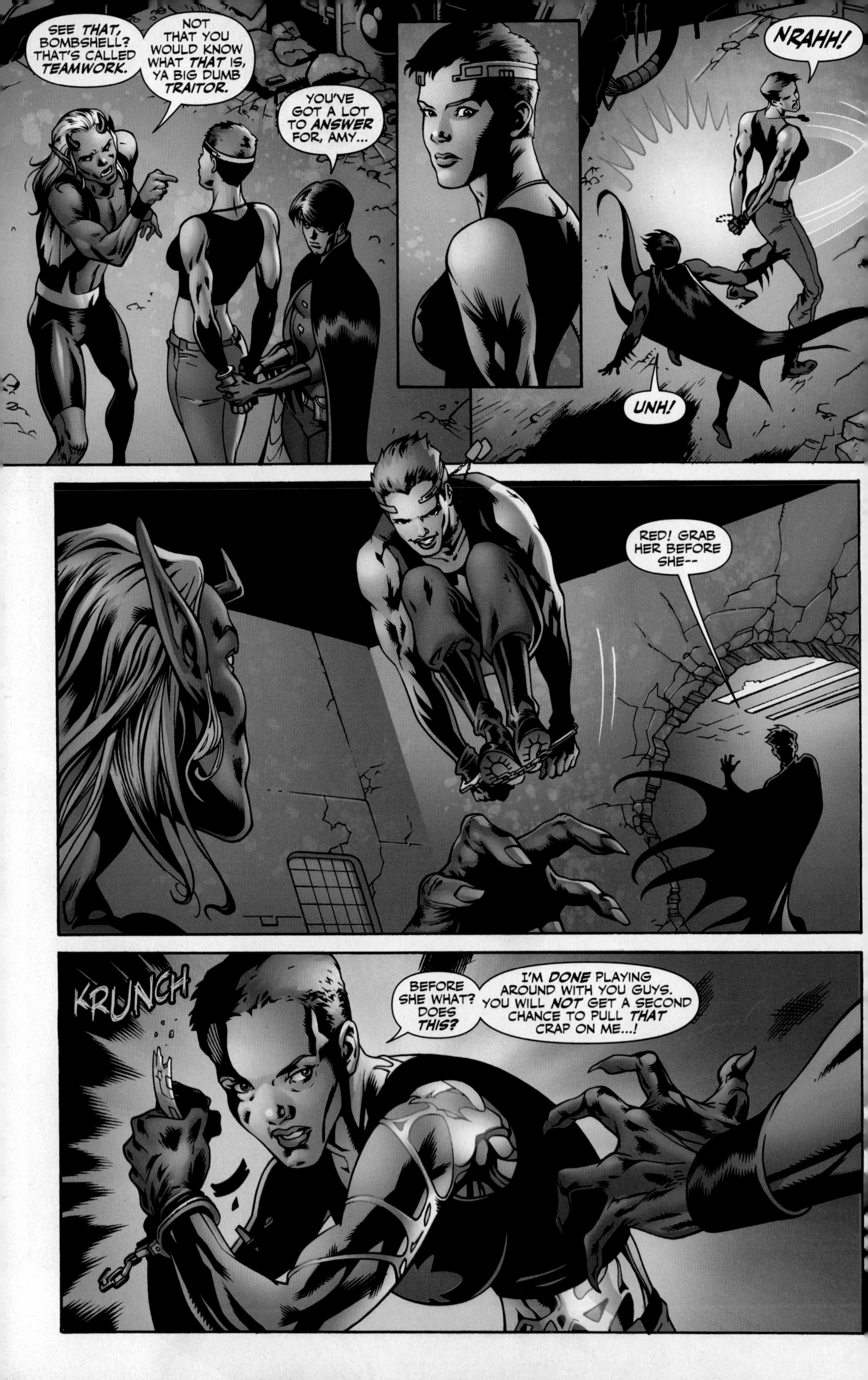
SEE THAT, BOMBSHELL? THAT'S CALLED TEAMWORK.
NOT THAT YOU WOULD KNOW WHAT THAT IS, YA BIG DUMB TRAITOR.
YOU'VE GOT A LOT TO ANSWER FOR, AMY...
NRAHH!
UNH!
RED! GRAB HER BEFORE SHE--
KRUNCH
BEFORE SHE WHAT? DOES THIS?
I'M DONE PLAYING AROUND WITH YOU GUYS. YOU WILL NOT GET A SECOND CHANCE TO PULL THAT CRAP ON ME...!

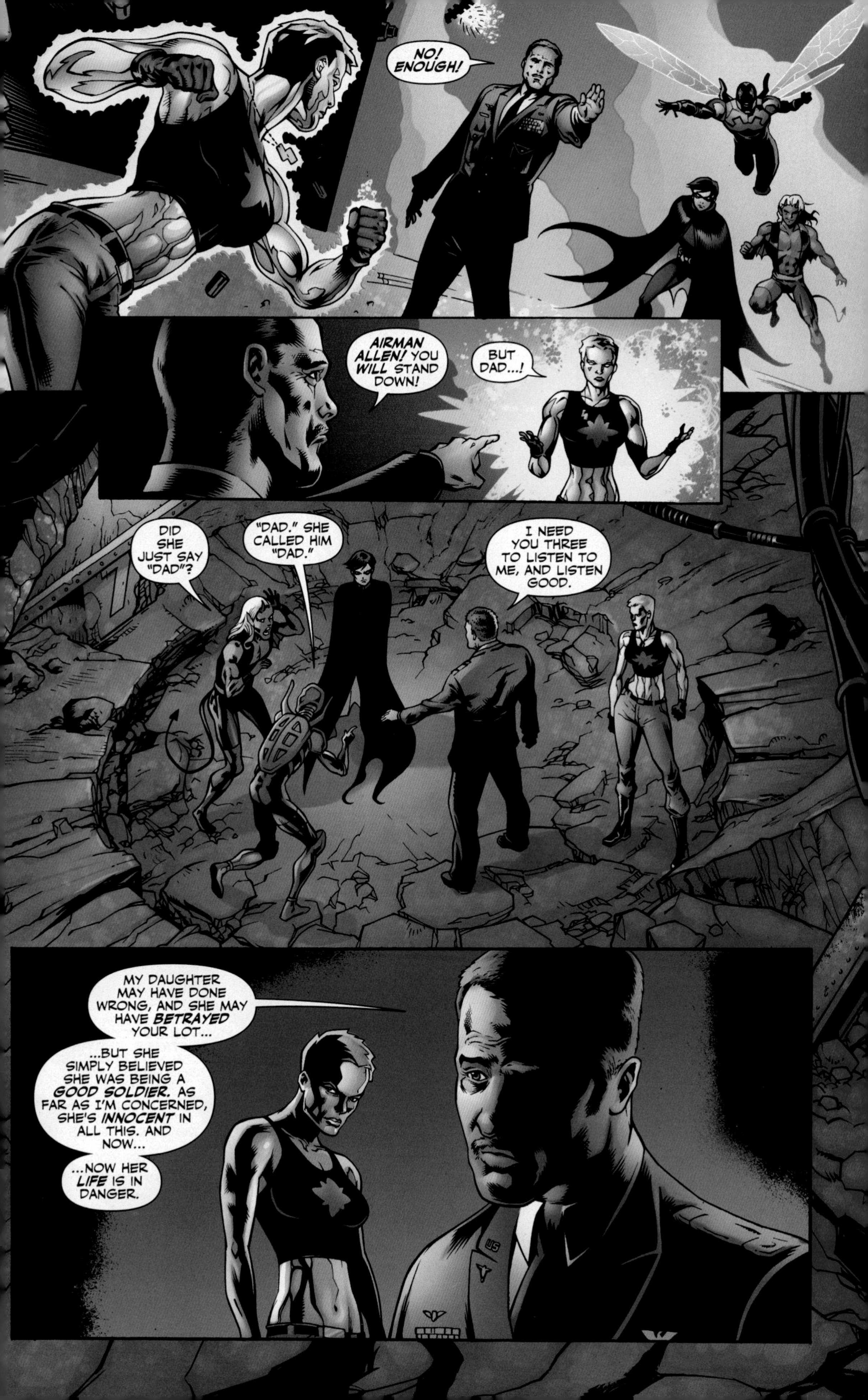
NO! ENOUGH!
AIRMAN ALLEN! YOU WILL STAND DOWN!
BUT DAD...!
DID SHE JUST SAY "DAD"?
"DAD." SHE CALLED HIM "DAD."
I NEED YOU THREE TO LISTEN TO ME, AND LISTEN GOOD.
MY DAUGHTER MAY HAVE DONE WRONG, AND SHE MAY HAVE BETRAYED YOUR LOT...
...BUT SHE SIMPLY BELIEVED SHE WAS BEING A GOOD SOLDIER. AS FAR AS I'M CONCERNED, SHE'S INNOCENT IN ALL THIS. AND NOW...
...NOW HER LIFE IS IN DANGER.

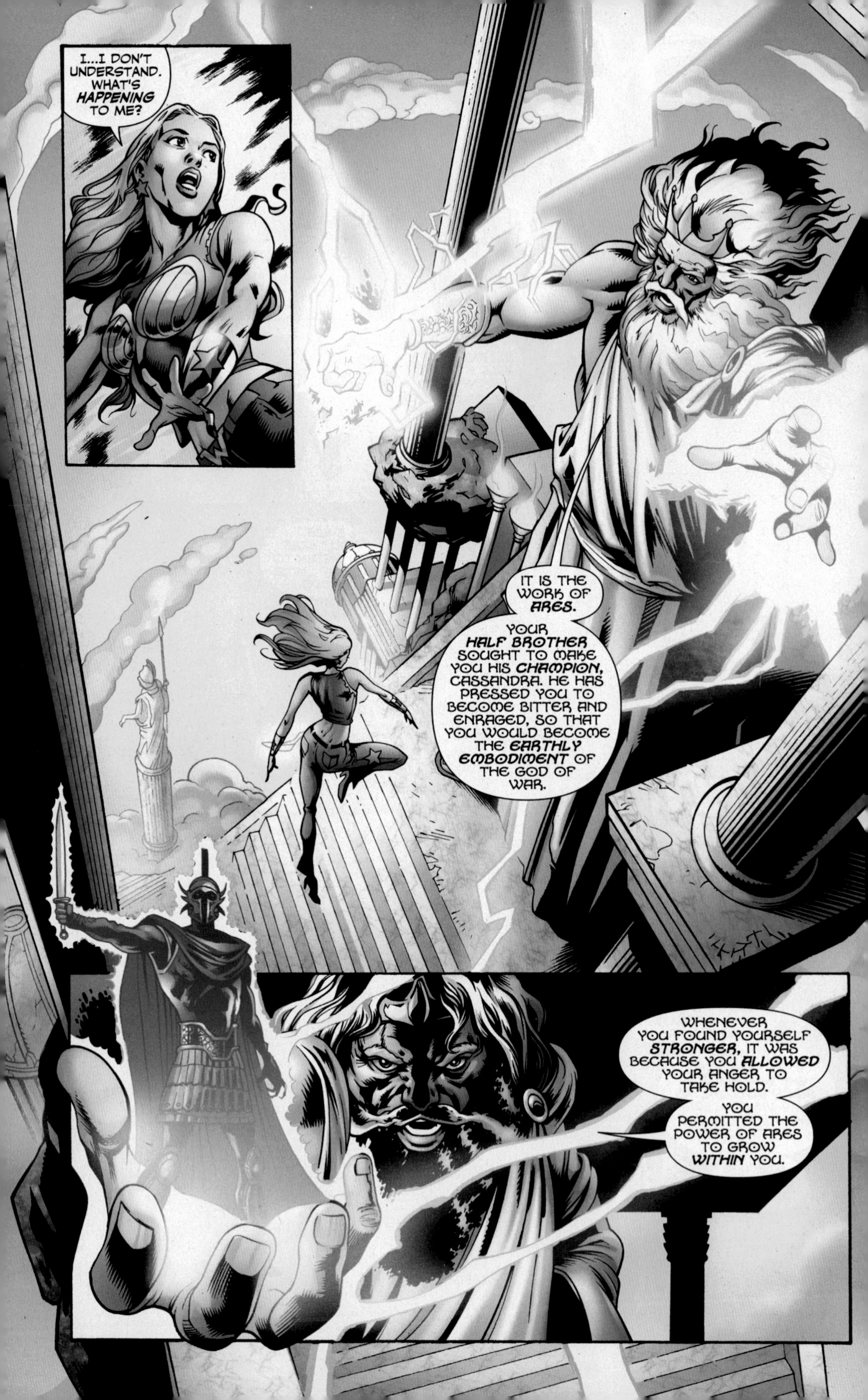

I...I DON'T UNDERSTAND. WHAT'S HAPPENING TO ME?
IT IS THE WORK OF ARES.
YOUR HALF BROTHER SOUGHT TO MAKE YOU HIS CHAMPION, CASSANDRA. HE HAS PRESSED YOU TO BECOME BITTER AND ENRAGED, SO THAT YOU WOULD BECOME THE EARTHLY EMBODIMENT OF THE GOD OF WAR.
WHENEVER YOU FOUND YOURSELF STRONGER, IT WAS BECAUSE YOU ALLOWED YOUR ANGER TO TAKE HOLD.
YOU PERMITTED THE POWER OF ARES TO GROW WITHIN YOU.

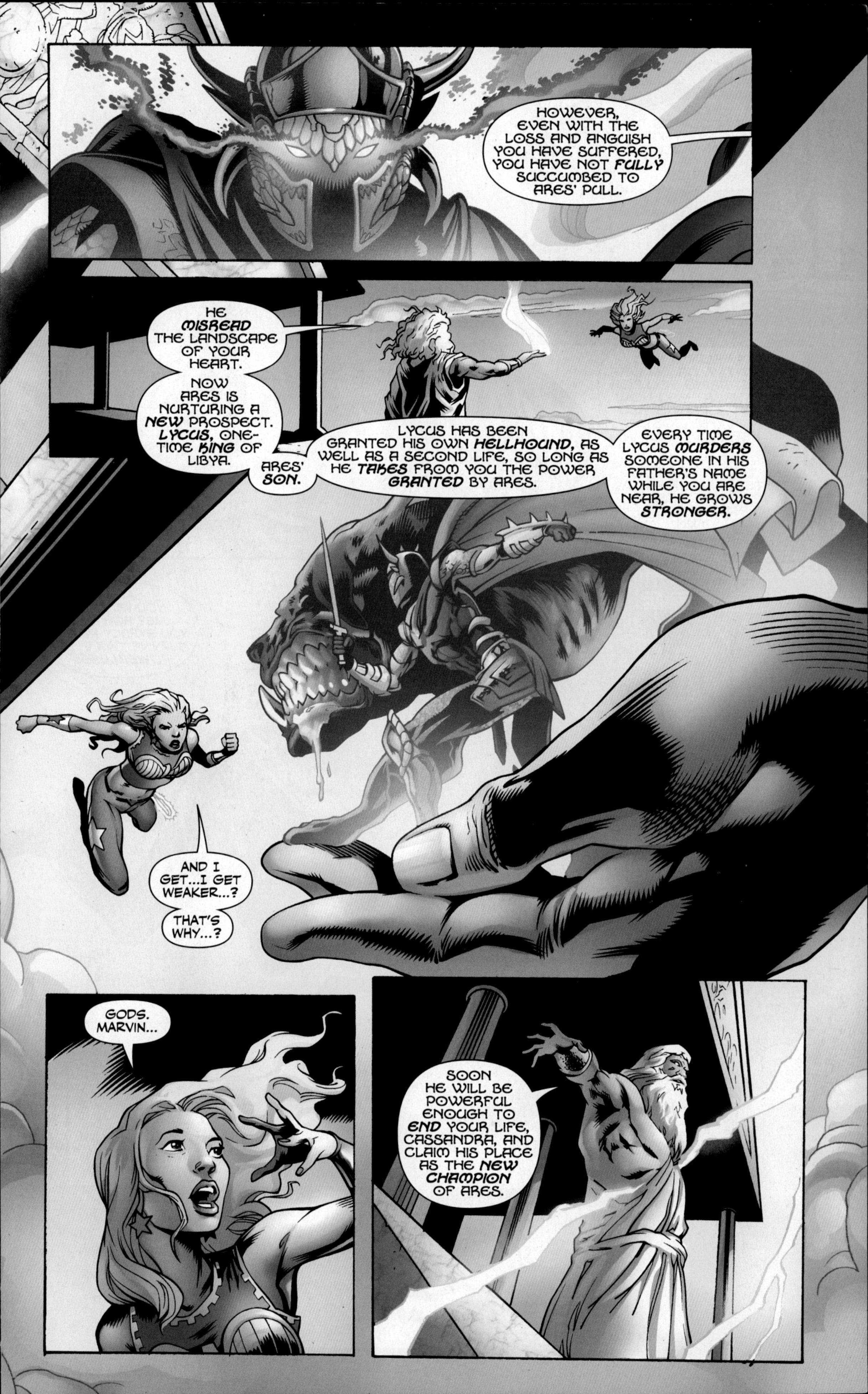
HOWEVER, EVEN WITH THE LOSS AND ANGUISH YOU HAVE SUFFERED, YOU HAVE NOT FULLY SUCCUMBED TO ARES' PULL.
HE MISREAD THE LANDSCAPE OF YOUR HEART.
NOW ARES IS NURTURING A NEW PROSPECT. LYCUS, ONE-TIME KING OF LIBYA.
ARES' SON.
LYCUS HAS BEEN GRANTED HIS OWN HELLHOUND, AS WELL AS A SECOND LIFE, SO LONG AS HE TAKES FROM YOU THE POWER GRANTED BY ARES.
EVERY TIME LYCUS MURDERS SOMEONE IN HIS FATHER'S NAME WHILE YOU ARE NEAR, HE GROWS STRONGER.
AND I GET...I GET WEAKER...?
THAT'S WHY...?
GODS. MARVIN...
SOON HE WILL BE POWERFUL ENOUGH TO END YOUR LIFE, CASSANDRA, AND CLAIM HIS PLACE AS THE NEW CHAMPION OF ARES.

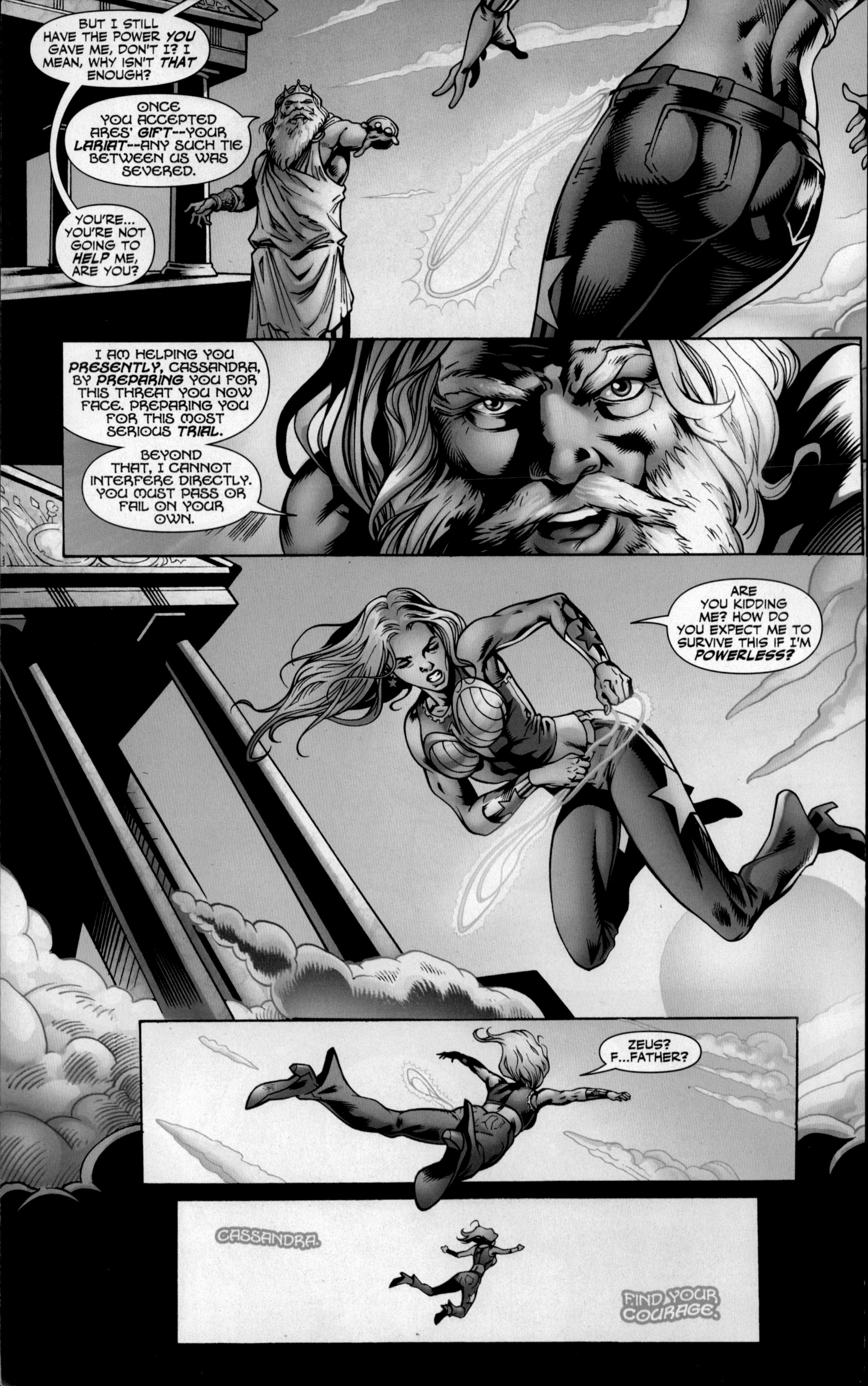
BUT I STILL HAVE THE POWER YOU GAVE ME, DON'T I? I MEAN, WHY ISN'T THAT ENOUGH?
ONCE YOU ACCEPTED ARES' GIFT--YOUR LARIAT--ANY SUCH TIE BETWEEN US WAS SEVERED.
YOU'RE... YOU'RE NOT GOING TO HELP ME, ARE YOU?
I AM HELPING YOU PRESENTLY, CASSANDRA, BY PREPARING YOU FOR THIS THREAT YOU NOW FACE. PREPARING YOU FOR THIS MOST SERIOUS TRIAL.
BEYOND THAT, I CANNOT INTERFERE DIRECTLY. YOU MUST PASS OR FAIL ON YOUR OWN.
ARE YOU KIDDING ME? HOW DO YOU EXPECT ME TO SURVIVE THIS IF I'M POWERLESS?
ZEUS? F...FATHER?
CASSANDRA.
FIND YOUR COURAGE.

"BE STRONG, MY DAUGHTER."

...EVEN WITH MY RESOURCES THERE'S BEEN ONLY SO *MUCH* I CAN DO. I'LL HAVE FAR MORE TRACTION IF I CAN FIND OUT WHO'S *ABUSING* PROJECT QUANTUM LIKE THIS.

YOU DO *BELIEVE* ME, DON'T YOU?

WHAT DO YOU THINK, AMY? DO *YOU* BELIEVE HIM?

I... I DON'T THINK HE'S LYING.

WELL...IN LIGHT OF EVERYTHING YOUR *DAD* HAS SAID, I THINK YOU SHOULD CONSIDER STAYING WITH US AT *TITANS TOWER*, AT LEAST UNTIL--

I *DON'T* NEED YOUR *PROTECTION.*

BUT YOU *DO* NEED A PLACE TO *STAY.* AND DESPITE THE NATURE OF YOUR *PAST* WITH US, I THINK WE'D *ALL* BE HAPPY TO HELP YOU *DEAL* WITH--

RIGHT. YOU'RE GONNA *TRUST* ME IN YOUR *HOME* JUST LIKE *THAT?* LISTEN HERE, LITTLE BIRDIE--

AMY SUE ALLEN. YOUR MOTHER DIDN'T RAISE YOU TO BE RUDE IN THE FACE OF KINDNESS, DID SHE?

GO WITH THEM. YOU'RE TOUGH. I KNOW IT. BUT IT'LL SURE BE A LOAD OFF *MY* MIND TO KNOW THAT WHILE I'M GETTING TO THE *BOTTOM* OF THIS, YOU'RE WITH *GOOD PEOPLE.*

YEAH. OKAY.

GOOD. I'M GLAD.

BOMBSHELL AT THE *TOWER?*

NOW WE'VE JUST GOT TO FIND OUT WHAT HAPPENED TO *CASSIE,* AND--

IT'S HER!

BEE-DEET

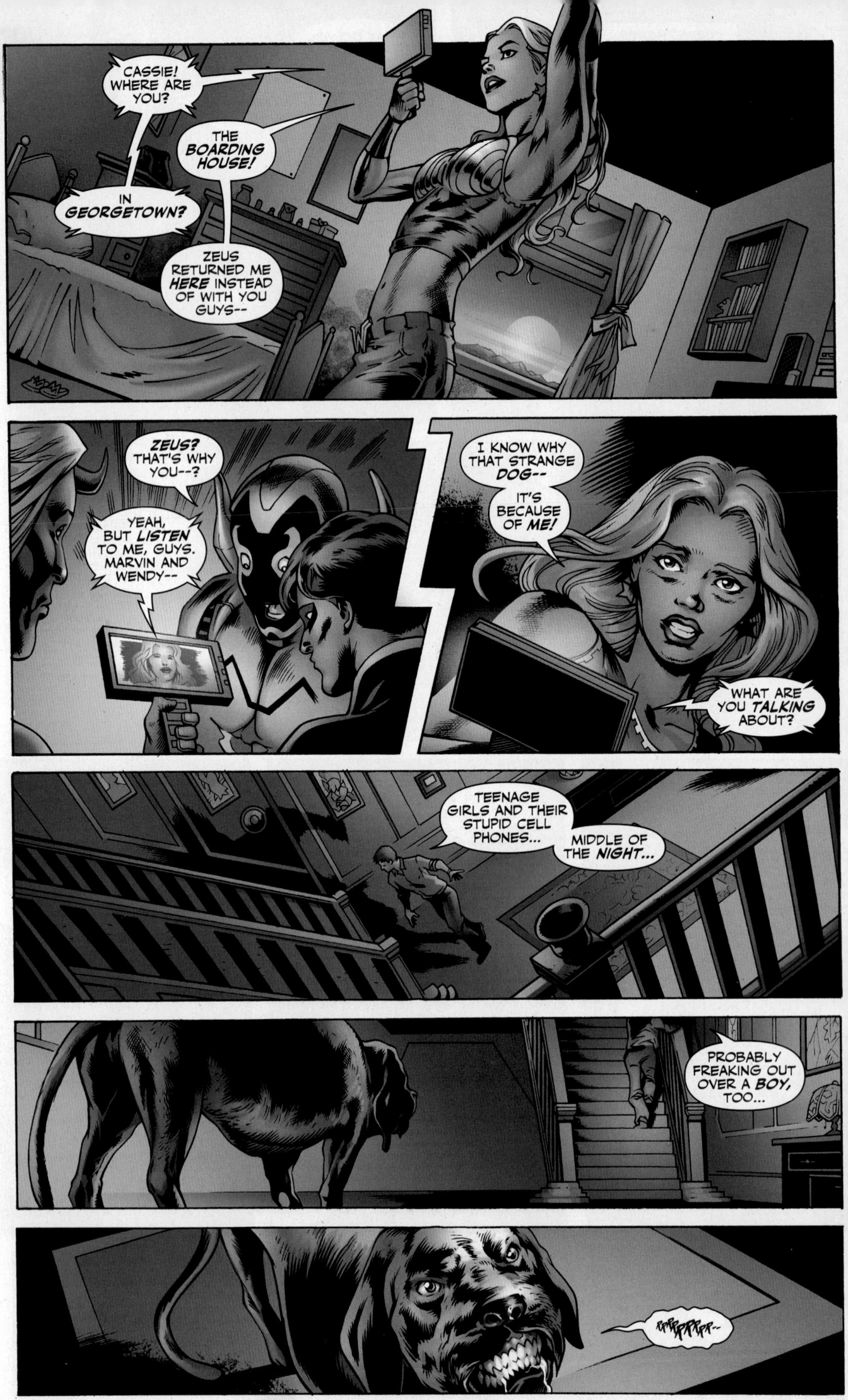
CASSIE! WHERE ARE YOU?
THE BOARDING HOUSE!
IN GEORGETOWN?
ZEUS RETURNED ME HERE INSTEAD OF WITH YOU GUYS--
ZEUS? THAT'S WHY YOU--?
YEAH, BUT LISTEN TO ME, GUYS. MARVIN AND WENDY--
I KNOW WHY THAT STRANGE DOG--
IT'S BECAUSE OF ME!
WHAT ARE YOU TALKING ABOUT?
TEENAGE GIRLS AND THEIR STUPID CELL PHONES...
MIDDLE OF THE NIGHT...
PROBABLY FREAKING OUT OVER A BOY, TOO...
RRRRRRRRR--

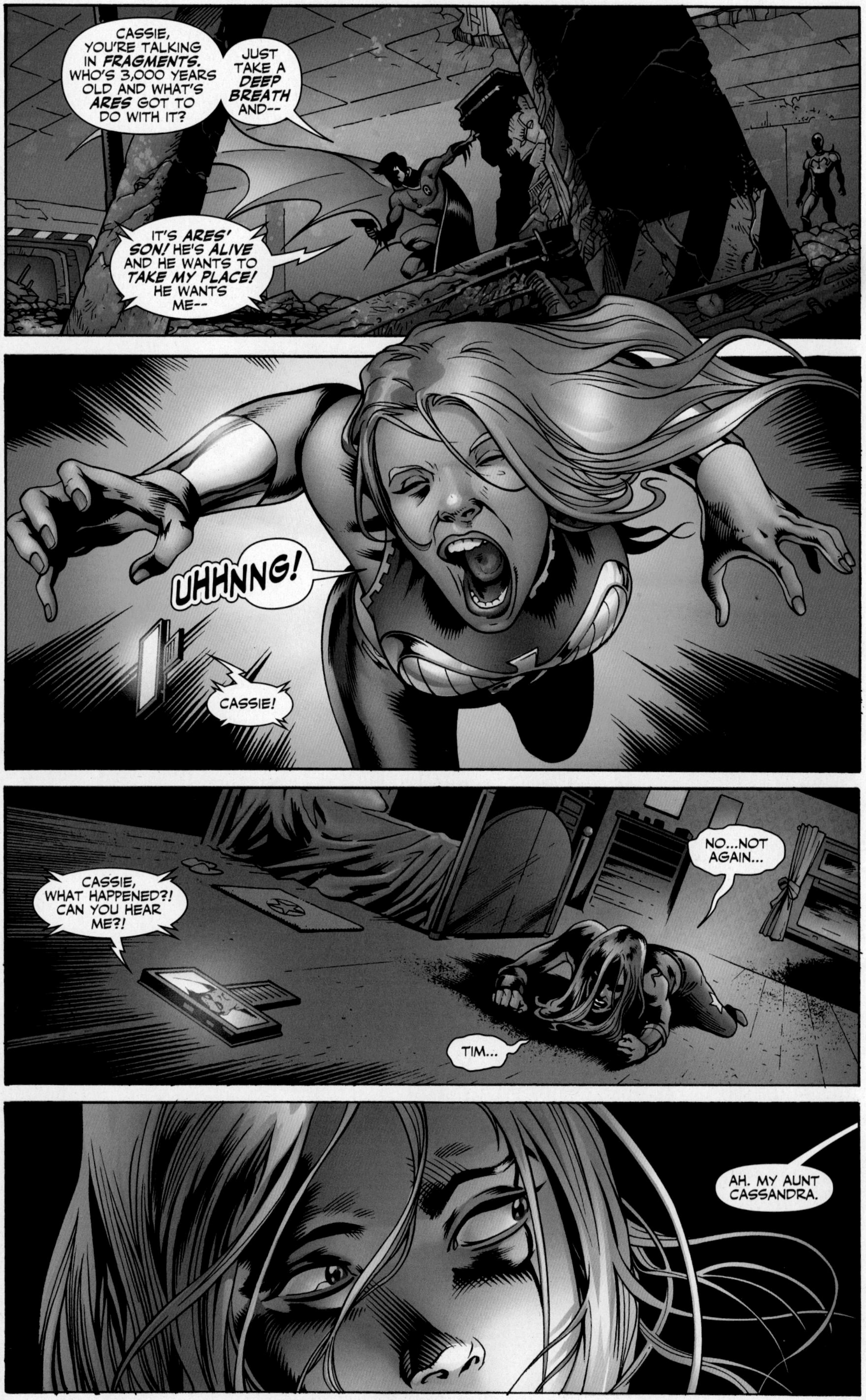
CASSIE, YOU'RE TALKING IN FRAGMENTS. WHO'S 3,000 YEARS OLD AND WHAT'S ARES GOT TO DO WITH IT?
JUST TAKE A DEEP BREATH AND--
IT'S ARES' SON! HE'S ALIVE AND HE WANTS TO TAKE MY PLACE! HE WANTS ME--
UHHNNG!
CASSIE!
CASSIE, WHAT HAPPENED?! CAN YOU HEAR ME?!
NO...NOT AGAIN...
TIM...
AH. MY AUNT CASSANDRA.

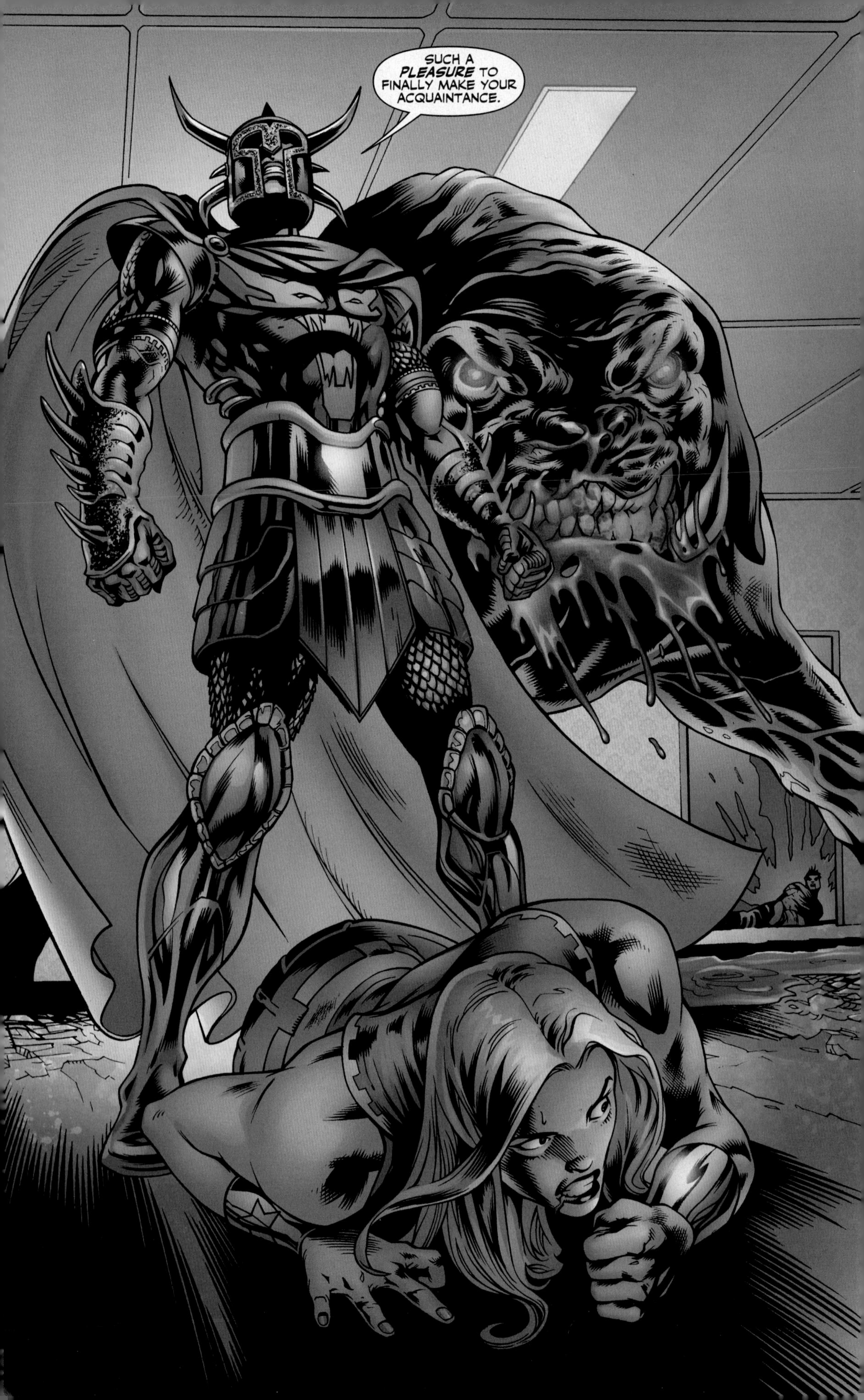
SUCH A PLEASURE TO FINALLY MAKE YOUR ACQUAINTANCE.

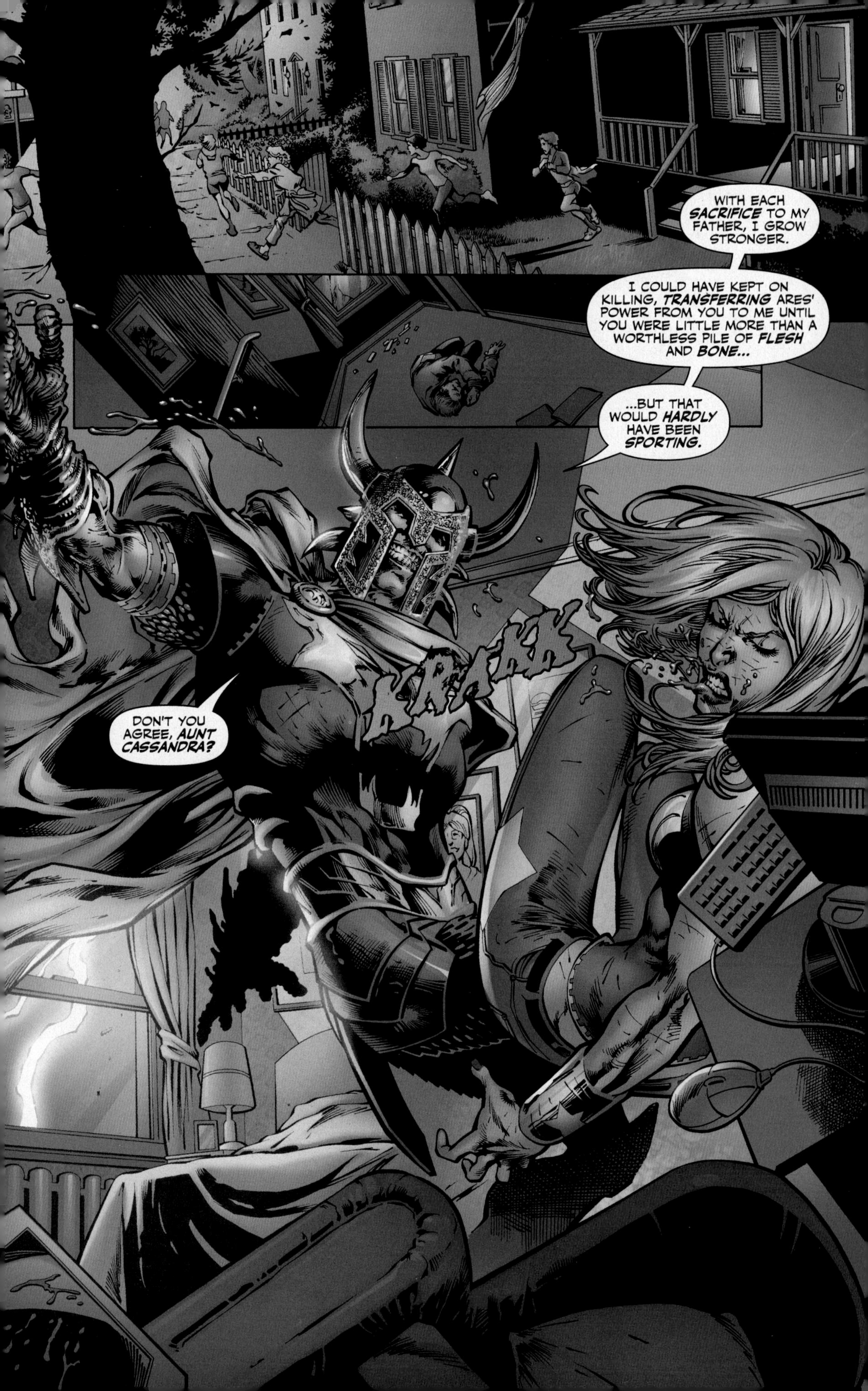
WITH EACH SACRIFICE TO MY FATHER, I GROW STRONGER.
I COULD HAVE KEPT ON KILLING, TRANSFERRING ARES' POWER FROM YOU TO ME UNTIL YOU WERE LITTLE MORE THAN A WORTHLESS PILE OF FLESH AND BONE...
...BUT THAT WOULD HARDLY HAVE BEEN SPORTING.
KRAKK
DON'T YOU AGREE, AUNT CASSANDRA?

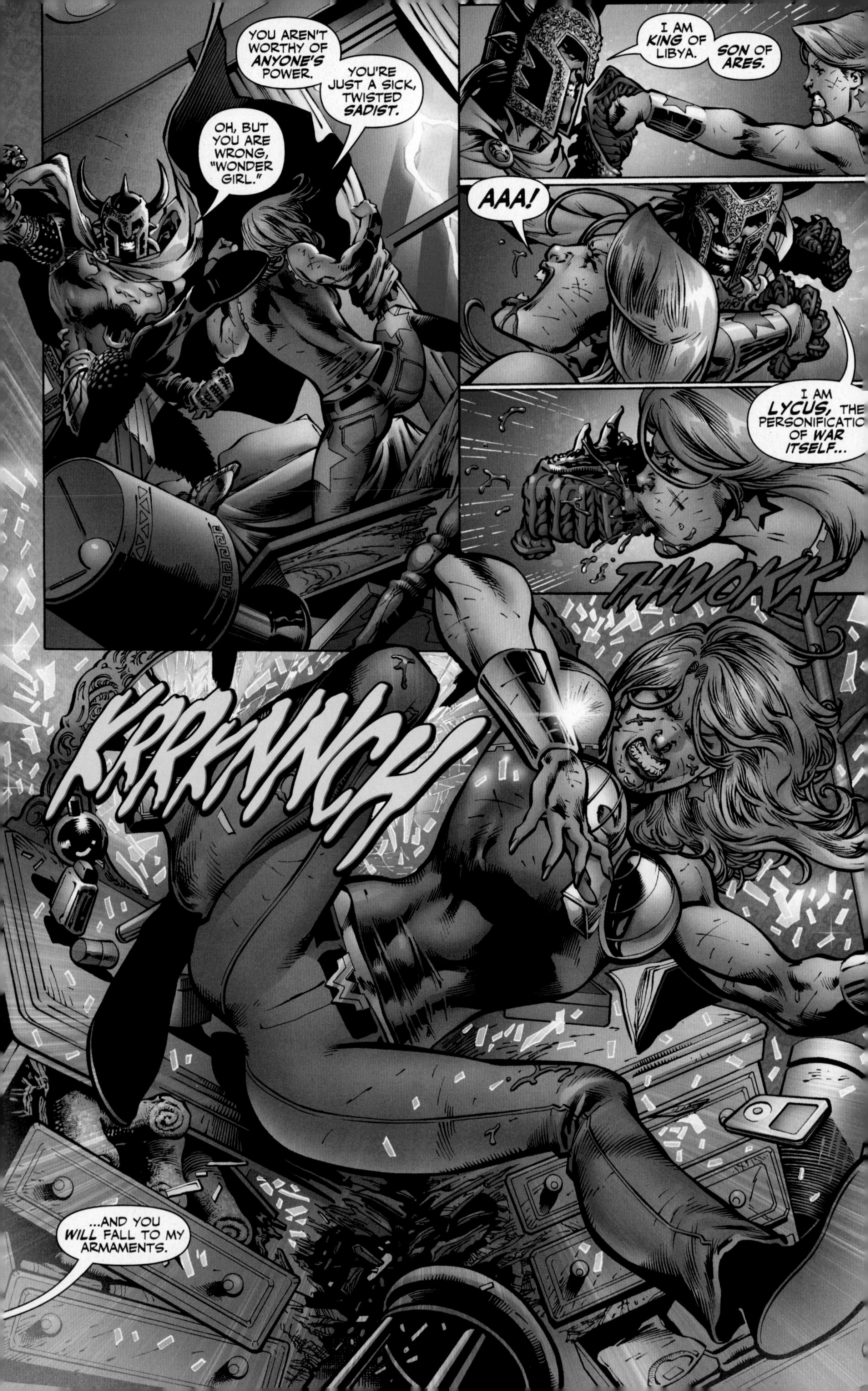

YOU AREN'T WORTHY OF ANYONE'S POWER.
YOU'RE JUST A SICK, TWISTED SADIST.
OH, BUT YOU ARE WRONG, "WONDER GIRL."
I AM KING OF LIBYA.
SON OF ARES.
AAA!
I AM LYCUS, THE PERSONIFICATIO OF WAR ITSELF...
THWOKK
KRRUNNCH
...AND YOU WILL FALL TO MY ARMAMENTS.

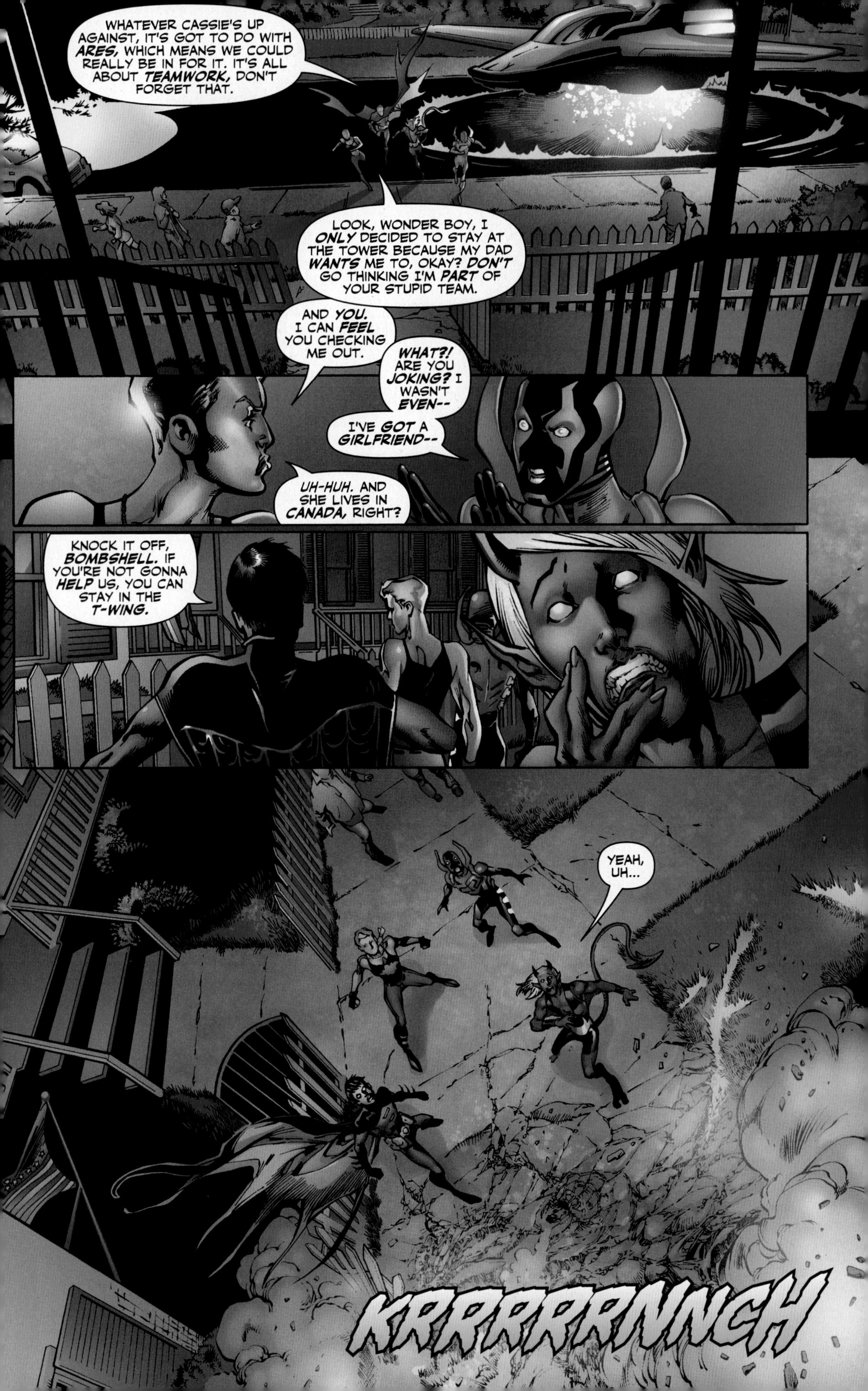
WHATEVER CASSIE'S UP AGAINST, IT'S GOT TO DO WITH ARES, WHICH MEANS WE COULD REALLY BE IN FOR IT. IT'S ALL ABOUT TEAMWORK, DON'T FORGET THAT.
LOOK, WONDER BOY, I ONLY DECIDED TO STAY AT THE TOWER BECAUSE MY DAD WANTS ME TO, OKAY? DON'T GO THINKING I'M PART OF YOUR STUPID TEAM.
AND YOU. I CAN FEEL YOU CHECKING ME OUT.
WHAT?! ARE YOU JOKING? I WASN'T EVEN--
I'VE GOT A GIRLFRIEND--
UH-HUH. AND SHE LIVES IN CANADA, RIGHT?
KNOCK IT OFF, BOMBSHELL. IF YOU'RE NOT GONNA HELP US, YOU CAN STAY IN THE T-WING.
YEAH, UH...
KRRRRRNNCH

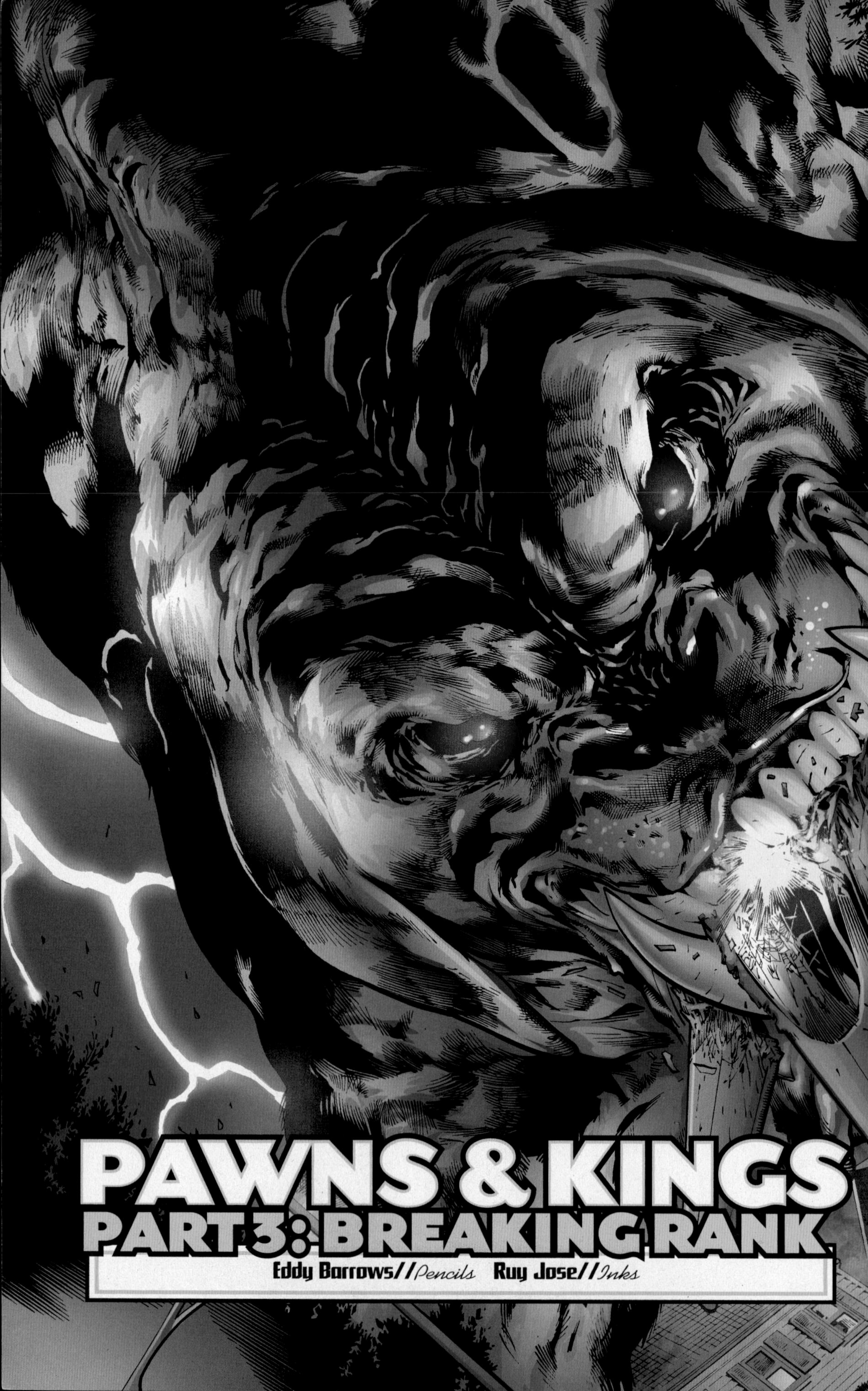
PAWNS & KINGS
PART 3: BREAKING RANK
Eddy Barrows//Pencils Ruy Jose//Inks

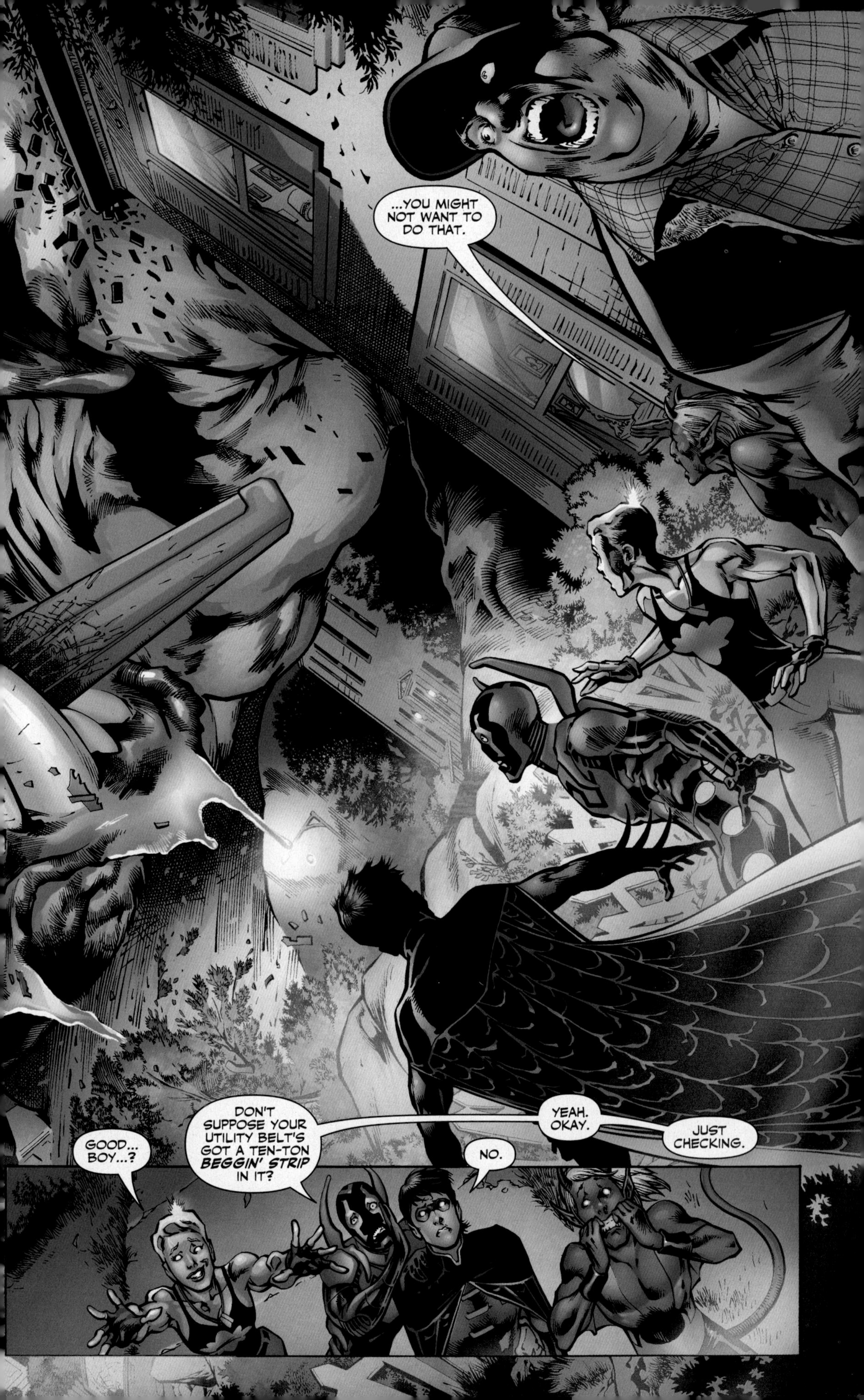
...YOU MIGHT NOT WANT TO DO THAT.
GOOD... BOY...?
DON'T SUPPOSE YOUR UTILITY BELT'S GOT A TEN-TON *BEGGIN' STRIP* IN IT?
NO.
YEAH. OKAY.
JUST CHECKING.

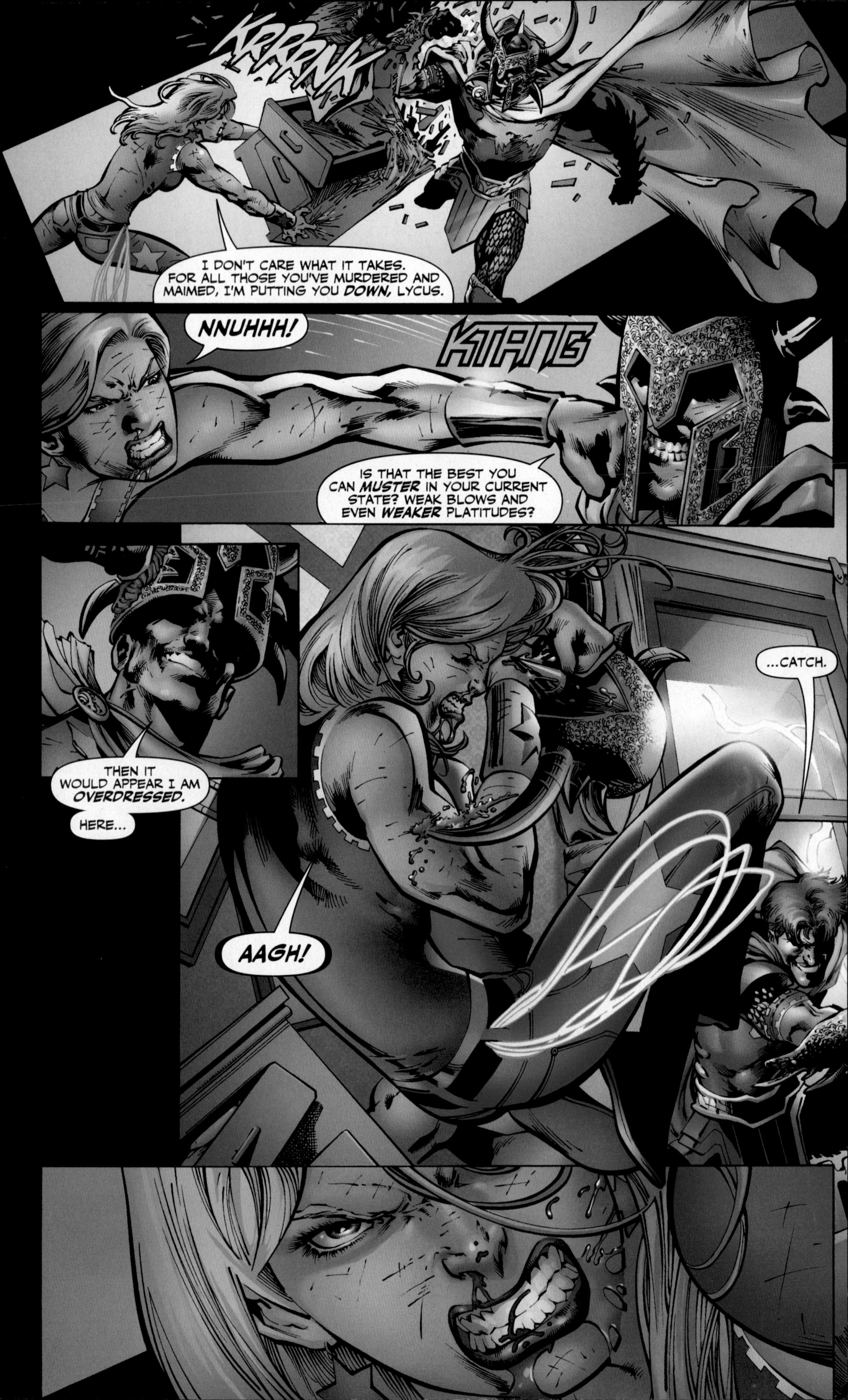
KRRRNK
I DON'T CARE WHAT IT TAKES. FOR ALL THOSE YOU'VE MURDERED AND MAIMED, I'M PUTTING YOU DOWN, LYCUS.
NNUHHH!
KTANG
IS THAT THE BEST YOU CAN MUSTER IN YOUR CURRENT STATE? WEAK BLOWS AND EVEN WEAKER PLATITUDES?
THEN IT WOULD APPEAR I AM OVERDRESSED.
HERE...
...CATCH.
AAGH!

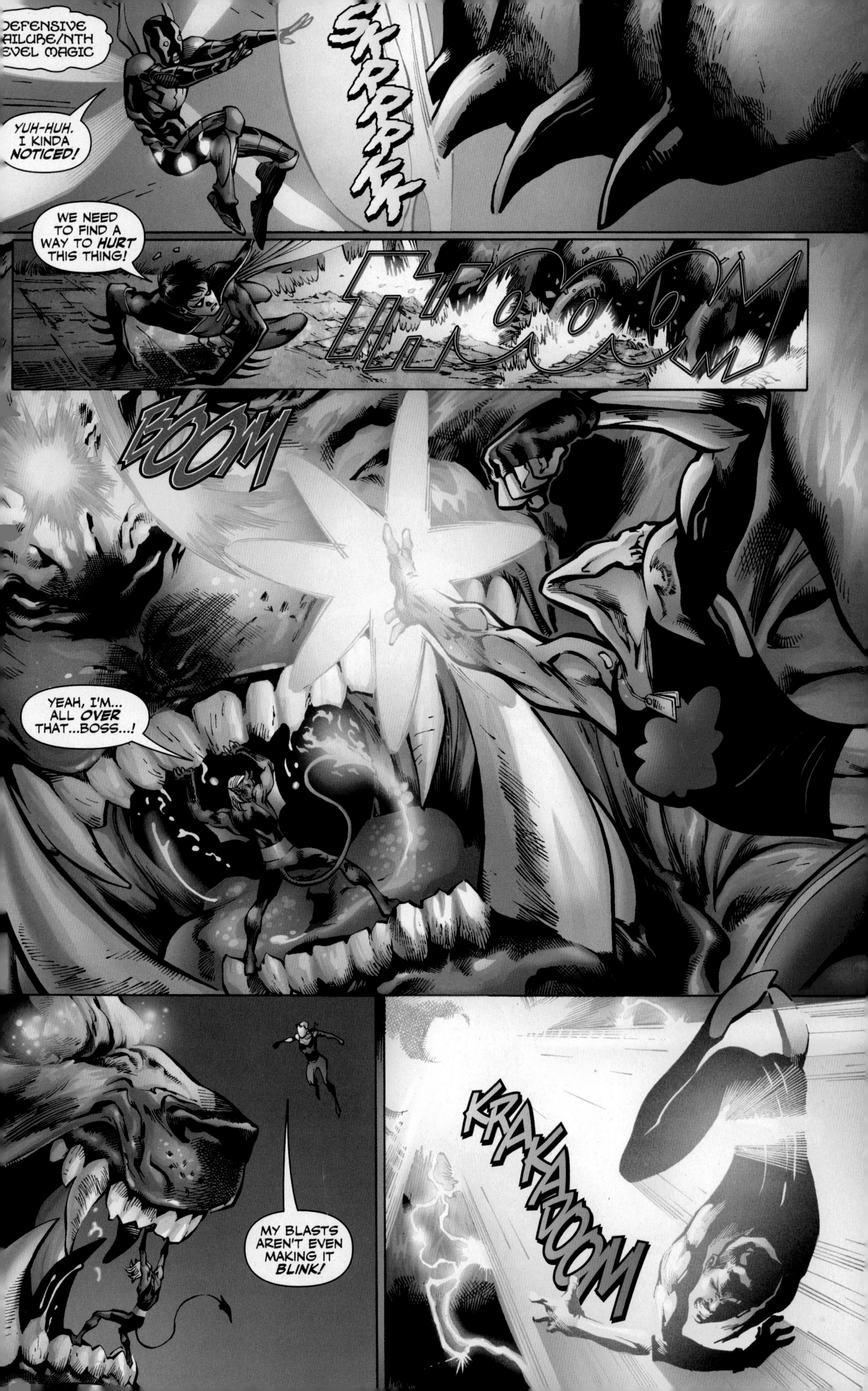

DEFENSIVE FAILURE/NTH LEVEL MAGIC
YUH-HUH. I KINDA NOTICED!
SKRRRRK
WE NEED TO FIND A WAY TO HURT THIS THING!
THOOOOM
BOOM
YEAH, I'M... ALL OVER THAT...BOSS...!
MY BLASTS AREN'T EVEN MAKING IT BLINK!
KRAKADOOM

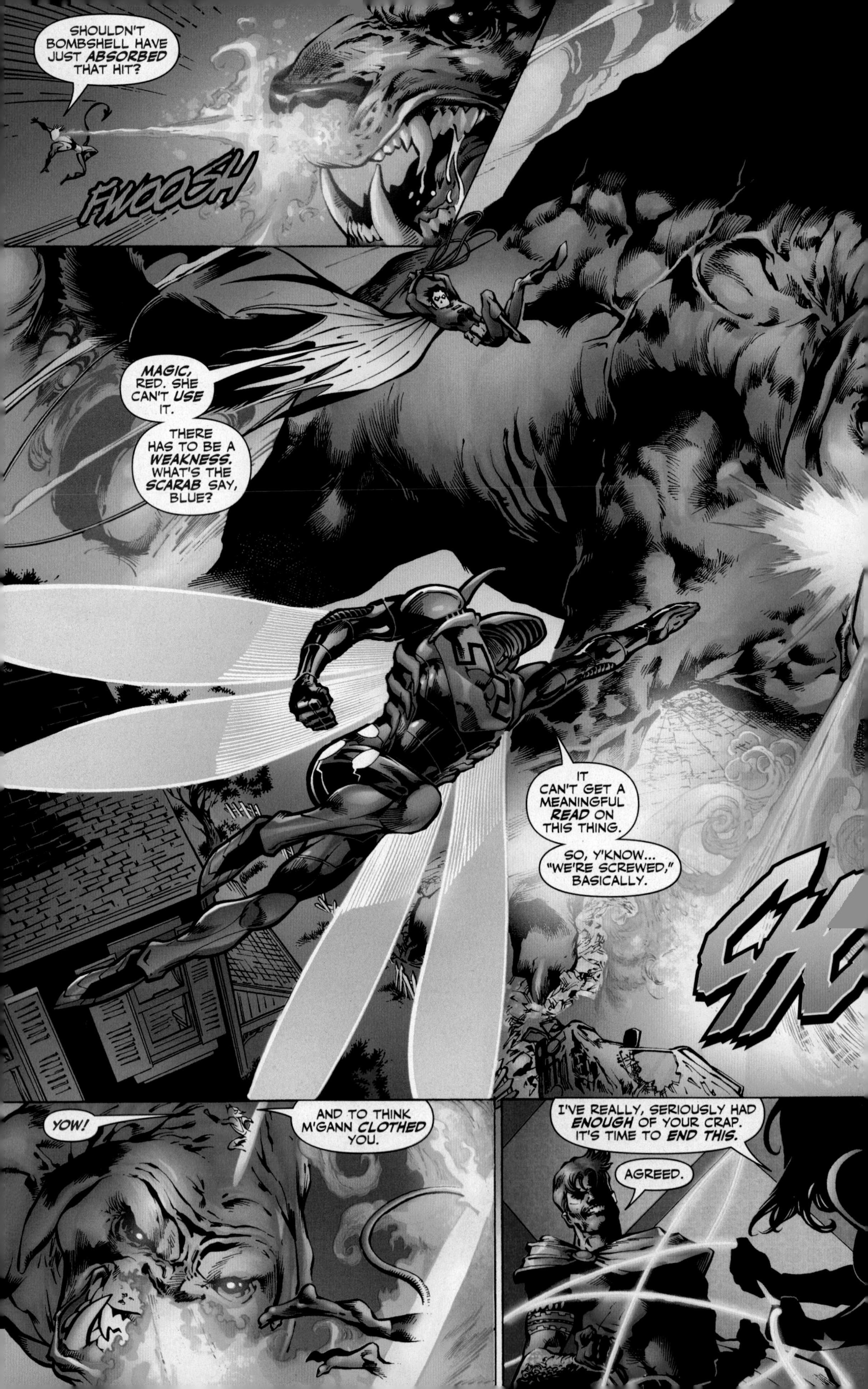

SHOULDN'T BOMBSHELL HAVE JUST ABSORBED THAT HIT?
FWOOSH
MAGIC, RED. SHE CAN'T USE IT.
THERE HAS TO BE A WEAKNESS. WHAT'S THE SCARAB SAY, BLUE?
IT CAN'T GET A MEANINGFUL READ ON THIS THING.
SO, Y'KNOW... "WE'RE SCREWED," BASICALLY.
YOW!
AND TO THINK M'GANN CLOTHED YOU.
I'VE REALLY, SERIOUSLY HAD ENOUGH OF YOUR CRAP. IT'S TIME TO END THIS.
AGREED.

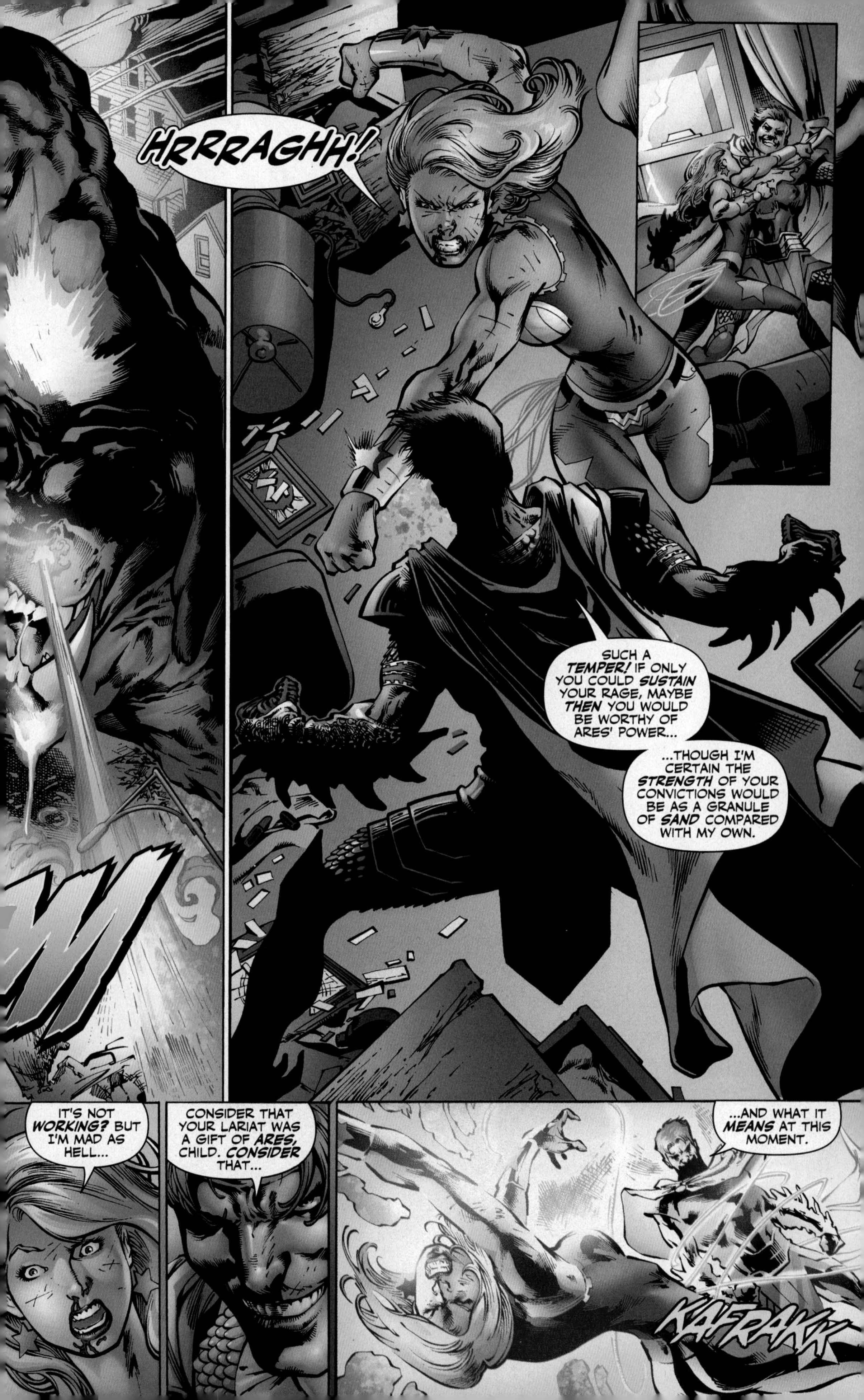
HRRRAGHH!
SUCH A TEMPER! IF ONLY YOU COULD SUSTAIN YOUR RAGE, MAYBE THEN YOU WOULD BE WORTHY OF ARES' POWER...
...THOUGH I'M CERTAIN THE STRENGTH OF YOUR CONVICTIONS WOULD BE AS A GRANULE OF SAND COMPARED WITH MY OWN.
IT'S NOT WORKING? BUT I'M MAD AS HELL...
CONSIDER THAT YOUR LARIAT WAS A GIFT OF ARES, CHILD. CONSIDER THAT...
...AND WHAT IT MEANS AT THIS MOMENT.
KAFRAKK

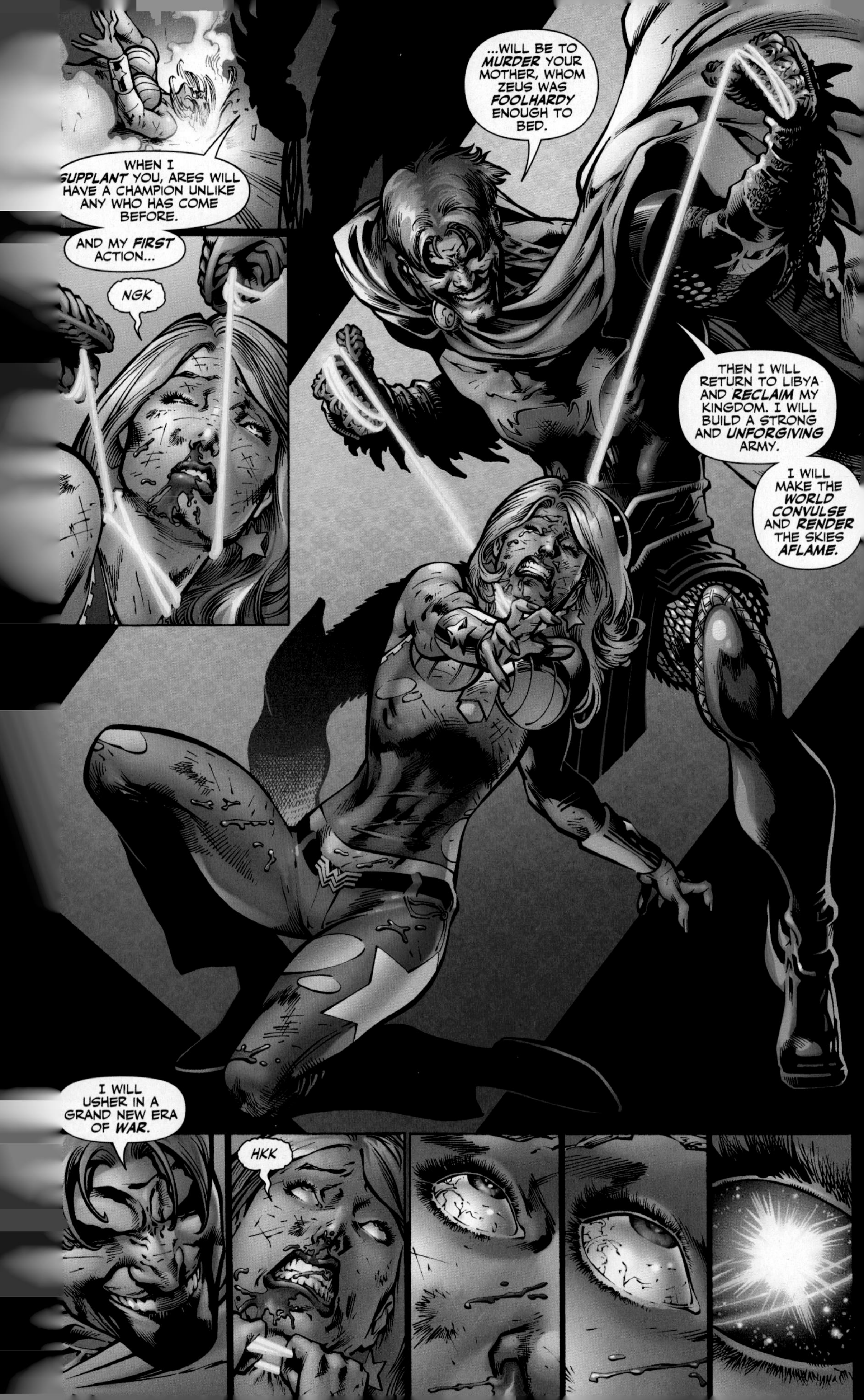
WHEN I SUPPLANT YOU, ARES WILL HAVE A CHAMPION UNLIKE ANY WHO HAS COME BEFORE.
AND MY FIRST ACTION...
NGK
...WILL BE TO MURDER YOUR MOTHER, WHOM ZEUS WAS FOOLHARDY ENOUGH TO BED.
THEN I WILL RETURN TO LIBYA AND RECLAIM MY KINGDOM. I WILL BUILD A STRONG AND UNFORGIVING ARMY.
I WILL MAKE THE WORLD CONVULSE AND RENDER THE SKIES AFLAME.
I WILL USHER IN A GRAND NEW ERA OF WAR.
HKK

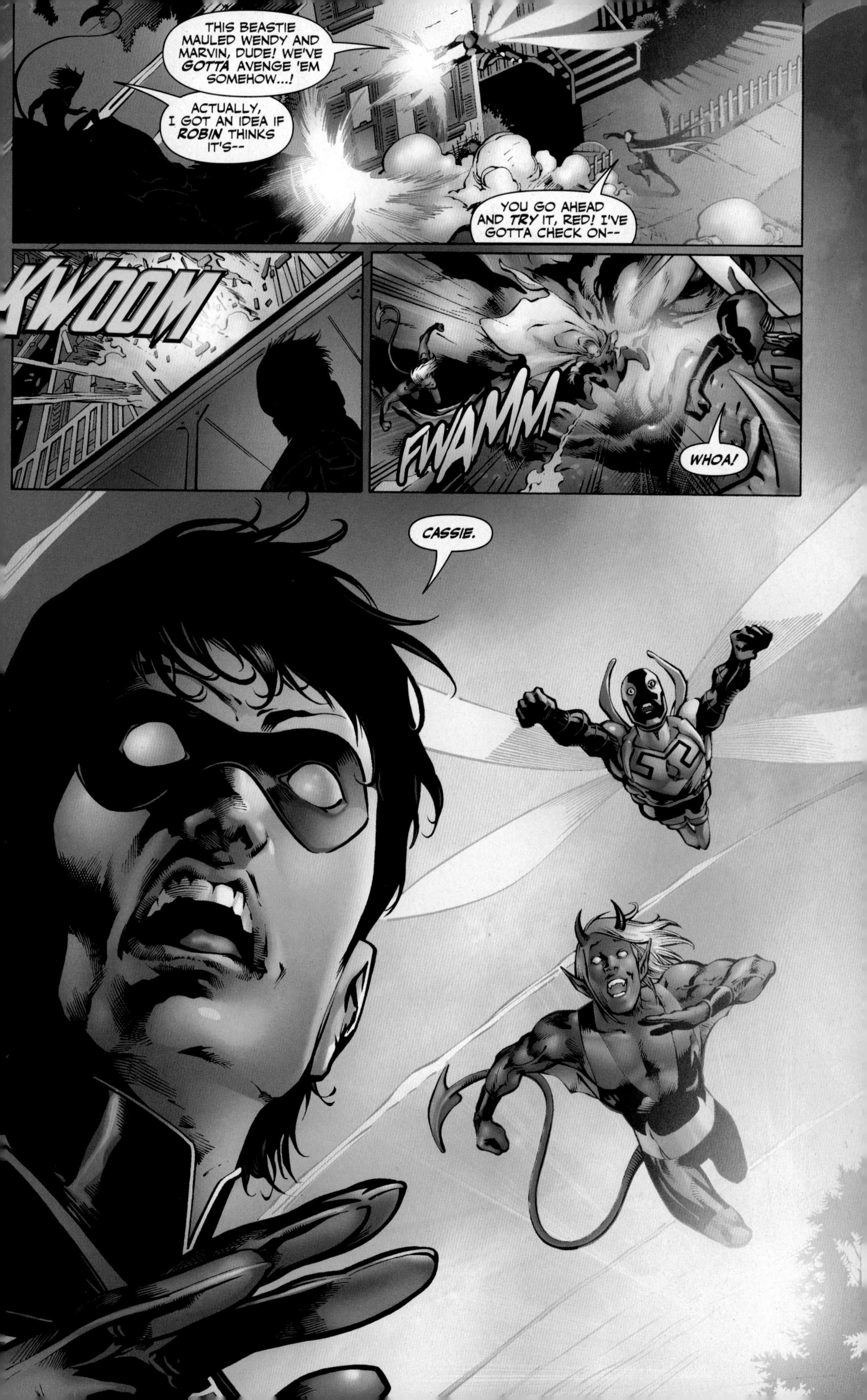
THIS BEASTIE MAULED WENDY AND MARVIN, DUDE! WE'VE GOTTA AVENGE 'EM SOMEHOW...!
ACTUALLY, I GOT AN IDEA IF ROBIN THINKS IT'S--
YOU GO AHEAD AND TRY IT, RED! I'VE GOTTA CHECK ON--
KWOOM
FWAMM
WHOA!
CASSIE.

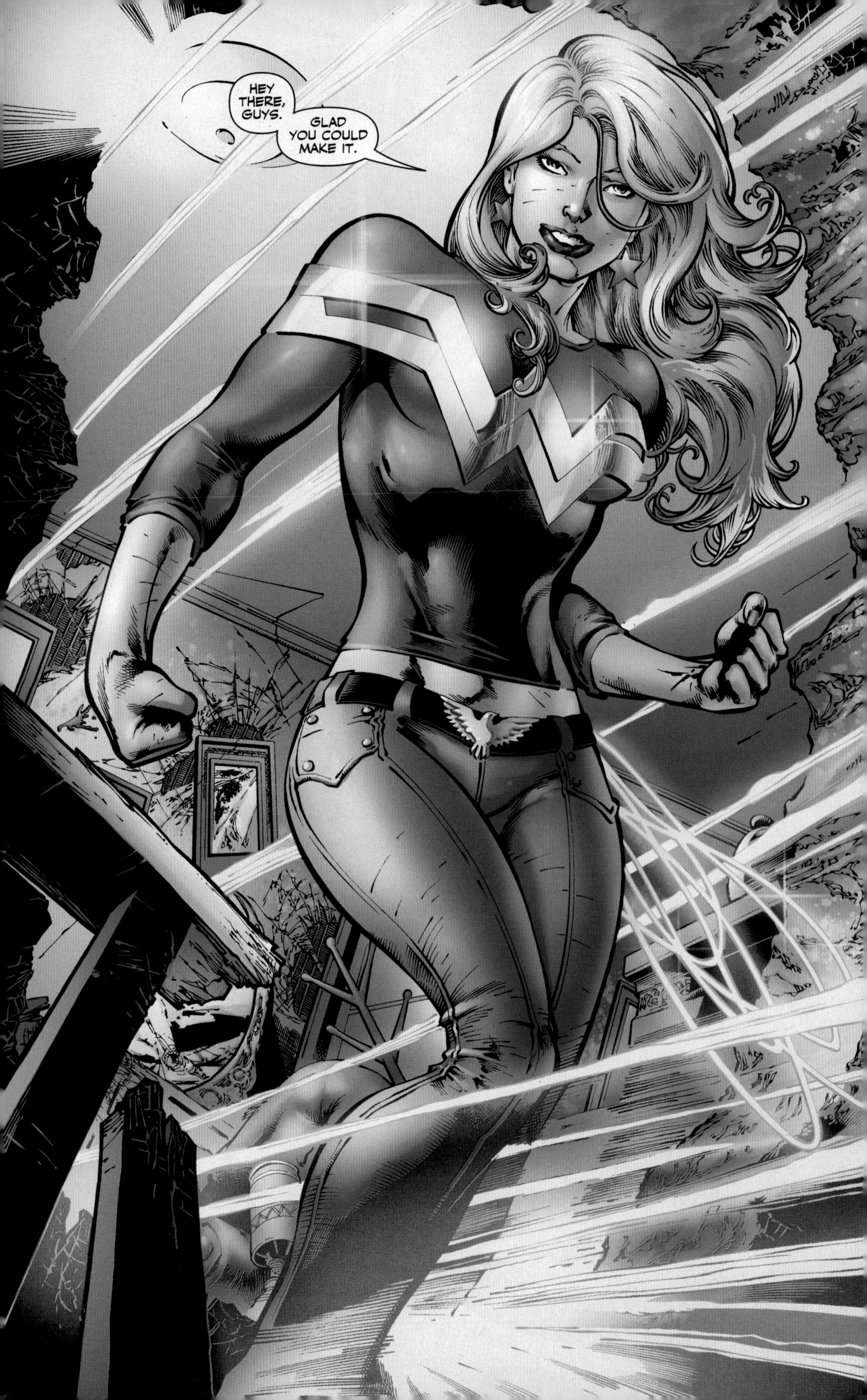
HEY THERE, GUYS.
GLAD YOU COULD MAKE IT.

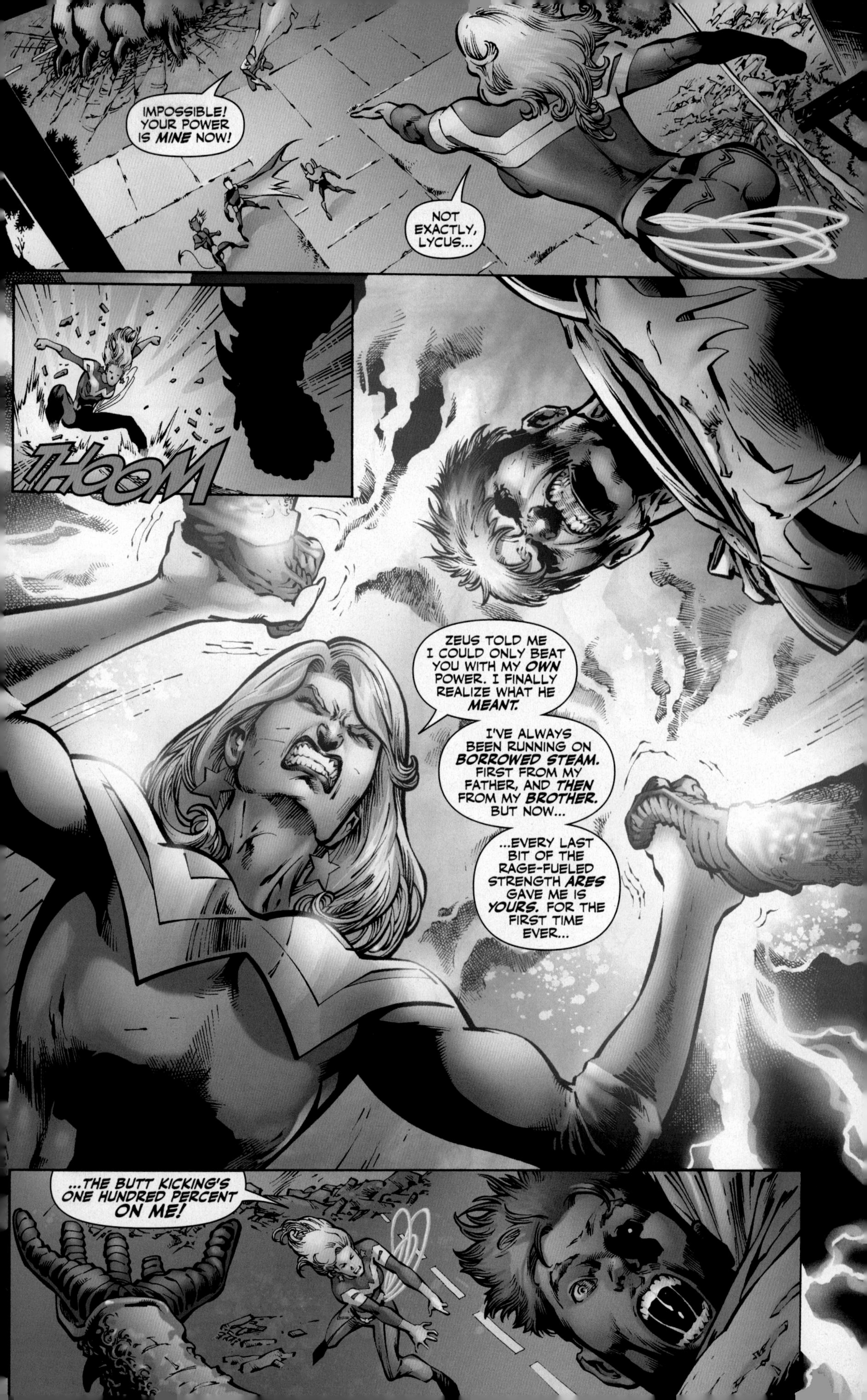
IMPOSSIBLE! YOUR POWER IS MINE NOW!
NOT EXACTLY, LYCUS...
THOOM
ZEUS TOLD ME I COULD ONLY BEAT YOU WITH MY OWN POWER. I FINALLY REALIZE WHAT HE MEANT.
I'VE ALWAYS BEEN RUNNING ON BORROWED STEAM. FIRST FROM MY FATHER, AND THEN FROM MY BROTHER. BUT NOW...
...EVERY LAST BIT OF THE RAGE-FUELED STRENGTH ARES GAVE ME IS YOURS. FOR THE FIRST TIME EVER...
...THE BUTT KICKING'S ONE HUNDRED PERCENT ON ME!

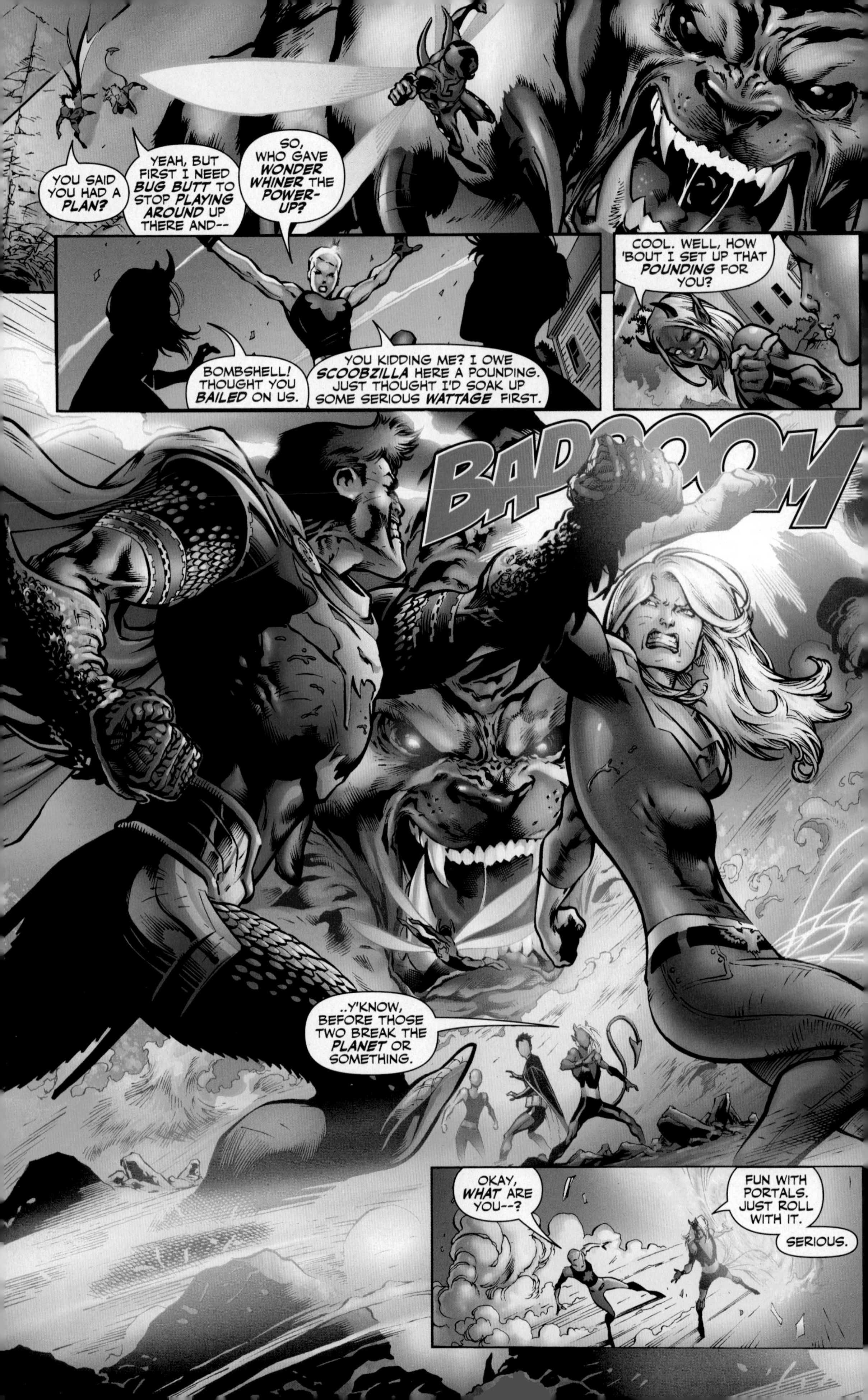
YOU SAID YOU HAD A PLAN?
YEAH, BUT FIRST I NEED BUG BUTT TO STOP PLAYING AROUND UP THERE AND--
SO, WHO GAVE WONDER WHINER THE POWER-UP?
BOMBSHELL! THOUGHT YOU BAILED ON US.
YOU KIDDING ME? I OWE SCOOBZILLA HERE A POUNDING. JUST THOUGHT I'D SOAK UP SOME SERIOUS WATTAGE FIRST.
COOL. WELL, HOW 'BOUT I SET UP THAT POUNDING FOR YOU?
BADOOOM
..Y'KNOW, BEFORE THOSE TWO BREAK THE PLANET OR SOMETHING.
OKAY, WHAT ARE YOU--?
FUN WITH PORTALS. JUST ROLL WITH IT.
SERIOUS.

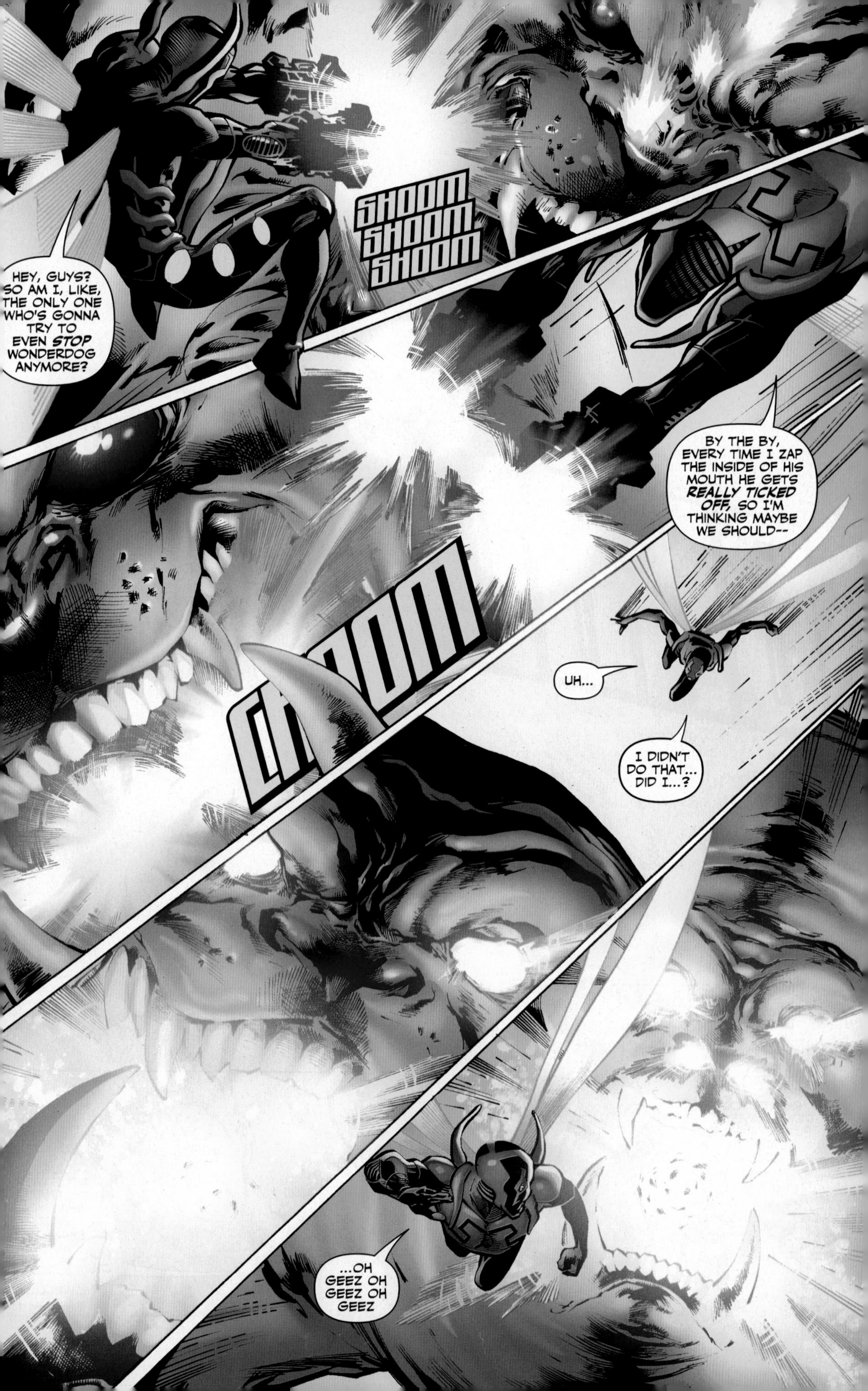
HEY, GUYS? SO AM I, LIKE, THE ONLY ONE WHO'S GONNA TRY TO EVEN STOP WONDERDOG ANYMORE?
SHOOM SHOOM SHOOM
BY THE BY, EVERY TIME I ZAP THE INSIDE OF HIS MOUTH HE GETS REALLY TICKED OFF, SO I'M THINKING MAYBE WE SHOULD--
UH...
I DIDN'T DO THAT... DID I...?
...OH GEEZ OH GEEZ OH GEEZ

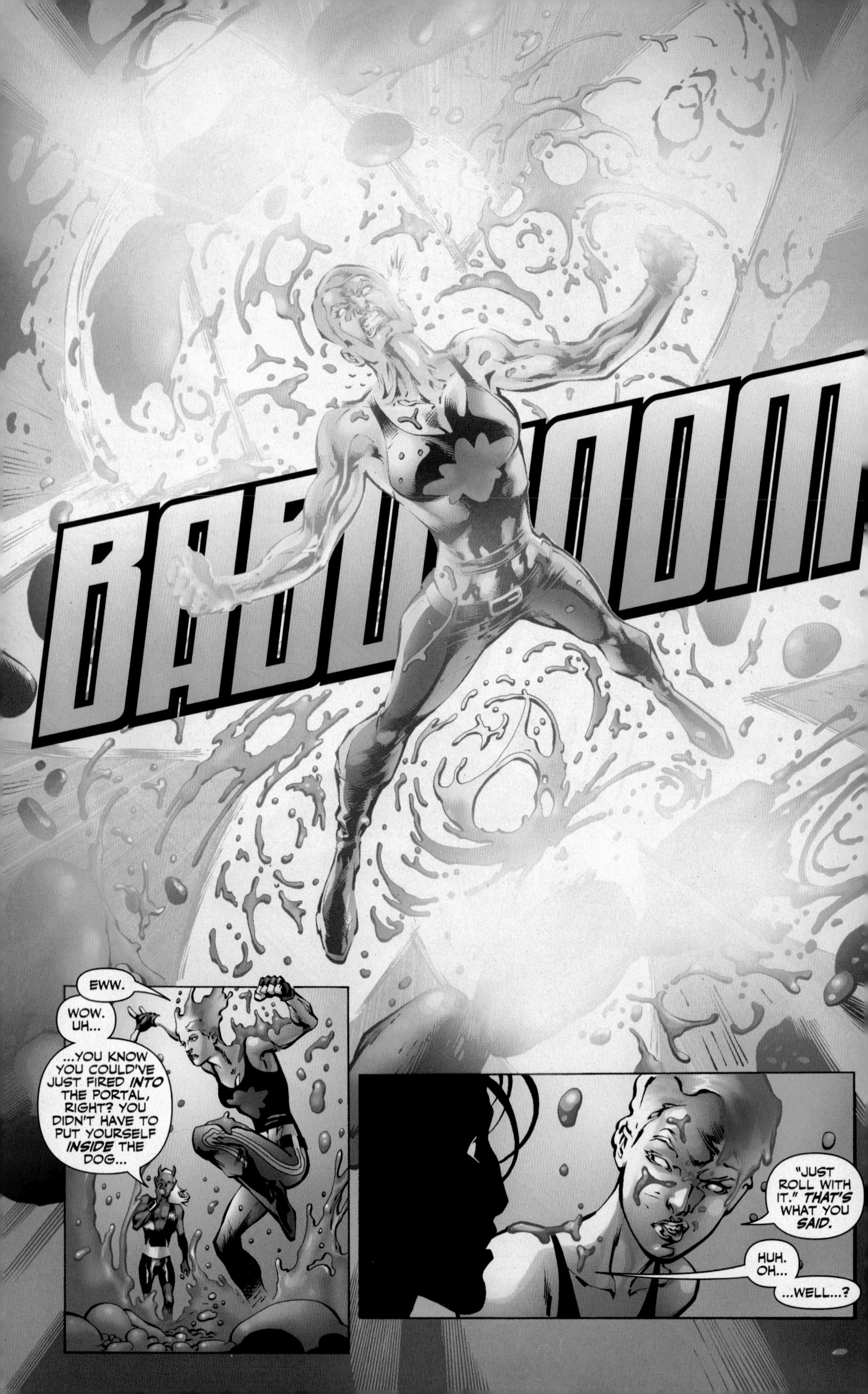
BABOOOM
EWW.
WOW. UH...
...YOU KNOW YOU COULD'VE JUST FIRED *INTO* THE PORTAL, RIGHT? YOU DIDN'T HAVE TO PUT YOURSELF *INSIDE* THE DOG...
"JUST ROLL WITH IT." *THAT'S* WHAT YOU *SAID.*
HUH. OH...
...WELL...?

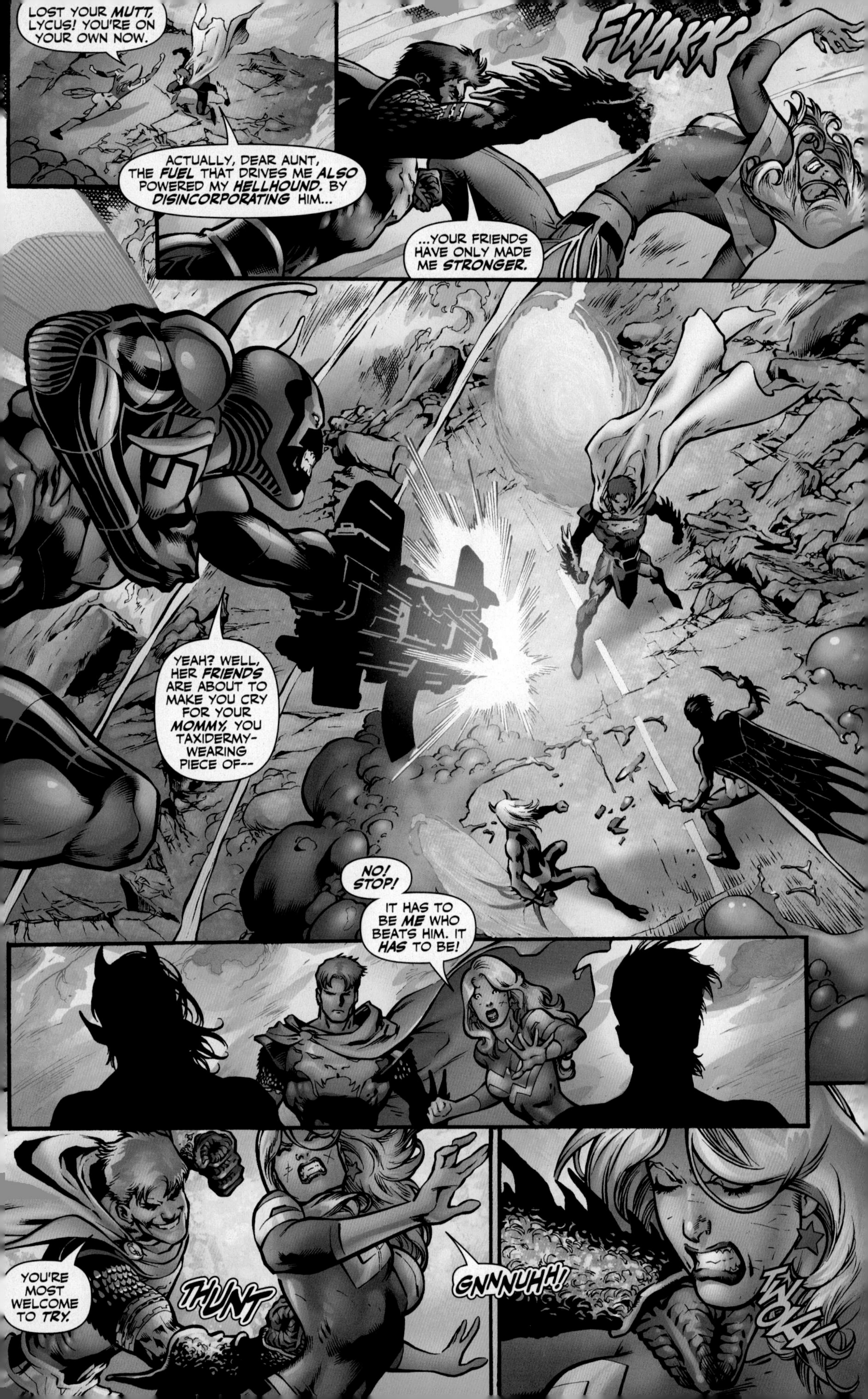
LOST YOUR MUTT, LYCUS! YOU'RE ON YOUR OWN NOW.
FWARK
ACTUALLY, DEAR AUNT, THE FUEL THAT DRIVES ME ALSO POWERED MY HELLHOUND. BY DISINCORPORATING HIM...
...YOUR FRIENDS HAVE ONLY MADE ME STRONGER.
YEAH? WELL, HER FRIENDS ARE ABOUT TO MAKE YOU CRY FOR YOUR MOMMY, YOU TAXIDERMY-WEARING PIECE OF--
NO! STOP!
IT HAS TO BE ME WHO BEATS HIM. IT HAS TO BE!
YOU'RE MOST WELCOME TO TRY.
THUNT
GNNNUHH!
TNOKK

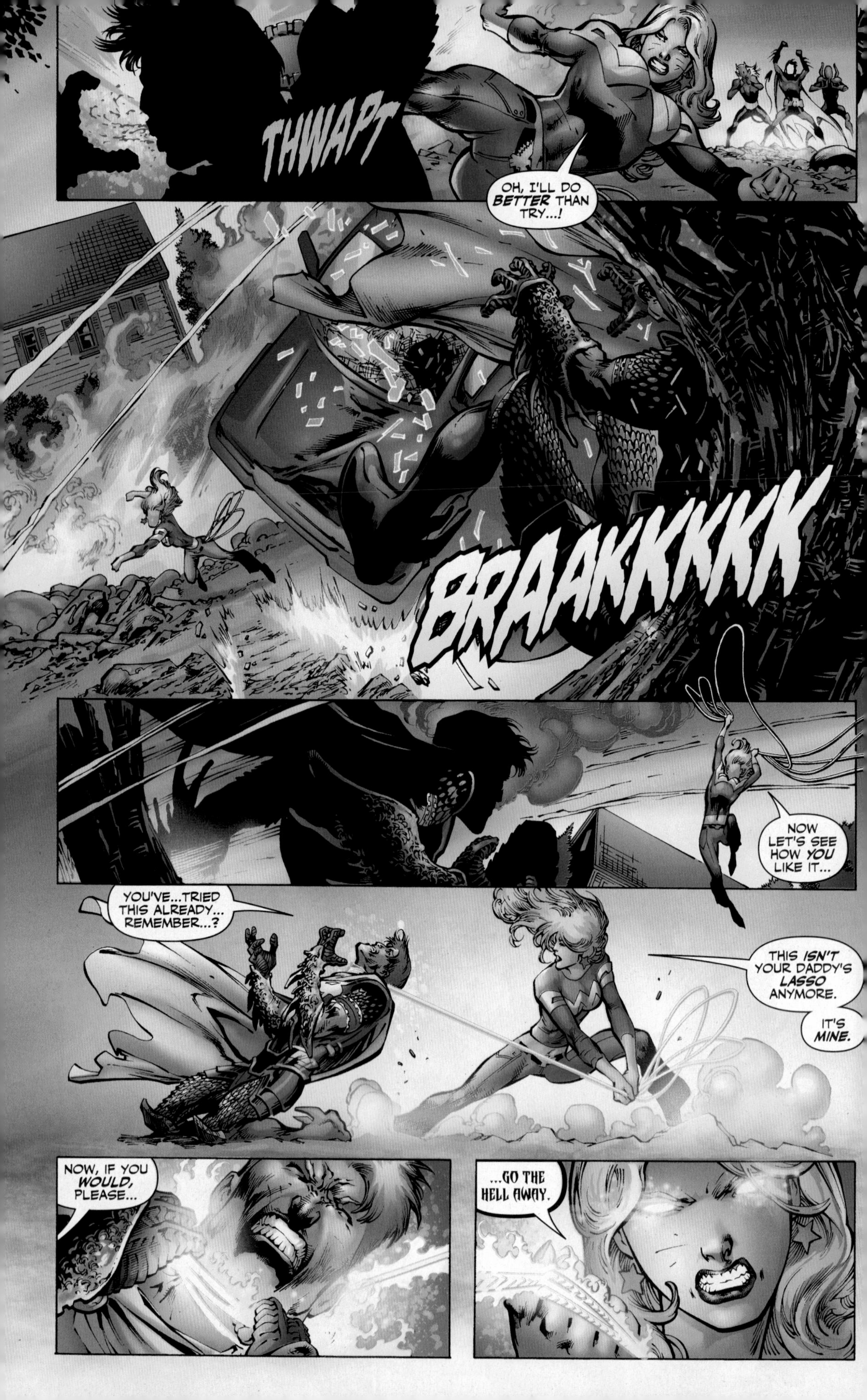
THWAPT
OH, I'LL DO BETTER THAN TRY...!
BRAAKKKKK
NOW LET'S SEE HOW YOU LIKE IT...
YOU'VE...TRIED THIS ALREADY... REMEMBER...?
THIS ISN'T YOUR DADDY'S LASSO ANYMORE.
IT'S MINE.
NOW, IF YOU WOULD, PLEASE...
...GO THE HELL AWAY.

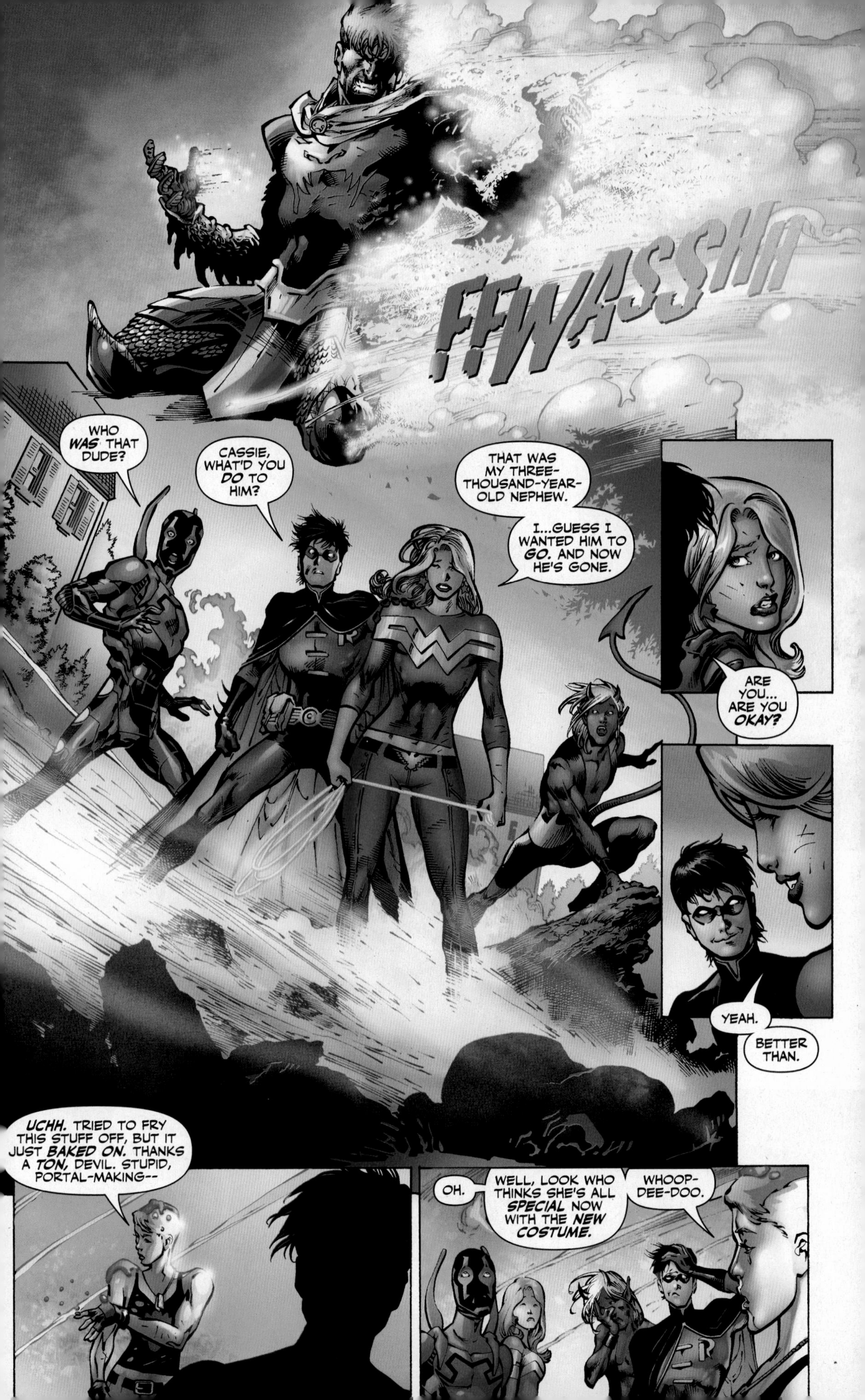
FFWASSHH
WHO WAS THAT DUDE?
CASSIE, WHAT'D YOU DO TO HIM?
THAT WAS MY THREE-THOUSAND-YEAR-OLD NEPHEW.
I...GUESS I WANTED HIM TO GO. AND NOW HE'S GONE.
ARE YOU... ARE YOU OKAY?
YEAH.
BETTER THAN.
UCHH. TRIED TO FRY THIS STUFF OFF, BUT IT JUST BAKED ON. THANKS A TON, DEVIL. STUPID, PORTAL-MAKING--
OH.
WELL, LOOK WHO THINKS SHE'S ALL SPECIAL NOW WITH THE NEW COSTUME.
WHOOP-DEE-DOO.

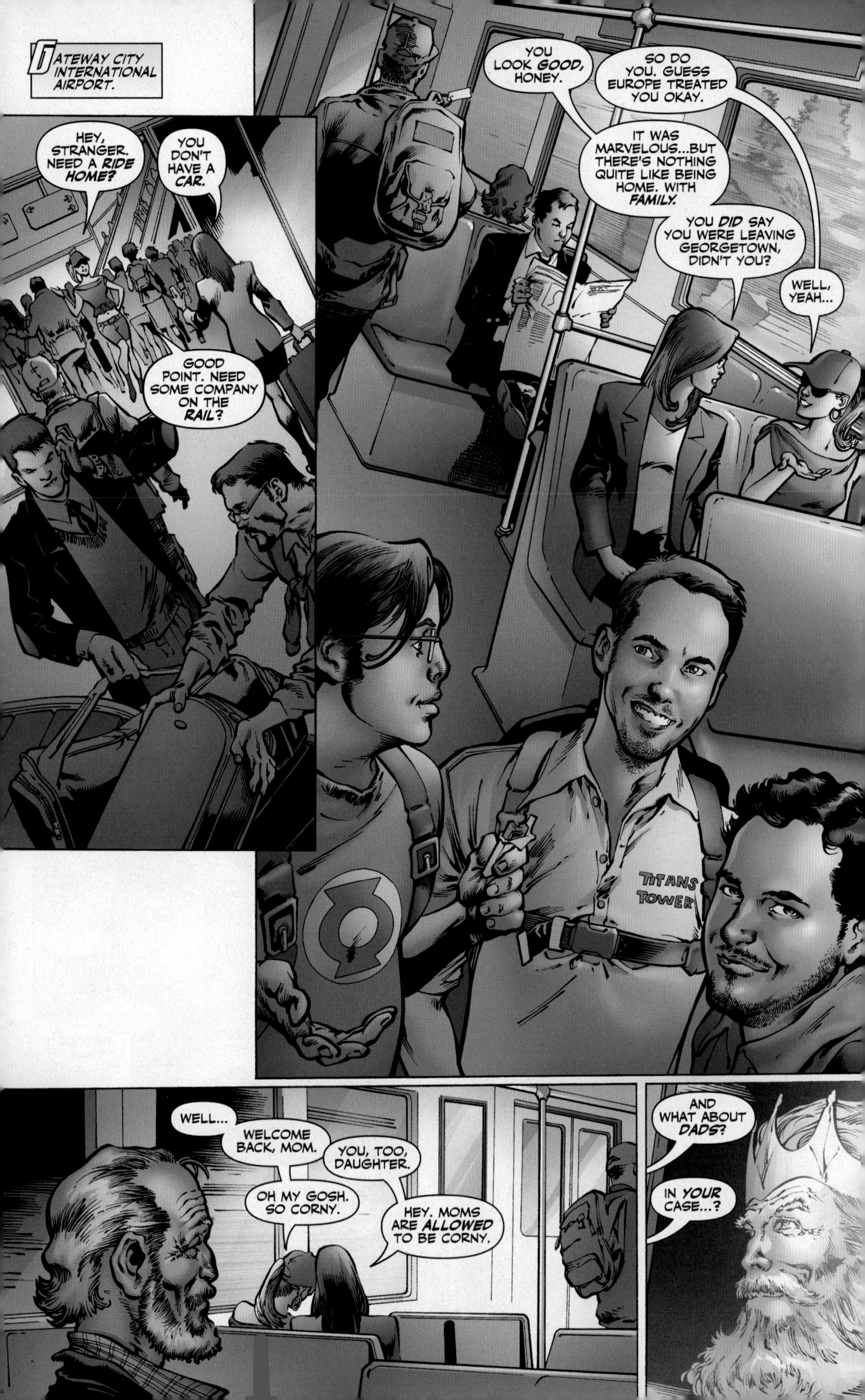
GATEWAY CITY INTERNATIONAL AIRPORT.
HEY, STRANGER. NEED A RIDE HOME?
YOU DON'T HAVE A CAR.
GOOD POINT. NEED SOME COMPANY ON THE RAIL?
YOU LOOK GOOD, HONEY.
SO DO YOU. GUESS EUROPE TREATED YOU OKAY.
IT WAS MARVELOUS...BUT THERE'S NOTHING QUITE LIKE BEING HOME. WITH FAMILY.
YOU DID SAY YOU WERE LEAVING GEORGETOWN, DIDN'T YOU?
WELL, YEAH...
TITANS TOWER
WELL...
WELCOME BACK, MOM.
YOU, TOO, DAUGHTER.
OH MY GOSH. SO CORNY.
HEY. MOMS ARE ALLOWED TO BE CORNY.
AND WHAT ABOUT DADS?
IN YOUR CASE...?

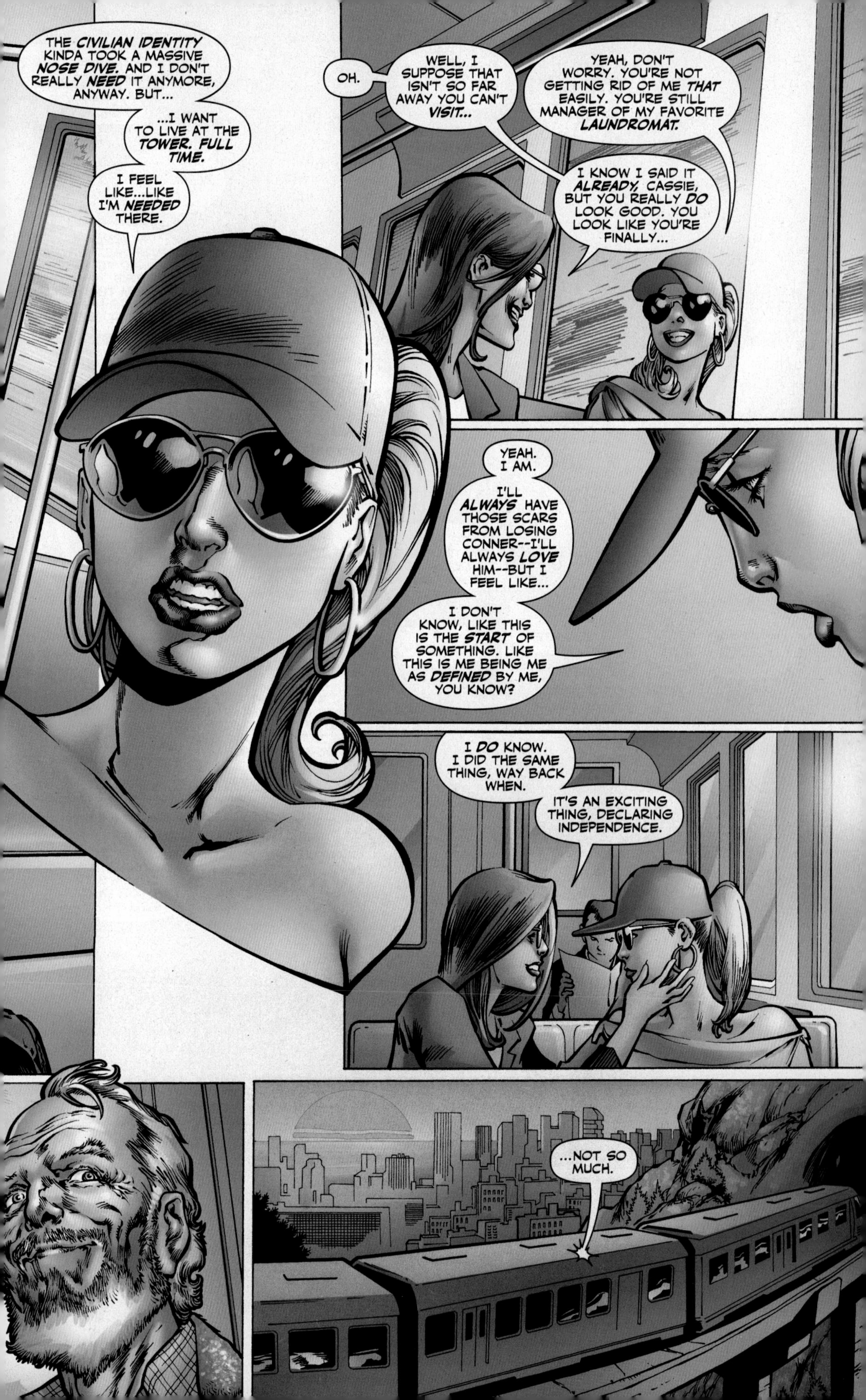
THE CIVILIAN IDENTITY KINDA TOOK A MASSIVE NOSE DIVE. AND I DON'T REALLY NEED IT ANYMORE, ANYWAY. BUT...
...I WANT TO LIVE AT THE TOWER. FULL TIME.
I FEEL LIKE...LIKE I'M NEEDED THERE.
OH.
WELL, I SUPPOSE THAT ISN'T SO FAR AWAY YOU CAN'T VISIT...
YEAH, DON'T WORRY. YOU'RE NOT GETTING RID OF ME THAT EASILY. YOU'RE STILL MANAGER OF MY FAVORITE LAUNDROMAT.
I KNOW I SAID IT ALREADY, CASSIE, BUT YOU REALLY DO LOOK GOOD. YOU LOOK LIKE YOU'RE FINALLY...
YEAH. I AM.
I'LL ALWAYS HAVE THOSE SCARS FROM LOSING CONNER--I'LL ALWAYS LOVE HIM--BUT I FEEL LIKE...
I DON'T KNOW, LIKE THIS IS THE START OF SOMETHING. LIKE THIS IS ME BEING ME AS DEFINED BY ME, YOU KNOW?
I DO KNOW. I DID THE SAME THING, WAY BACK WHEN.
IT'S AN EXCITING THING, DECLARING INDEPENDENCE.
...NOT SO MUCH.

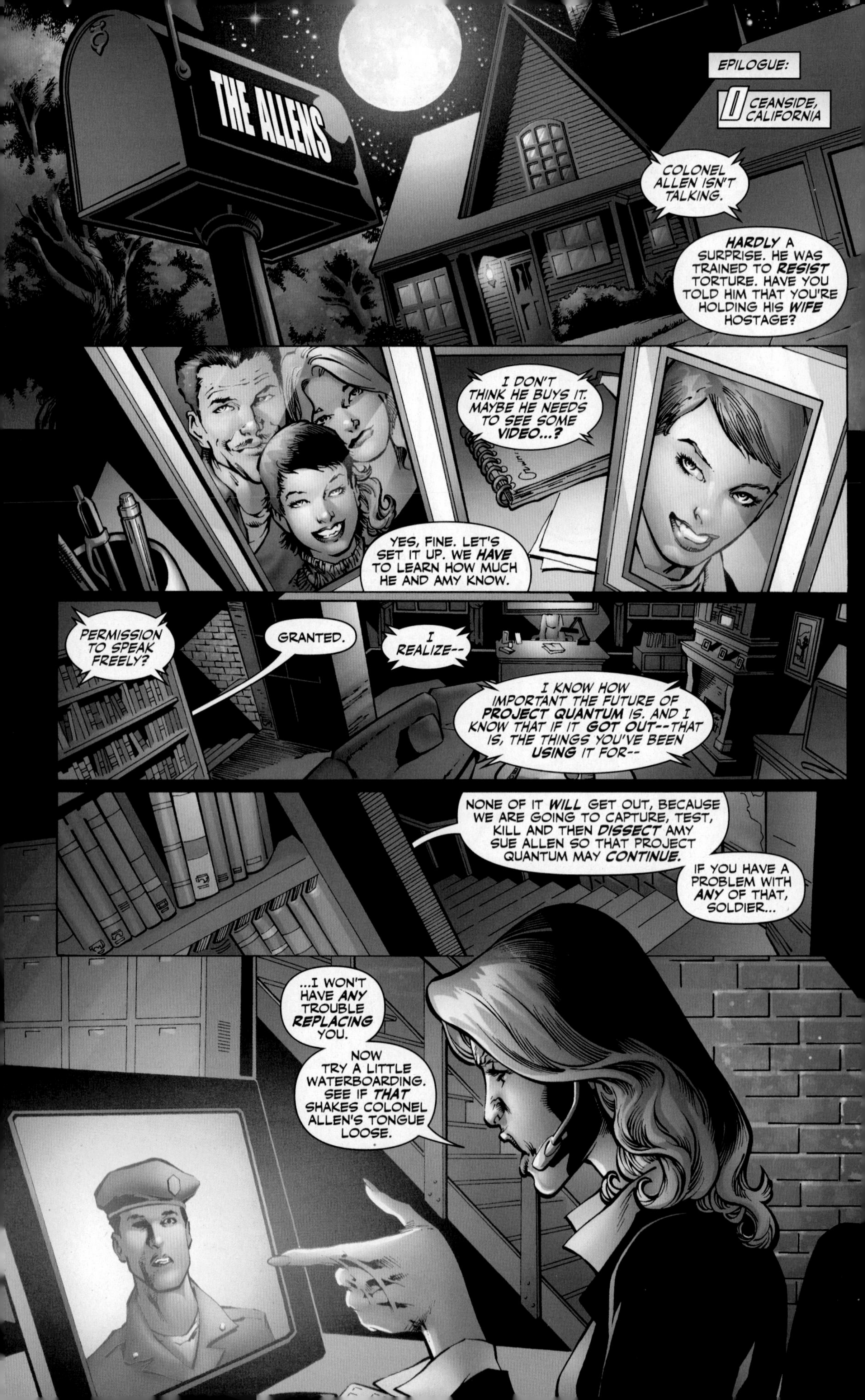
THE ALLENS
EPILOGUE:
OCEANSIDE, CALIFORNIA
COLONEL ALLEN ISN'T TALKING.
HARDLY A SURPRISE. HE WAS TRAINED TO RESIST TORTURE. HAVE YOU TOLD HIM THAT YOU'RE HOLDING HIS WIFE HOSTAGE?
I DON'T THINK HE BUYS IT. MAYBE HE NEEDS TO SEE SOME VIDEO...?
YES, FINE. LET'S SET IT UP. WE HAVE TO LEARN HOW MUCH HE AND AMY KNOW.
PERMISSION TO SPEAK FREELY?
GRANTED.
I REALIZE--
I KNOW HOW IMPORTANT THE FUTURE OF PROJECT QUANTUM IS. AND I KNOW THAT IF IT GOT OUT--THAT IS, THE THINGS YOU'VE BEEN USING IT FOR--
NONE OF IT WILL GET OUT, BECAUSE WE ARE GOING TO CAPTURE, TEST, KILL AND THEN DISSECT AMY SUE ALLEN SO THAT PROJECT QUANTUM MAY CONTINUE.
IF YOU HAVE A PROBLEM WITH ANY OF THAT, SOLDIER...
...I WON'T HAVE ANY TROUBLE REPLACING YOU.
NOW TRY A LITTLE WATERBOARDING. SEE IF THAT SHAKES COLONEL ALLEN'S TONGUE LOOSE.

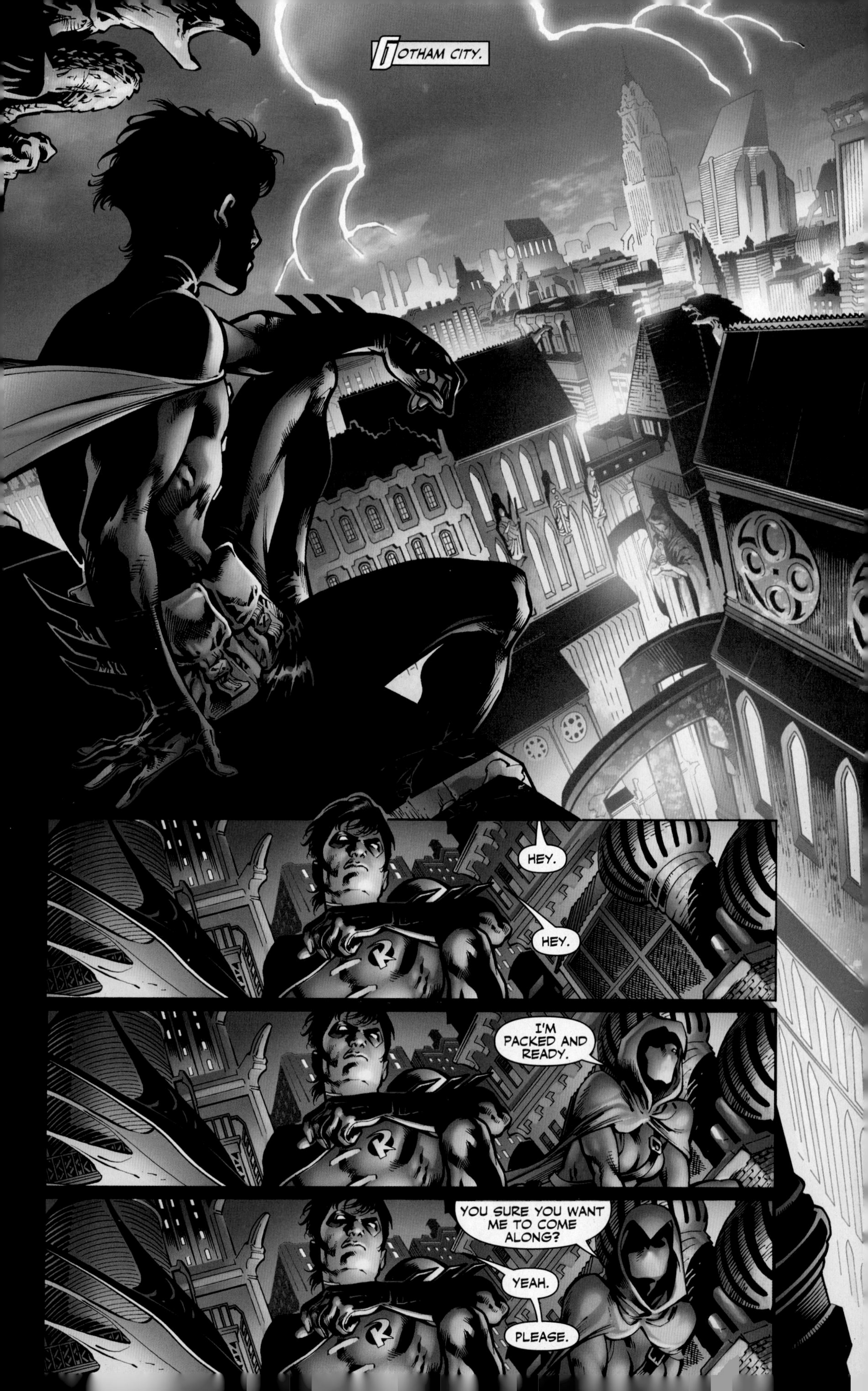
GOTHAM CITY.
HEY.
HEY.
I'M PACKED AND READY.
YOU SURE YOU WANT ME TO COME ALONG?
YEAH.
PLEASE.

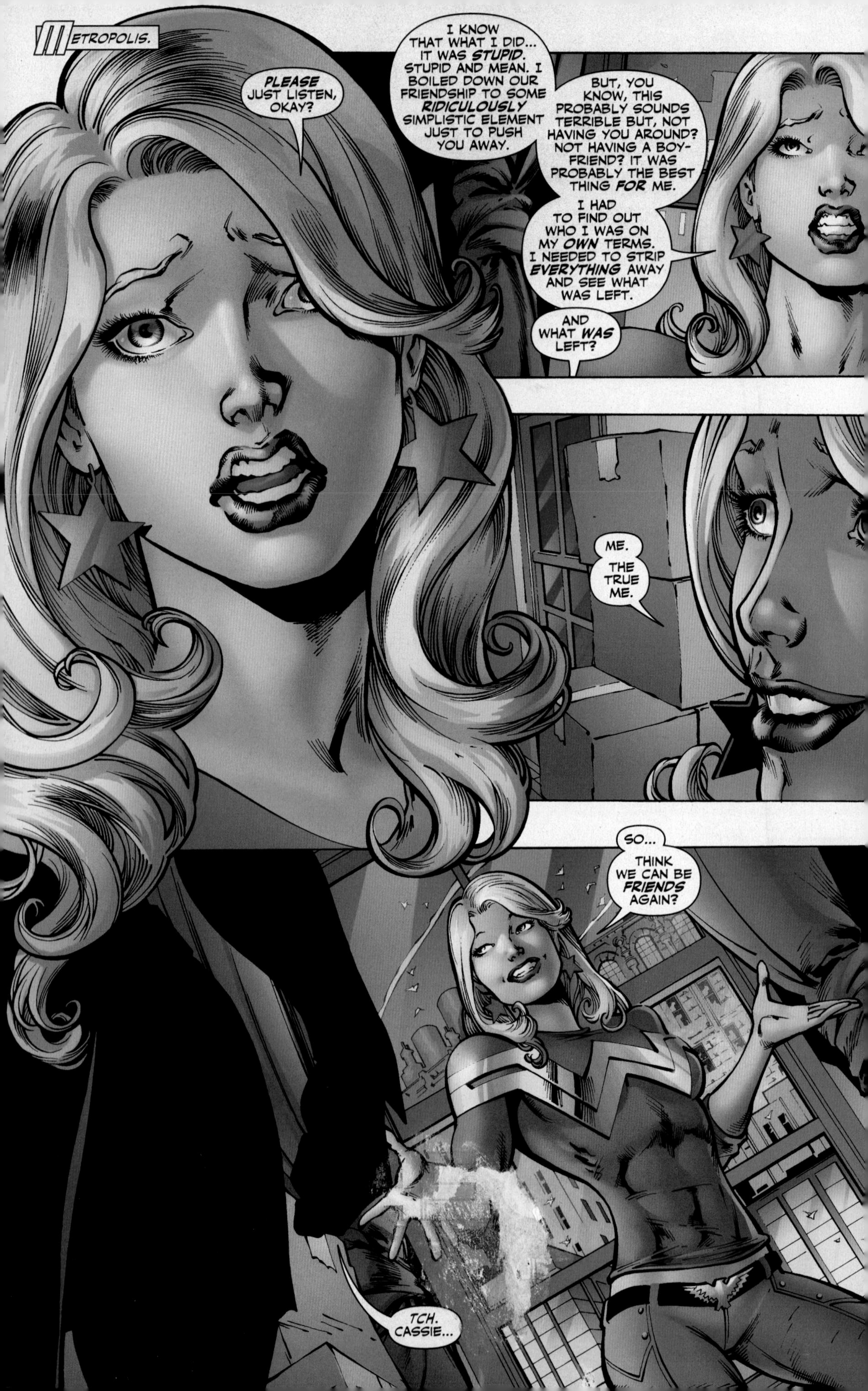
METROPOLIS.
PLEASE JUST LISTEN, OKAY?
I KNOW THAT WHAT I DID... IT WAS STUPID. STUPID AND MEAN. I BOILED DOWN OUR FRIENDSHIP TO SOME RIDICULOUSLY SIMPLISTIC ELEMENT JUST TO PUSH YOU AWAY.
BUT, YOU KNOW, THIS PROBABLY SOUNDS TERRIBLE BUT, NOT HAVING YOU AROUND? NOT HAVING A BOY-FRIEND? IT WAS PROBABLY THE BEST THING FOR ME.
I HAD TO FIND OUT WHO I WAS ON MY OWN TERMS. I NEEDED TO STRIP EVERYTHING AWAY AND SEE WHAT WAS LEFT.
AND WHAT WAS LEFT?
ME. THE TRUE ME.
SO... THINK WE CAN BE FRIENDS AGAIN?
TCH. CASSIE...

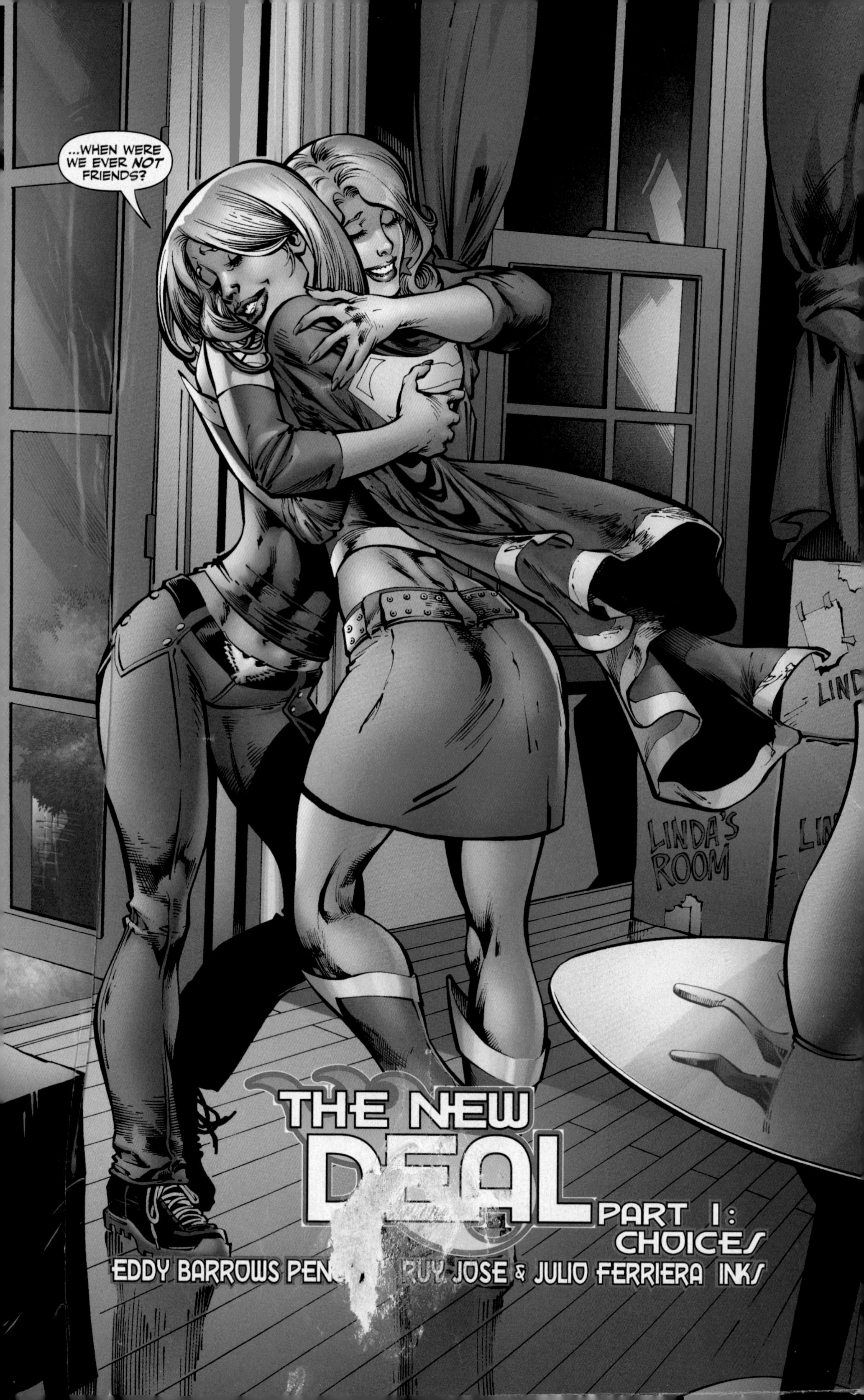

...WHEN WERE WE EVER *NOT* FRIENDS?
LINDA'S ROOM
THE NEW DEAL
PART 1: CHOICES
EDDY BARROWS PEN
RUY JOSE & JULIO FERRIERA INKS

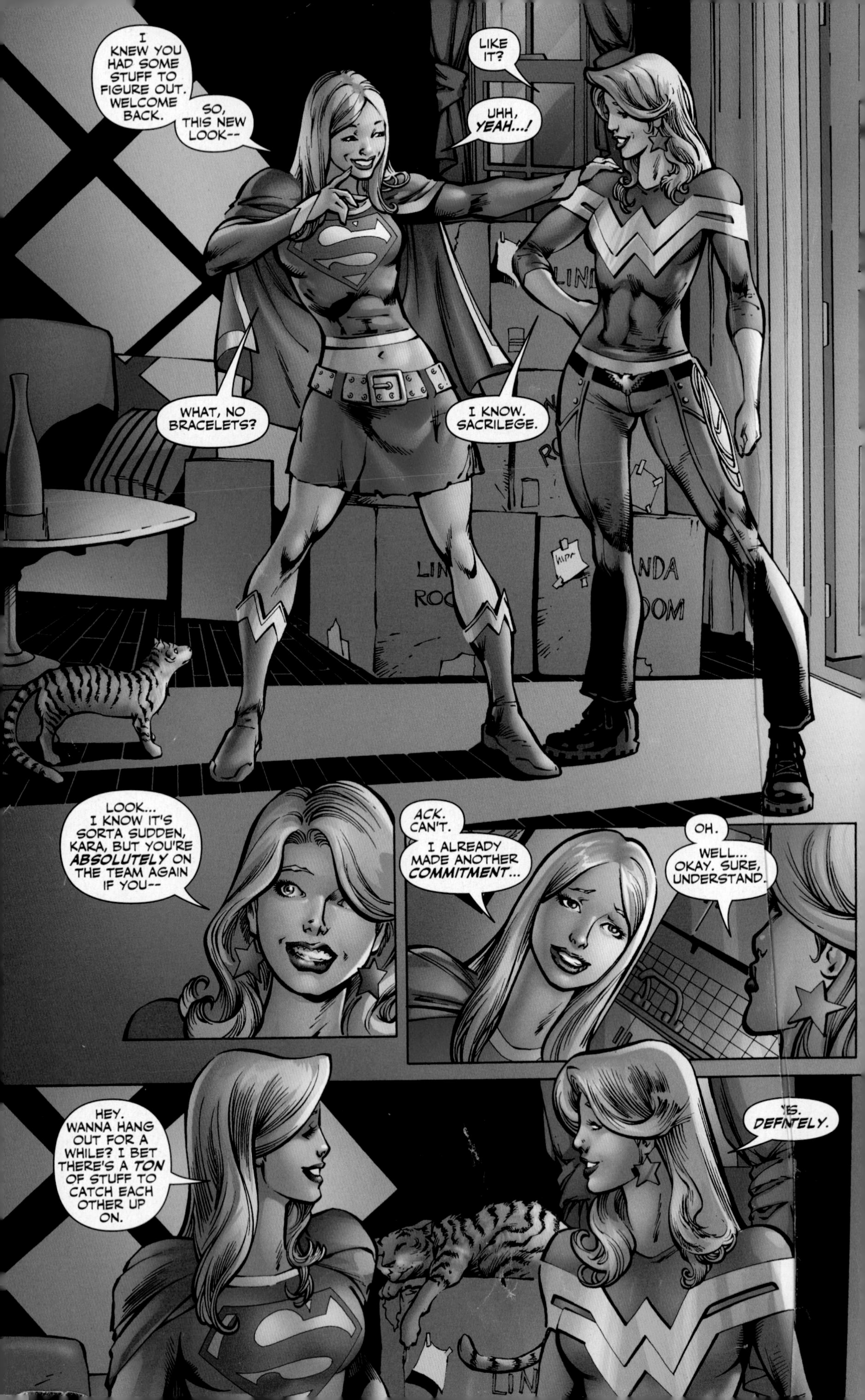
I KNEW YOU HAD SOME STUFF TO FIGURE OUT. WELCOME BACK.
SO, THIS NEW LOOK--
LIKE IT?
UHH, *YEAH...!*
WHAT, NO BRACELETS?
I KNOW. SACRILEGE.
LOOK... I KNOW IT'S SORTA SUDDEN, KARA, BUT YOU'RE *ABSOLUTELY* ON THE TEAM AGAIN IF YOU--
ACK. CAN'T.
I ALREADY MADE ANOTHER *COMMITMENT*...
OH.
WELL... OKAY. SURE, UNDERSTAND.
HEY. WANNA HANG OUT FOR A WHILE? I BET THERE'S A *TON* OF STUFF TO CATCH EACH OTHER UP ON.
YES. *DEFINTELY.*

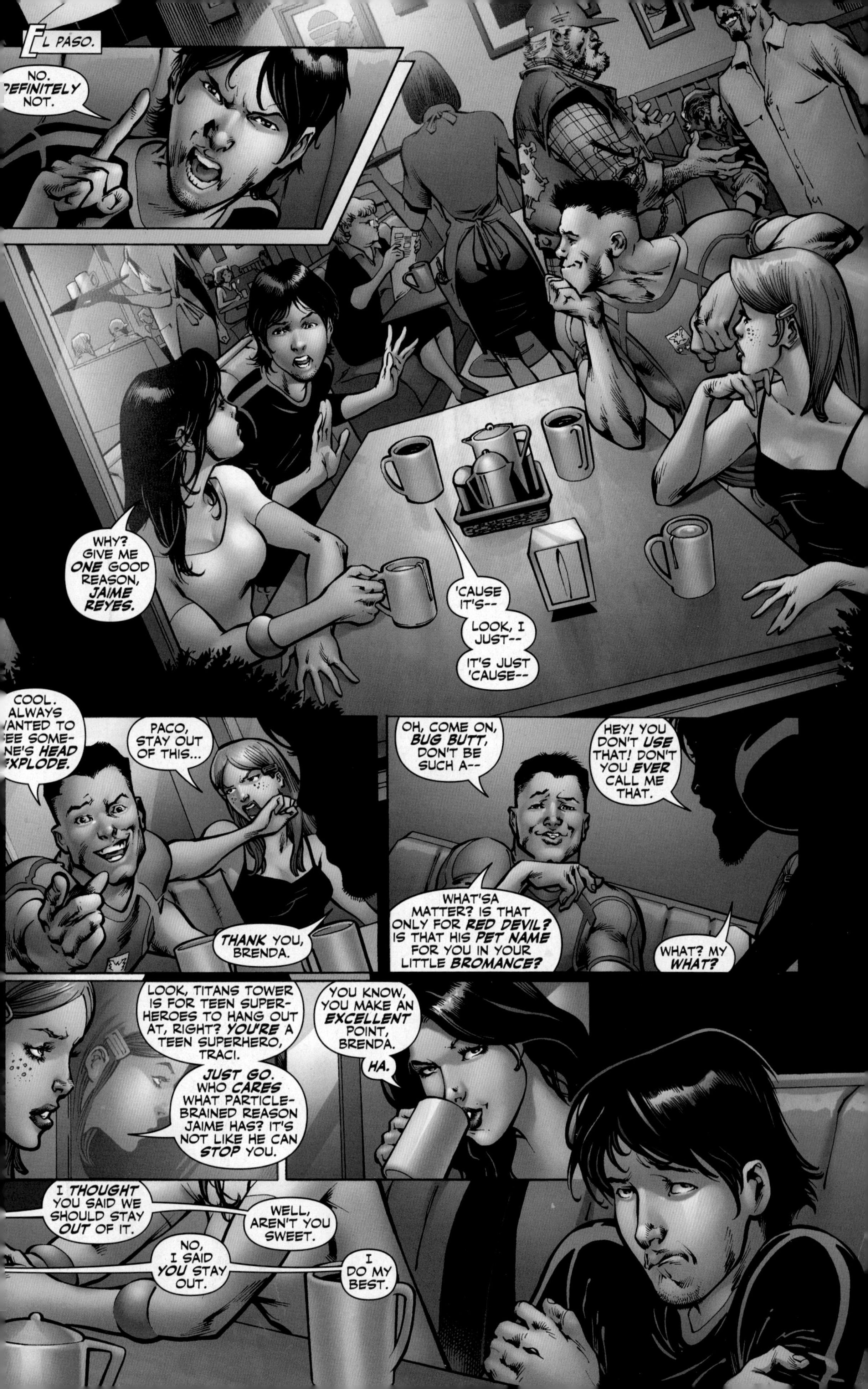
EL PASO.
NO. DEFINITELY NOT.
WHY? GIVE ME ONE GOOD REASON, JAIME REYES.
'CAUSE IT'S--
LOOK, I JUST--
IT'S JUST 'CAUSE--
COOL. ALWAYS WANTED TO SEE SOME-ONE'S HEAD EXPLODE.
PACO, STAY OUT OF THIS...
THANK YOU, BRENDA.
OH, COME ON, BUG BUTT, DON'T BE SUCH A--
HEY! YOU DON'T USE THAT! DON'T YOU EVER CALL ME THAT.
WHAT'SA MATTER? IS THAT ONLY FOR RED DEVIL? IS THAT HIS PET NAME FOR YOU IN YOUR LITTLE BROMANCE?
WHAT? MY WHAT?
LOOK, TITANS TOWER IS FOR TEEN SUPER-HEROES TO HANG OUT AT, RIGHT? YOU'RE A TEEN SUPERHERO, TRACI.
JUST GO. WHO CARES WHAT PARTICLE-BRAINED REASON JAIME HAS? IT'S NOT LIKE HE CAN STOP YOU.
YOU KNOW, YOU MAKE AN EXCELLENT POINT, BRENDA.
HA.
I THOUGHT YOU SAID WE SHOULD STAY OUT OF IT.
WELL, AREN'T YOU SWEET.
NO, I SAID YOU STAY OUT.
I DO MY BEST.

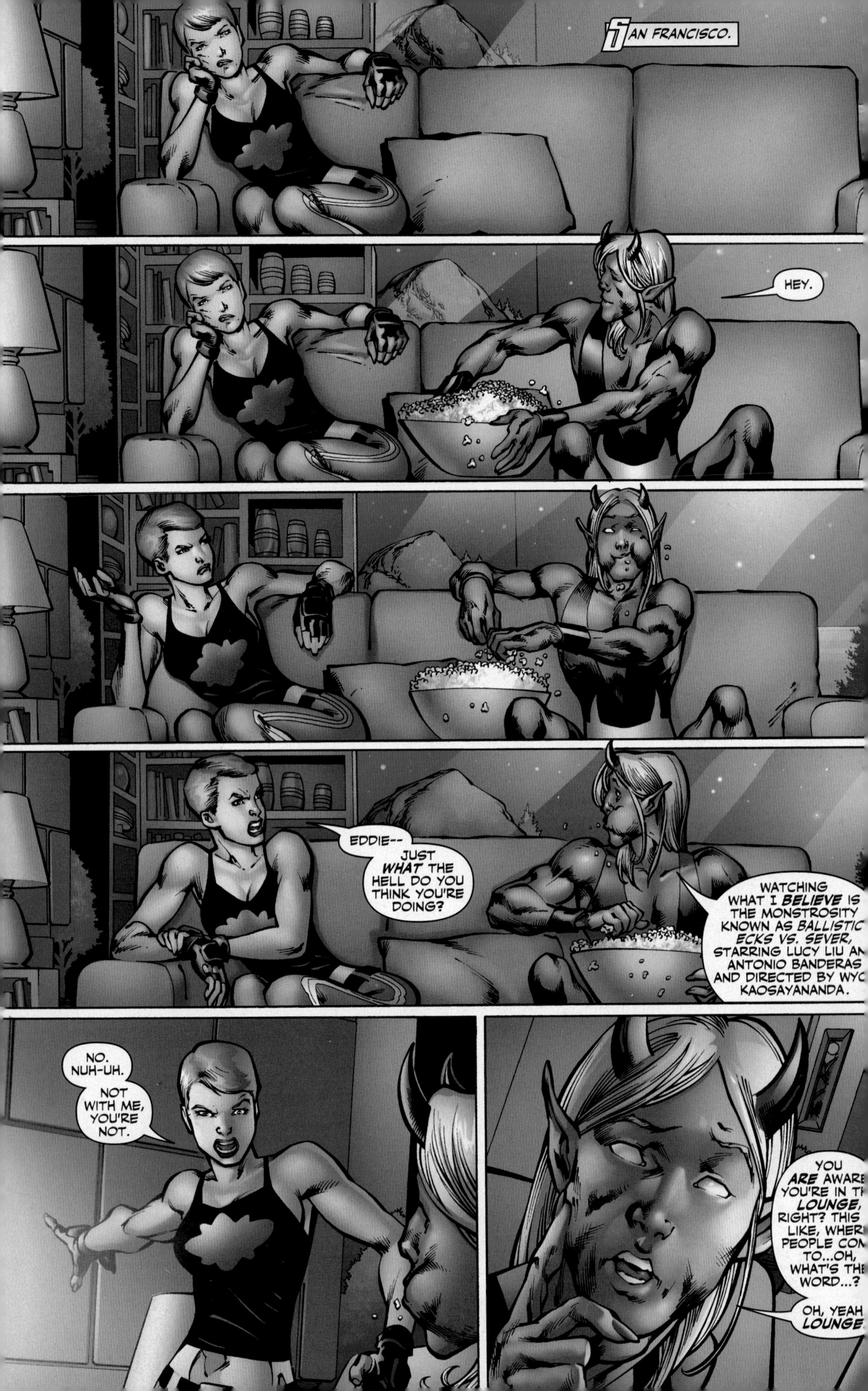
SAN FRANCISCO.
HEY.
EDDIE-- JUST WHAT THE HELL DO YOU THINK YOU'RE DOING?
WATCHING WHAT I BELIEVE IS THE MONSTROSITY KNOWN AS BALLISTIC ECKS VS. SEVER, STARRING LUCY LIU AN ANTONIO BANDERAS AND DIRECTED BY WYC KAOSAYANANDA.
NO. NUH-UH.
NOT WITH ME, YOU'RE NOT.
YOU ARE AWARE YOU'RE IN TH LOUNGE, RIGHT? THIS LIKE, WHER PEOPLE CON TO...OH, WHAT'S THE WORD...?
OH, YEAH LOUNGE.

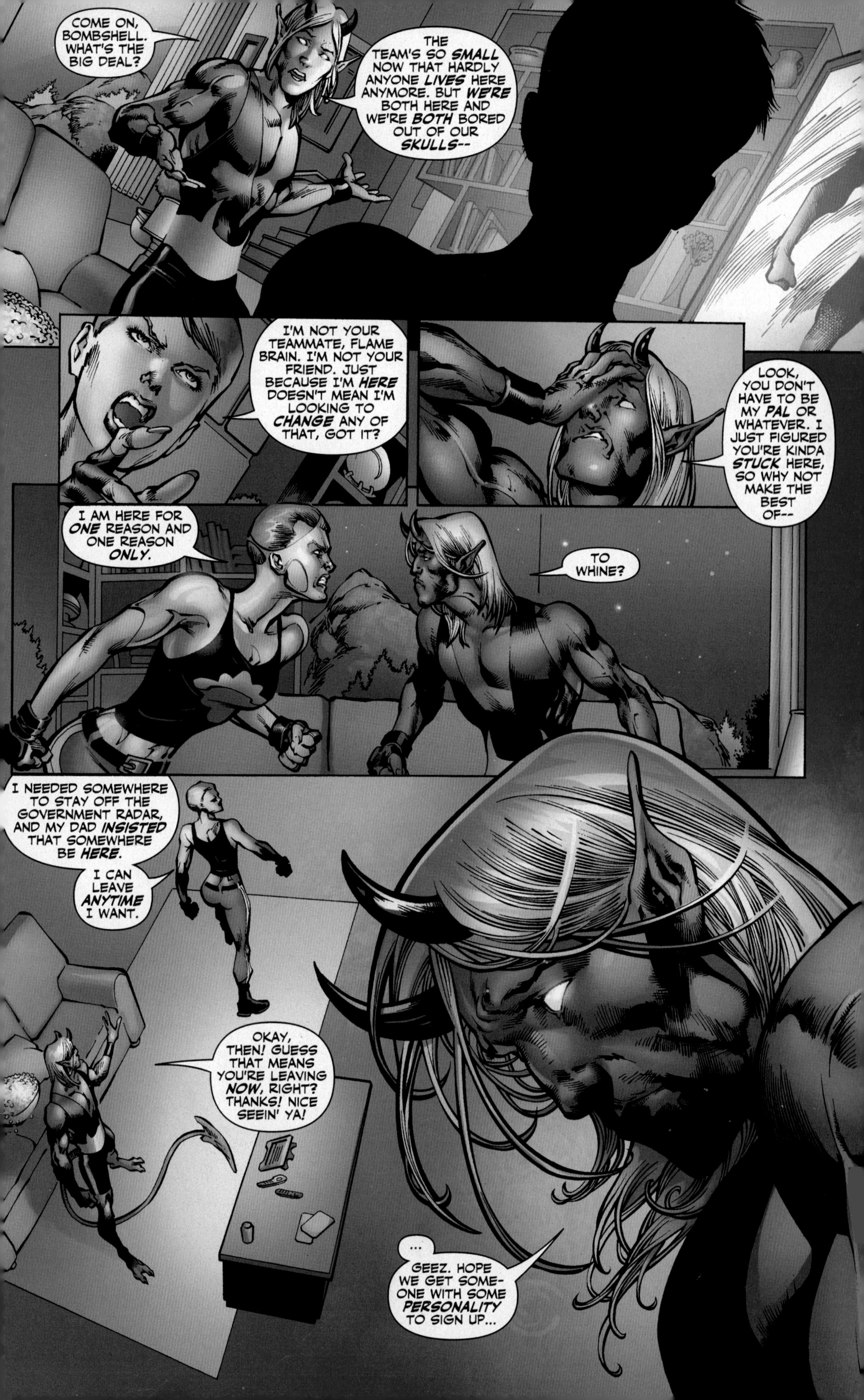
COME ON, BOMBSHELL. WHAT'S THE BIG DEAL?
THE TEAM'S SO *SMALL* NOW THAT HARDLY ANYONE *LIVES* HERE ANYMORE. BUT *WE'RE* BOTH HERE AND WE'RE *BOTH* BORED OUT OF OUR *SKULLS*--
I'M NOT YOUR TEAMMATE, FLAME BRAIN. I'M NOT YOUR FRIEND. JUST BECAUSE I'M *HERE* DOESN'T MEAN I'M LOOKING TO *CHANGE* ANY OF THAT, GOT IT?
LOOK, YOU DON'T HAVE TO BE MY *PAL* OR WHATEVER. I JUST FIGURED YOU'RE KINDA *STUCK* HERE, SO WHY NOT MAKE THE BEST OF--
I AM HERE FOR *ONE* REASON AND ONE REASON *ONLY*.
TO WHINE?
I NEEDED SOMEWHERE TO STAY OFF THE GOVERNMENT RADAR, AND MY DAD *INSISTED* THAT SOMEWHERE BE *HERE*.
I CAN LEAVE *ANYTIME* I WANT.
OKAY, THEN! GUESS THAT MEANS YOU'RE LEAVING *NOW*, RIGHT? THANKS! NICE SEEIN' YA!
...
GEEZ. HOPE WE GET SOME-ONE WITH SOME *PERSONALITY* TO SIGN UP...

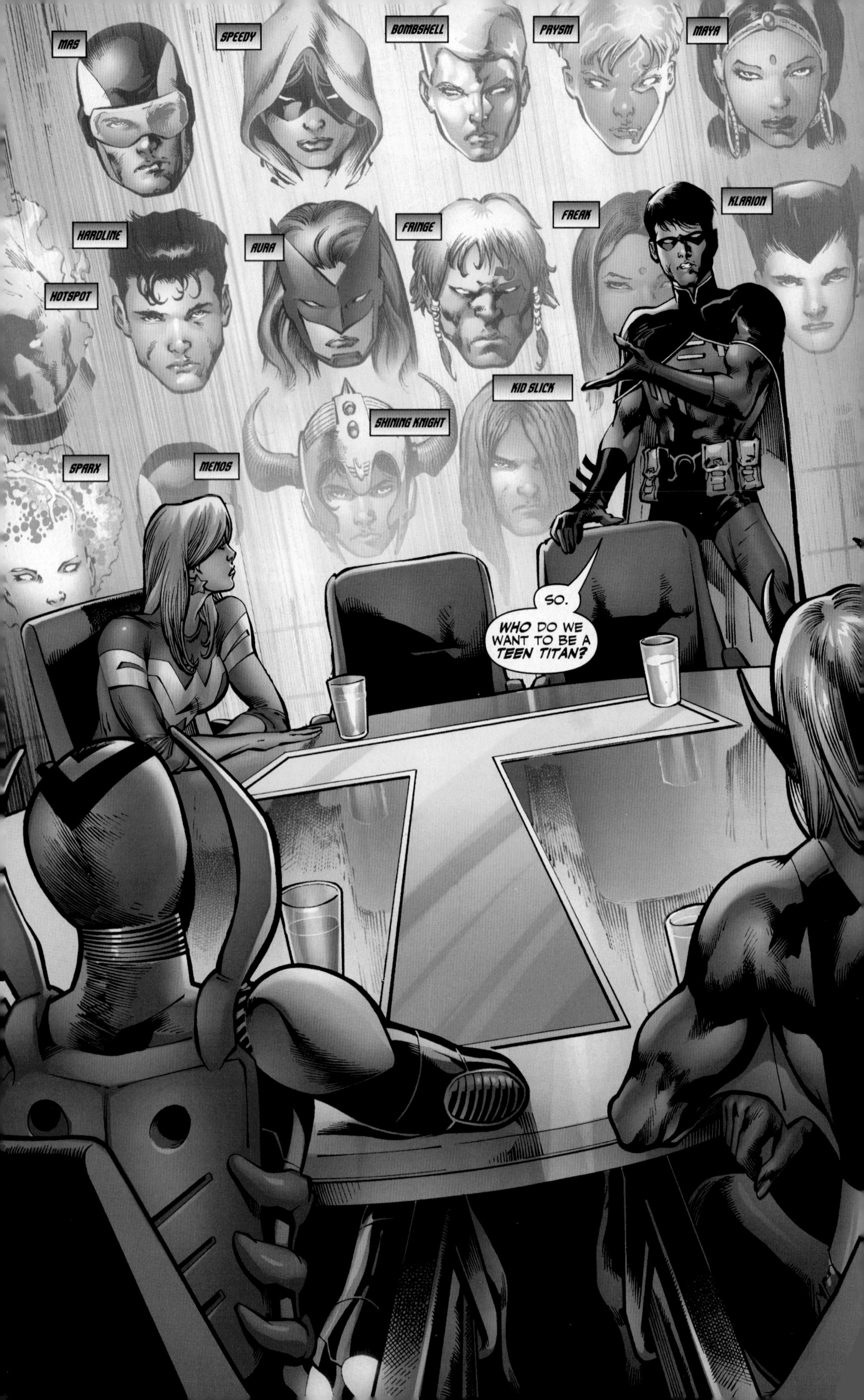
MAS
SPEEDY
BOMBSHELL
PRYSM
MAYA
HARDLINE
AURA
FRINGE
FREAK
KLARION
HOTSPOT
KID SLICK
SHINING KNIGHT
SPARX
MENOS
SO.
WHO DO WE WANT TO BE A TEEN TITAN?

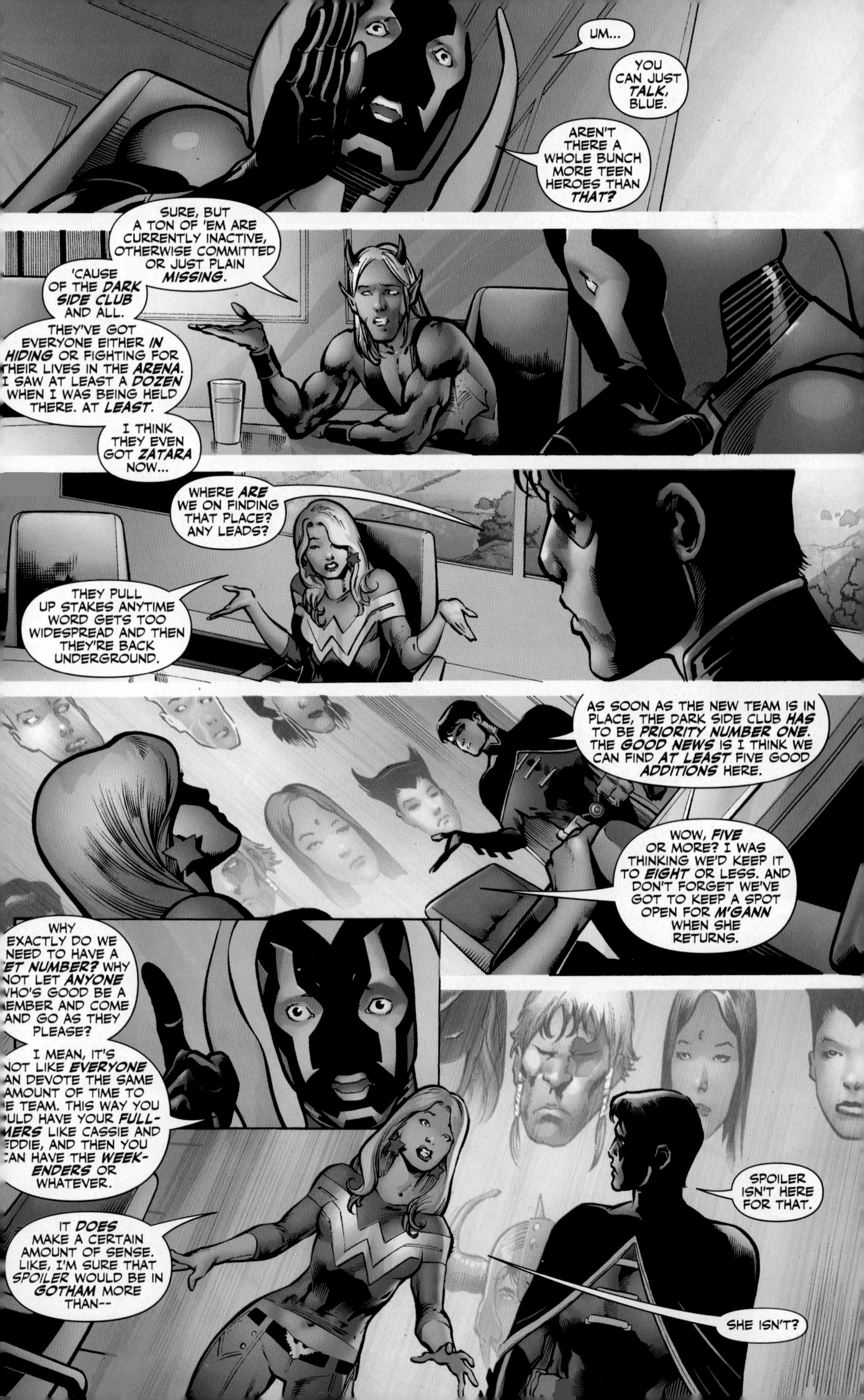

UM...
YOU CAN JUST TALK, BLUE.
AREN'T THERE A WHOLE BUNCH MORE TEEN HEROES THAN THAT?
SURE, BUT A TON OF 'EM ARE CURRENTLY INACTIVE, OTHERWISE COMMITTED OR JUST PLAIN MISSING.
'CAUSE OF THE DARK SIDE CLUB AND ALL.
THEY'VE GOT EVERYONE EITHER IN HIDING OR FIGHTING FOR THEIR LIVES IN THE ARENA. I SAW AT LEAST A DOZEN WHEN I WAS BEING HELD THERE. AT LEAST.
I THINK THEY EVEN GOT ZATARA NOW...
WHERE ARE WE ON FINDING THAT PLACE? ANY LEADS?
THEY PULL UP STAKES ANYTIME WORD GETS TOO WIDESPREAD AND THEN THEY'RE BACK UNDERGROUND.
AS SOON AS THE NEW TEAM IS IN PLACE, THE DARK SIDE CLUB HAS TO BE PRIORITY NUMBER ONE. THE GOOD NEWS IS I THINK WE CAN FIND AT LEAST FIVE GOOD ADDITIONS HERE.
WOW, FIVE OR MORE? I WAS THINKING WE'D KEEP IT TO EIGHT OR LESS. AND DON'T FORGET WE'VE GOT TO KEEP A SPOT OPEN FOR M'GANN WHEN SHE RETURNS.
WHY EXACTLY DO WE NEED TO HAVE A ET NUMBER? WHY NOT LET ANYONE WHO'S GOOD BE A EMBER AND COME AND GO AS THEY PLEASE?
I MEAN, IT'S NOT LIKE EVERYONE AN DEVOTE THE SAME AMOUNT OF TIME TO E TEAM. THIS WAY YOU ULD HAVE YOUR FULL-MERS LIKE CASSIE AND EDDIE, AND THEN YOU AN HAVE THE WEEK-ENDERS OR WHATEVER.
IT DOES MAKE A CERTAIN AMOUNT OF SENSE. LIKE, I'M SURE THAT SPOILER WOULD BE IN GOTHAM MORE THAN--
SPOILER ISN'T HERE FOR THAT.
SHE ISN'T?

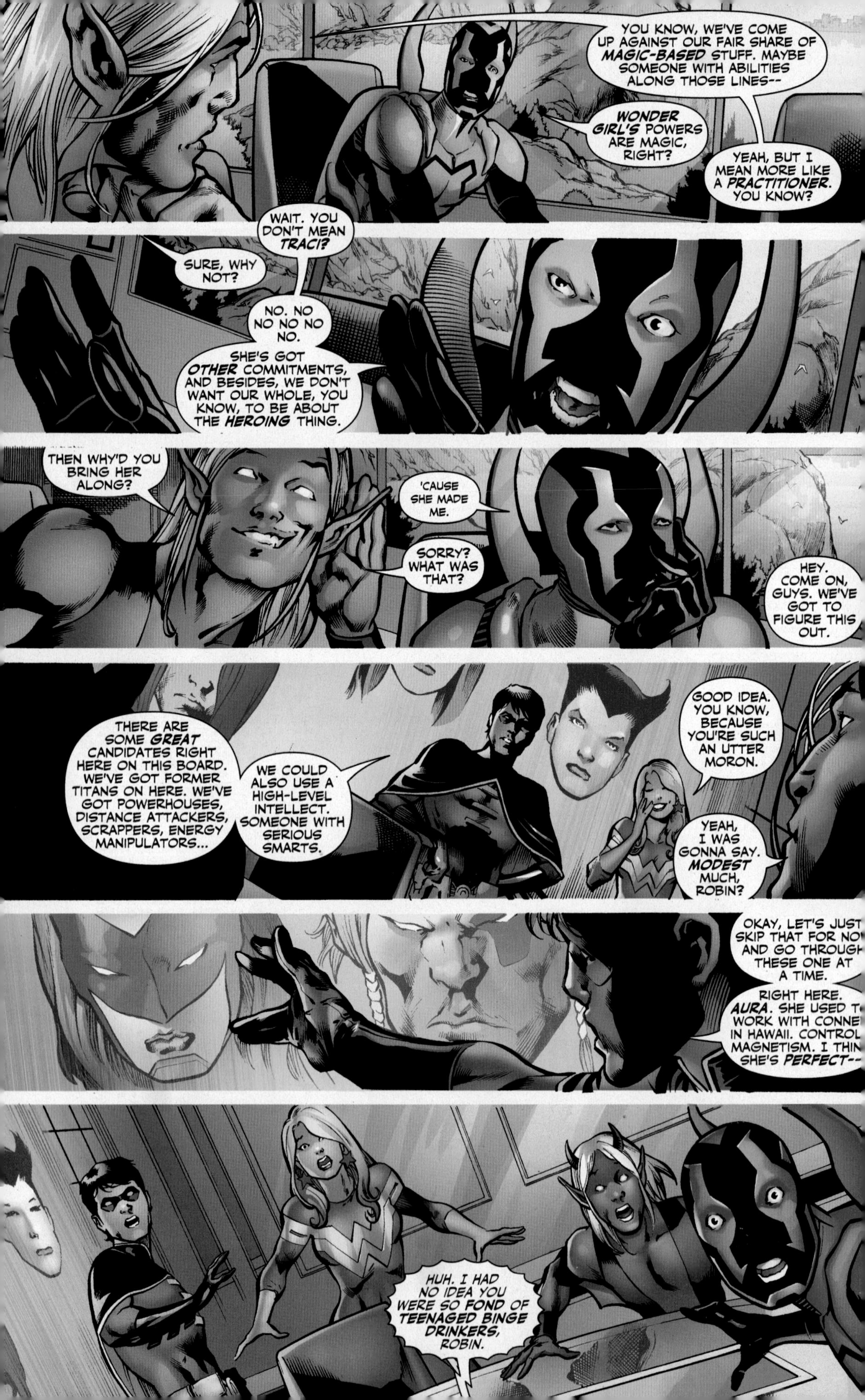

YOU KNOW, WE'VE COME UP AGAINST OUR FAIR SHARE OF MAGIC-BASED STUFF. MAYBE SOMEONE WITH ABILITIES ALONG THOSE LINES--
WONDER GIRL'S POWERS ARE MAGIC, RIGHT?
YEAH, BUT I MEAN MORE LIKE A PRACTITIONER. YOU KNOW?
SURE, WHY NOT?
WAIT. YOU DON'T MEAN TRACI?
NO. NO NO NO NO NO.
SHE'S GOT OTHER COMMITMENTS, AND BESIDES, WE DON'T WANT OUR WHOLE, YOU KNOW, TO BE ABOUT THE HEROING THING.
THEN WHY'D YOU BRING HER ALONG?
'CAUSE SHE MADE ME.
SORRY? WHAT WAS THAT?
HEY. COME ON, GUYS. WE'VE GOT TO FIGURE THIS OUT.
THERE ARE SOME GREAT CANDIDATES RIGHT HERE ON THIS BOARD. WE'VE GOT FORMER TITANS ON HERE. WE'VE GOT POWERHOUSES, DISTANCE ATTACKERS, SCRAPPERS, ENERGY MANIPULATORS...
WE COULD ALSO USE A HIGH-LEVEL INTELLECT. SOMEONE WITH SERIOUS SMARTS.
GOOD IDEA. YOU KNOW, BECAUSE YOU'RE SUCH AN UTTER MORON.
YEAH, I WAS GONNA SAY. MODEST MUCH, ROBIN?
OKAY, LET'S JUST SKIP THAT FOR NO AND GO THROUGH THESE ONE AT A TIME.
RIGHT HERE. AURA. SHE USED T WORK WITH CONNE IN HAWAII. CONTROL MAGNETISM. I THIN SHE'S PERFECT--
HUH. I HAD NO IDEA YOU WERE SO FOND OF TEENAGED BINGE DRINKERS, ROBIN.

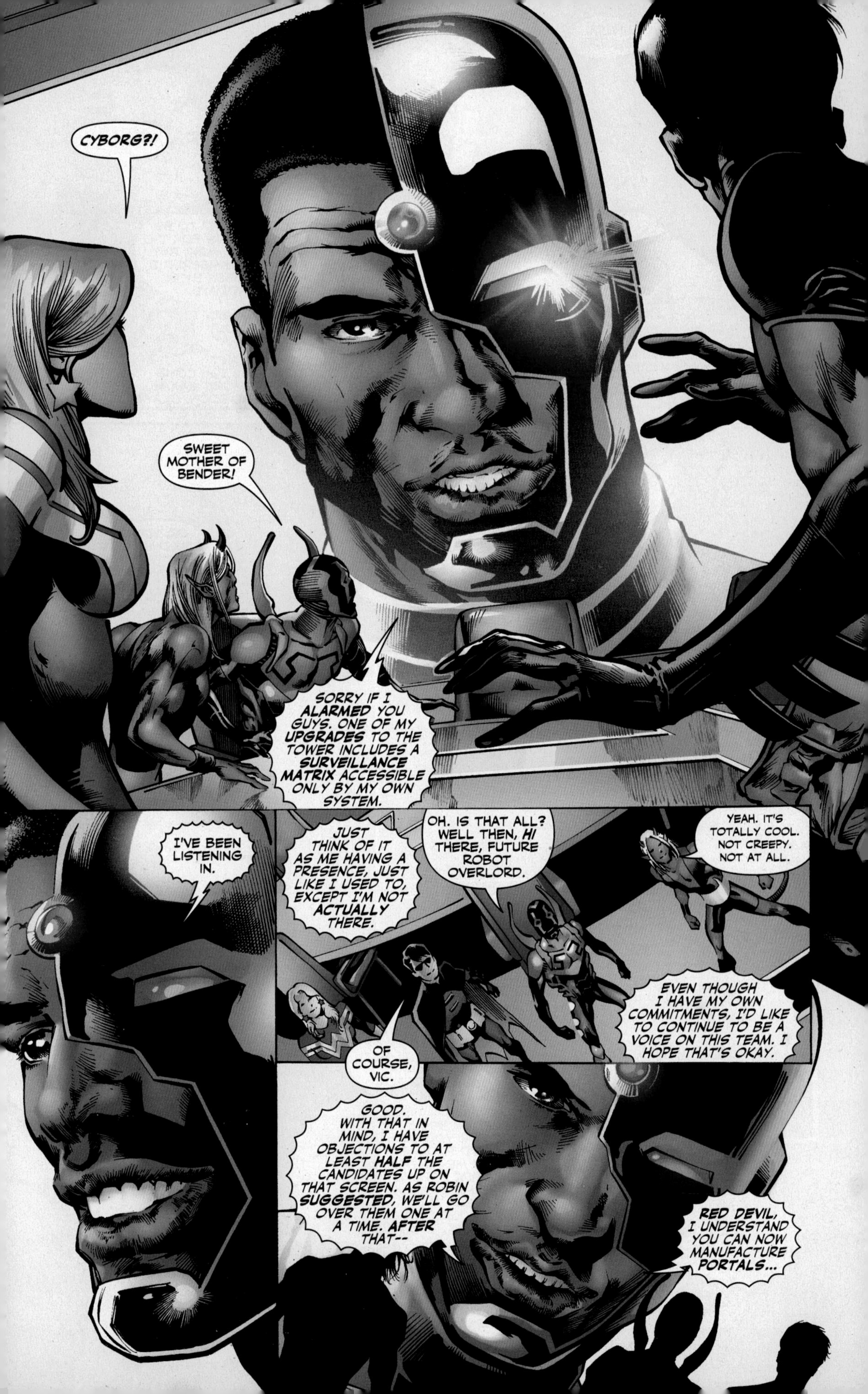
CYBORG?!
SWEET MOTHER OF BENDER!
SORRY IF I ALARMED YOU GUYS. ONE OF MY UPGRADES TO THE TOWER INCLUDES A SURVEILLANCE MATRIX ACCESSIBLE ONLY BY MY OWN SYSTEM.
I'VE BEEN LISTENING IN.
JUST THINK OF IT AS ME HAVING A PRESENCE, JUST LIKE I USED TO, EXCEPT I'M NOT ACTUALLY THERE.
OH. IS THAT ALL? WELL THEN, HI THERE, FUTURE ROBOT OVERLORD.
YEAH. IT'S TOTALLY COOL. NOT CREEPY. NOT AT ALL.
EVEN THOUGH I HAVE MY OWN COMMITMENTS, I'D LIKE TO CONTINUE TO BE A VOICE ON THIS TEAM. I HOPE THAT'S OKAY.
OF COURSE, VIC.
GOOD. WITH THAT IN MIND, I HAVE OBJECTIONS TO AT LEAST HALF THE CANDIDATES UP ON THAT SCREEN. AS ROBIN SUGGESTED, WE'LL GO OVER THEM ONE AT A TIME. AFTER THAT--
RED DEVIL, I UNDERSTAND YOU CAN NOW MANUFACTURE PORTALS...

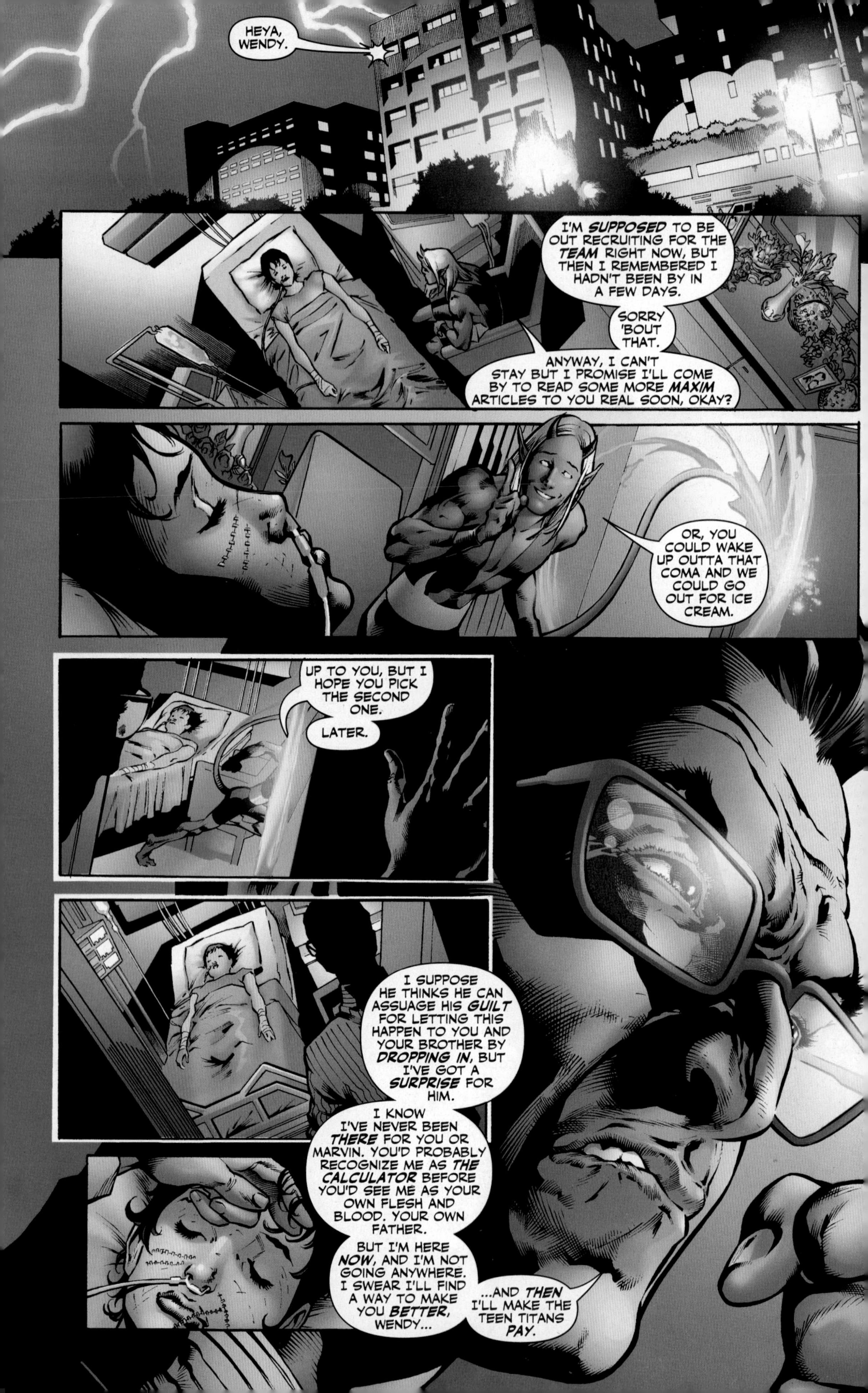
HEYA, WENDY.
I'M SUPPOSED TO BE OUT RECRUITING FOR THE TEAM RIGHT NOW, BUT THEN I REMEMBERED I HADN'T BEEN BY IN A FEW DAYS.
SORRY 'BOUT THAT.
ANYWAY, I CAN'T STAY BUT I PROMISE I'LL COME BY TO READ SOME MORE MAXIM ARTICLES TO YOU REAL SOON, OKAY?
OR, YOU COULD WAKE UP OUTTA THAT COMA AND WE COULD GO OUT FOR ICE CREAM.
UP TO YOU, BUT I HOPE YOU PICK THE SECOND ONE.
LATER.
I SUPPOSE HE THINKS HE CAN ASSUAGE HIS GUILT FOR LETTING THIS HAPPEN TO YOU AND YOUR BROTHER BY DROPPING IN, BUT I'VE GOT A SURPRISE FOR HIM.
I KNOW I'VE NEVER BEEN THERE FOR YOU OR MARVIN. YOU'D PROBABLY RECOGNIZE ME AS THE CALCULATOR BEFORE YOU'D SEE ME AS YOUR OWN FLESH AND BLOOD. YOUR OWN FATHER.
BUT I'M HERE NOW, AND I'M NOT GOING ANYWHERE. I SWEAR I'LL FIND A WAY TO MAKE YOU BETTER, WENDY...
...AND THEN I'LL MAKE THE TEEN TITANS PAY.

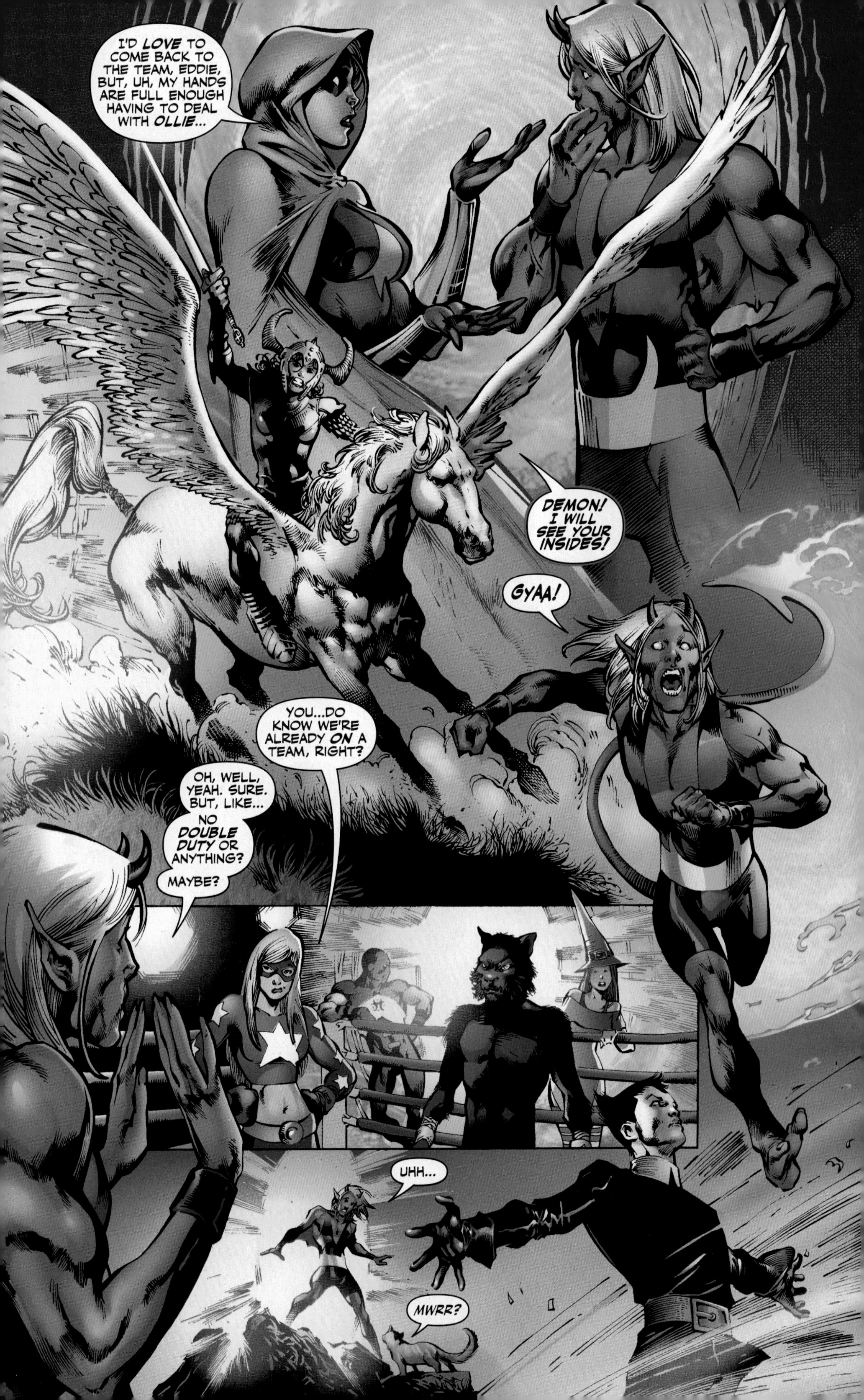
I'D LOVE TO COME BACK TO THE TEAM, EDDIE, BUT, UH, MY HANDS ARE FULL ENOUGH HAVING TO DEAL WITH OLLIE...
DEMON! I WILL SEE YOUR INSIDES!
GYAA!
YOU...DO KNOW WE'RE ALREADY ON A TEAM, RIGHT?
OH, WELL, YEAH. SURE. BUT, LIKE... NO DOUBLE DUTY OR ANYTHING?
MAYBE?
UHH...
MWRR?

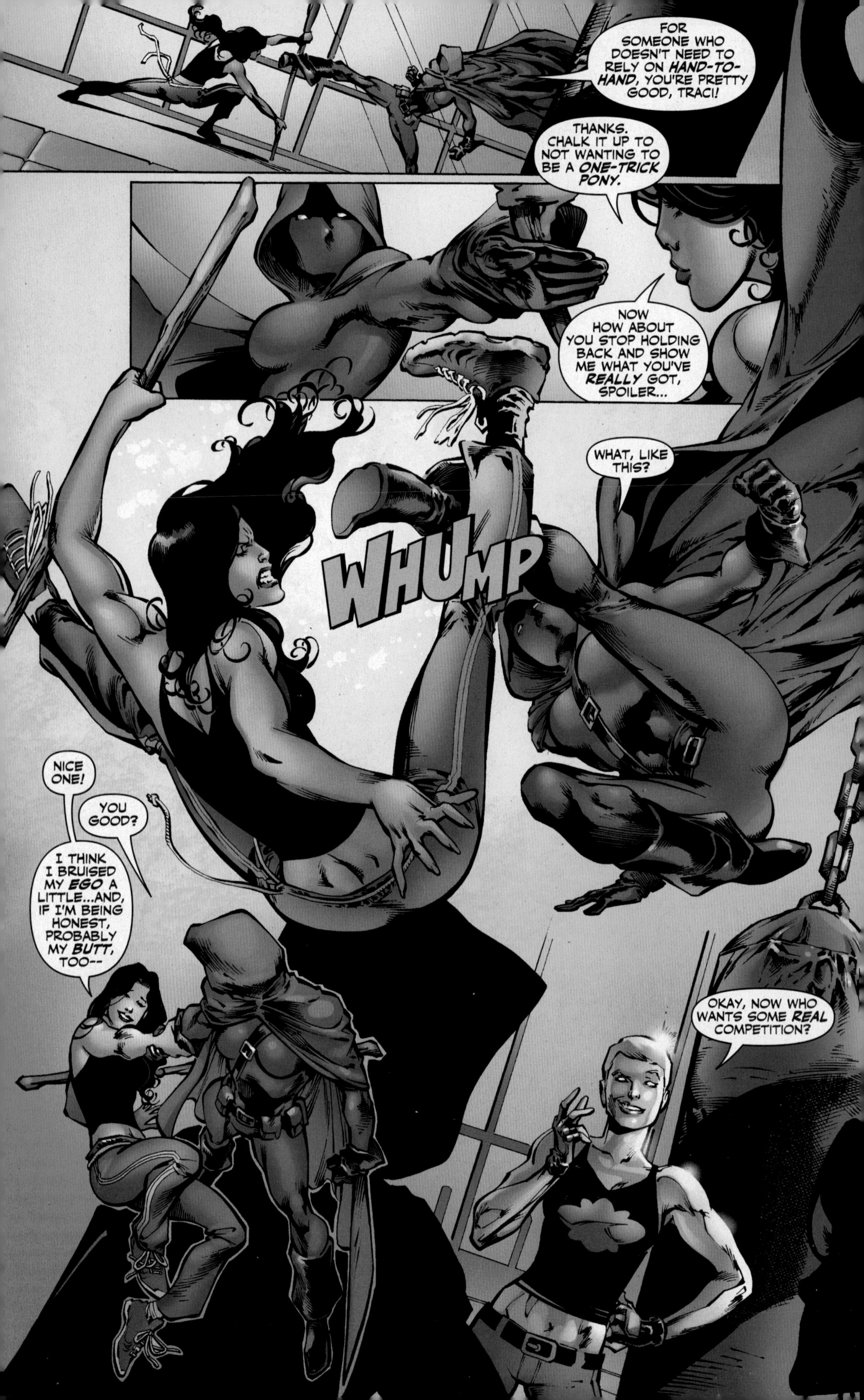
FOR SOMEONE WHO DOESN'T NEED TO RELY ON *HAND-TO-HAND*, YOU'RE PRETTY GOOD, TRACI!
THANKS. CHALK IT UP TO NOT WANTING TO BE A *ONE-TRICK PONY*.
NOW HOW ABOUT YOU STOP HOLDING BACK AND SHOW ME WHAT YOU'VE *REALLY* GOT, SPOILER...
WHAT, LIKE THIS?
WHUMP
NICE ONE!
YOU GOOD?
I THINK I BRUISED MY *EGO* A LITTLE...AND, IF I'M BEING HONEST, PROBABLY MY *BUTT*, TOO--
OKAY, NOW WHO WANTS SOME *REAL* COMPETITION?

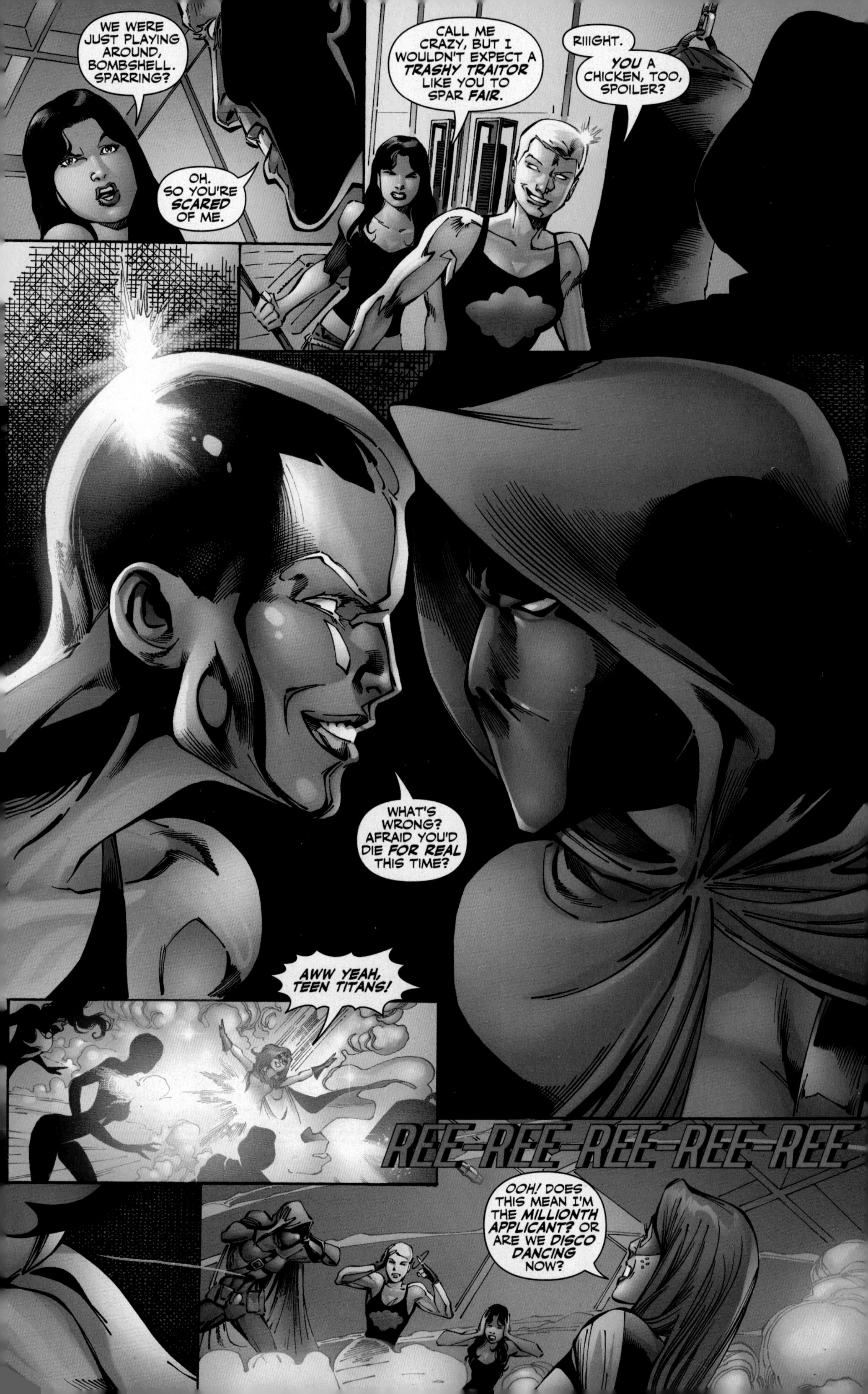
WE WERE JUST PLAYING AROUND, BOMBSHELL. SPARRING?
OH. SO YOU'RE SCARED OF ME.
CALL ME CRAZY, BUT I WOULDN'T EXPECT A TRASHY TRAITOR LIKE YOU TO SPAR FAIR.
RIIIGHT.
YOU A CHICKEN, TOO, SPOILER?
WHAT'S WRONG? AFRAID YOU'D DIE FOR REAL THIS TIME?
AWW YEAH, TEEN TITANS!
REE-REE-REE-REE-REE
OOH! DOES THIS MEAN I'M THE MILLIONTH APPLICANT? OR ARE WE DISCO DANCING NOW?

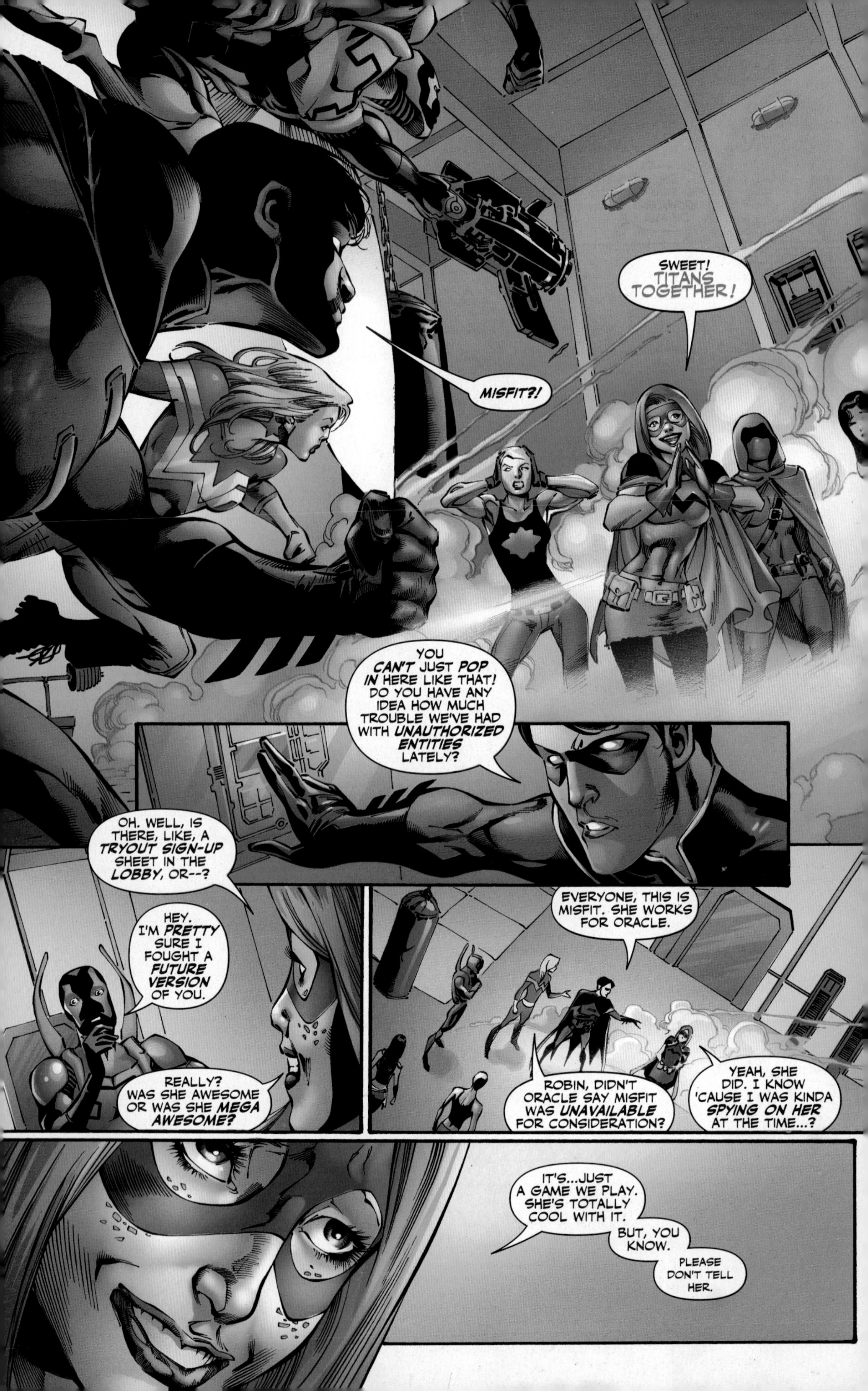
SWEET! TITANS TOGETHER!
MISFIT?!
YOU CAN'T JUST POP IN HERE LIKE THAT! DO YOU HAVE ANY IDEA HOW MUCH TROUBLE WE'VE HAD WITH UNAUTHORIZED ENTITIES LATELY?
OH. WELL, IS THERE, LIKE, A TRYOUT SIGN-UP SHEET IN THE LOBBY, OR--?
HEY. I'M PRETTY SURE I FOUGHT A FUTURE VERSION OF YOU.
REALLY? WAS SHE AWESOME OR WAS SHE MEGA AWESOME?
EVERYONE, THIS IS MISFIT. SHE WORKS FOR ORACLE.
ROBIN, DIDN'T ORACLE SAY MISFIT WAS UNAVAILABLE FOR CONSIDERATION?
YEAH, SHE DID. I KNOW 'CAUSE I WAS KINDA SPYING ON HER AT THE TIME...?
IT'S...JUST A GAME WE PLAY. SHE'S TOTALLY COOL WITH IT.
BUT, YOU KNOW.
PLEASE DON'T TELL HER.

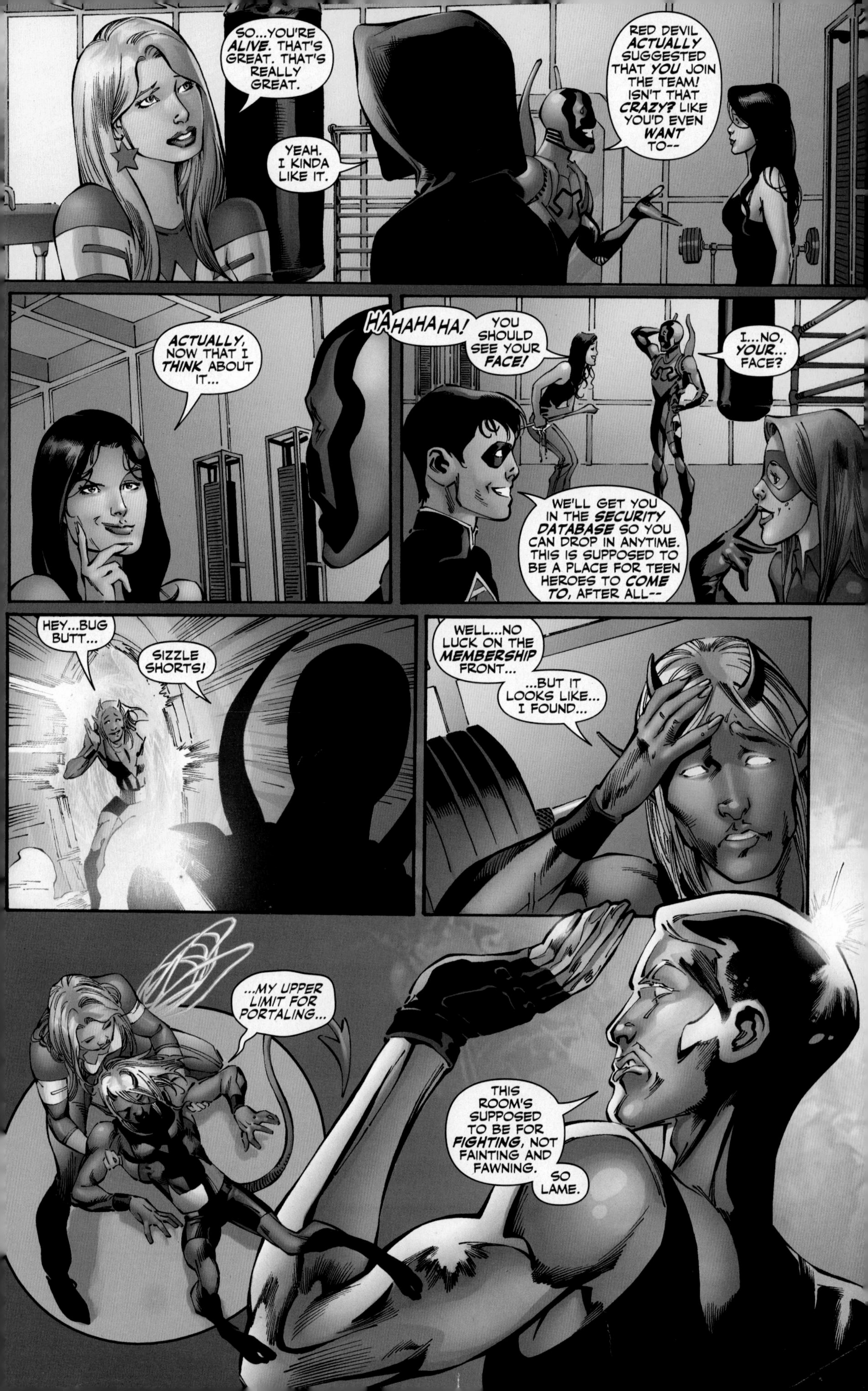
SO...YOU'RE ALIVE. THAT'S GREAT. THAT'S REALLY GREAT.
YEAH. I KINDA LIKE IT.
RED DEVIL ACTUALLY SUGGESTED THAT YOU JOIN THE TEAM! ISN'T THAT CRAZY? LIKE YOU'D EVEN WANT TO--
ACTUALLY, NOW THAT I THINK ABOUT IT...
HAHAHAHA!
YOU SHOULD SEE YOUR FACE!
I...NO, YOUR... FACE?
WE'LL GET YOU IN THE SECURITY DATABASE SO YOU CAN DROP IN ANYTIME. THIS IS SUPPOSED TO BE A PLACE FOR TEEN HEROES TO COME TO, AFTER ALL--
HEY...BUG BUTT...
SIZZLE SHORTS!
WELL...NO LUCK ON THE MEMBERSHIP FRONT...
...BUT IT LOOKS LIKE... I FOUND...
...MY UPPER LIMIT FOR PORTALING...
THIS ROOM'S SUPPOSED TO BE FOR FIGHTING, NOT FAINTING AND FAWNING.
SO LAME.

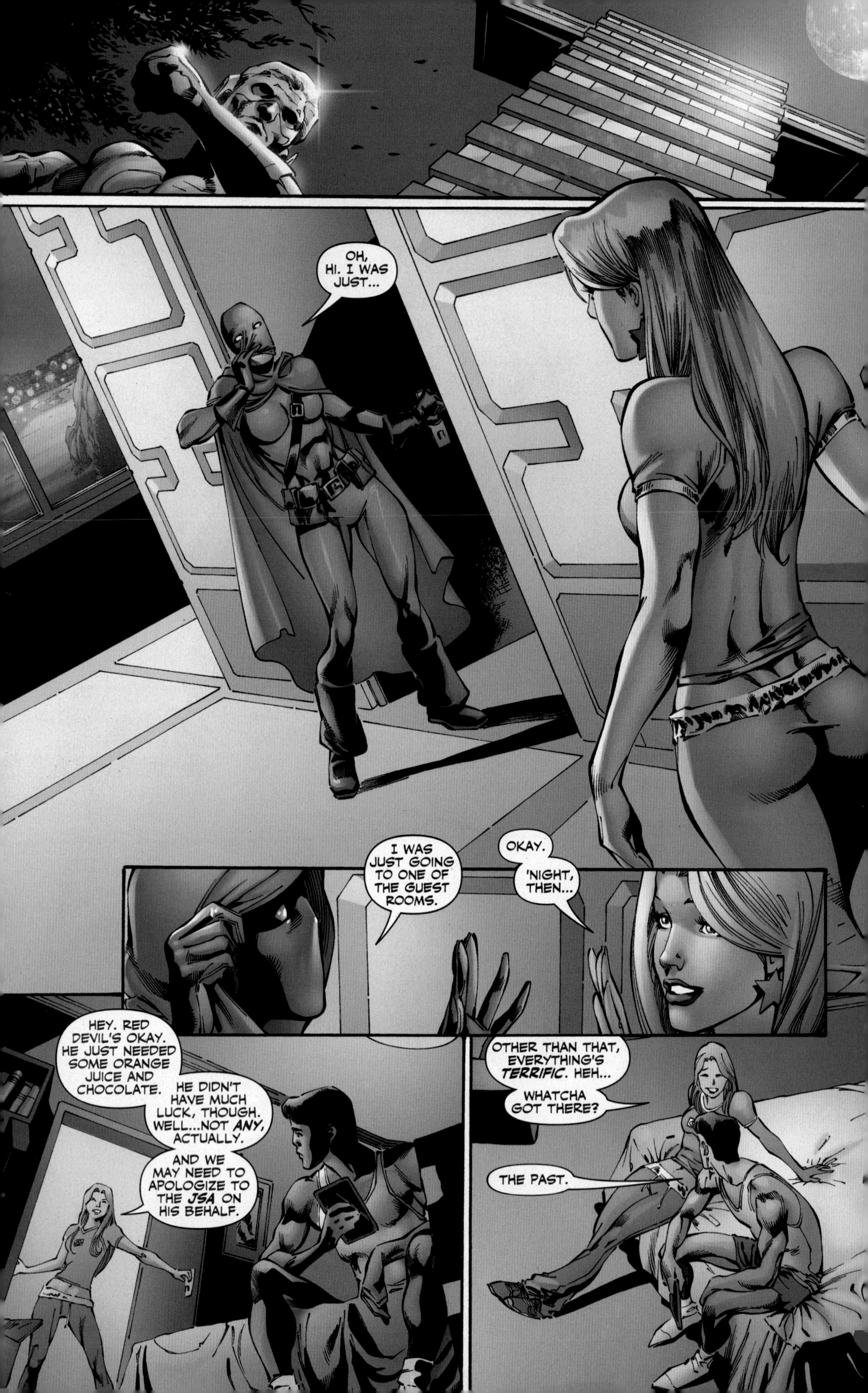

OH, HI. I WAS JUST...
I WAS JUST GOING TO ONE OF THE GUEST ROOMS.
OKAY.
'NIGHT, THEN...
HEY. RED DEVIL'S OKAY. HE JUST NEEDED SOME ORANGE JUICE AND CHOCOLATE.
HE DIDN'T HAVE MUCH LUCK, THOUGH. WELL...NOT ANY, ACTUALLY.
AND WE MAY NEED TO APOLOGIZE TO THE JSA ON HIS BEHALF.
OTHER THAN THAT, EVERYTHING'S TERRIFIC. HEH...
WHATCHA GOT THERE?
THE PAST.

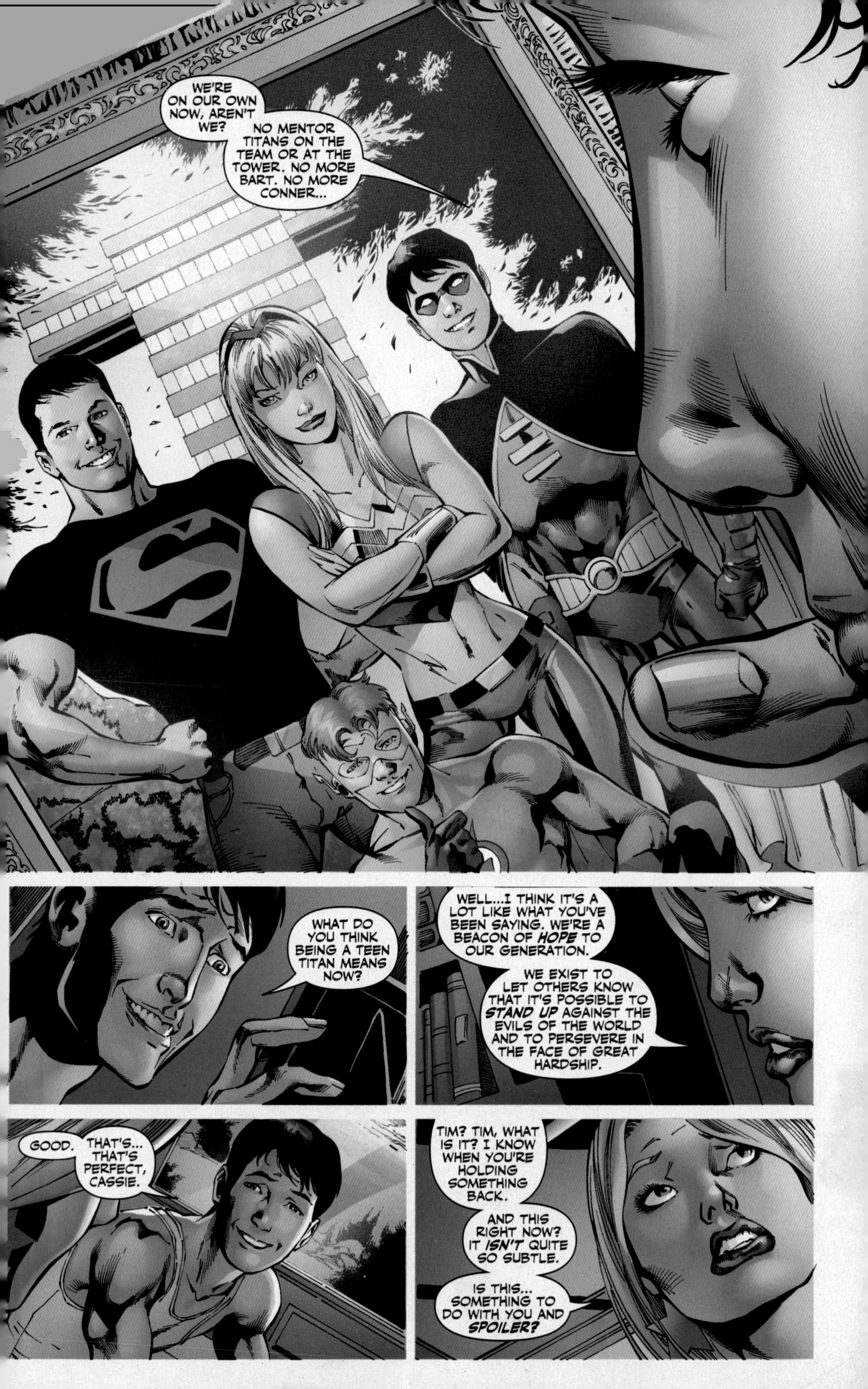
WE'RE ON OUR OWN NOW, AREN'T WE?
NO MENTOR TITANS ON THE TEAM OR AT THE TOWER. NO MORE BART. NO MORE CONNER...
WHAT DO YOU THINK BEING A TEEN TITAN MEANS NOW?
WELL...I THINK IT'S A LOT LIKE WHAT YOU'VE BEEN SAYING. WE'RE A BEACON OF *HOPE* TO OUR GENERATION.
WE EXIST TO LET OTHERS KNOW THAT IT'S POSSIBLE TO *STAND UP* AGAINST THE EVILS OF THE WORLD AND TO PERSEVERE IN THE FACE OF GREAT HARDSHIP.
GOOD.
THAT'S... THAT'S PERFECT, CASSIE.
TIM? TIM, WHAT IS IT? I KNOW WHEN YOU'RE HOLDING SOMETHING BACK.
AND THIS RIGHT NOW? IT *ISN'T* QUITE SO SUBTLE.
IS THIS... SOMETHING TO DO WITH YOU AND *SPOILER?*

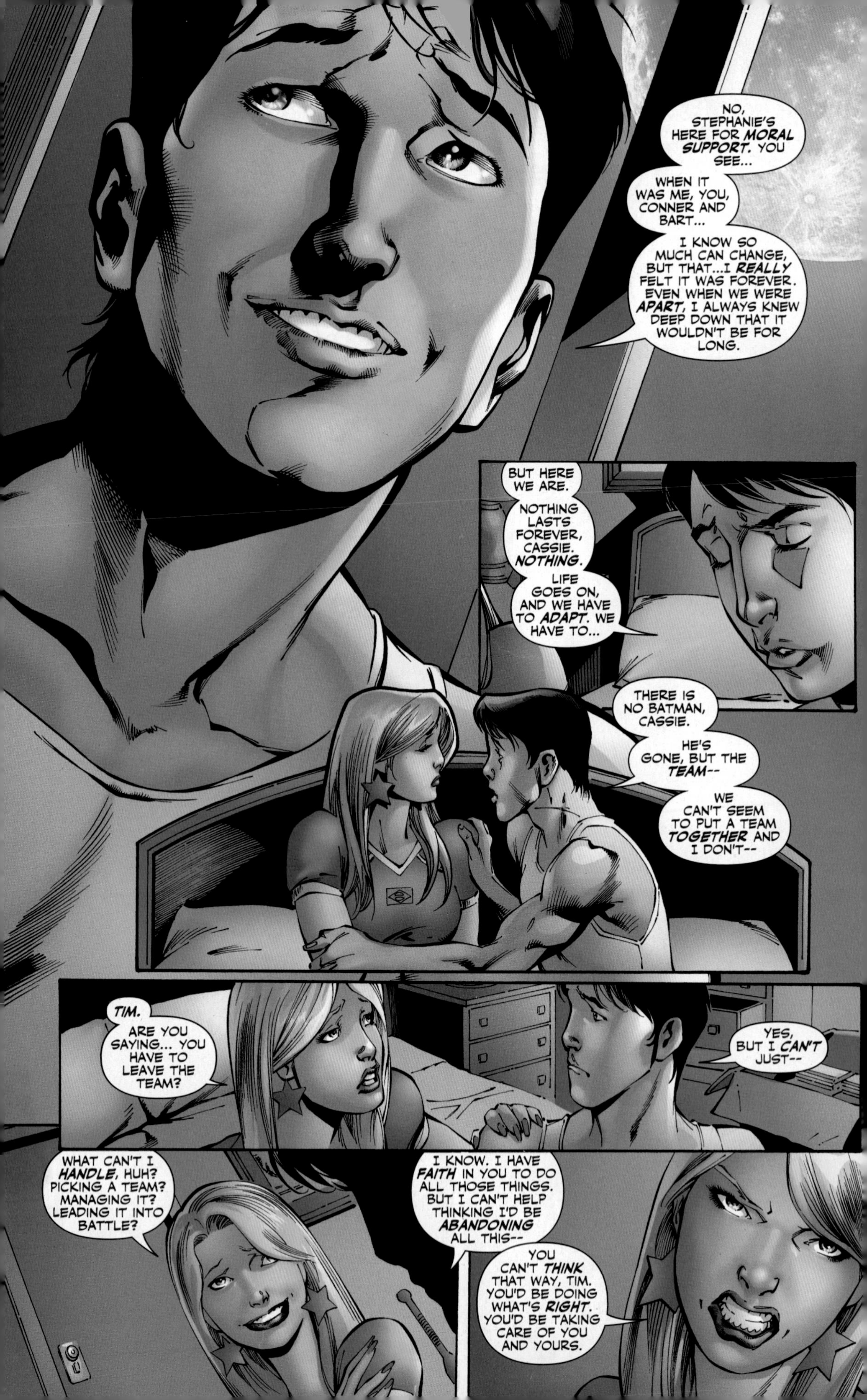
NO, STEPHANIE'S HERE FOR MORAL SUPPORT. YOU SEE...
WHEN IT WAS ME, YOU, CONNER AND BART...
I KNOW SO MUCH CAN CHANGE, BUT THAT...I REALLY FELT IT WAS FOREVER. EVEN WHEN WE WERE APART, I ALWAYS KNEW DEEP DOWN THAT IT WOULDN'T BE FOR LONG.
BUT HERE WE ARE.
NOTHING LASTS FOREVER, CASSIE. NOTHING.
LIFE GOES ON, AND WE HAVE TO ADAPT. WE HAVE TO...
THERE IS NO BATMAN, CASSIE.
HE'S GONE, BUT THE TEAM--
WE CAN'T SEEM TO PUT A TEAM TOGETHER AND I DON'T--
TIM.
ARE YOU SAYING... YOU HAVE TO LEAVE THE TEAM?
YES, BUT I CAN'T JUST--
WHAT CAN'T I HANDLE, HUH? PICKING A TEAM? MANAGING IT? LEADING IT INTO BATTLE?
I KNOW. I HAVE FAITH IN YOU TO DO ALL THOSE THINGS. BUT I CAN'T HELP THINKING I'D BE ABANDONING ALL THIS--
YOU CAN'T THINK THAT WAY, TIM. YOU'D BE DOING WHAT'S RIGHT. YOU'D BE TAKING CARE OF YOU AND YOURS.

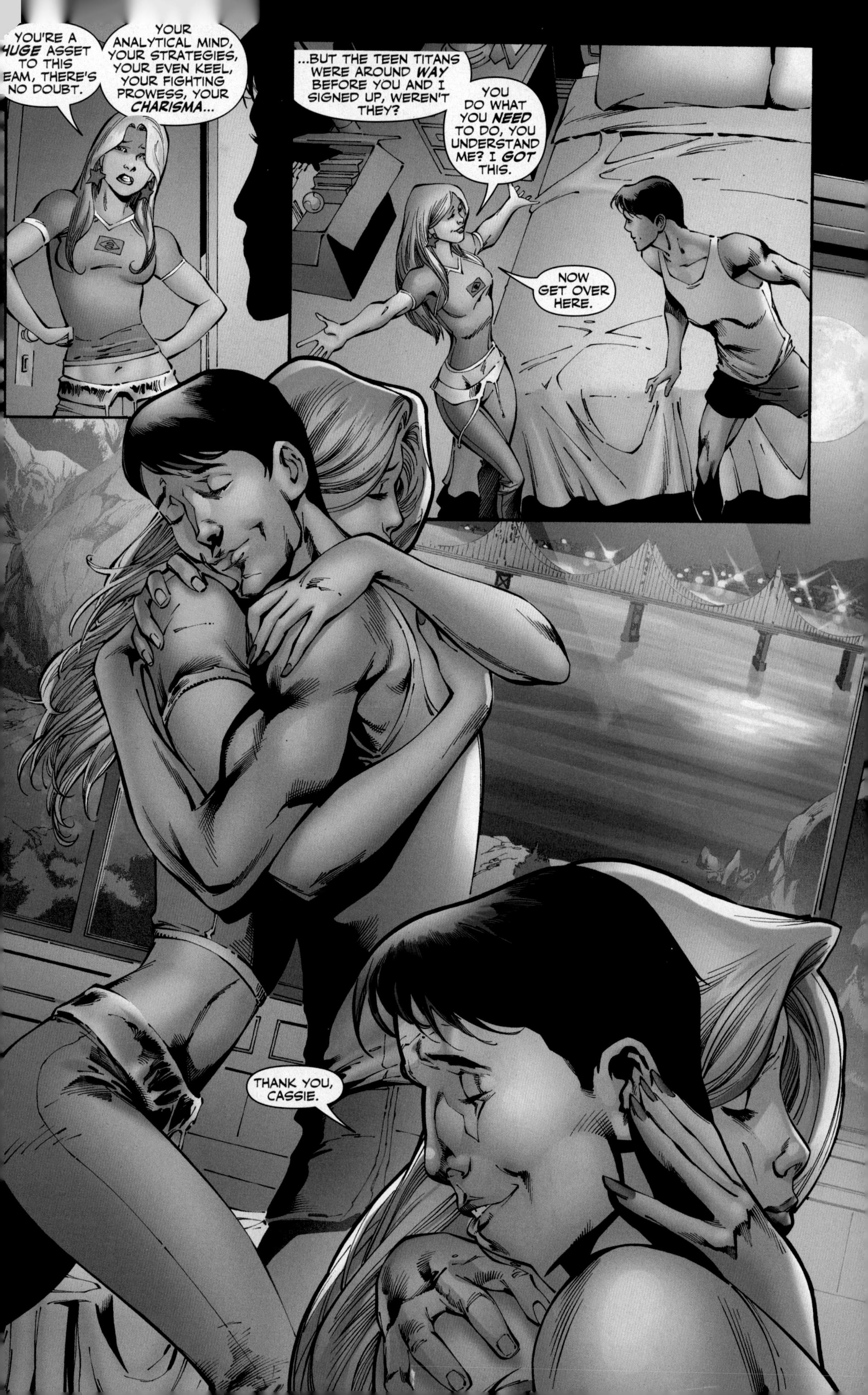
YOU'RE A HUGE ASSET TO THIS EAM, THERE'S NO DOUBT.
YOUR ANALYTICAL MIND, YOUR STRATEGIES, YOUR EVEN KEEL, YOUR FIGHTING PROWESS, YOUR CHARISMA...
...BUT THE TEEN TITANS WERE AROUND WAY BEFORE YOU AND I SIGNED UP, WEREN'T THEY?
YOU DO WHAT YOU NEED TO DO, YOU UNDERSTAND ME? I GOT THIS.
NOW GET OVER HERE.
THANK YOU, CASSIE.

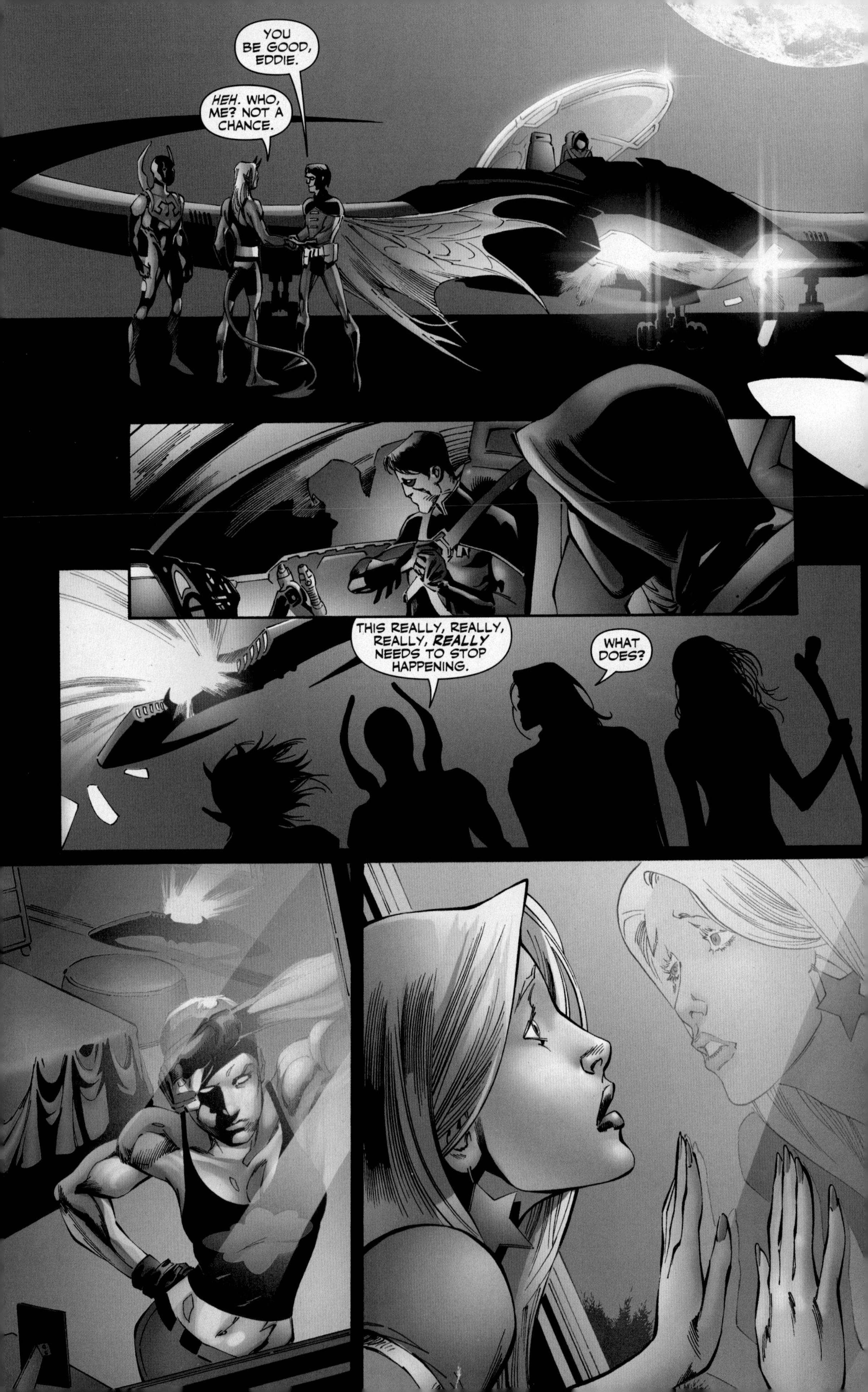
YOU BE GOOD, EDDIE.
HEH. WHO, ME? NOT A CHANCE.
THIS REALLY, REALLY, REALLY, REALLY NEEDS TO STOP HAPPENING.
WHAT DOES?

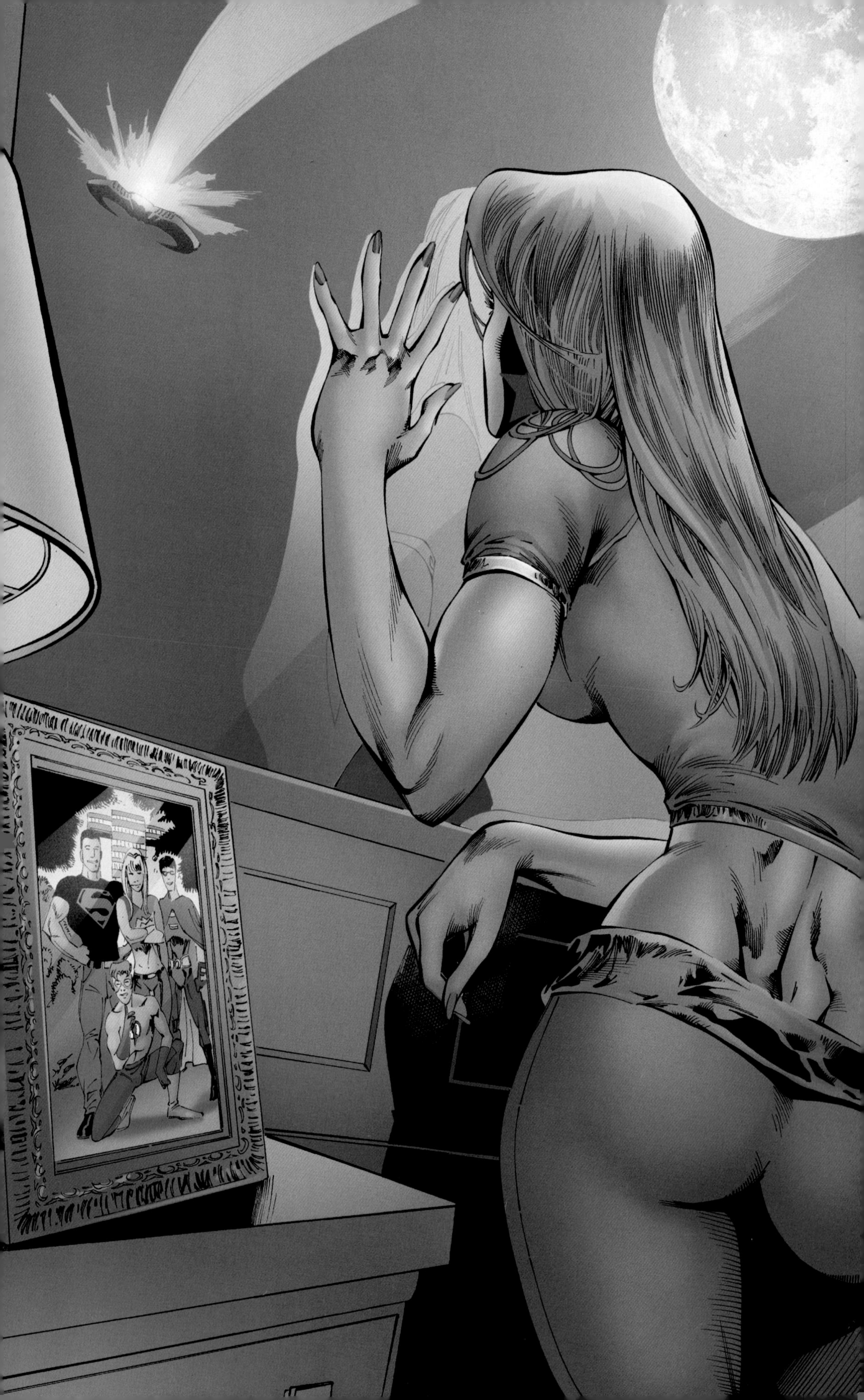

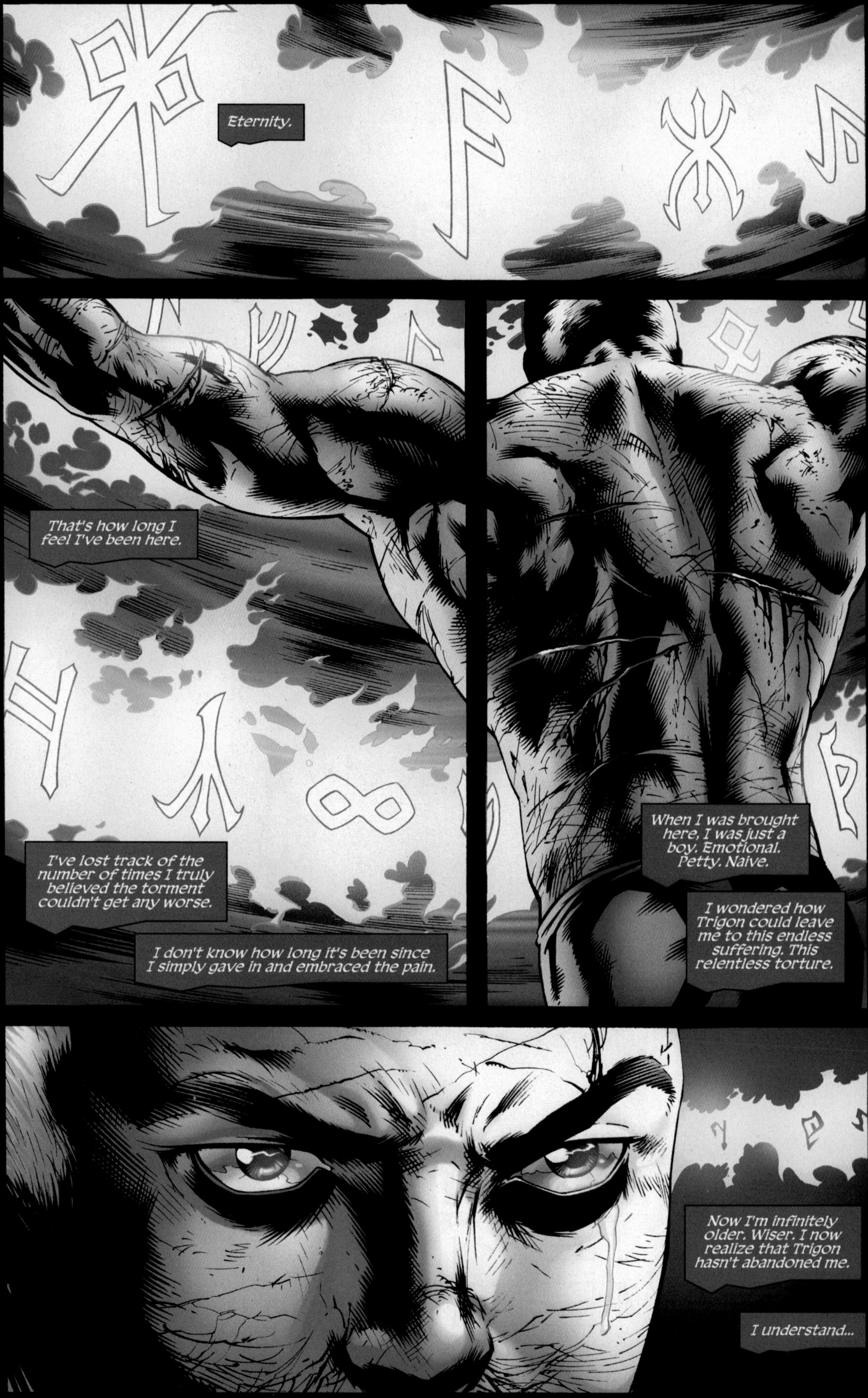
Eternity.
That's how long I feel I've been here.
I've lost track of the number of times I truly believed the torment couldn't get any worse.
I don't know how long it's been since I simply gave in and embraced the pain.
When I was brought here, I was just a boy. Emotional. Petty. Naive.
I wondered how Trigon could leave me to this endless suffering. This relentless torture.
Now I'm infinitely older. Wiser. I now realize that Trigon hasn't abandoned me.
I understand...

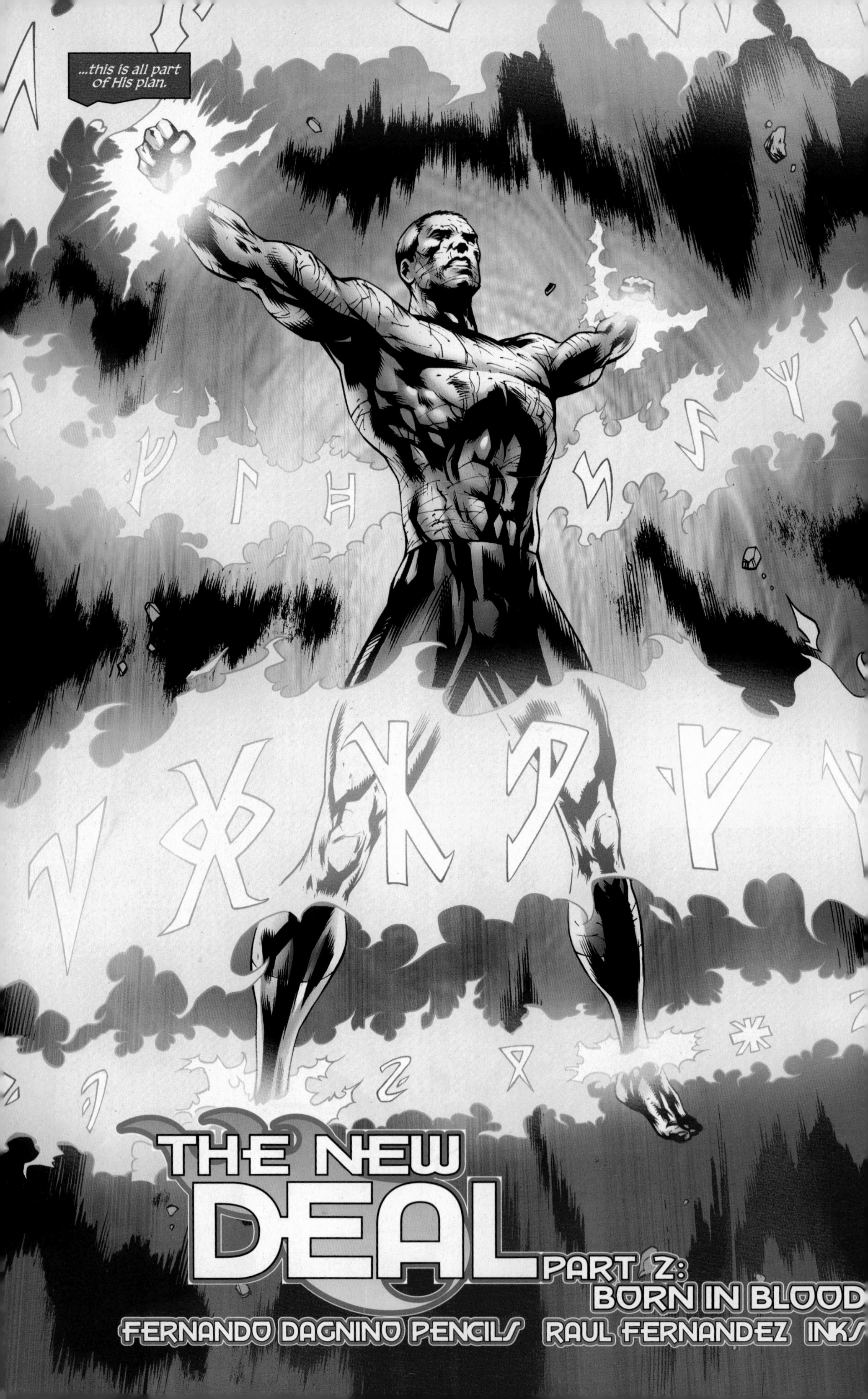
...this is all part of His plan.
THE NEW DEAL
PART 2: BORN IN BLOOD
FERNANDO DAGNINO PENCILS RAUL FERNANDEZ INKS

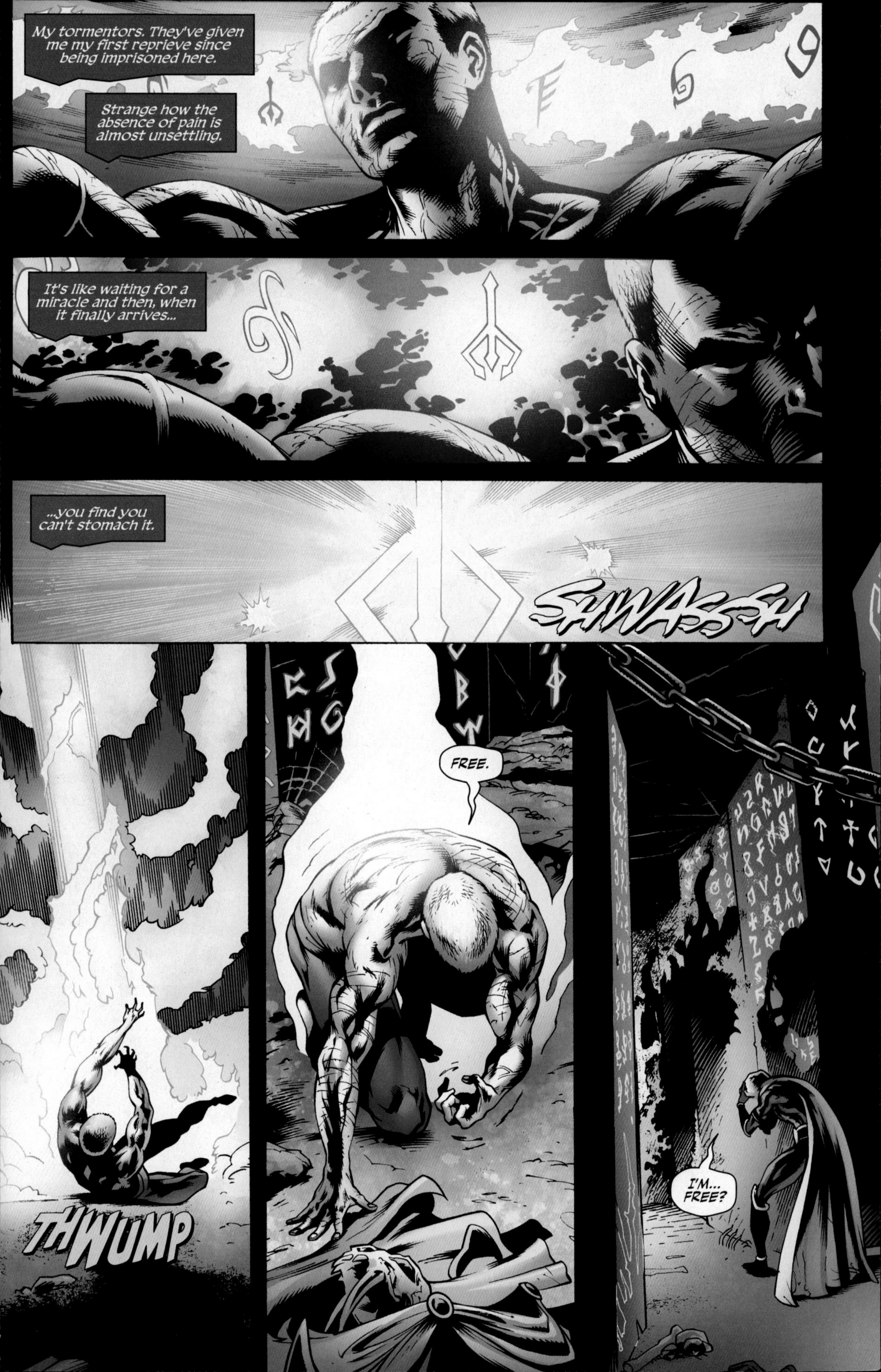
My tormentors. They've given me my first reprieve since being imprisoned here.
Strange how the absence of pain is almost unsettling.
It's like waiting for a miracle and then, when it finally arrives...
...you find you can't stomach it.
SHWASSH
THWUMP
FREE.
I'M... FREE?

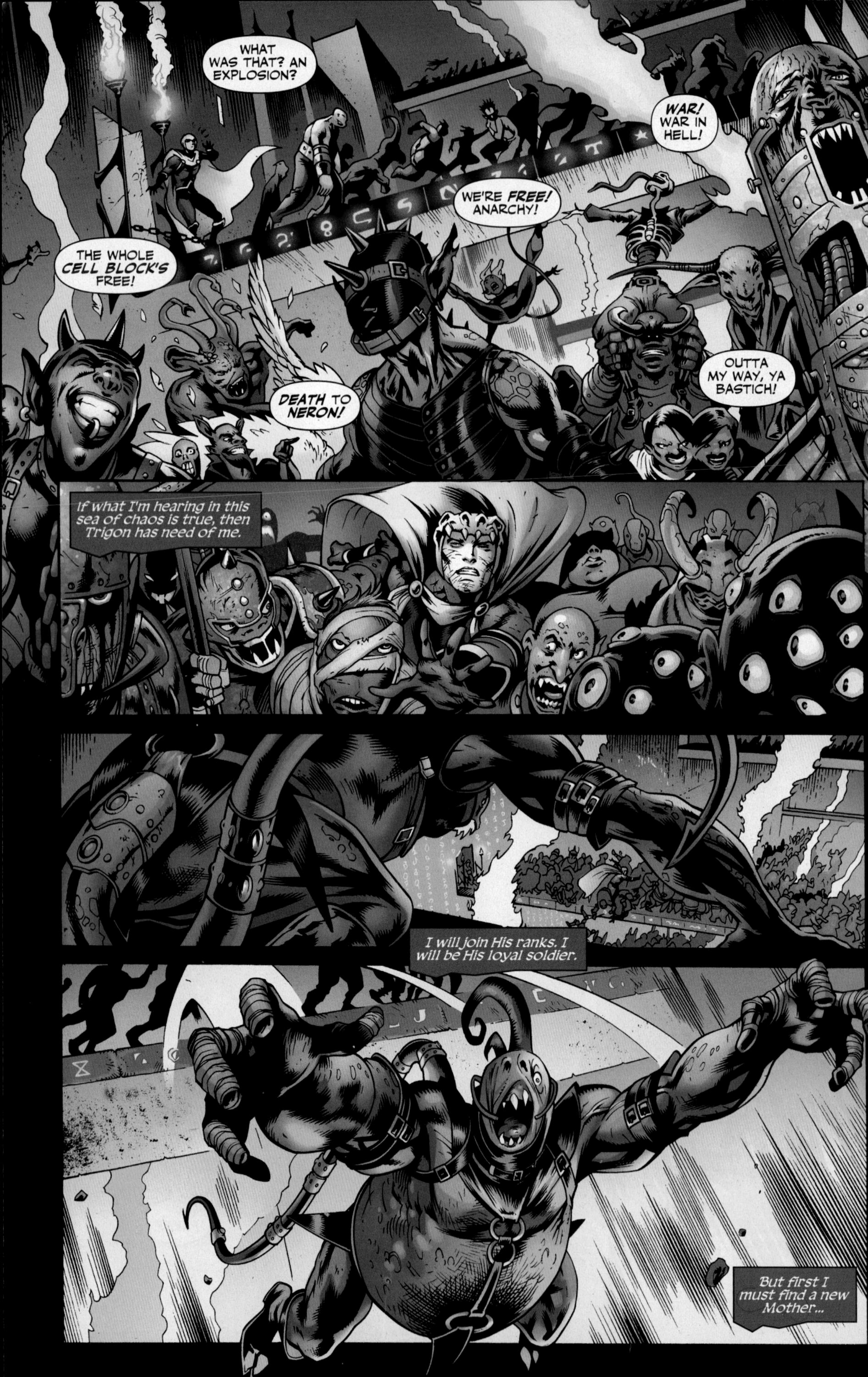
WHAT WAS THAT? AN EXPLOSION?
WAR! WAR IN HELL!
WE'RE FREE! ANARCHY!
THE WHOLE CELL BLOCK'S FREE!
DEATH TO NERON!
OUTTA MY WAY, YA BASTICH!
If what I'm hearing in this sea of chaos is true, then Trigon has need of me.
I will join His ranks. I will be His loyal soldier.
But first I must find a new Mother...

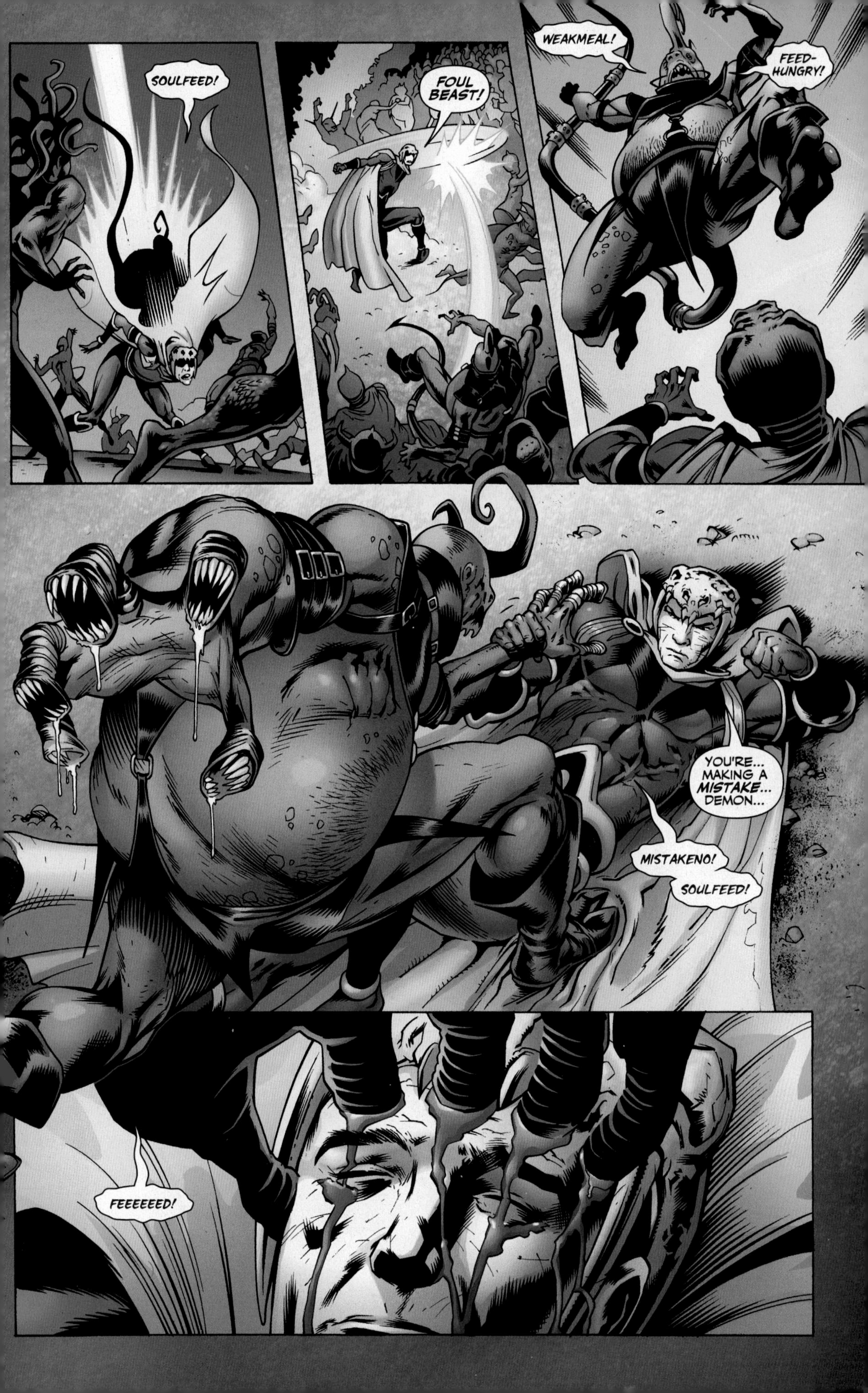
SOULFEED!
FOUL BEAST!
WEAKMEAL!
FEED-HUNGRY!
YOU'RE... MAKING A MISTAKE... DEMON...
MISTAKENO!
SOULFEED!
FEEEEEED!

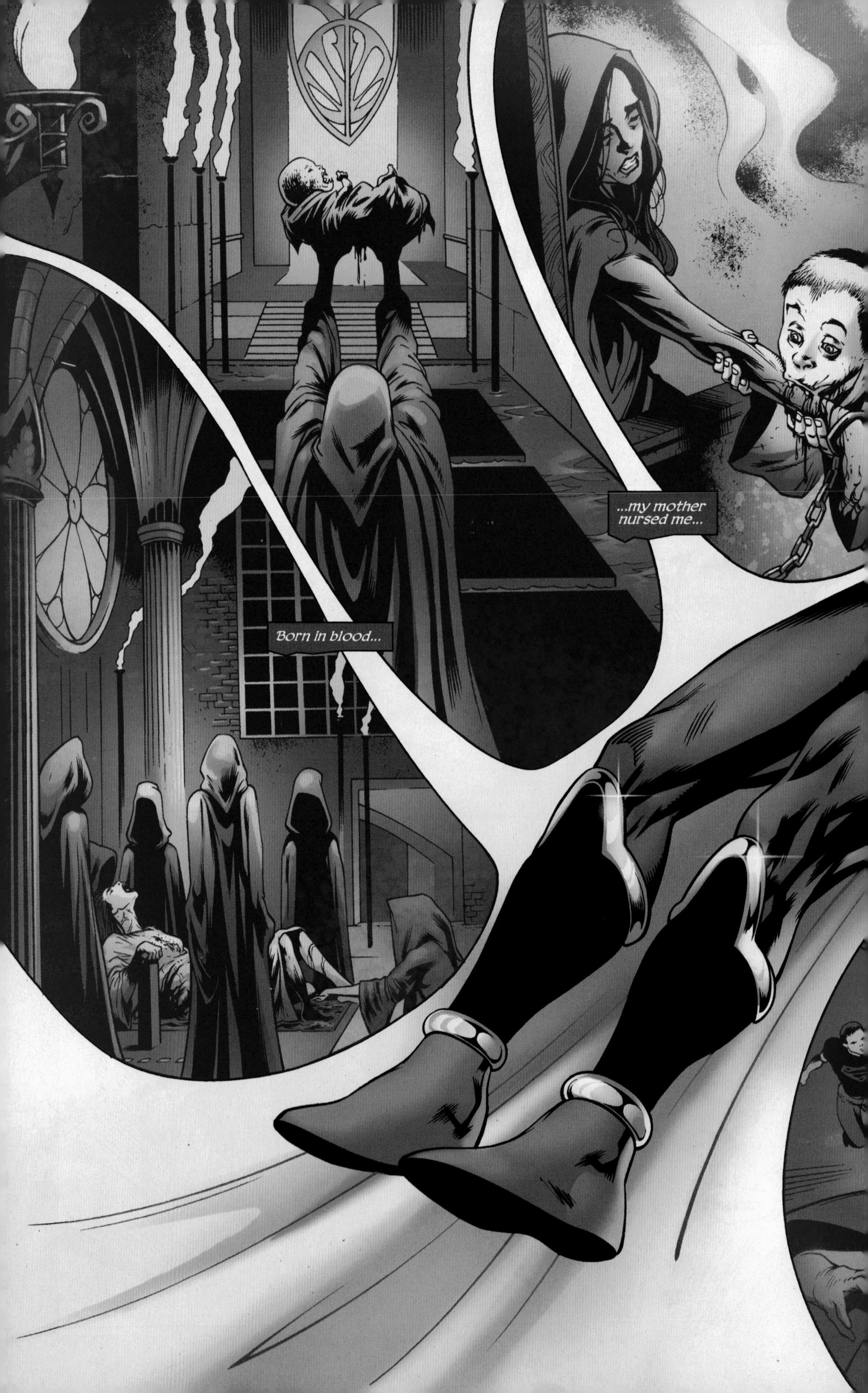
Born in blood...
...my mother nursed me...

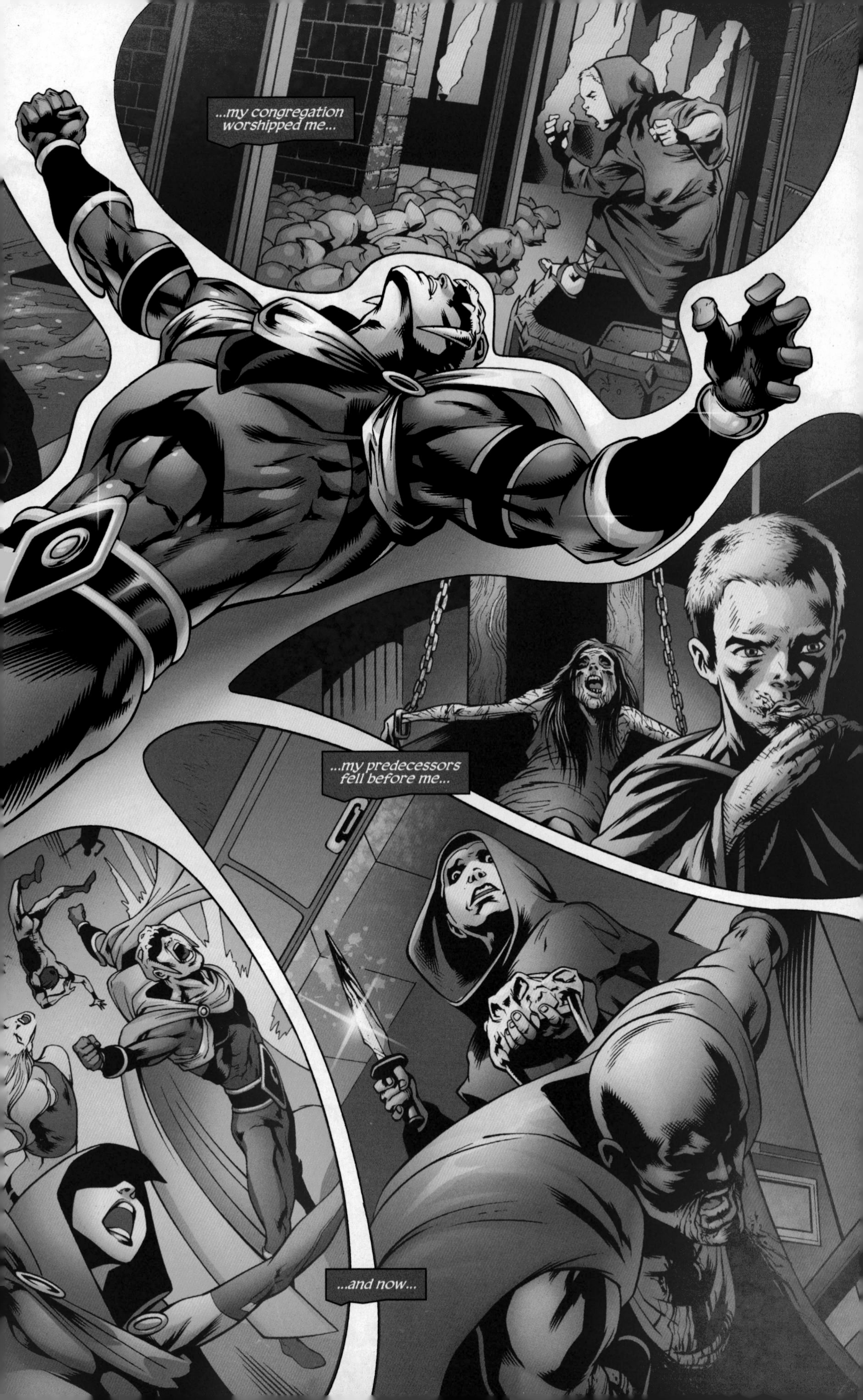
...my congregation worshipped me...
...my predecessors fell before me...
...and now...

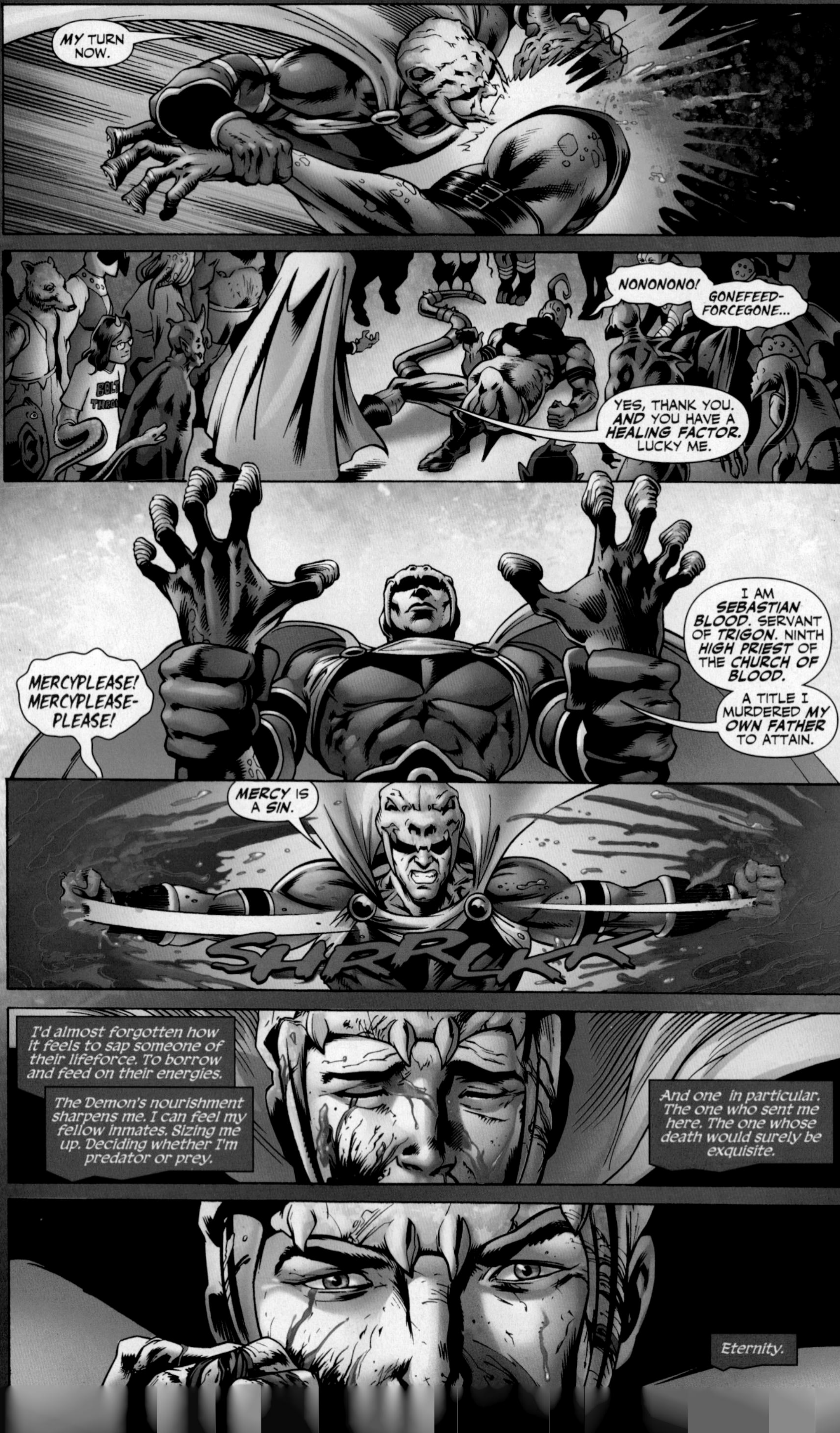
MY TURN NOW.
NONONONO!
GONEFEED-FORCEGONE...
YES, THANK YOU. AND YOU HAVE A HEALING FACTOR. LUCKY ME.
I AM SEBASTIAN BLOOD. SERVANT OF TRIGON. NINTH HIGH PRIEST OF THE CHURCH OF BLOOD.
A TITLE I MURDERED MY OWN FATHER TO ATTAIN.
MERCYPLEASE! MERCYPLEASE-PLEASE!
MERCY IS A SIN.
SHRRLKK
I'd almost forgotten how it feels to sap someone of their lifeforce. To borrow and feed on their energies.
The Demon's nourishment sharpens me. I can feel my fellow inmates. Sizing me up. Deciding whether I'm predator or prey.
And one in particular. The one who sent me here. The one whose death would surely be exquisite.
Eternity.

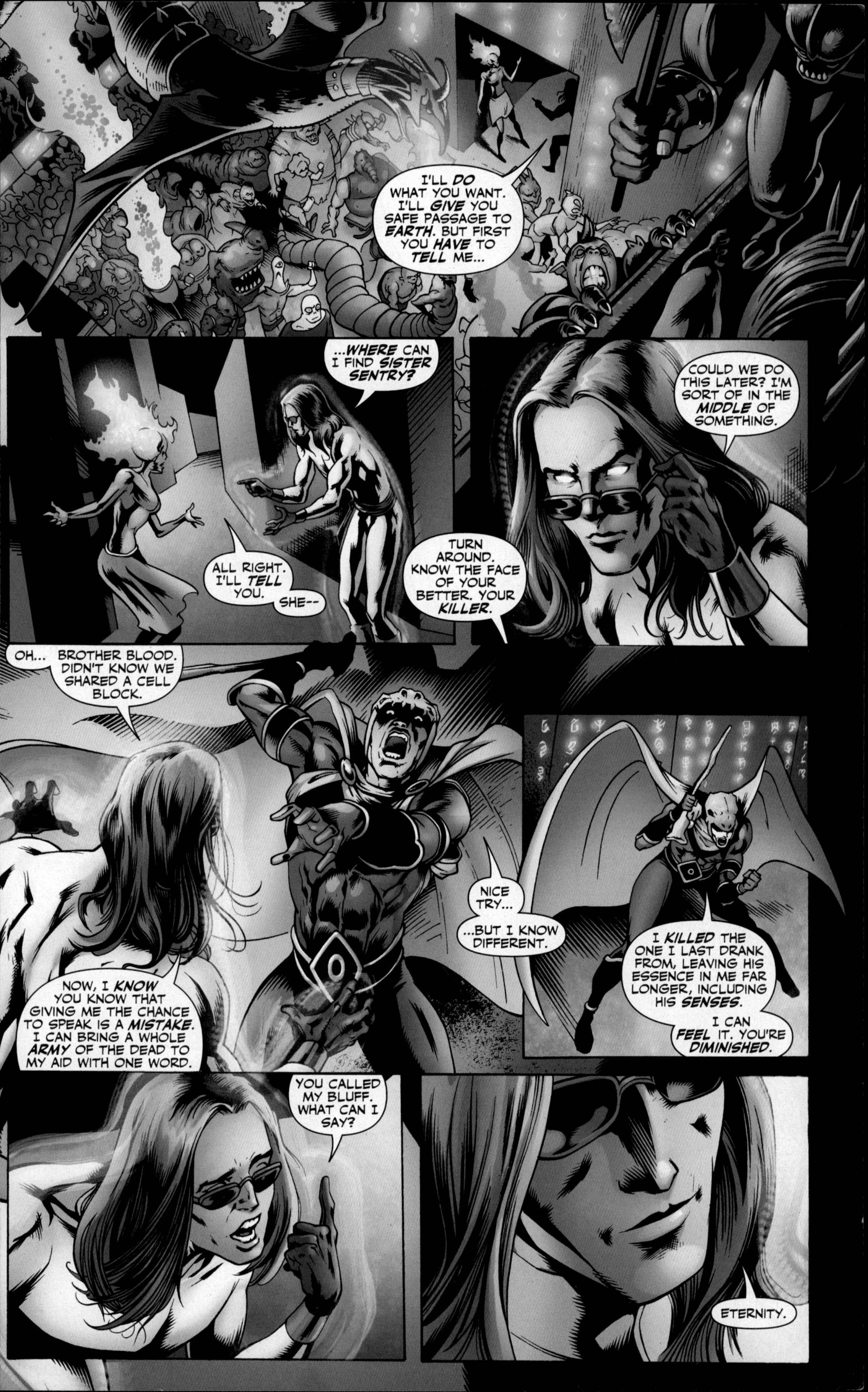
I'LL DO WHAT YOU WANT. I'LL GIVE YOU SAFE PASSAGE TO EARTH. BUT FIRST YOU HAVE TO TELL ME...
...WHERE CAN I FIND SISTER SENTRY?
ALL RIGHT. I'LL TELL YOU.
SHE--
COULD WE DO THIS LATER? I'M SORT OF IN THE MIDDLE OF SOMETHING.
TURN AROUND. KNOW THE FACE OF YOUR BETTER. YOUR KILLER.
OH... BROTHER BLOOD. DIDN'T KNOW WE SHARED A CELL BLOCK.
NOW, I KNOW YOU KNOW THAT GIVING ME THE CHANCE TO SPEAK IS A MISTAKE. I CAN BRING A WHOLE ARMY OF THE DEAD TO MY AID WITH ONE WORD.
NICE TRY...
...BUT I KNOW DIFFERENT.
I KILLED THE ONE I LAST DRANK FROM, LEAVING HIS ESSENCE IN ME FAR LONGER, INCLUDING HIS SENSES.
I CAN FEEL IT. YOU'RE DIMINISHED.
YOU CALLED MY BLUFF. WHAT CAN I SAY?
ETERNITY.

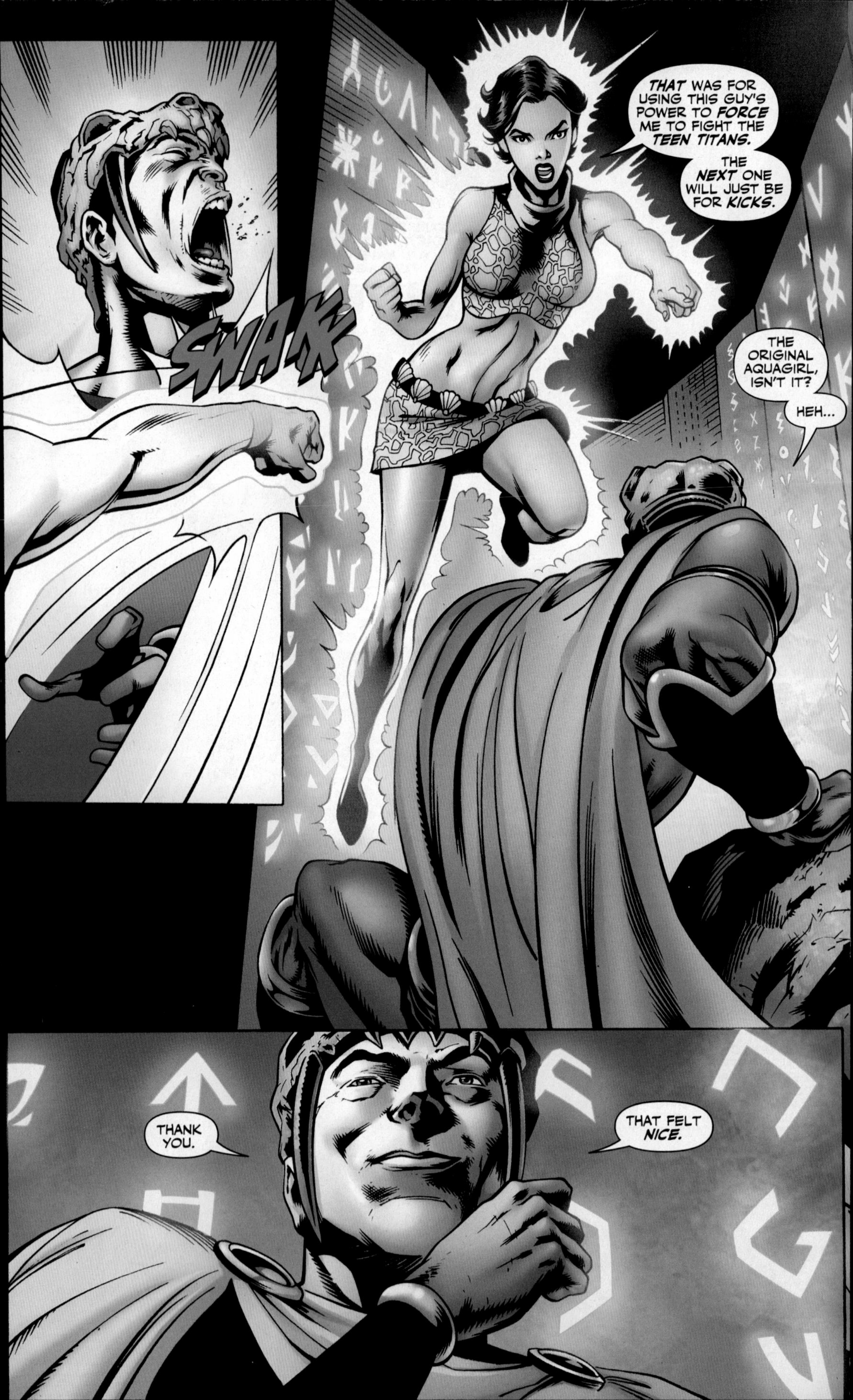
SWAK
THAT WAS FOR USING THIS GUY'S POWER TO FORCE ME TO FIGHT THE TEEN TITANS.
THE NEXT ONE WILL JUST BE FOR KICKS.
THE ORIGINAL AQUAGIRL, ISN'T IT?
HEH...
THANK YOU.
THAT FELT NICE.

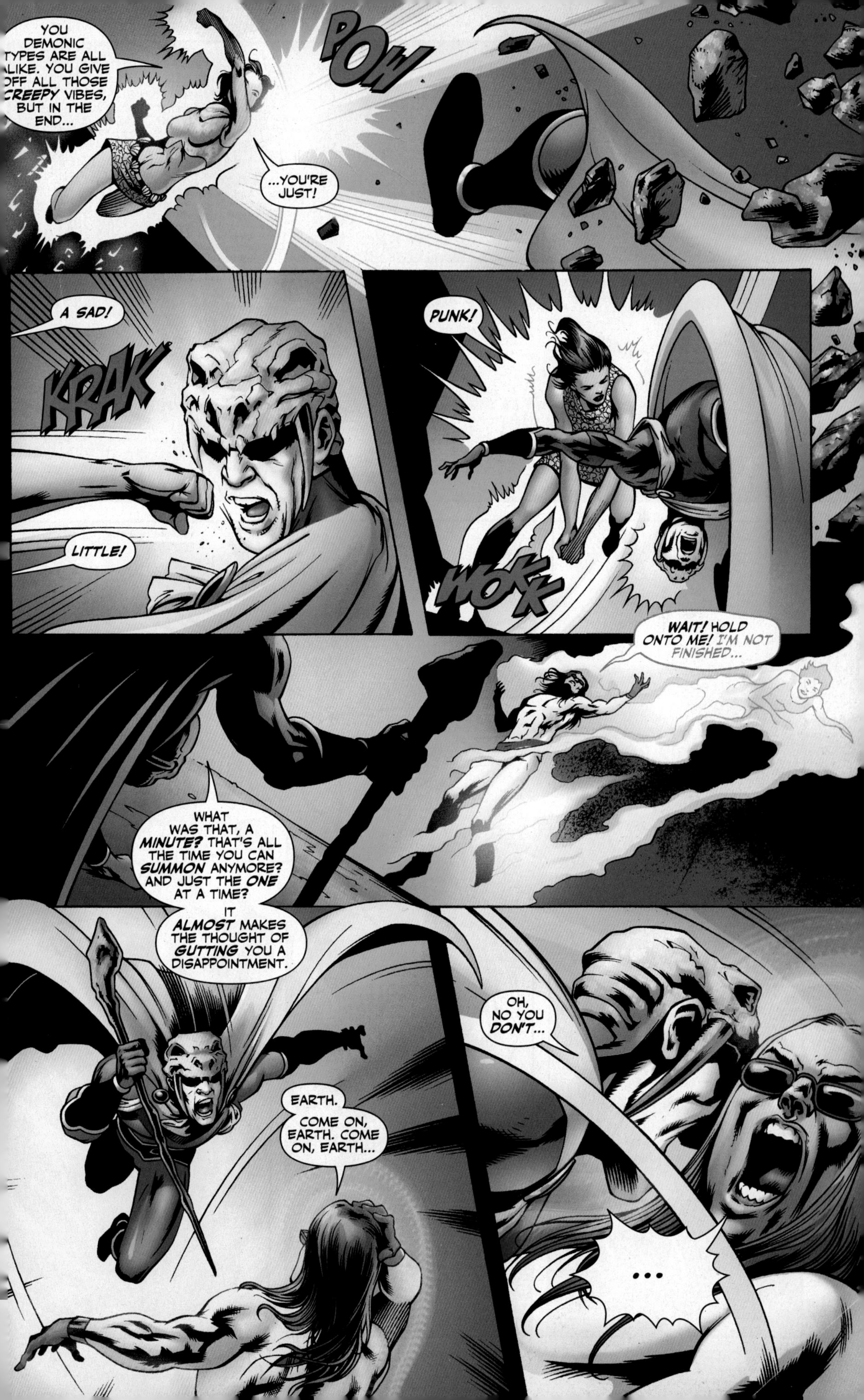
YOU DEMONIC TYPES ARE ALL ALIKE. YOU GIVE OFF ALL THOSE CREEPY VIBES, BUT IN THE END...
POW
...YOU'RE JUST!
A SAD!
KRAK
LITTLE!
PUNK!
WOKK
WAIT! HOLD ONTO ME! I'M NOT FINISHED...
WHAT WAS THAT, A MINUTE? THAT'S ALL THE TIME YOU CAN SUMMON ANYMORE? AND JUST THE ONE AT A TIME?
IT ALMOST MAKES THE THOUGHT OF GUTTING YOU A DISAPPOINTMENT.
EARTH.
COME ON, EARTH. COME ON, EARTH...
OH, NO YOU DON'T...
...

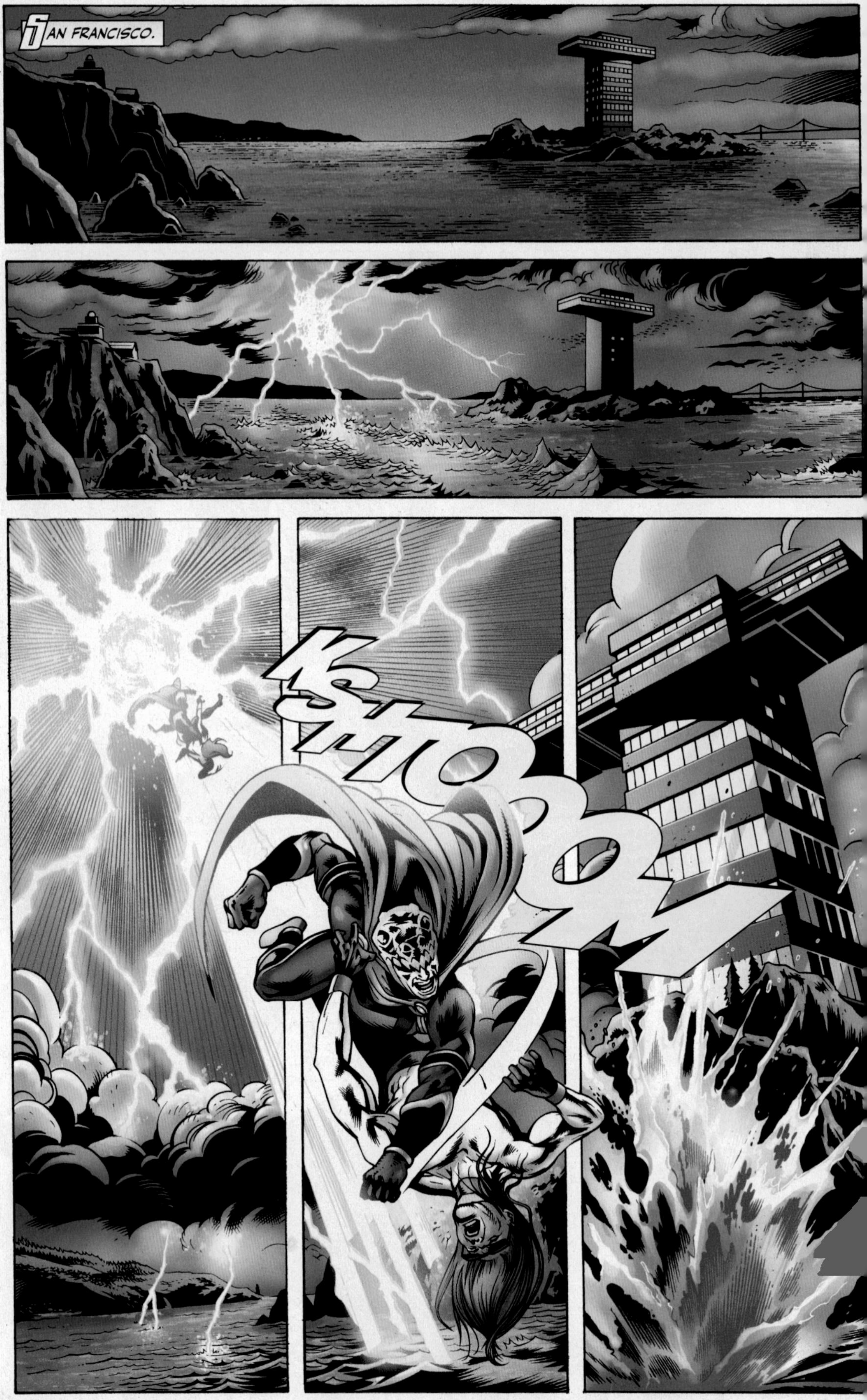
SAN FRANCISCO.
KSHOOOM

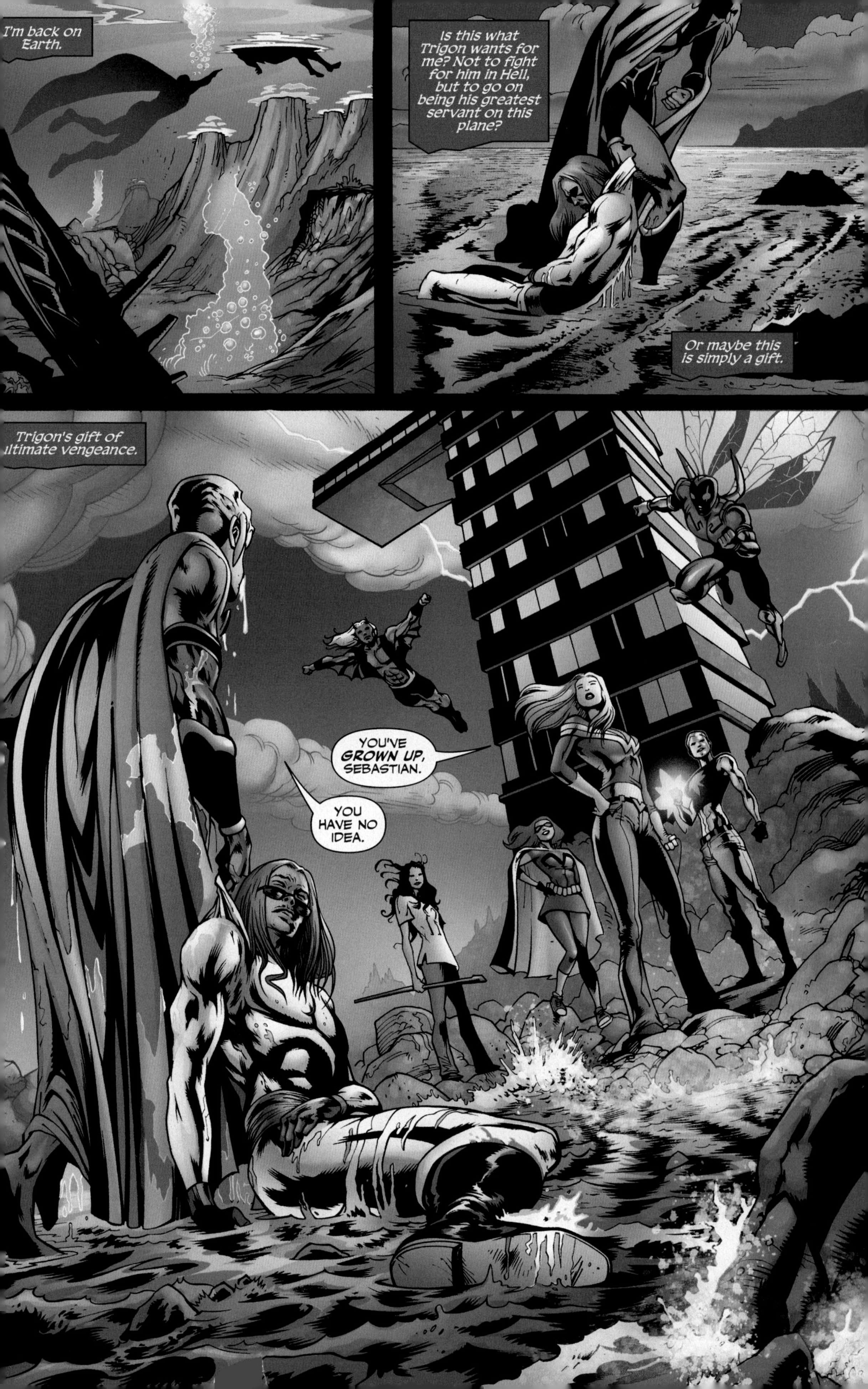
I'm back on Earth.
Is this what Trigon wants for me? Not to fight for him in Hell, but to go on being his greatest servant on this plane?
Or maybe this is simply a gift.
Trigon's gift of ultimate vengeance.
YOU'VE GROWN UP, SEBASTIAN.
YOU HAVE NO IDEA.

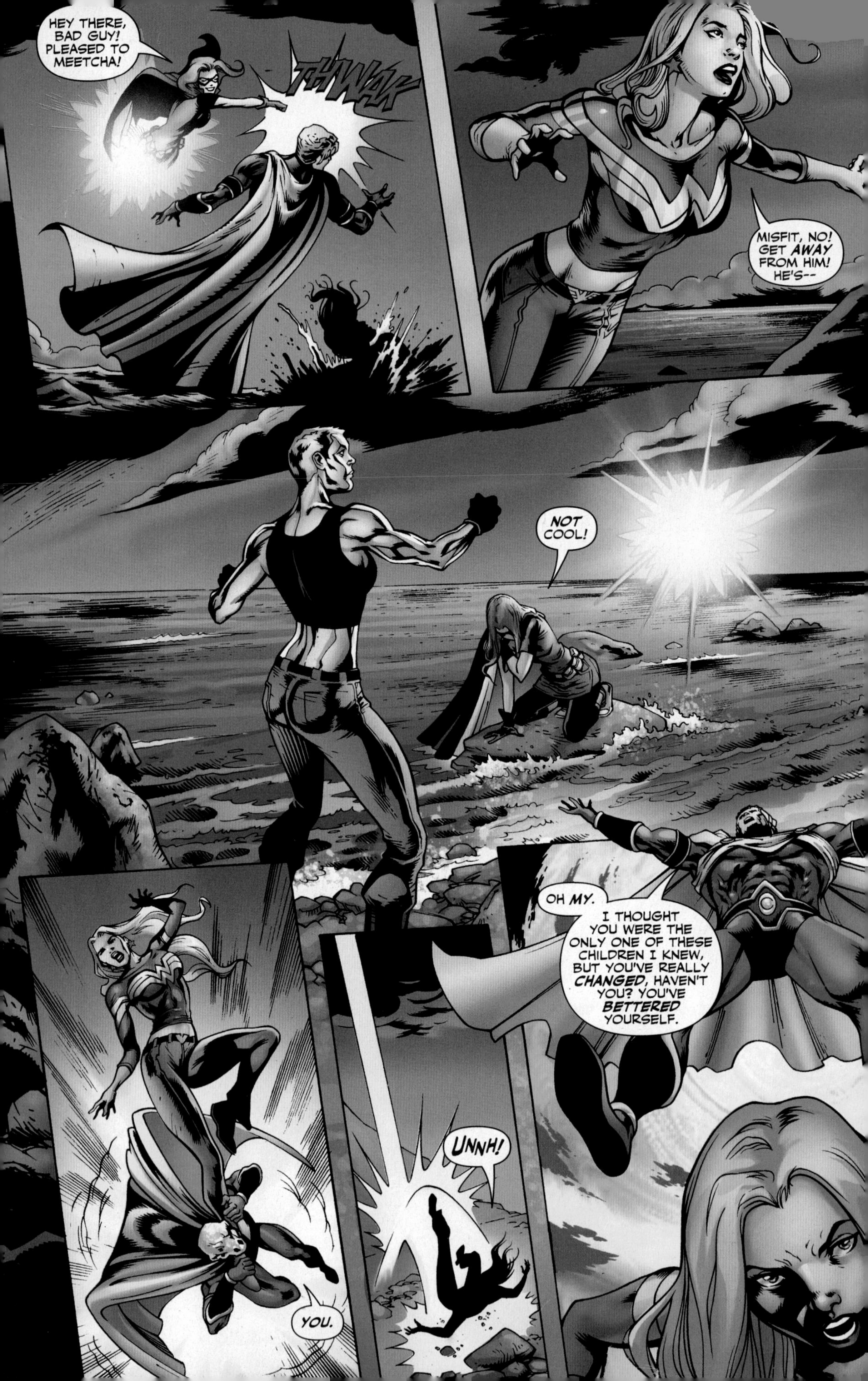
HEY THERE, BAD GUY! PLEASED TO MEETCHA!
THWAK
MISFIT, NO! GET AWAY FROM HIM! HE'S--
NOT COOL!
OH MY.
I THOUGHT YOU WERE THE ONLY ONE OF THESE CHILDREN I KNEW, BUT YOU'VE REALLY CHANGED, HAVEN'T YOU? YOU'VE BETTERED YOURSELF.
UNNH!
YOU.

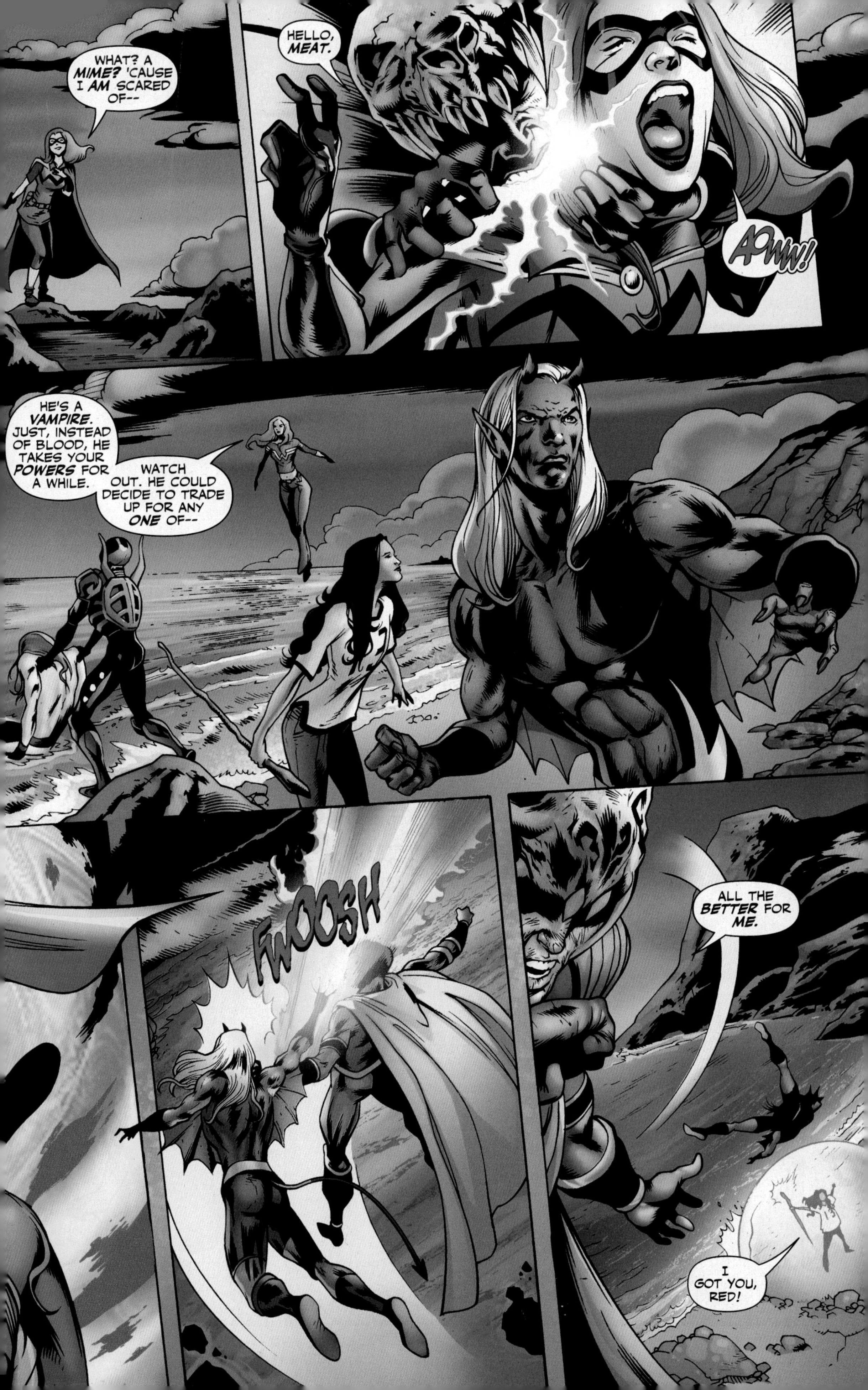
WHAT? A MIME? 'CAUSE I AM SCARED OF--
HELLO, MEAT.
AOWW!
HE'S A VAMPIRE. JUST, INSTEAD OF BLOOD, HE TAKES YOUR POWERS FOR A WHILE.
WATCH OUT. HE COULD DECIDE TO TRADE UP FOR ANY ONE OF--
FWOOSH
ALL THE BETTER FOR ME.
I GOT YOU, RED!

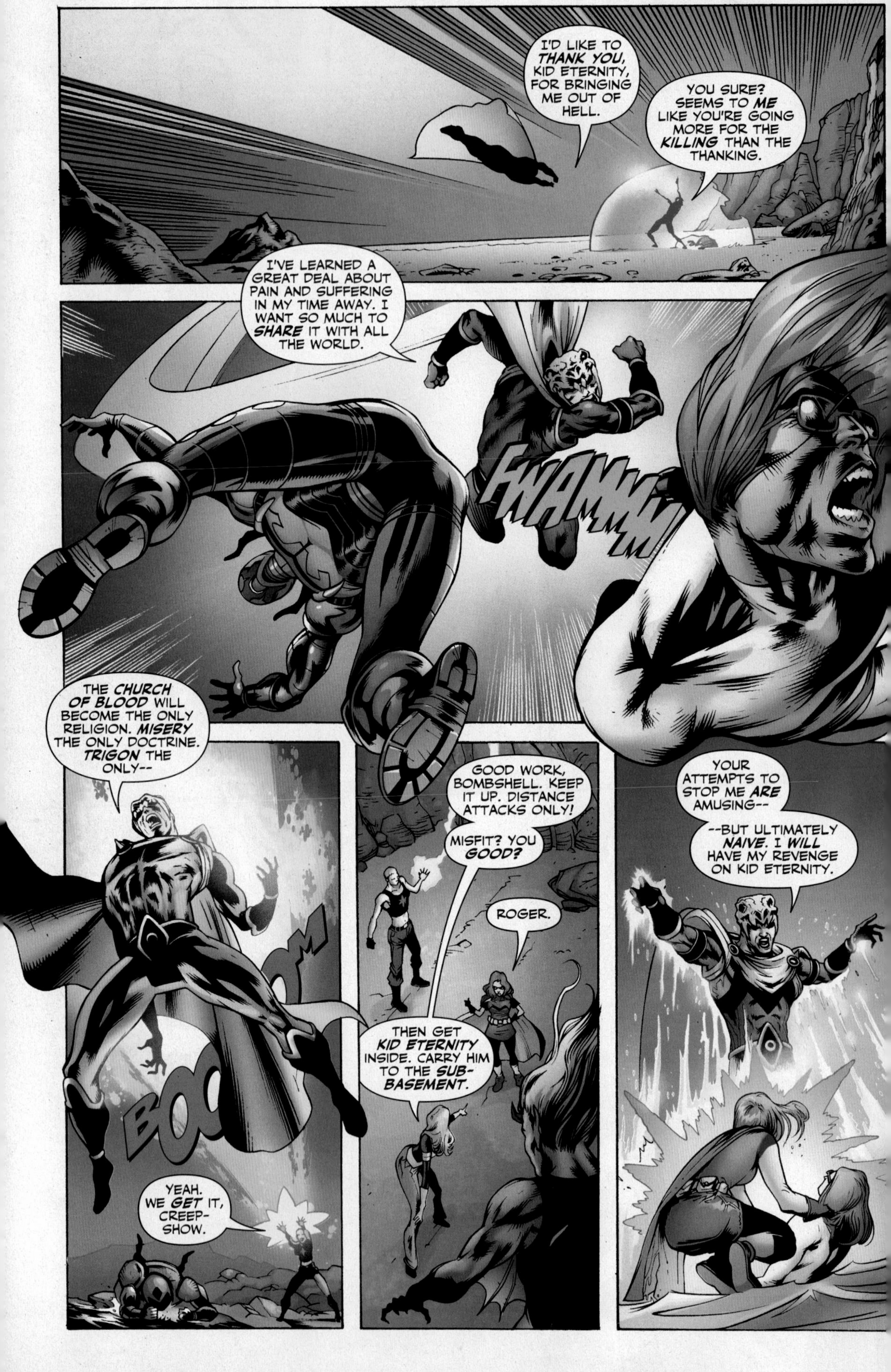
I'D LIKE TO THANK YOU, KID ETERNITY, FOR BRINGING ME OUT OF HELL.
YOU SURE? SEEMS TO ME LIKE YOU'RE GOING MORE FOR THE KILLING THAN THE THANKING.
I'VE LEARNED A GREAT DEAL ABOUT PAIN AND SUFFERING IN MY TIME AWAY. I WANT SO MUCH TO SHARE IT WITH ALL THE WORLD.
FWAMMM
THE CHURCH OF BLOOD WILL BECOME THE ONLY RELIGION. MISERY THE ONLY DOCTRINE. TRIGON THE ONLY--
BOOOM
YEAH. WE GET IT, CREEP-SHOW.
GOOD WORK, BOMBSHELL. KEEP IT UP. DISTANCE ATTACKS ONLY!
MISFIT? YOU GOOD?
ROGER.
THEN GET KID ETERNITY INSIDE. CARRY HIM TO THE SUB-BASEMENT.
YOUR ATTEMPTS TO STOP ME ARE AMUSING--
--BUT ULTIMATELY NAIVE. I WILL HAVE MY REVENGE ON KID ETERNITY.

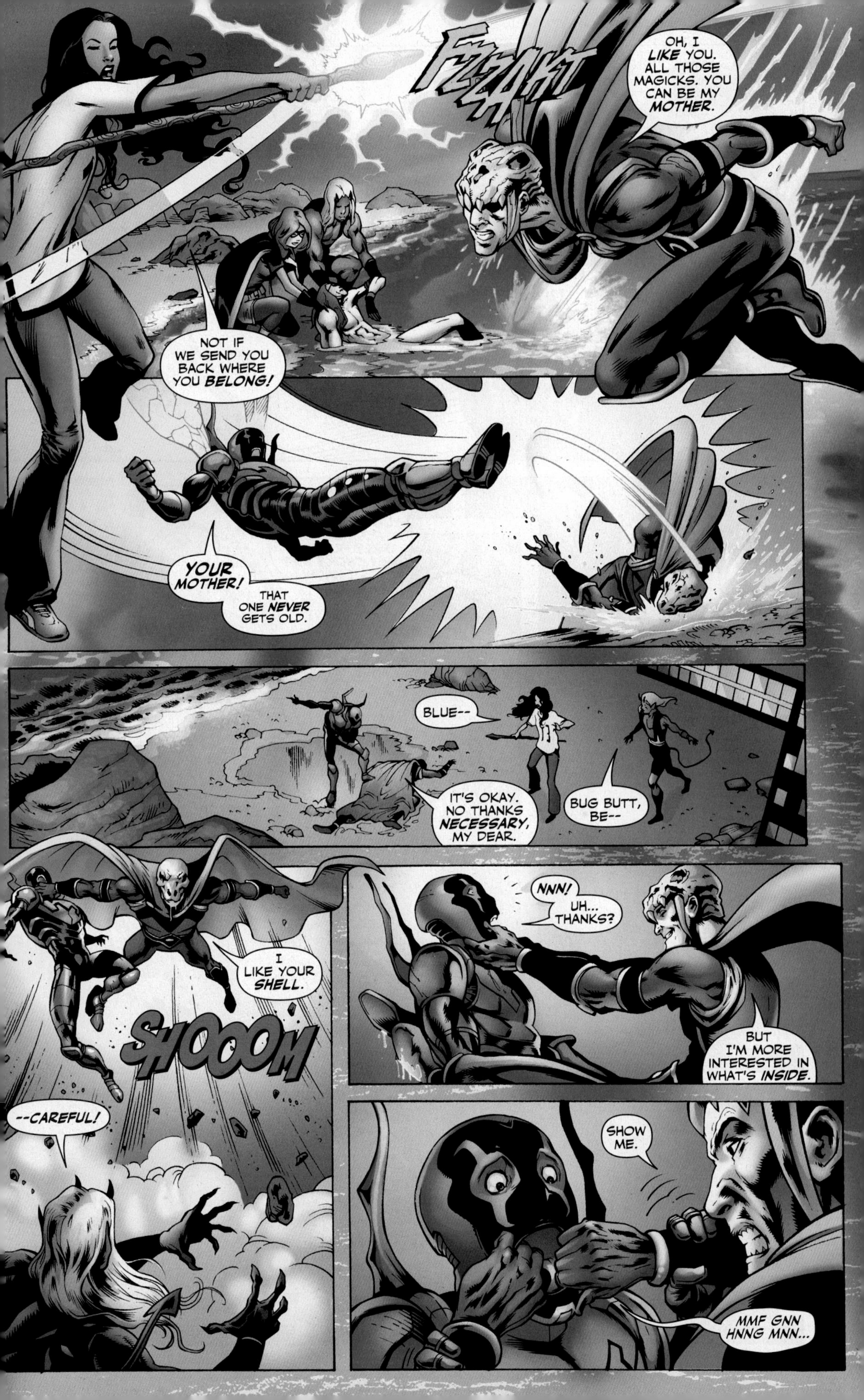
FZZAKT
OH, I LIKE YOU. ALL THOSE MAGICKS. YOU CAN BE MY MOTHER.
NOT IF WE SEND YOU BACK WHERE YOU BELONG!
YOUR MOTHER!
THAT ONE NEVER GETS OLD.
BLUE--
IT'S OKAY. NO THANKS NECESSARY, MY DEAR.
BUG BUTT, BE--
I LIKE YOUR SHELL.
SHOOOM
--CAREFUL!
NNN!
UH... THANKS?
BUT I'M MORE INTERESTED IN WHAT'S INSIDE.
SHOW ME.
MMF GNN HNNG MNN...

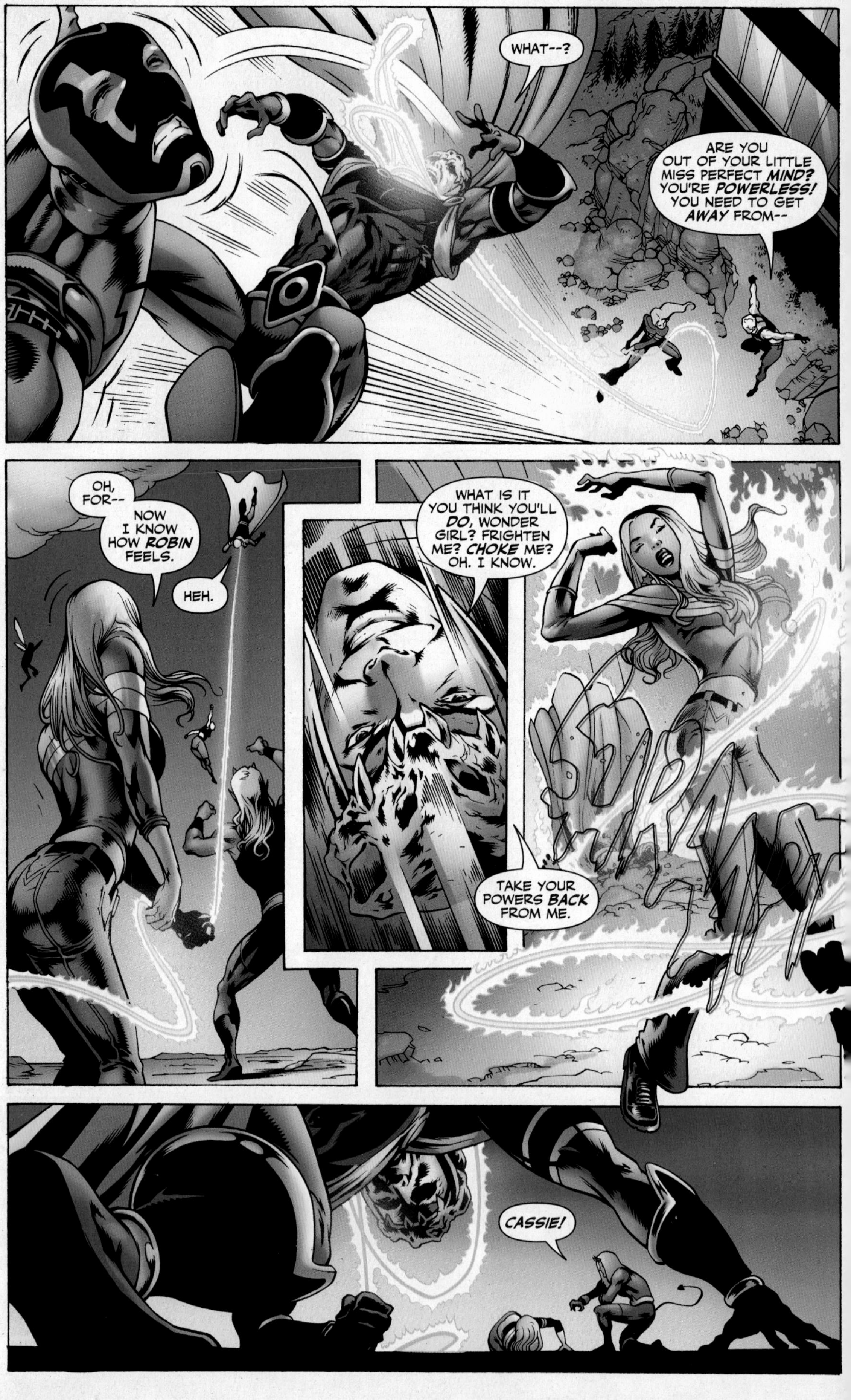
WHAT--?
ARE YOU OUT OF YOUR LITTLE MISS PERFECT MIND? YOU'RE POWERLESS! YOU NEED TO GET AWAY FROM--
OH, FOR--
NOW I KNOW HOW ROBIN FEELS.
HEH.
WHAT IS IT YOU THINK YOU'LL DO, WONDER GIRL? FRIGHTEN ME? CHOKE ME? OH. I KNOW.
TAKE YOUR POWERS BACK FROM ME.
CASSIE!

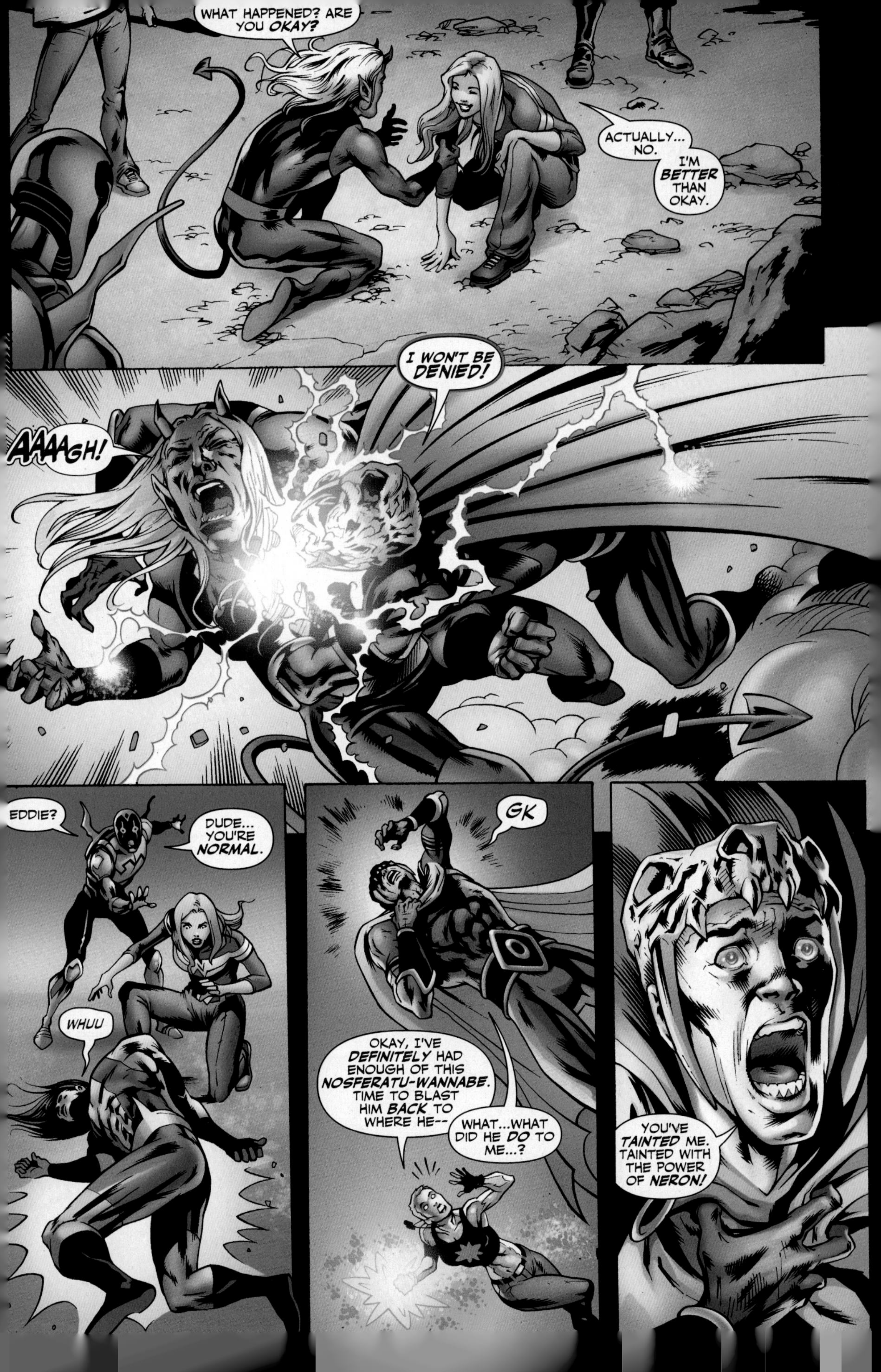
WHAT HAPPENED? ARE YOU OKAY?
ACTUALLY... NO.
I'M BETTER THAN OKAY.
I WON'T BE DENIED!
AAAAGH!
EDDIE?
DUDE... YOU'RE NORMAL.
WHUU
GK
OKAY, I'VE DEFINITELY HAD ENOUGH OF THIS NOSFERATU-WANNABE. TIME TO BLAST HIM BACK TO WHERE HE--
WHAT...WHAT DID HE DO TO ME...?
YOU'VE TAINTED ME. TAINTED WITH THE POWER OF NERON!

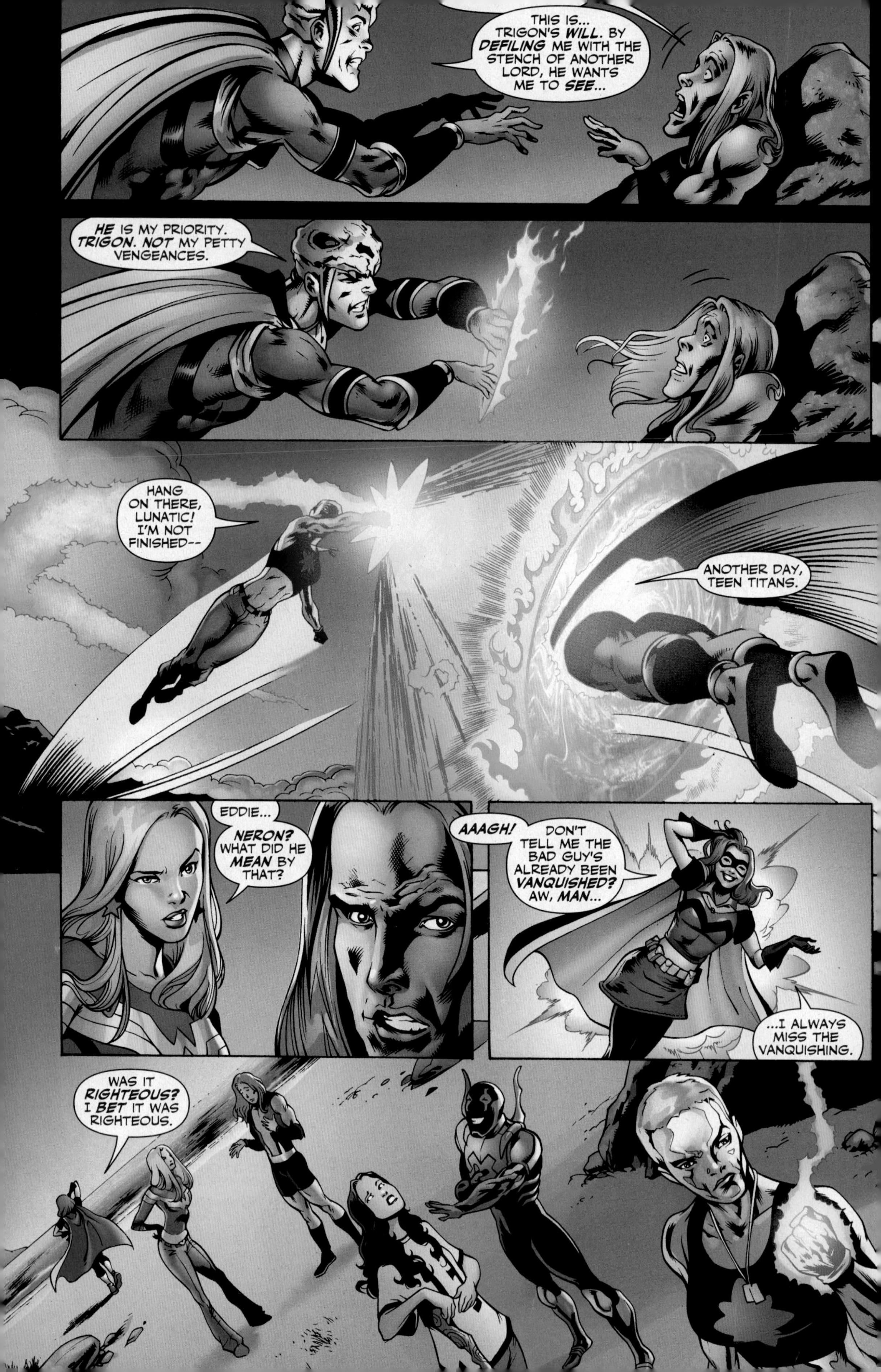
THIS IS... TRIGON'S WILL. BY DEFILING ME WITH THE STENCH OF ANOTHER LORD, HE WANTS ME TO SEE...
HE IS MY PRIORITY. TRIGON. NOT MY PETTY VENGEANCES.
HANG ON THERE, LUNATIC! I'M NOT FINISHED--
ANOTHER DAY, TEEN TITANS.
EDDIE...
NERON? WHAT DID HE MEAN BY THAT?
AAAGH!
DON'T TELL ME THE BAD GUY'S ALREADY BEEN VANQUISHED? AW, MAN...
...I ALWAYS MISS THE VANQUISHING.
WAS IT RIGHTEOUS? I BET IT WAS RIGHTEOUS.

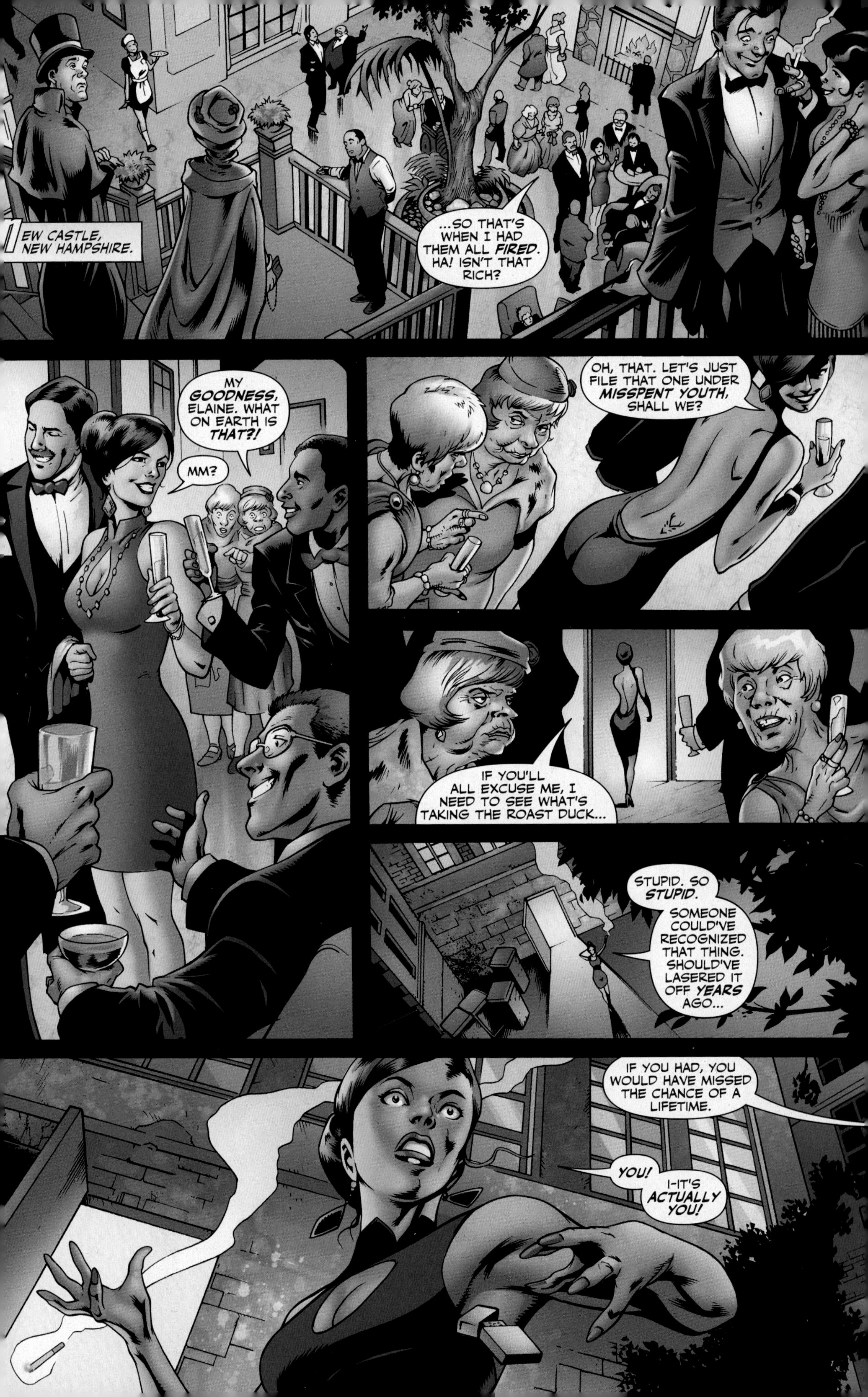
NEW CASTLE, NEW HAMPSHIRE.
...SO THAT'S WHEN I HAD THEM ALL FIRED. HA! ISN'T THAT RICH?
MY GOODNESS, ELAINE. WHAT ON EARTH IS THAT?!
MM?
OH, THAT. LET'S JUST FILE THAT ONE UNDER MISSPENT YOUTH, SHALL WE?
IF YOU'LL ALL EXCUSE ME, I NEED TO SEE WHAT'S TAKING THE ROAST DUCK...
STUPID. SO STUPID.
SOMEONE COULD'VE RECOGNIZED THAT THING. SHOULD'VE LASERED IT OFF YEARS AGO...
IF YOU HAD, YOU WOULD HAVE MISSED THE CHANCE OF A LIFETIME.
YOU!
I-IT'S ACTUALLY YOU!

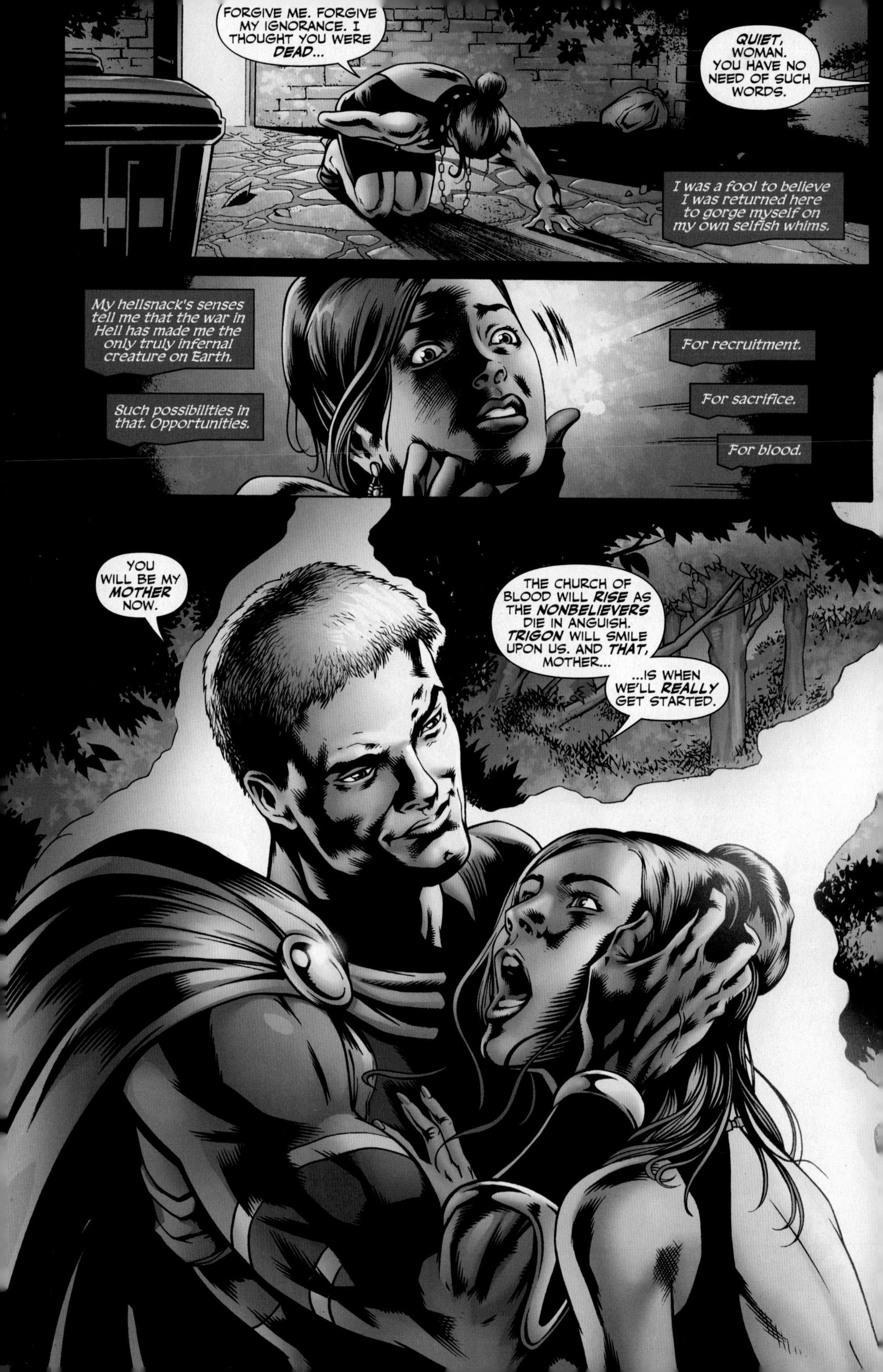
FORGIVE ME. FORGIVE MY IGNORANCE. I THOUGHT YOU WERE DEAD...
QUIET, WOMAN. YOU HAVE NO NEED OF SUCH WORDS.
I was a fool to believe I was returned here to gorge myself on my own selfish whims.
My hellsnack's senses tell me that the war in Hell has made me the only truly infernal creature on Earth.
Such possibilities in that. Opportunities.
For recruitment.
For sacrifice.
For blood.
YOU WILL BE MY MOTHER NOW.
THE CHURCH OF BLOOD WILL RISE AS THE NONBELIEVERS DIE IN ANGUISH. TRIGON WILL SMILE UPON US. AND THAT, MOTHER...
...IS WHEN WE'LL REALLY GET STARTED.

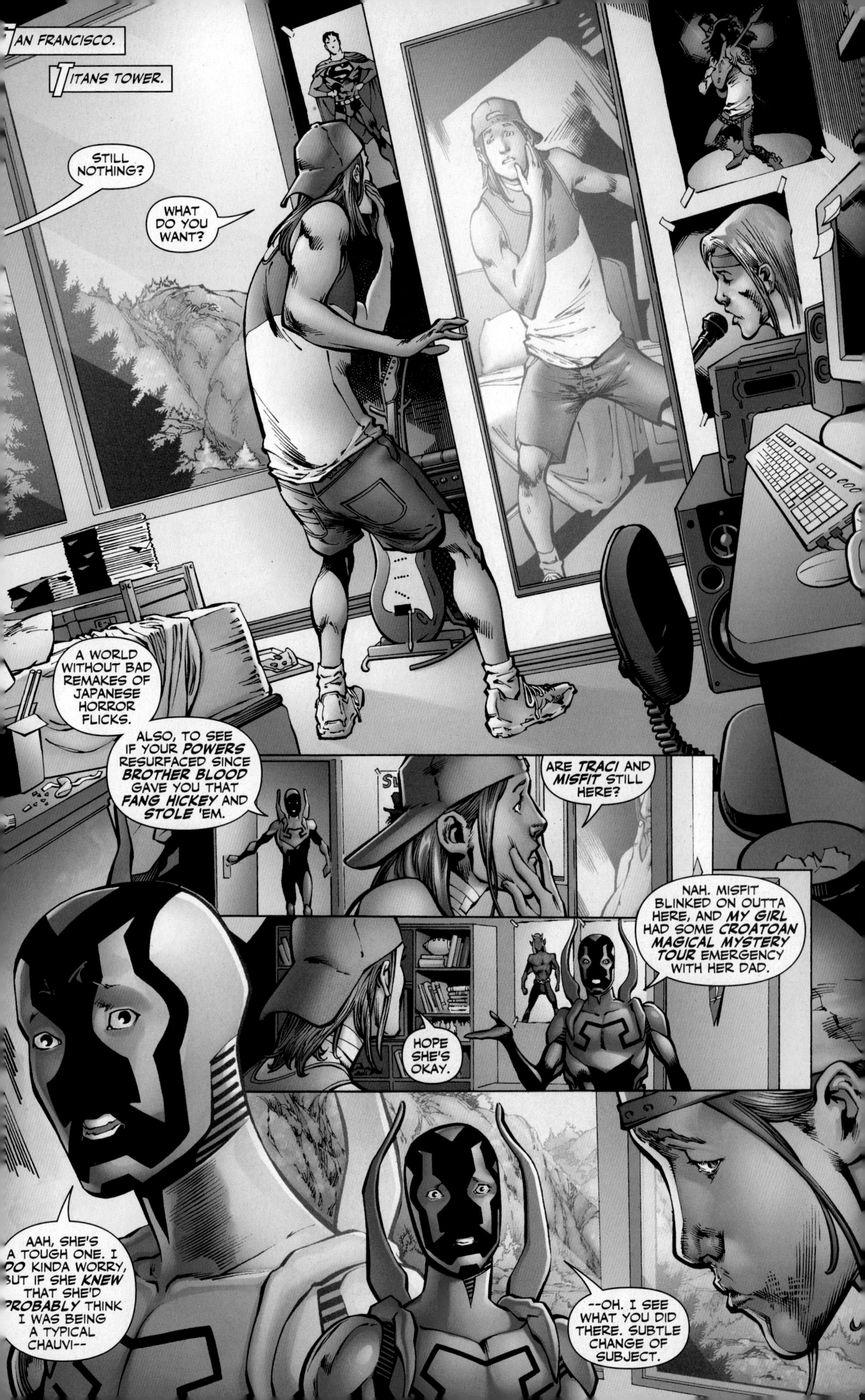

AN FRANCISCO.
TITANS TOWER.
STILL NOTHING?
WHAT DO YOU WANT?
A WORLD WITHOUT BAD REMAKES OF JAPANESE HORROR FLICKS.
ALSO, TO SEE IF YOUR POWERS RESURFACED SINCE BROTHER BLOOD GAVE YOU THAT FANG HICKEY AND STOLE 'EM.
ARE TRACI AND MISFIT STILL HERE?
NAH. MISFIT BLINKED ON OUTTA HERE, AND MY GIRL HAD SOME CROATOAN MAGICAL MYSTERY TOUR EMERGENCY WITH HER DAD.
HOPE SHE'S OKAY.
AAH, SHE'S A TOUGH ONE. I DO KINDA WORRY, BUT IF SHE KNEW THAT SHE'D PROBABLY THINK I WAS BEING A TYPICAL CHAUVI--
--OH. I SEE WHAT YOU DID THERE. SUBTLE CHANGE OF SUBJECT.

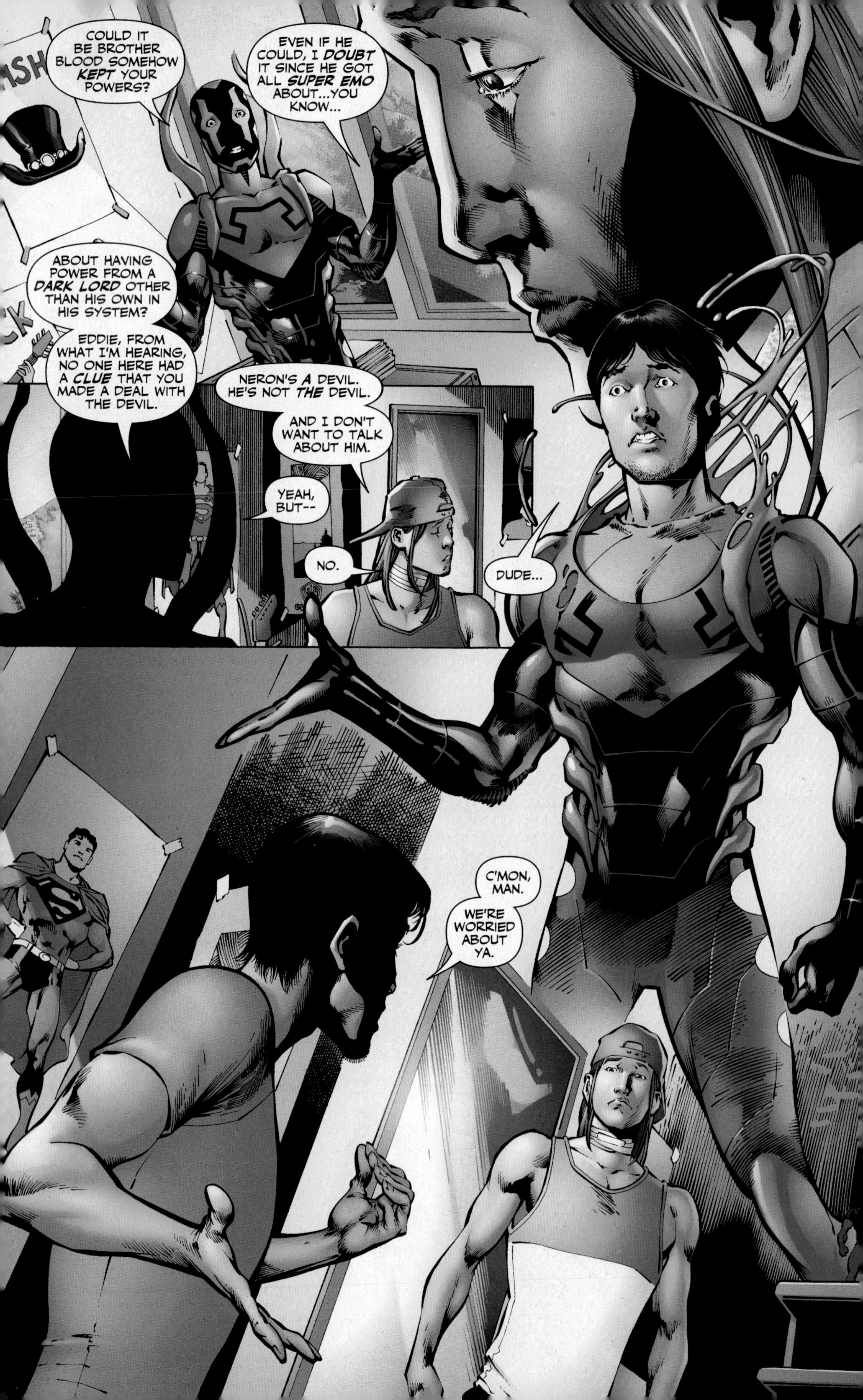

COULD IT BE BROTHER BLOOD SOMEHOW KEPT YOUR POWERS?
EVEN IF HE COULD, I DOUBT IT SINCE HE GOT ALL SUPER EMO ABOUT...YOU KNOW...
ABOUT HAVING POWER FROM A DARK LORD OTHER THAN HIS OWN IN HIS SYSTEM?
EDDIE, FROM WHAT I'M HEARING, NO ONE HERE HAD A CLUE THAT YOU MADE A DEAL WITH THE DEVIL.
NERON'S A DEVIL. HE'S NOT THE DEVIL.
AND I DON'T WANT TO TALK ABOUT HIM.
YEAH, BUT--
NO.
DUDE...
C'MON, MAN.
WE'RE WORRIED ABOUT YA.

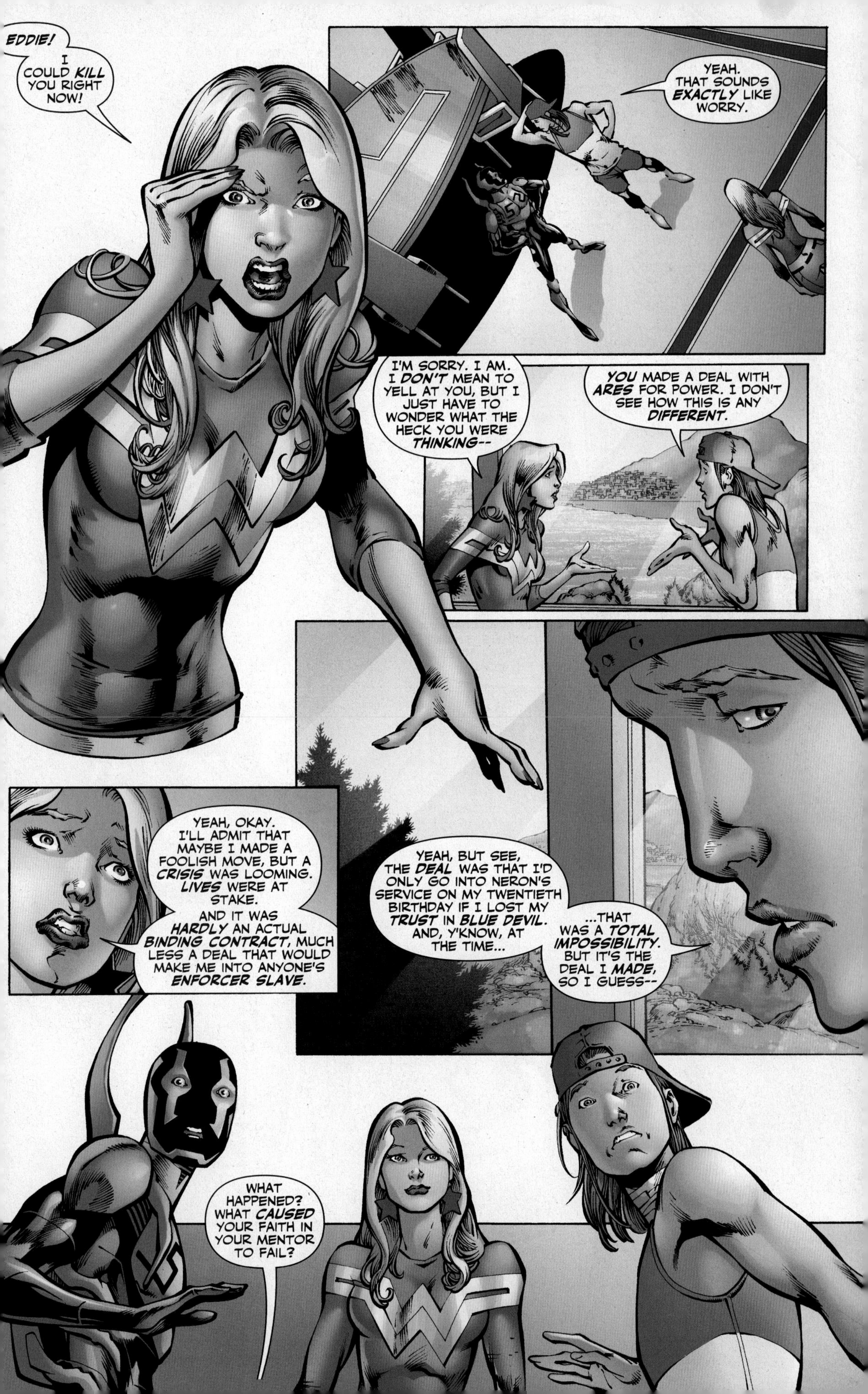
EDDIE! I COULD KILL YOU RIGHT NOW!
YEAH. THAT SOUNDS EXACTLY LIKE WORRY.
I'M SORRY. I AM. I DON'T MEAN TO YELL AT YOU, BUT I JUST HAVE TO WONDER WHAT THE HECK YOU WERE THINKING--
YOU MADE A DEAL WITH ARES FOR POWER. I DON'T SEE HOW THIS IS ANY DIFFERENT.
YEAH, OKAY. I'LL ADMIT THAT MAYBE I MADE A FOOLISH MOVE, BUT A CRISIS WAS LOOMING. LIVES WERE AT STAKE.
AND IT WAS HARDLY AN ACTUAL BINDING CONTRACT, MUCH LESS A DEAL THAT WOULD MAKE ME INTO ANYONE'S ENFORCER SLAVE.
YEAH, BUT SEE, THE DEAL WAS THAT I'D ONLY GO INTO NERON'S SERVICE ON MY TWENTIETH BIRTHDAY IF I LOST MY TRUST IN BLUE DEVIL. AND, Y'KNOW, AT THE TIME...
...THAT WAS A TOTAL IMPOSSIBILITY. BUT IT'S THE DEAL I MADE, SO I GUESS--
WHAT HAPPENED? WHAT CAUSED YOUR FAITH IN YOUR MENTOR TO FAIL?

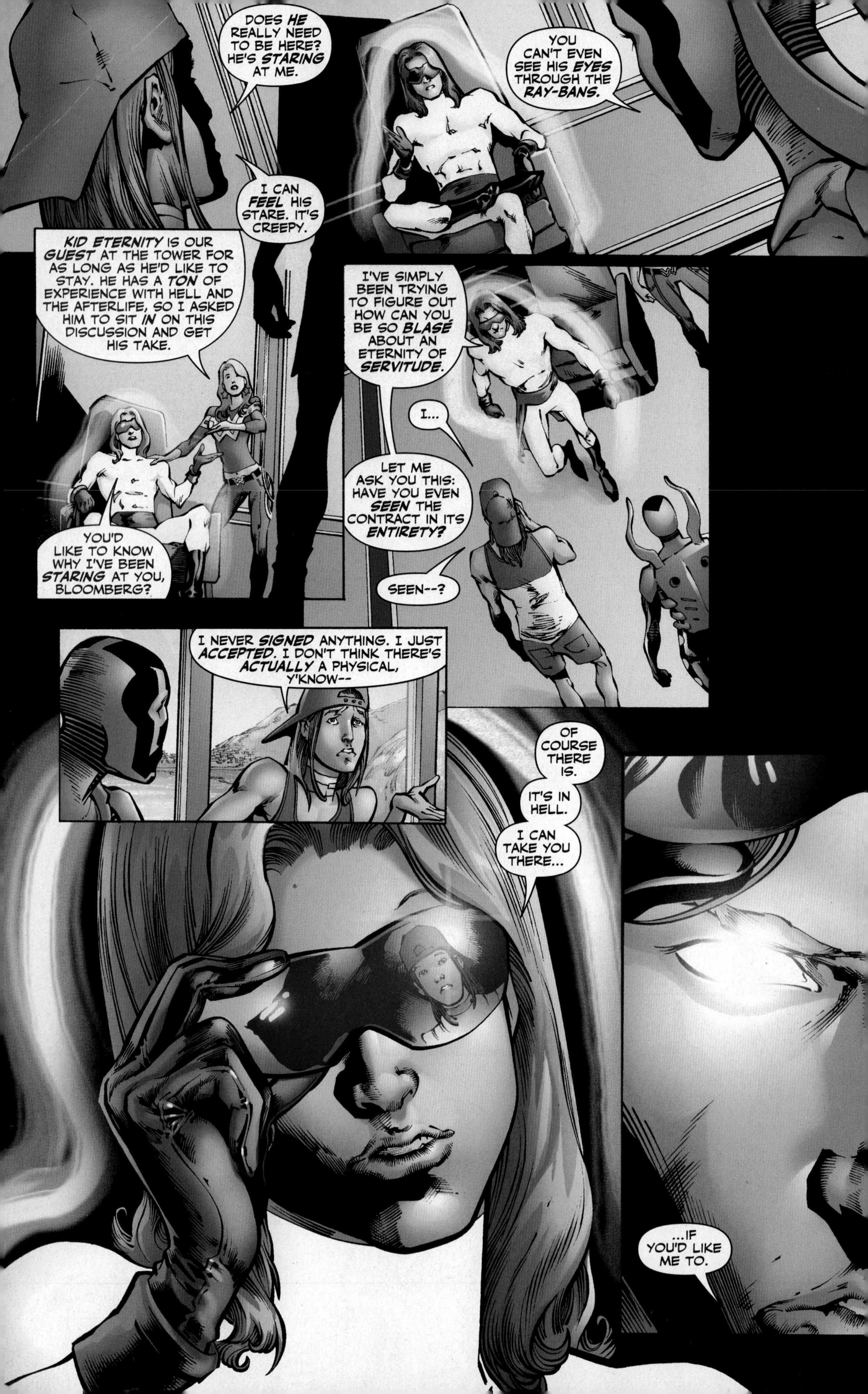
DOES HE REALLY NEED TO BE HERE? HE'S STARING AT ME.
YOU CAN'T EVEN SEE HIS EYES THROUGH THE RAY-BANS.
I CAN FEEL HIS STARE. IT'S CREEPY.
KID ETERNITY IS OUR GUEST AT THE TOWER FOR AS LONG AS HE'D LIKE TO STAY. HE HAS A TON OF EXPERIENCE WITH HELL AND THE AFTERLIFE, SO I ASKED HIM TO SIT IN ON THIS DISCUSSION AND GET HIS TAKE.
YOU'D LIKE TO KNOW WHY I'VE BEEN STARING AT YOU, BLOOMBERG?
I'VE SIMPLY BEEN TRYING TO FIGURE OUT HOW CAN YOU BE SO BLASÉ ABOUT AN ETERNITY OF SERVITUDE.
I...
LET ME ASK YOU THIS: HAVE YOU EVEN SEEN THE CONTRACT IN ITS ENTIRETY?
SEEN--?
I NEVER SIGNED ANYTHING. I JUST ACCEPTED. I DON'T THINK THERE'S ACTUALLY A PHYSICAL, Y'KNOW--
OF COURSE THERE IS.
IT'S IN HELL.
I CAN TAKE YOU THERE...
...IF YOU'D LIKE ME TO.

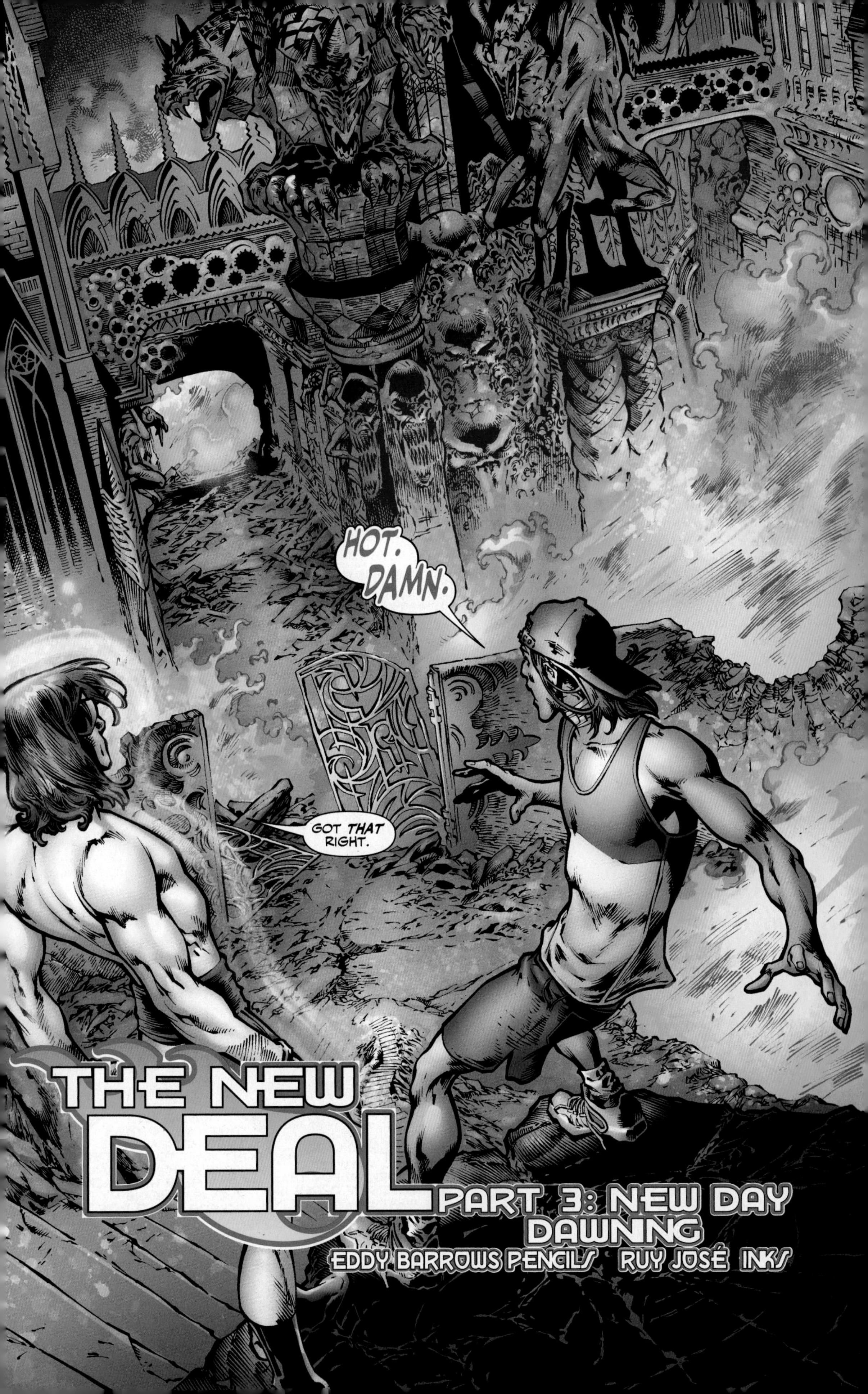
HOT. DAMN.
GOT THAT RIGHT.
THE NEW DEAL
PART 3: NEW DAY DAWNING
EDDY BARROWS PENCILS RUY JOSÉ INKS

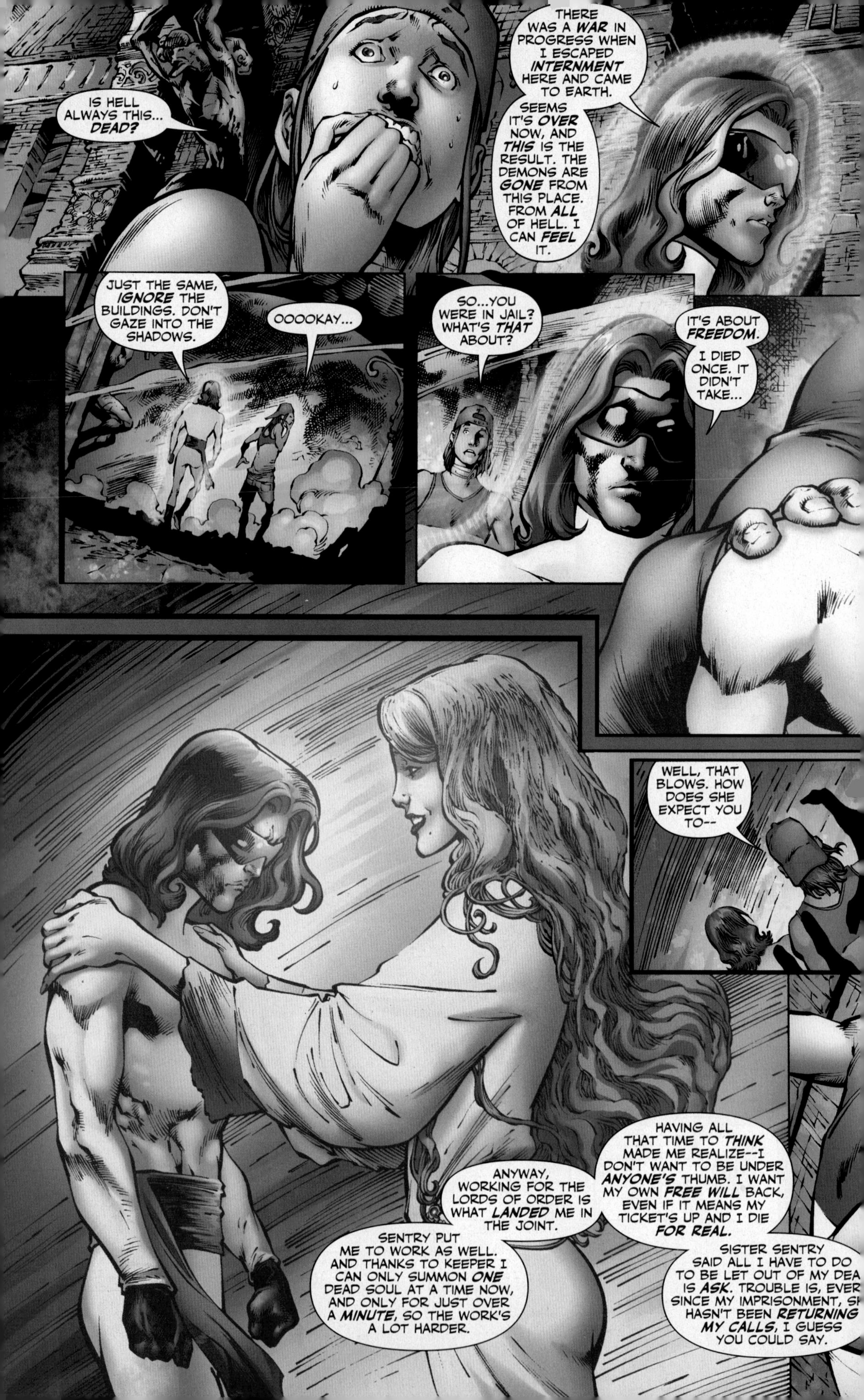

IS HELL ALWAYS THIS... DEAD?
THERE WAS A WAR IN PROGRESS WHEN I ESCAPED INTERNMENT HERE AND CAME TO EARTH.
SEEMS IT'S OVER NOW, AND THIS IS THE RESULT. THE DEMONS ARE GONE FROM THIS PLACE. FROM ALL OF HELL. I CAN FEEL IT.
JUST THE SAME, IGNORE THE BUILDINGS. DON'T GAZE INTO THE SHADOWS.
OOOOKAY...
SO...YOU WERE IN JAIL? WHAT'S THAT ABOUT?
IT'S ABOUT FREEDOM.
I DIED ONCE. IT DIDN'T TAKE...
WELL, THAT BLOWS. HOW DOES SHE EXPECT YOU TO--
ANYWAY, WORKING FOR THE LORDS OF ORDER IS WHAT LANDED ME IN THE JOINT.
SENTRY PUT ME TO WORK AS WELL. AND THANKS TO KEEPER I CAN ONLY SUMMON ONE DEAD SOUL AT A TIME NOW, AND ONLY FOR JUST OVER A MINUTE, SO THE WORK'S A LOT HARDER.
HAVING ALL THAT TIME TO THINK MADE ME REALIZE--I DON'T WANT TO BE UNDER ANYONE'S THUMB. I WANT MY OWN FREE WILL BACK, EVEN IF IT MEANS MY TICKET'S UP AND I DIE FOR REAL.
SISTER SENTRY SAID ALL I HAVE TO DO TO BE LET OUT OF MY DEA IS ASK. TROUBLE IS, EVER SINCE MY IMPRISONMENT, SI HASN'T BEEN RETURNING MY CALLS, I GUESS YOU COULD SAY.

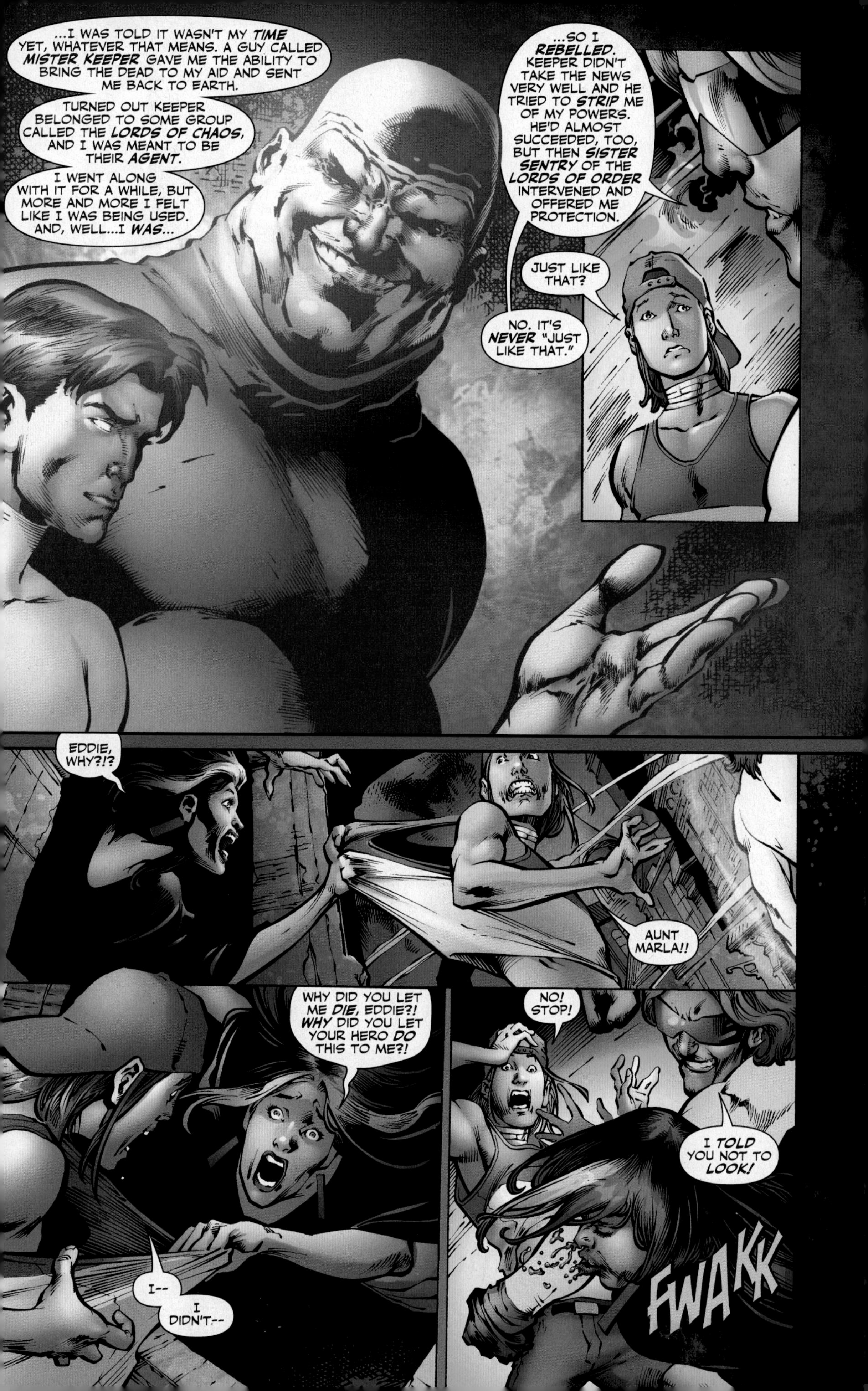
...I WAS TOLD IT WASN'T MY TIME YET, WHATEVER THAT MEANS. A GUY CALLED MISTER KEEPER GAVE ME THE ABILITY TO BRING THE DEAD TO MY AID AND SENT ME BACK TO EARTH.
TURNED OUT KEEPER BELONGED TO SOME GROUP CALLED THE LORDS OF CHAOS, AND I WAS MEANT TO BE THEIR AGENT.
I WENT ALONG WITH IT FOR A WHILE, BUT MORE AND MORE I FELT LIKE I WAS BEING USED. AND, WELL...I WAS...
...SO I REBELLED. KEEPER DIDN'T TAKE THE NEWS VERY WELL AND HE TRIED TO STRIP ME OF MY POWERS. HE'D ALMOST SUCCEEDED, TOO, BUT THEN SISTER SENTRY OF THE LORDS OF ORDER INTERVENED AND OFFERED ME PROTECTION.
JUST LIKE THAT?
NO. IT'S NEVER "JUST LIKE THAT."
EDDIE, WHY?!?
AUNT MARLA!!
WHY DID YOU LET ME DIE, EDDIE?! WHY DID YOU LET YOUR HERO DO THIS TO ME?!
I--
I DIDN'T--
NO! STOP!
I TOLD YOU NOT TO LOOK!
FWAKK

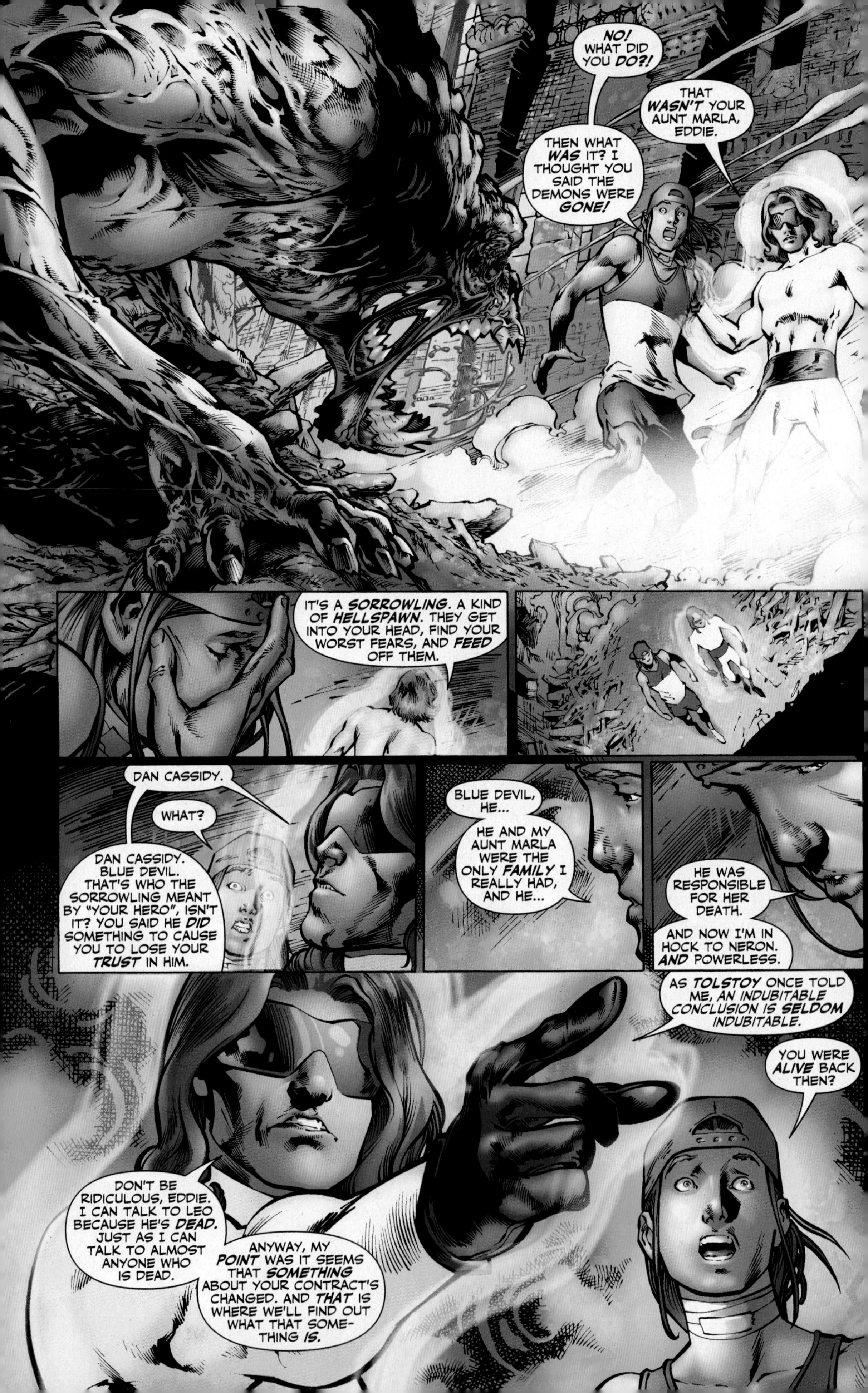
NO! WHAT DID YOU DO?!
THAT WASN'T YOUR AUNT MARLA, EDDIE.
THEN WHAT WAS IT? I THOUGHT YOU SAID THE DEMONS WERE GONE!
IT'S A SORROWLING. A KIND OF HELLSPAWN. THEY GET INTO YOUR HEAD, FIND YOUR WORST FEARS, AND FEED OFF THEM.
DAN CASSIDY.
WHAT?
DAN CASSIDY. BLUE DEVIL. THAT'S WHO THE SORROWLING MEANT BY "YOUR HERO", ISN'T IT? YOU SAID HE DID SOMETHING TO CAUSE YOU TO LOSE YOUR TRUST IN HIM.
BLUE DEVIL, HE...
HE AND MY AUNT MARLA WERE THE ONLY FAMILY I REALLY HAD, AND HE...
HE WAS RESPONSIBLE FOR HER DEATH.
AND NOW I'M IN HOCK TO NERON. AND POWERLESS.
AS TOLSTOY ONCE TOLD ME, AN INDUBITABLE CONCLUSION IS SELDOM INDUBITABLE.
YOU WERE ALIVE BACK THEN?
DON'T BE RIDICULOUS, EDDIE. I CAN TALK TO LEO BECAUSE HE'S DEAD. JUST AS I CAN TALK TO ALMOST ANYONE WHO IS DEAD.
ANYWAY, MY POINT WAS IT SEEMS THAT SOMETHING ABOUT YOUR CONTRACT'S CHANGED. AND THAT IS WHERE WE'LL FIND OUT WHAT THAT SOME-THING IS.

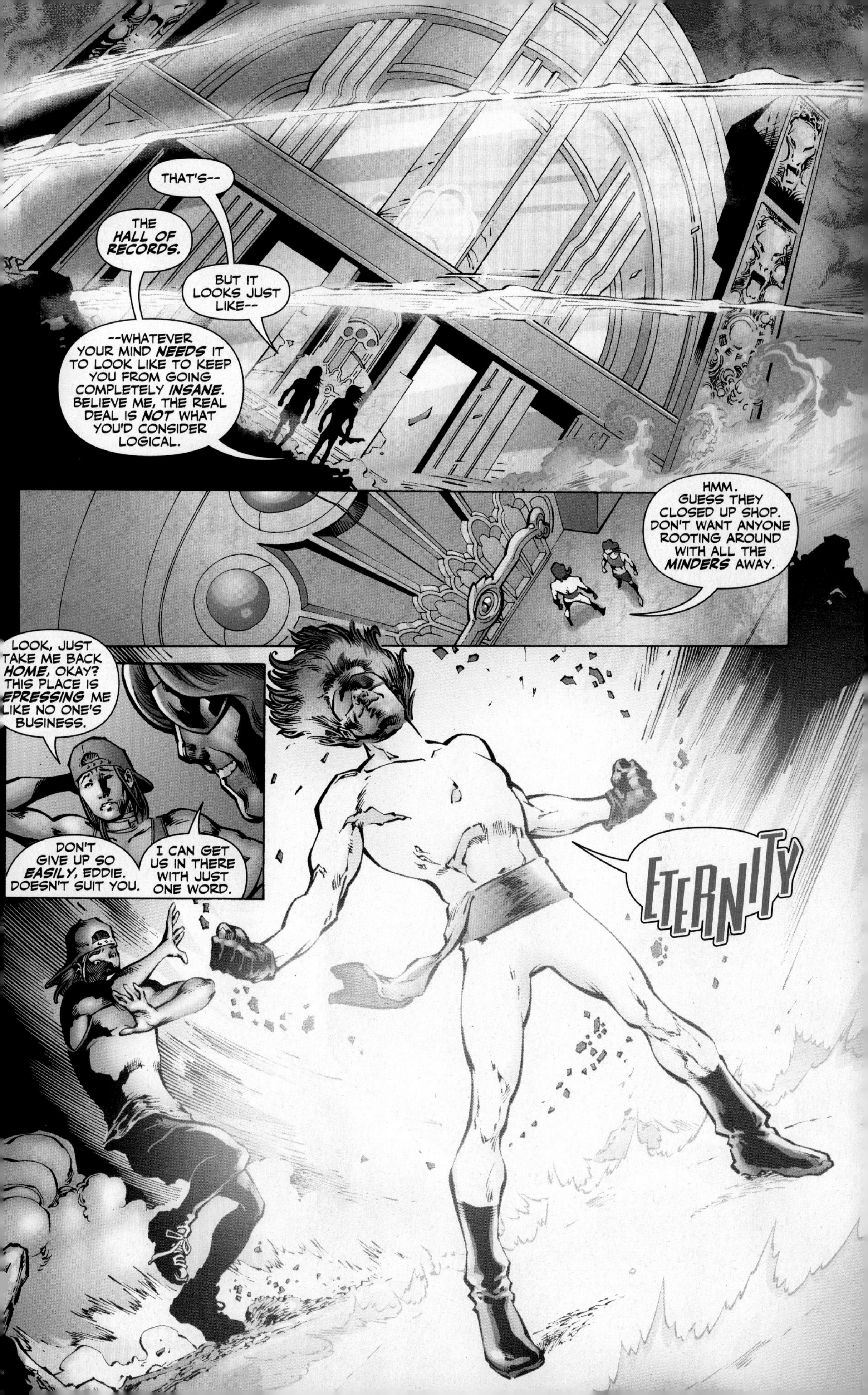
THAT'S--
THE HALL OF RECORDS.
BUT IT LOOKS JUST LIKE--
--WHATEVER YOUR MIND NEEDS IT TO LOOK LIKE TO KEEP YOU FROM GOING COMPLETELY INSANE. BELIEVE ME, THE REAL DEAL IS NOT WHAT YOU'D CONSIDER LOGICAL.
HMM. GUESS THEY CLOSED UP SHOP. DON'T WANT ANYONE ROOTING AROUND WITH ALL THE MINDERS AWAY.
LOOK, JUST TAKE ME BACK HOME, OKAY? THIS PLACE IS EPRESSING ME LIKE NO ONE'S BUSINESS.
DON'T GIVE UP SO EASILY, EDDIE. DOESN'T SUIT YOU.
I CAN GET US IN THERE WITH JUST ONE WORD.
ETERNITY

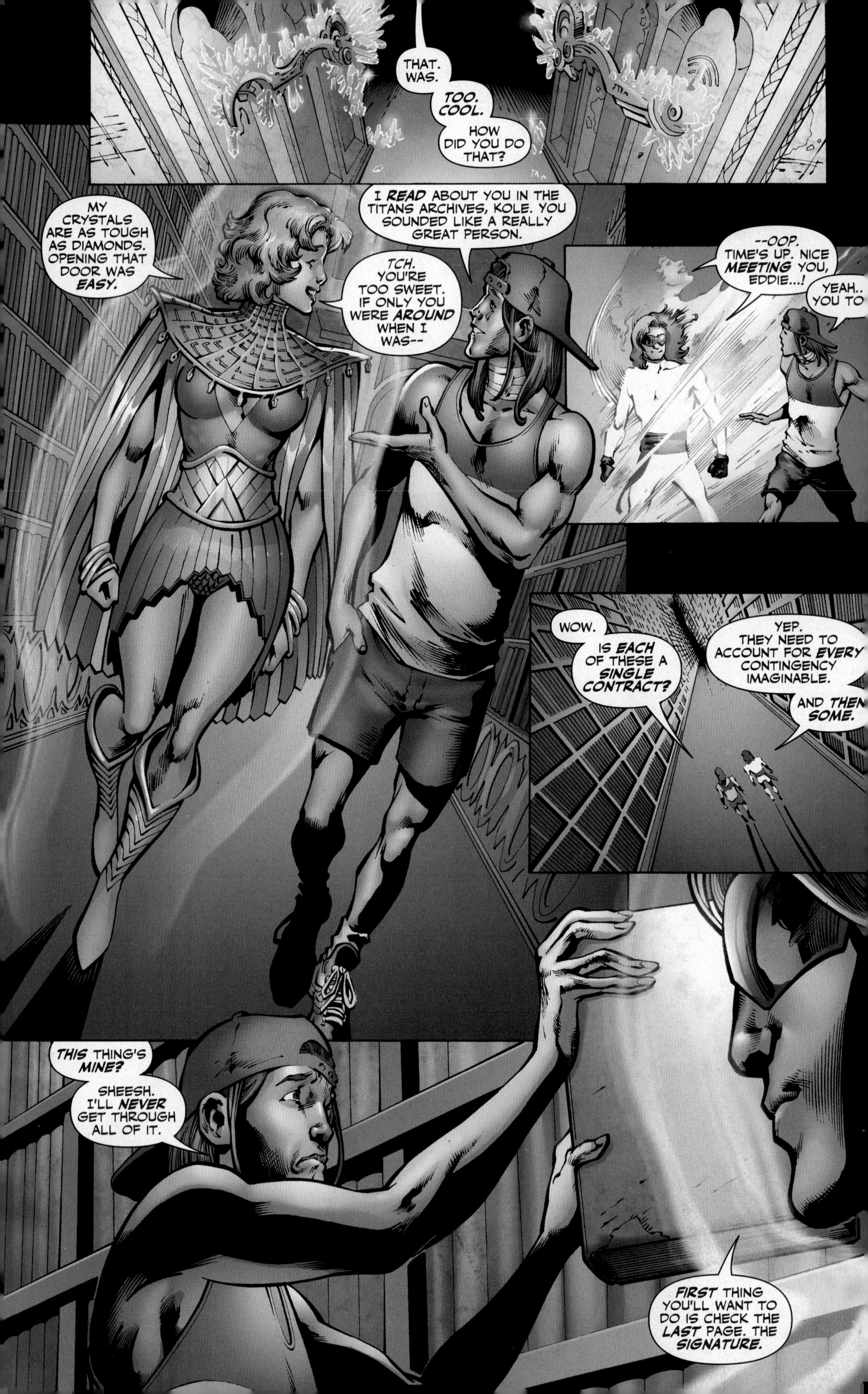
THAT. WAS. TOO. COOL.
HOW DID YOU DO THAT?
MY CRYSTALS ARE AS TOUGH AS DIAMONDS. OPENING THAT DOOR WAS EASY.
I READ ABOUT YOU IN THE TITANS ARCHIVES, KOLE. YOU SOUNDED LIKE A REALLY GREAT PERSON.
TCH. YOU'RE TOO SWEET. IF ONLY YOU WERE AROUND WHEN I WAS--
--OOP. TIME'S UP. NICE MEETING YOU, EDDIE...!
YEAH.. YOU TO
WOW.
IS EACH OF THESE A SINGLE CONTRACT?
YEP. THEY NEED TO ACCOUNT FOR EVERY CONTINGENCY IMAGINABLE.
AND THEN SOME.
THIS THING'S MINE?
SHEESH. I'LL NEVER GET THROUGH ALL OF IT.
FIRST THING YOU'LL WANT TO DO IS CHECK THE LAST PAGE. THE SIGNATURE.

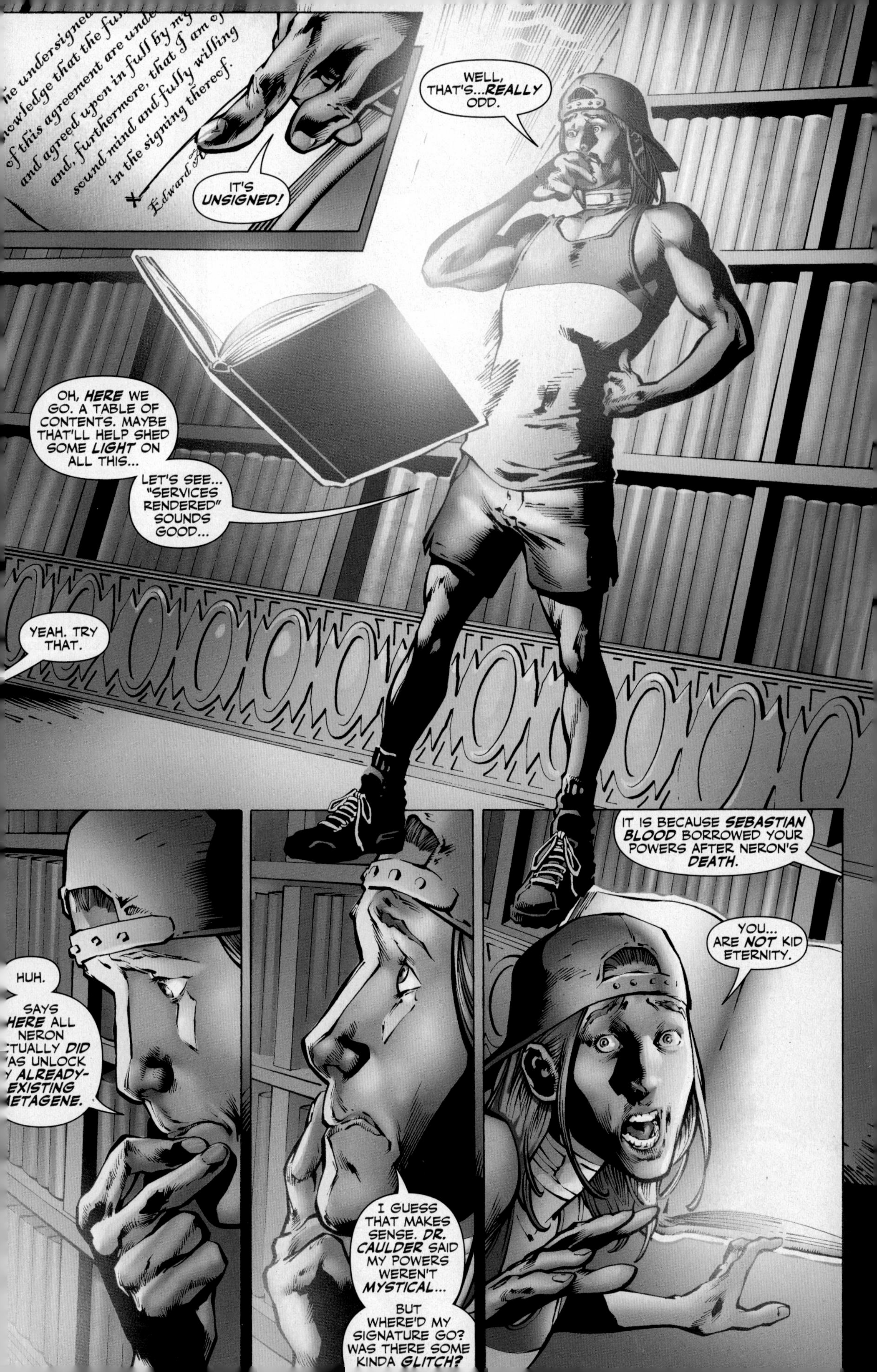

...the undersigned... acknowledge that the fu... of this agreement are unde... and agreed upon in full by my... and, furthermore, that I am of sound mind and fully willing in the signing thereof.
Edward
IT'S UNSIGNED!
WELL, THAT'S...REALLY ODD.
OH, HERE WE GO. A TABLE OF CONTENTS. MAYBE THAT'LL HELP SHED SOME LIGHT ON ALL THIS...
LET'S SEE... "SERVICES RENDERED" SOUNDS GOOD...
YEAH. TRY THAT.
HUH.
SAYS HERE ALL NERON ACTUALLY DID WAS UNLOCK MY ALREADY-EXISTING METAGENE.
I GUESS THAT MAKES SENSE. DR. CAULDER SAID MY POWERS WEREN'T MYSTICAL...
BUT WHERE'D MY SIGNATURE GO? WAS THERE SOME KINDA GLITCH?
IT IS BECAUSE SEBASTIAN BLOOD BORROWED YOUR POWERS AFTER NERON'S DEATH.
YOU... ARE NOT KID ETERNITY.

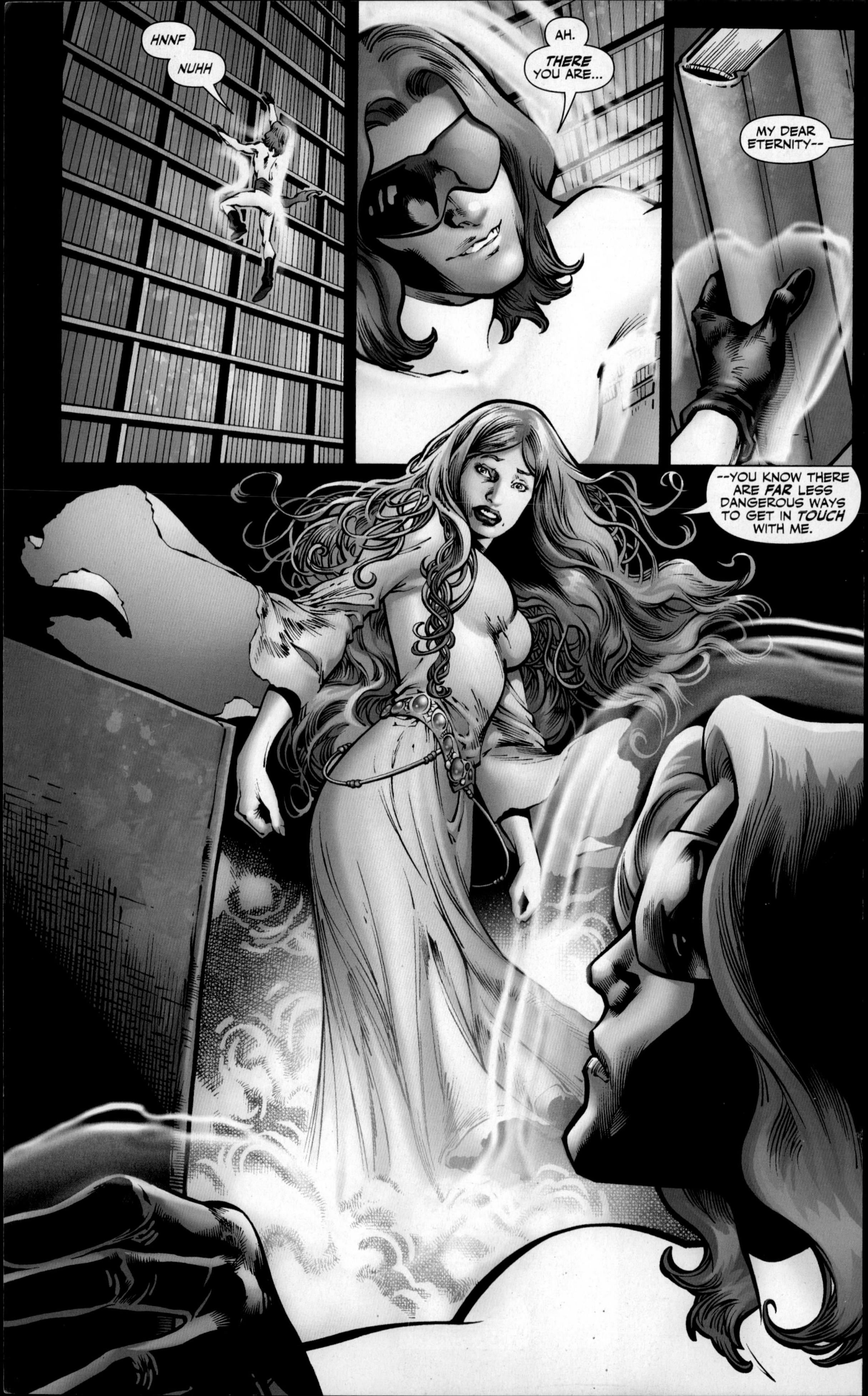
HNNF
NUHH
AH. THERE YOU ARE...
MY DEAR ETERNITY--
--YOU KNOW THERE ARE FAR LESS DANGEROUS WAYS TO GET IN TOUCH WITH ME.

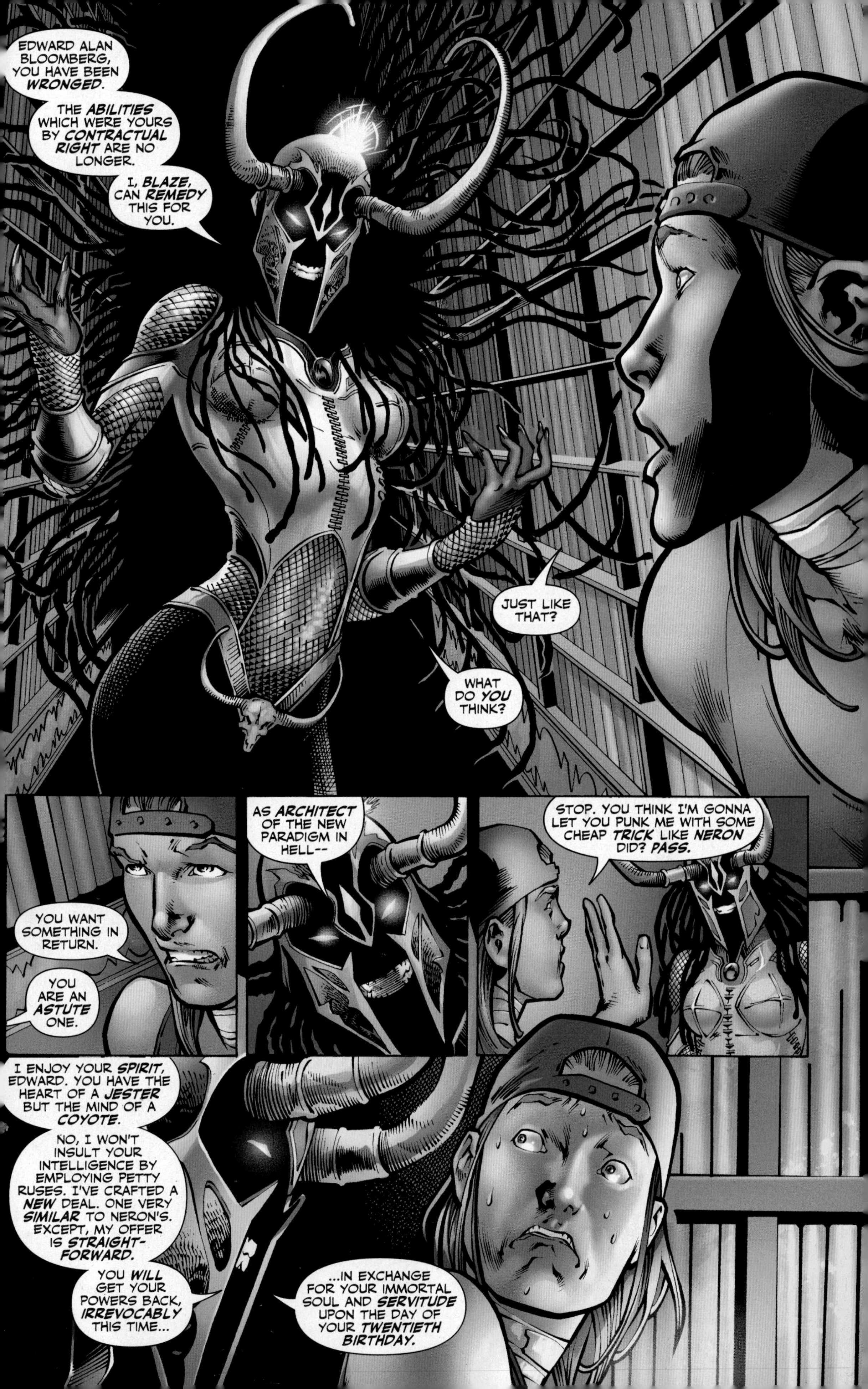

EDWARD ALAN BLOOMBERG, YOU HAVE BEEN WRONGED.
THE ABILITIES WHICH WERE YOURS BY CONTRACTUAL RIGHT ARE NO LONGER.
I, BLAZE, CAN REMEDY THIS FOR YOU.
JUST LIKE THAT?
WHAT DO YOU THINK?
YOU WANT SOMETHING IN RETURN.
YOU ARE AN ASTUTE ONE.
AS ARCHITECT OF THE NEW PARADIGM IN HELL--
STOP. YOU THINK I'M GONNA LET YOU PUNK ME WITH SOME CHEAP TRICK LIKE NERON DID? PASS.
I ENJOY YOUR SPIRIT, EDWARD. YOU HAVE THE HEART OF A JESTER BUT THE MIND OF A COYOTE.
NO, I WON'T INSULT YOUR INTELLIGENCE BY EMPLOYING PETTY RUSES. I'VE CRAFTED A NEW DEAL. ONE VERY SIMILAR TO NERON'S. EXCEPT, MY OFFER IS STRAIGHT-FORWARD.
YOU WILL GET YOUR POWERS BACK, IRREVOCABLY THIS TIME...
...IN EXCHANGE FOR YOUR IMMORTAL SOUL AND SERVITUDE UPON THE DAY OF YOUR TWENTIETH BIRTHDAY.

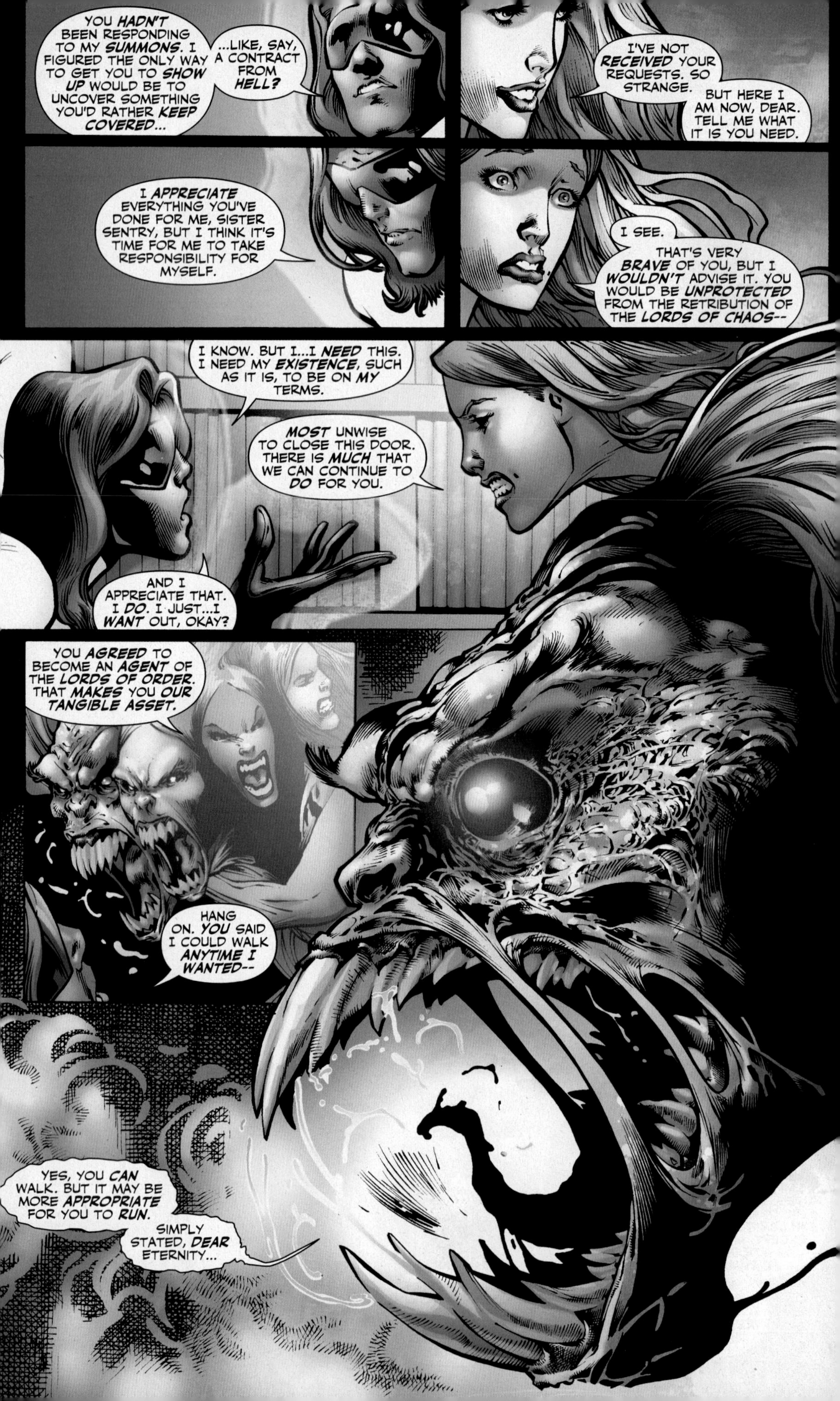
YOU HADN'T BEEN RESPONDING TO MY SUMMONS. I FIGURED THE ONLY WAY TO GET YOU TO SHOW UP WOULD BE TO UNCOVER SOMETHING YOU'D RATHER KEEP COVERED...
...LIKE, SAY, A CONTRACT FROM HELL?
I'VE NOT RECEIVED YOUR REQUESTS. SO STRANGE.
BUT HERE I AM NOW, DEAR. TELL ME WHAT IT IS YOU NEED.
I APPRECIATE EVERYTHING YOU'VE DONE FOR ME, SISTER SENTRY, BUT I THINK IT'S TIME FOR ME TO TAKE RESPONSIBILITY FOR MYSELF.
I SEE.
THAT'S VERY BRAVE OF YOU, BUT I WOULDN'T ADVISE IT. YOU WOULD BE UNPROTECTED FROM THE RETRIBUTION OF THE LORDS OF CHAOS--
I KNOW. BUT I...I NEED THIS. I NEED MY EXISTENCE, SUCH AS IT IS, TO BE ON MY TERMS.
MOST UNWISE TO CLOSE THIS DOOR. THERE IS MUCH THAT WE CAN CONTINUE TO DO FOR YOU.
AND I APPRECIATE THAT. I DO. I JUST...I WANT OUT, OKAY?
YOU AGREED TO BECOME AN AGENT OF THE LORDS OF ORDER. THAT MAKES YOU OUR TANGIBLE ASSET.
HANG ON. YOU SAID I COULD WALK ANYTIME I WANTED--
YES, YOU CAN WALK. BUT IT MAY BE MORE APPROPRIATE FOR YOU TO RUN.
SIMPLY STATED, DEAR ETERNITY...

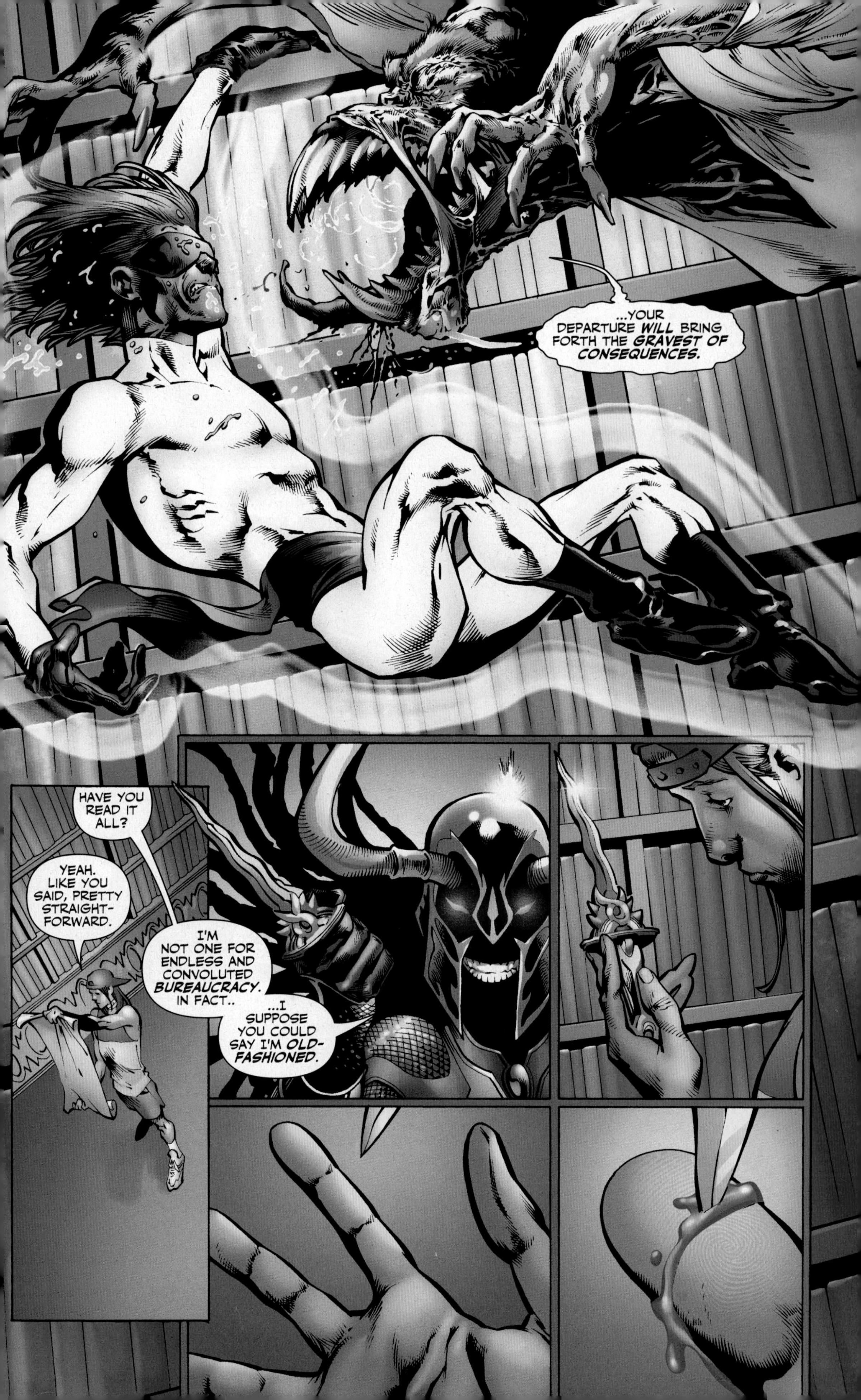
...YOUR DEPARTURE WILL BRING FORTH THE GRAVEST OF CONSEQUENCES.
HAVE YOU READ IT ALL?
YEAH. LIKE YOU SAID, PRETTY STRAIGHT-FORWARD.
I'M NOT ONE FOR ENDLESS AND CONVOLUTED BUREAUCRACY. IN FACT..
...I SUPPOSE YOU COULD SAY I'M OLD-FASHIONED.

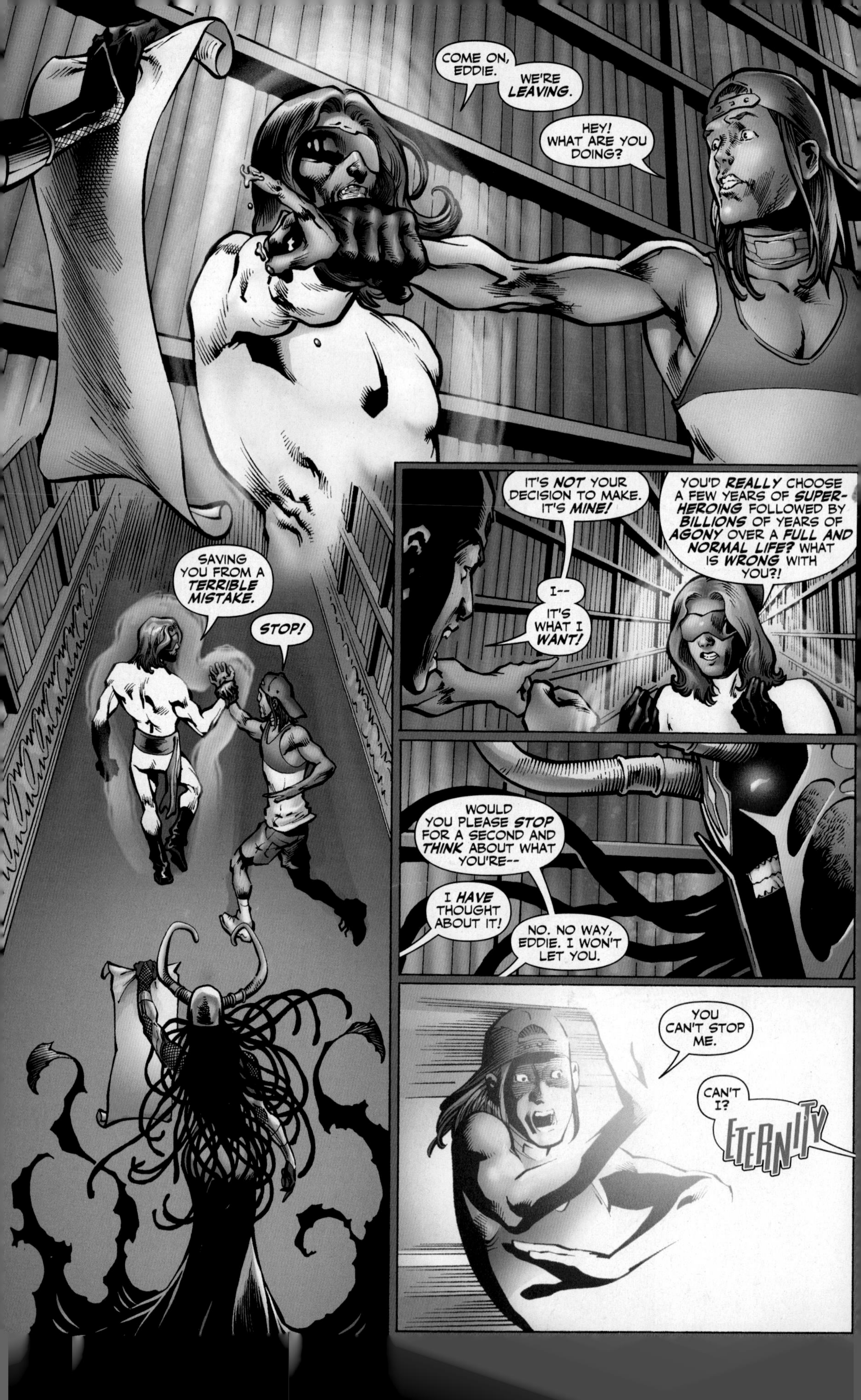
COME ON, EDDIE.
WE'RE LEAVING.
HEY! WHAT ARE YOU DOING?
SAVING YOU FROM A TERRIBLE MISTAKE.
STOP!
IT'S NOT YOUR DECISION TO MAKE. IT'S MINE!
YOU'D REALLY CHOOSE A FEW YEARS OF SUPER-HEROING FOLLOWED BY BILLIONS OF YEARS OF AGONY OVER A FULL AND NORMAL LIFE? WHAT IS WRONG WITH YOU?!
I--
IT'S WHAT I WANT!
WOULD YOU PLEASE STOP FOR A SECOND AND THINK ABOUT WHAT YOU'RE--
I HAVE THOUGHT ABOUT IT!
NO. NO WAY, EDDIE. I WON'T LET YOU.
YOU CAN'T STOP ME.
CAN'T I?
ETERNITY

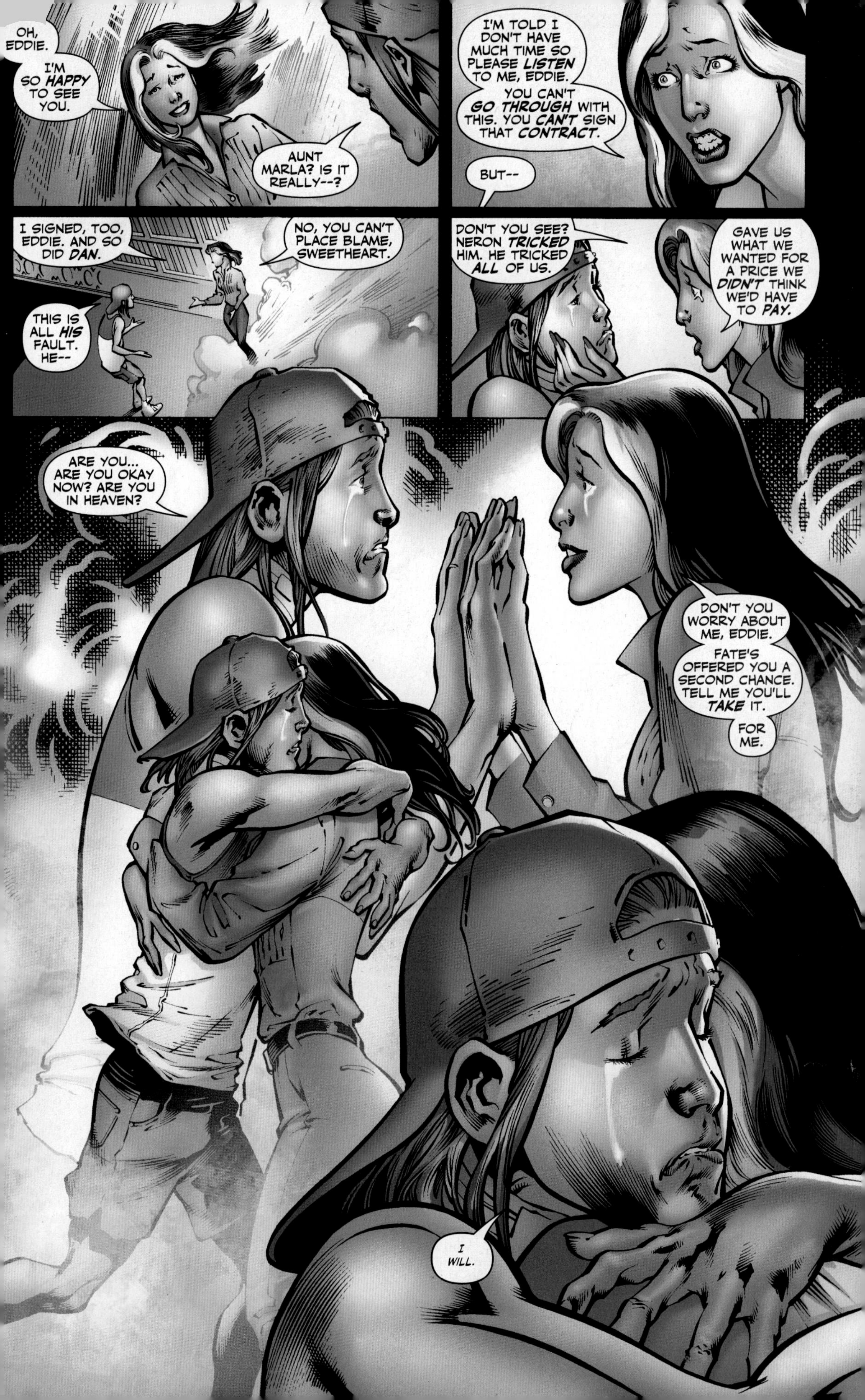
OH, EDDIE.
I'M SO HAPPY TO SEE YOU.
AUNT MARLA? IS IT REALLY--?
I'M TOLD I DON'T HAVE MUCH TIME SO PLEASE LISTEN TO ME, EDDIE.
YOU CAN'T GO THROUGH WITH THIS. YOU CAN'T SIGN THAT CONTRACT.
BUT--
I SIGNED, TOO, EDDIE. AND SO DID DAN.
THIS IS ALL HIS FAULT. HE--
NO, YOU CAN'T PLACE BLAME, SWEETHEART.
DON'T YOU SEE? NERON TRICKED HIM. HE TRICKED ALL OF US.
GAVE US WHAT WE WANTED FOR A PRICE WE DIDN'T THINK WE'D HAVE TO PAY.
ARE YOU... ARE YOU OKAY NOW? ARE YOU IN HEAVEN?
DON'T YOU WORRY ABOUT ME, EDDIE.
FATE'S OFFERED YOU A SECOND CHANCE. TELL ME YOU'LL TAKE IT.
FOR ME.
I WILL.

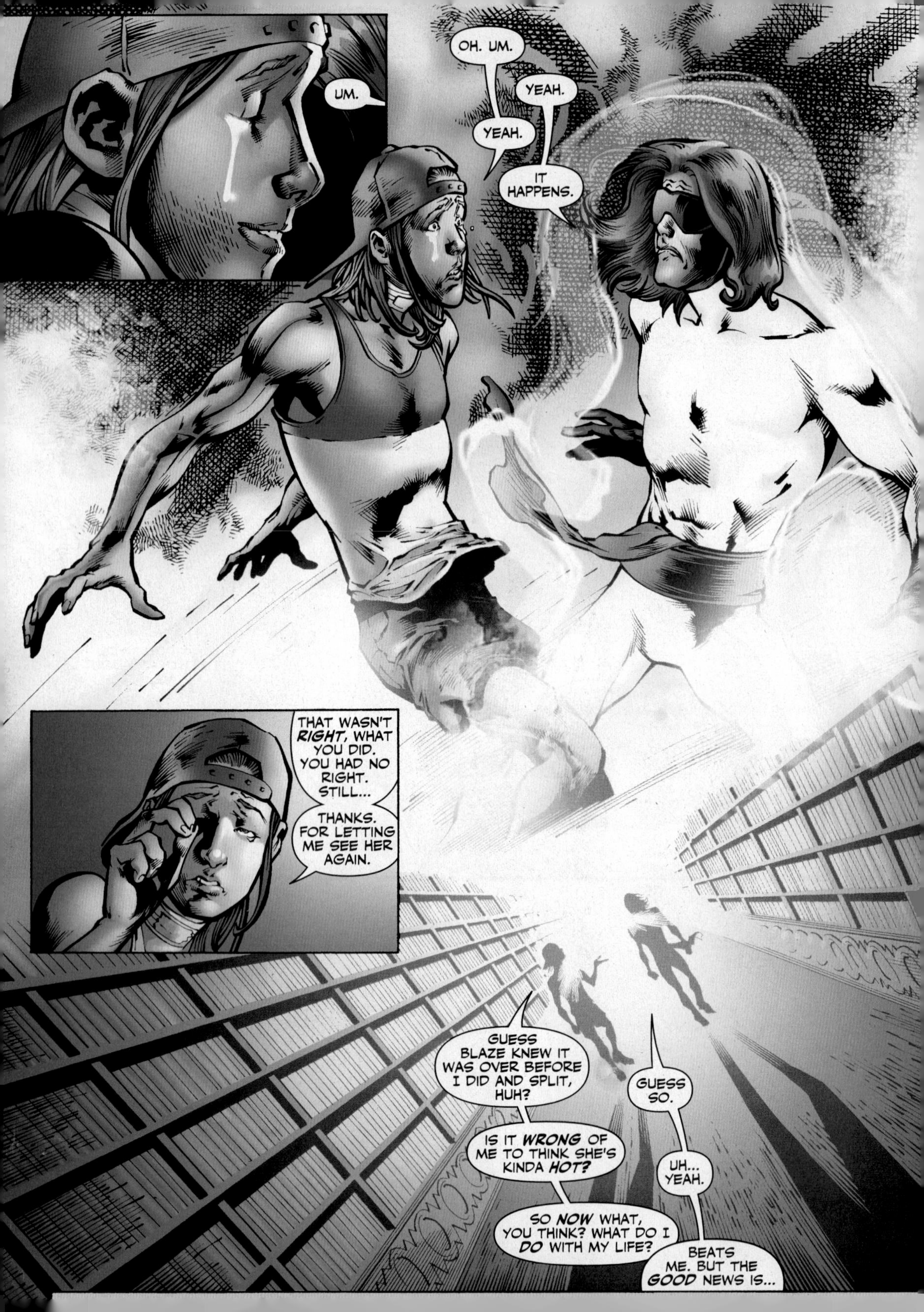
UM.
OH. UM.
YEAH.
YEAH.
IT HAPPENS.
THAT WASN'T RIGHT, WHAT YOU DID. YOU HAD NO RIGHT. STILL...
THANKS. FOR LETTING ME SEE HER AGAIN.
GUESS BLAZE KNEW IT WAS OVER BEFORE I DID AND SPLIT, HUH?
GUESS SO.
IS IT WRONG OF ME TO THINK SHE'S KINDA HOT?
UH... YEAH.
SO NOW WHAT, YOU THINK? WHAT DO I DO WITH MY LIFE?
BEATS ME. BUT THE GOOD NEWS IS...

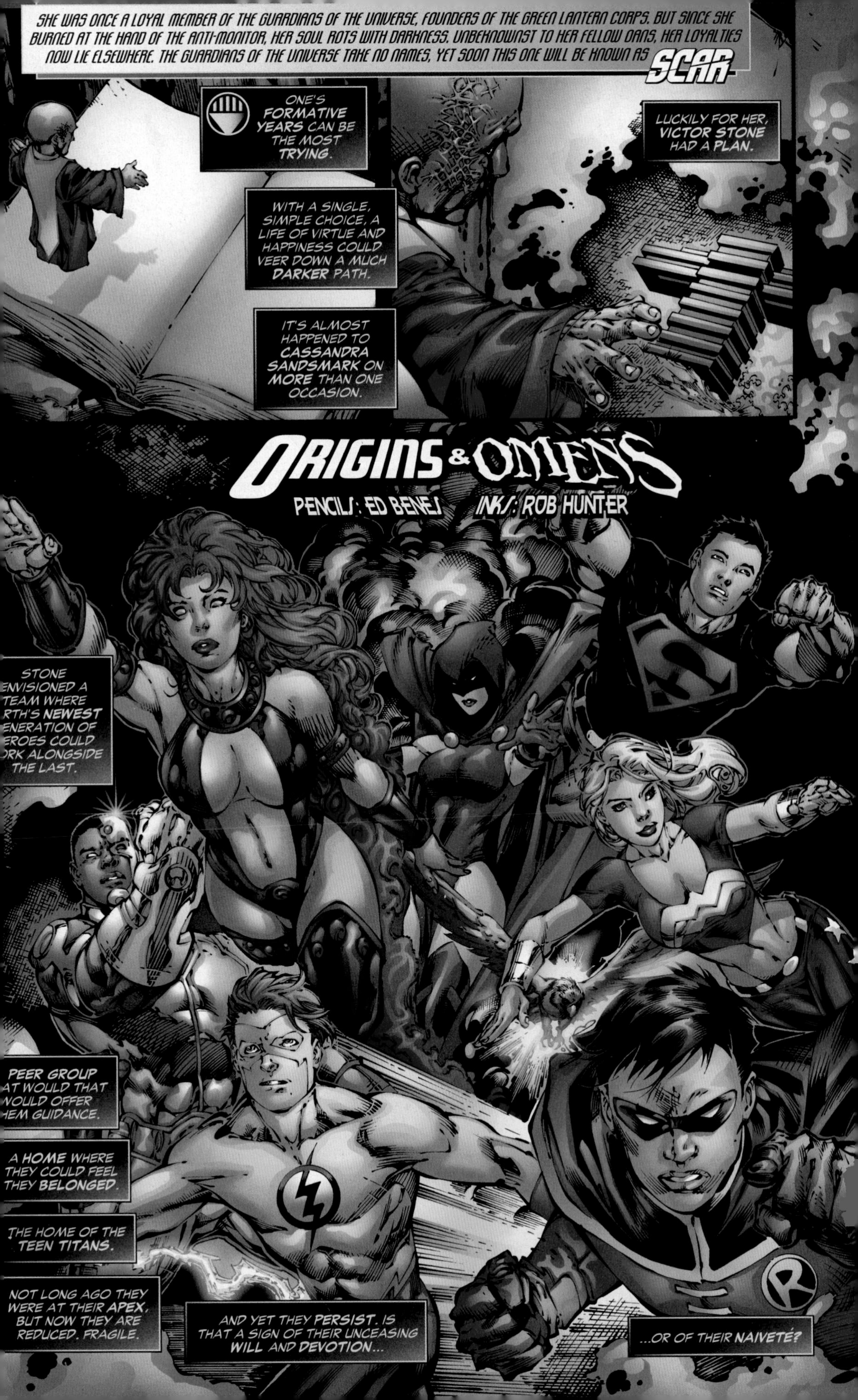
SHE WAS ONCE A LOYAL MEMBER OF THE GUARDIANS OF THE UNIVERSE, FOUNDERS OF THE GREEN LANTERN CORPS. BUT SINCE SHE BURNED AT THE HAND OF THE ANTI-MONITOR, HER SOUL ROTS WITH DARKNESS. UNBEKNOWNST TO HER FELLOW OANS, HER LOYALTIES NOW LIE ELSEWHERE. THE GUARDIANS OF THE UNIVERSE TAKE NO NAMES, YET SOON THIS ONE WILL BE KNOWN AS SCAR
ONE'S FORMATIVE YEARS CAN BE THE MOST TRYING.
WITH A SINGLE, SIMPLE CHOICE, A LIFE OF VIRTUE AND HAPPINESS COULD VEER DOWN A MUCH DARKER PATH.
IT'S ALMOST HAPPENED TO CASSANDRA SANDSMARK ON MORE THAN ONE OCCASION.
LUCKILY FOR HER, VICTOR STONE HAD A PLAN.
ORIGINS & OMENS
PENCILS: ED BENES INKS: ROB HUNTER
STONE ENVISIONED A TEAM WHERE RTH'S NEWEST ENERATION OF EROES COULD ORK ALONGSIDE THE LAST.
PEER GROUP AT WOULD THAT WOULD OFFER HEM GUIDANCE.
A HOME WHERE THEY COULD FEEL THEY BELONGED.
THE HOME OF THE TEEN TITANS.
NOT LONG AGO THEY WERE AT THEIR APEX, BUT NOW THEY ARE REDUCED. FRAGILE.
AND YET THEY PERSIST. IS THAT A SIGN OF THEIR UNCEASING WILL AND DEVOTION...
...OR OF THEIR NAIVETÉ?

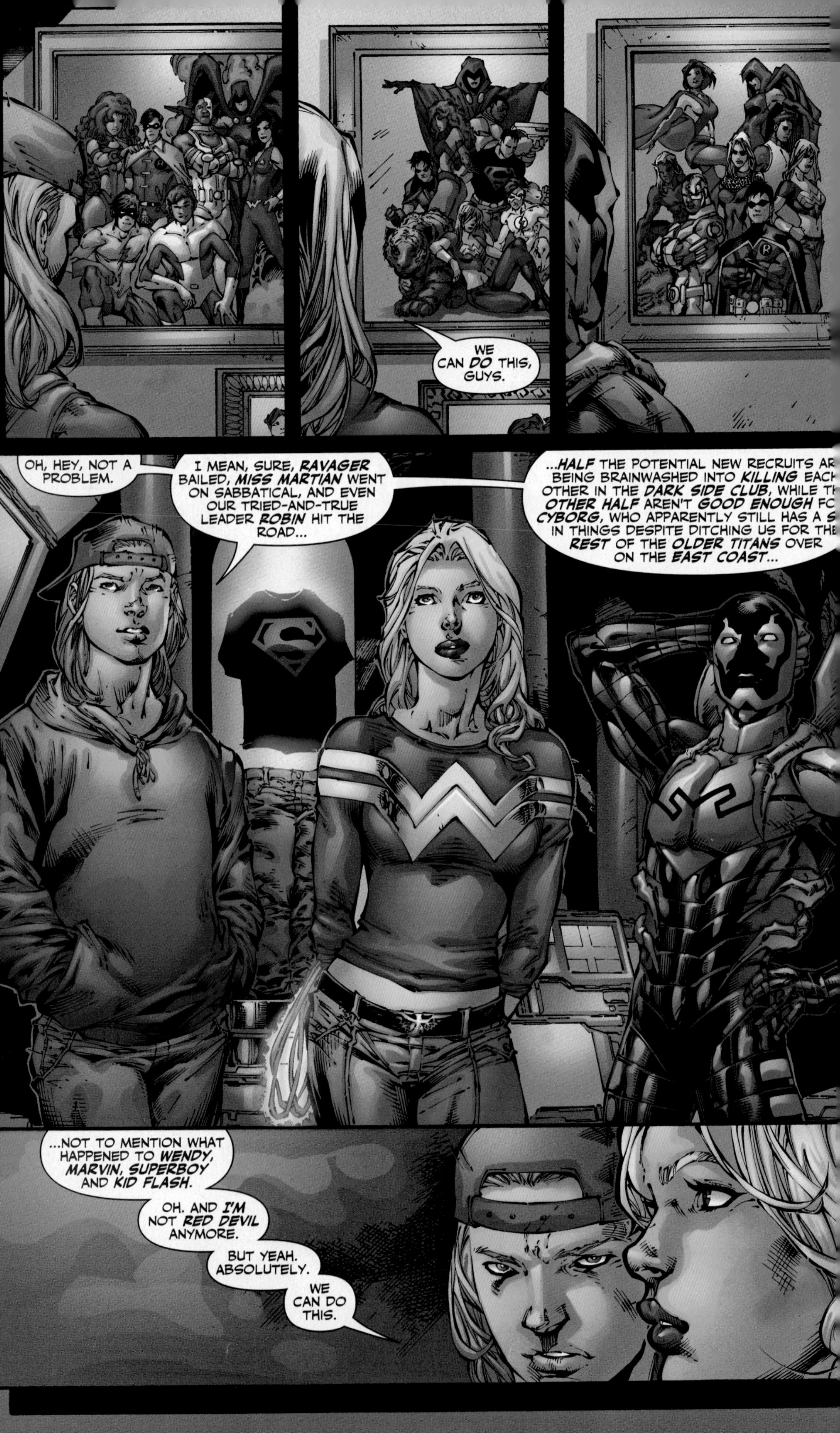
WE CAN DO THIS, GUYS.
OH, HEY, NOT A PROBLEM.
I MEAN, SURE, RAVAGER BAILED, MISS MARTIAN WENT ON SABBATICAL, AND EVEN OUR TRIED-AND-TRUE LEADER ROBIN HIT THE ROAD...
...HALF THE POTENTIAL NEW RECRUITS AR BEING BRAINWASHED INTO KILLING EACH OTHER IN THE DARK SIDE CLUB, WHILE TH OTHER HALF AREN'T GOOD ENOUGH FO CYBORG, WHO APPARENTLY STILL HAS A S IN THINGS DESPITE DITCHING US FOR THE REST OF THE OLDER TITANS OVER ON THE EAST COAST...
...NOT TO MENTION WHAT HAPPENED TO WENDY, MARVIN, SUPERBOY AND KID FLASH.
OH. AND I'M NOT RED DEVIL ANYMORE.
BUT YEAH. ABSOLUTELY.
WE CAN DO THIS.

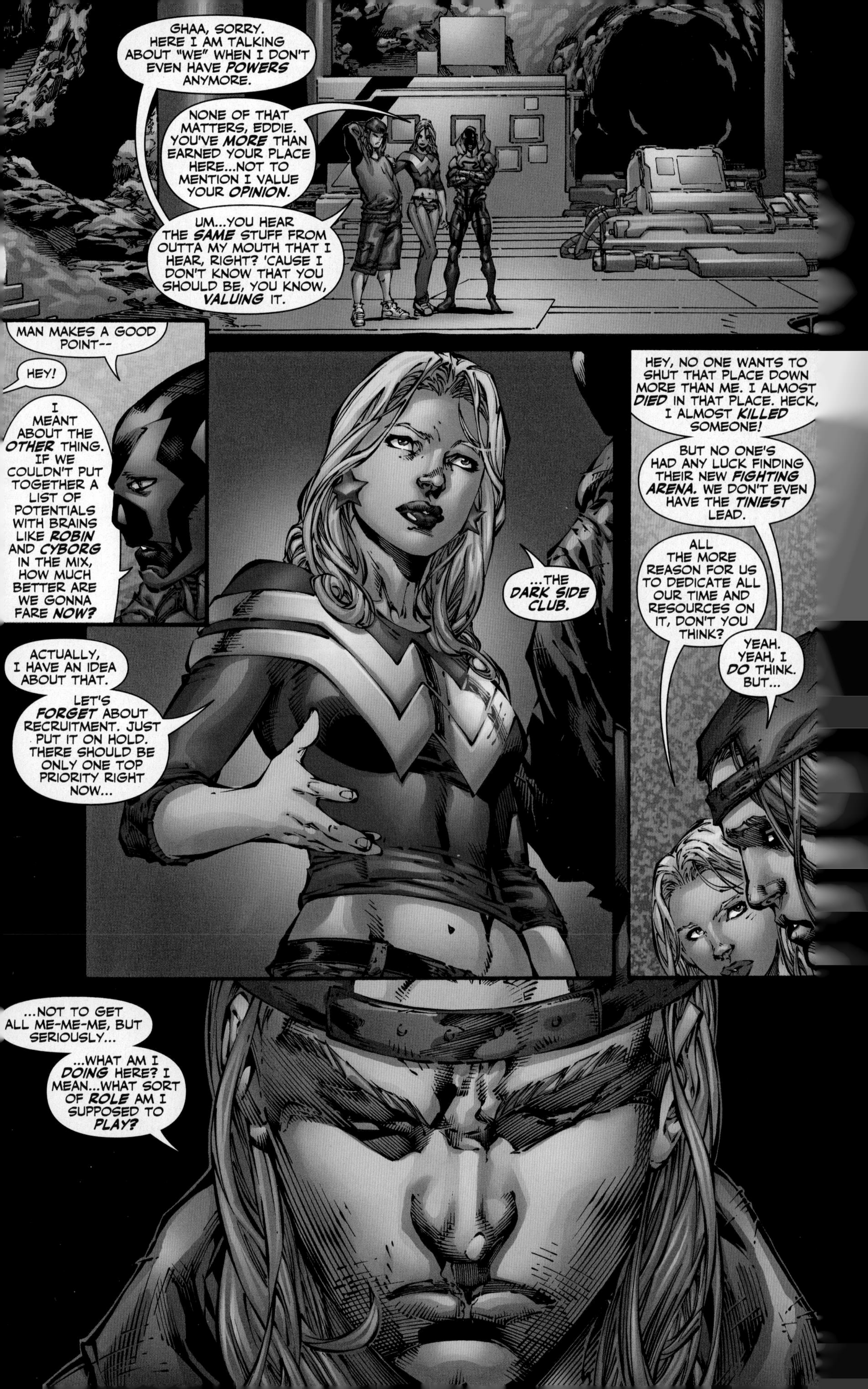
GHAA, SORRY. HERE I AM TALKING ABOUT "WE" WHEN I DON'T EVEN HAVE POWERS ANYMORE.
NONE OF THAT MATTERS, EDDIE. YOU'VE MORE THAN EARNED YOUR PLACE HERE...NOT TO MENTION I VALUE YOUR OPINION.
UM...YOU HEAR THE SAME STUFF FROM OUTTA MY MOUTH THAT I HEAR, RIGHT? 'CAUSE I DON'T KNOW THAT YOU SHOULD BE, YOU KNOW, VALUING IT.
MAN MAKES A GOOD POINT--
HEY!
I MEANT ABOUT THE OTHER THING. IF WE COULDN'T PUT TOGETHER A LIST OF POTENTIALS WITH BRAINS LIKE ROBIN AND CYBORG IN THE MIX, HOW MUCH BETTER ARE WE GONNA FARE NOW?
ACTUALLY, I HAVE AN IDEA ABOUT THAT.
LET'S FORGET ABOUT RECRUITMENT. JUST PUT IT ON HOLD. THERE SHOULD BE ONLY ONE TOP PRIORITY RIGHT NOW...
...THE DARK SIDE CLUB.
HEY, NO ONE WANTS TO SHUT THAT PLACE DOWN MORE THAN ME. I ALMOST DIED IN THAT PLACE. HECK, I ALMOST KILLED SOMEONE!
BUT NO ONE'S HAD ANY LUCK FINDING THEIR NEW FIGHTING ARENA. WE DON'T EVEN HAVE THE TINIEST LEAD.
ALL THE MORE REASON FOR US TO DEDICATE ALL OUR TIME AND RESOURCES ON IT, DON'T YOU THINK?
YEAH. YEAH, I DO THINK. BUT...
...NOT TO GET ALL ME-ME-ME, BUT SERIOUSLY...
...WHAT AM I DOING HERE? I MEAN...WHAT SORT OF ROLE AM I SUPPOSED TO PLAY?

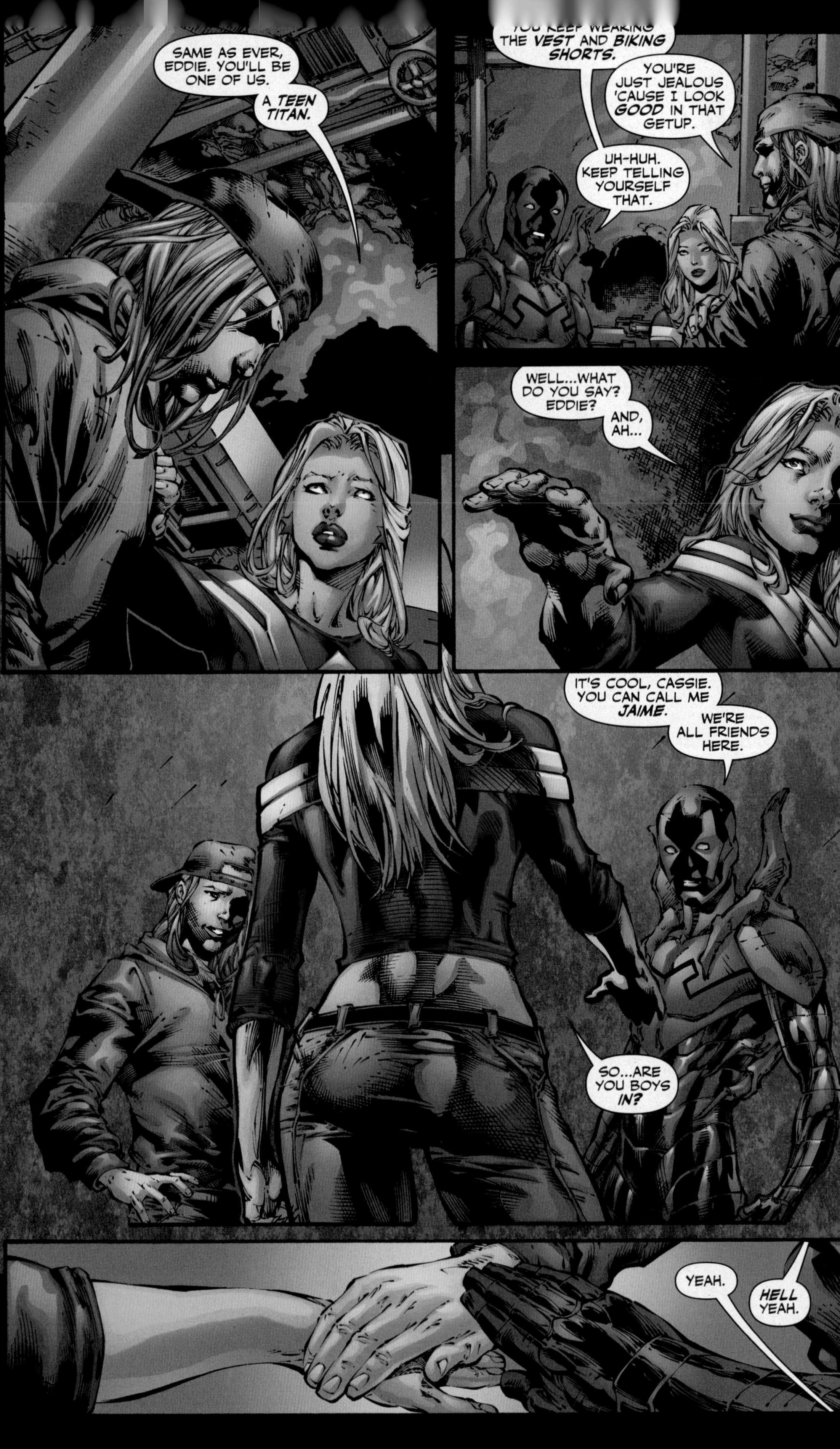
SAME AS EVER, EDDIE. YOU'LL BE ONE OF US.
A TEEN TITAN.
YOU KEEP WEARING THE VEST AND BIKING SHORTS.
YOU'RE JUST JEALOUS 'CAUSE I LOOK GOOD IN THAT GETUP.
UH-HUH. KEEP TELLING YOURSELF THAT.
WELL...WHAT DO YOU SAY? EDDIE?
AND, AH...
IT'S COOL, CASSIE. YOU CAN CALL ME JAIME.
WE'RE ALL FRIENDS HERE.
SO...ARE YOU BOYS IN?
YEAH.
HELL YEAH.

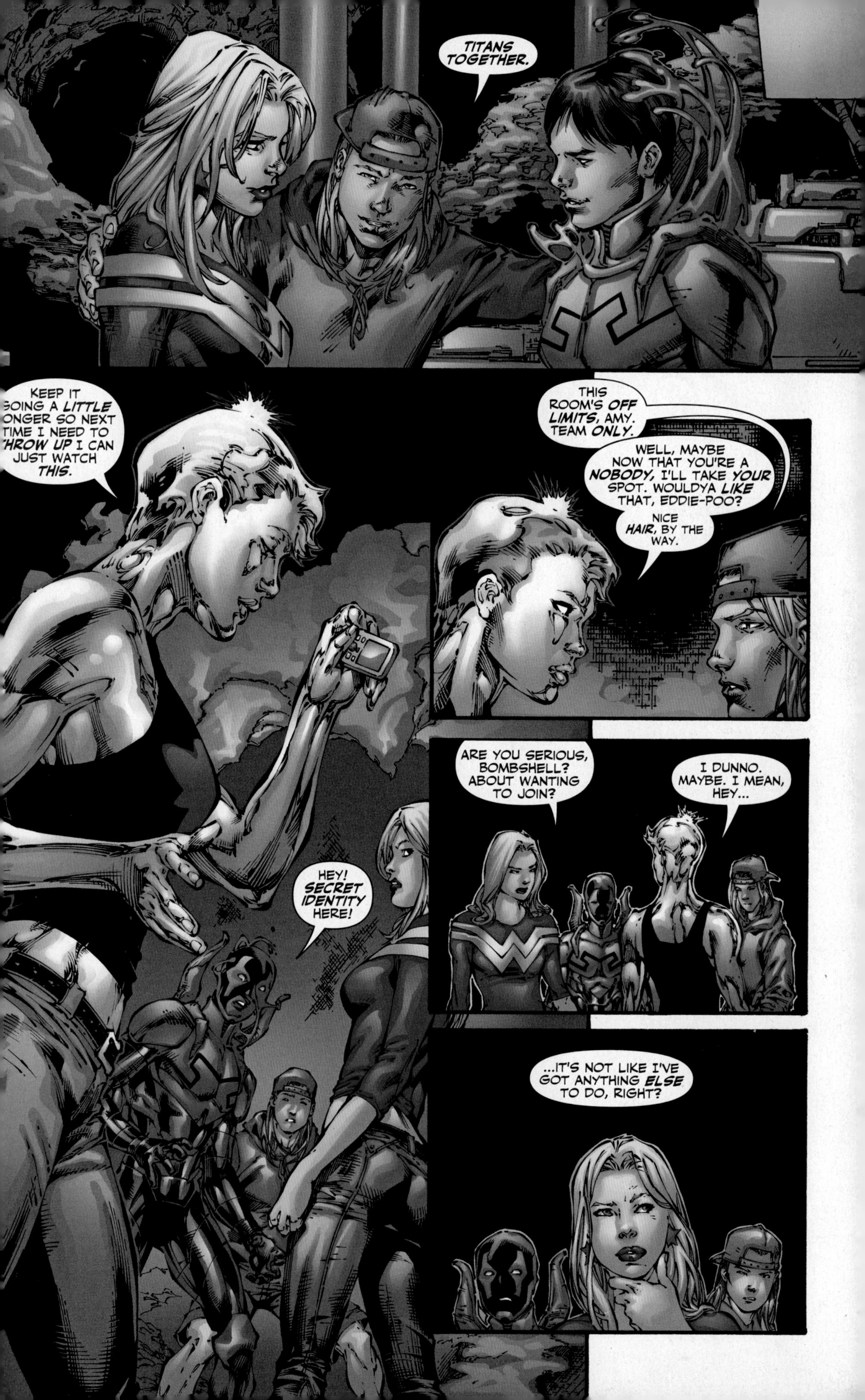
TITANS TOGETHER.
KEEP IT GOING A LITTLE LONGER SO NEXT TIME I NEED TO THROW UP I CAN JUST WATCH THIS.
THIS ROOM'S OFF LIMITS, AMY. TEAM ONLY.
WELL, MAYBE NOW THAT YOU'RE A NOBODY, I'LL TAKE YOUR SPOT. WOULDYA LIKE THAT, EDDIE-POO?
NICE HAIR, BY THE WAY.
HEY! SECRET IDENTITY HERE!
ARE YOU SERIOUS, BOMBSHELL? ABOUT WANTING TO JOIN?
I DUNNO. MAYBE. I MEAN, HEY...
...IT'S NOT LIKE I'VE GOT ANYTHING ELSE TO DO, RIGHT?

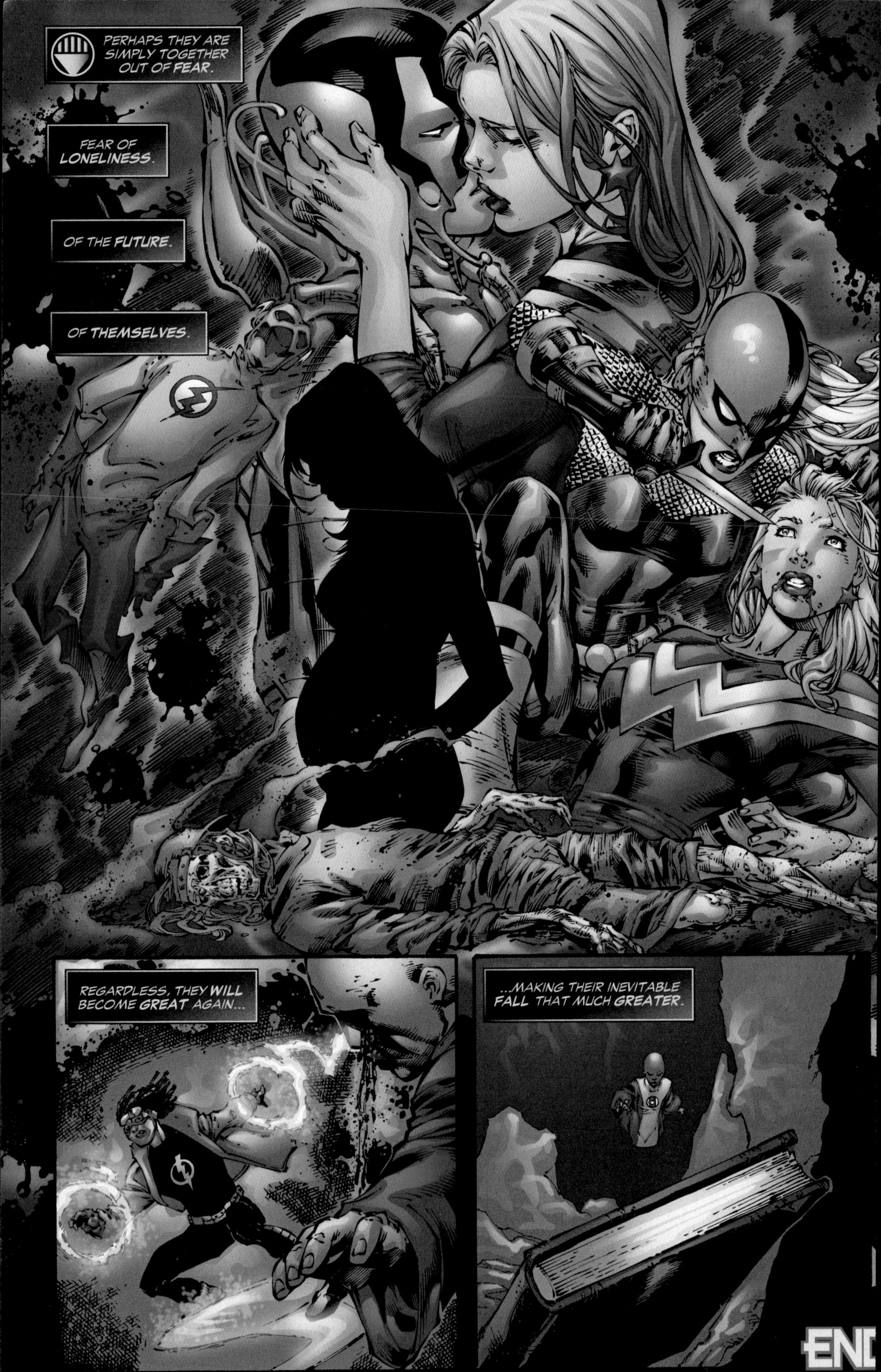
PERHAPS THEY ARE SIMPLY TOGETHER OUT OF FEAR.
FEAR OF LONELINESS.
OF THE FUTURE.
OF THEMSELVES.
REGARDLESS, THEY WILL BECOME GREAT AGAIN...
...MAKING THEIR INEVITABLE FALL THAT MUCH GREATER.
END

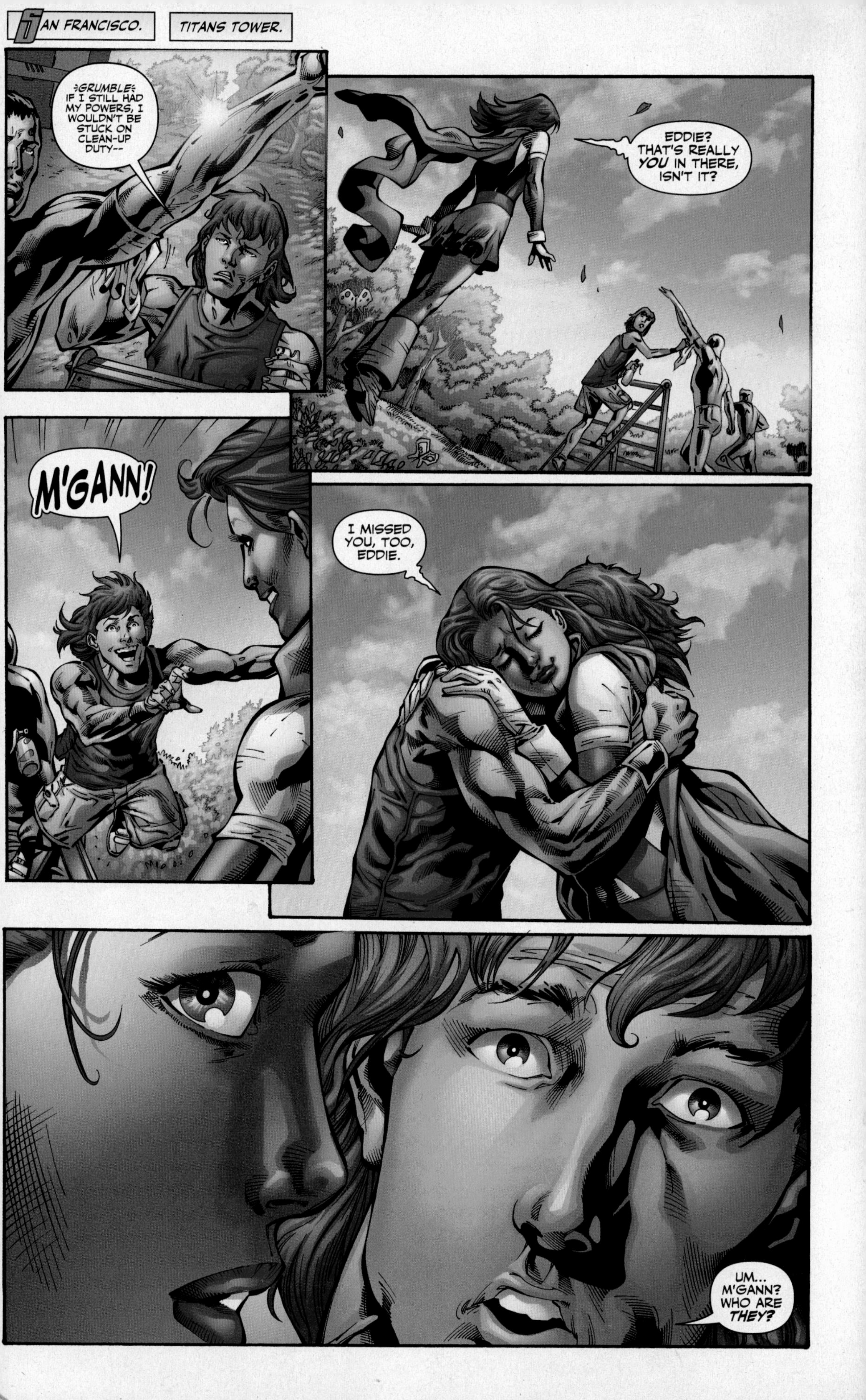
SAN FRANCISCO.
TITANS TOWER.
GRUMBLE IF I STILL HAD MY POWERS, I WOULDN'T BE STUCK ON CLEAN-UP DUTY--
EDDIE? THAT'S REALLY YOU IN THERE, ISN'T IT?
M'GANN!
I MISSED YOU, TOO, EDDIE.
UM... M'GANN? WHO ARE THEY?

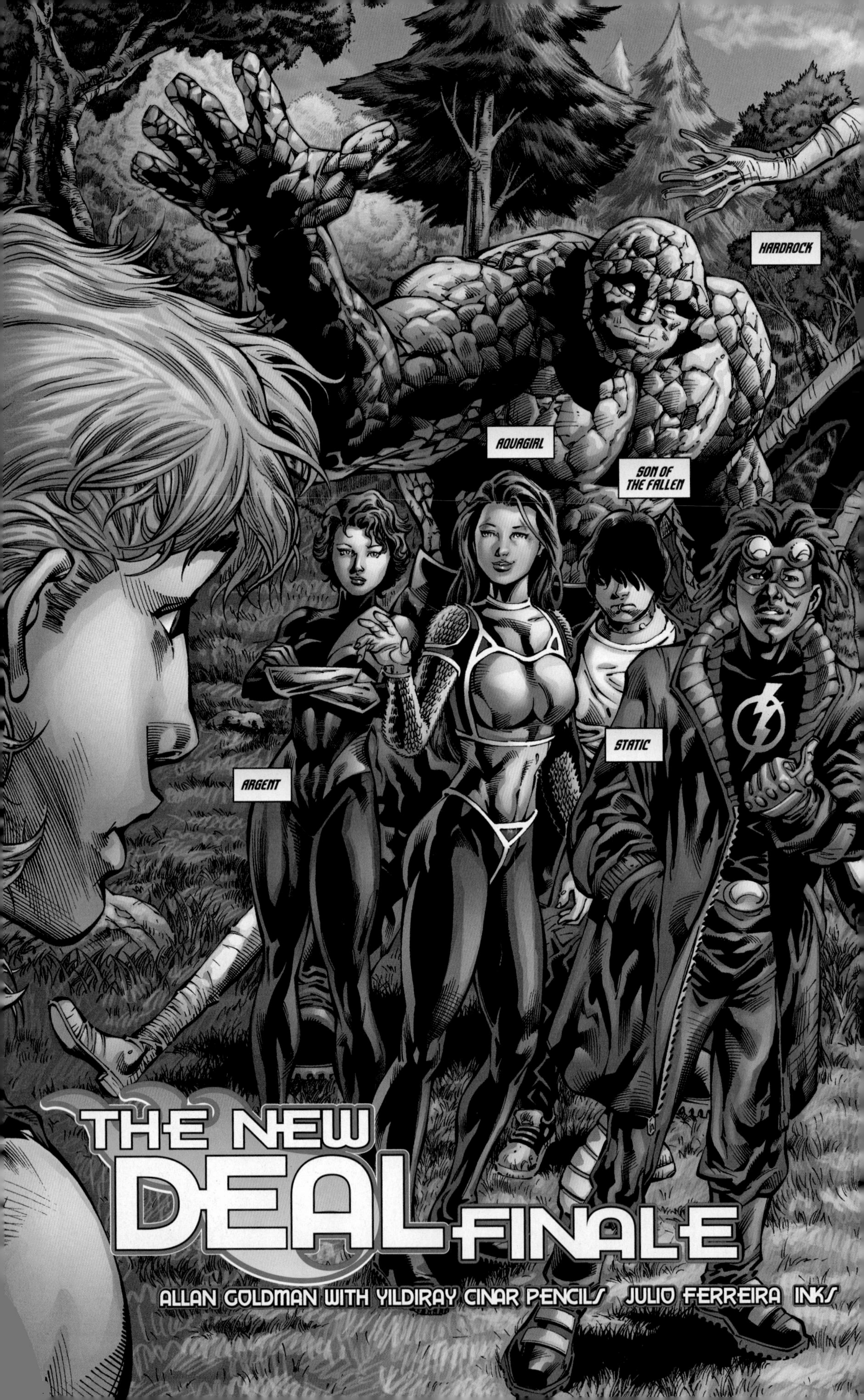
HARDROCK
AQUAGIRL
SON OF THE FALLEN
STATIC
ARGENT
THE NEW DEAL FINALE
ALLAN GOLDMAN WITH YILDIRAY CINAR PENCILS JULIO FERREIRA INKS

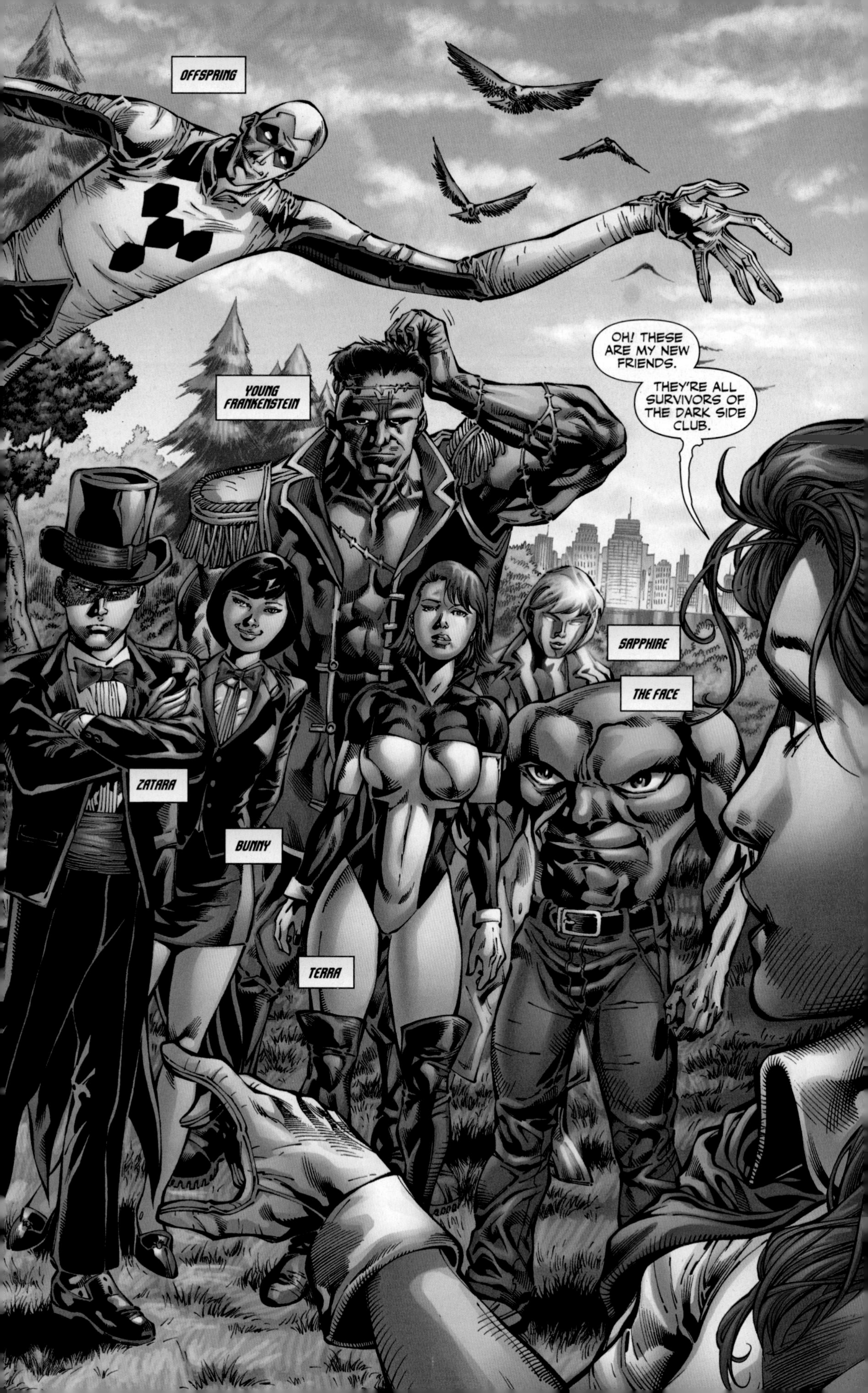
OFFSPRING
OH! THESE ARE MY NEW FRIENDS.
THEY'RE ALL SURVIVORS OF THE DARK SIDE CLUB.
YOUNG FRANKENSTEIN
SAPPHIRE
THE FACE
ZATARA
BUNNY
TERRA

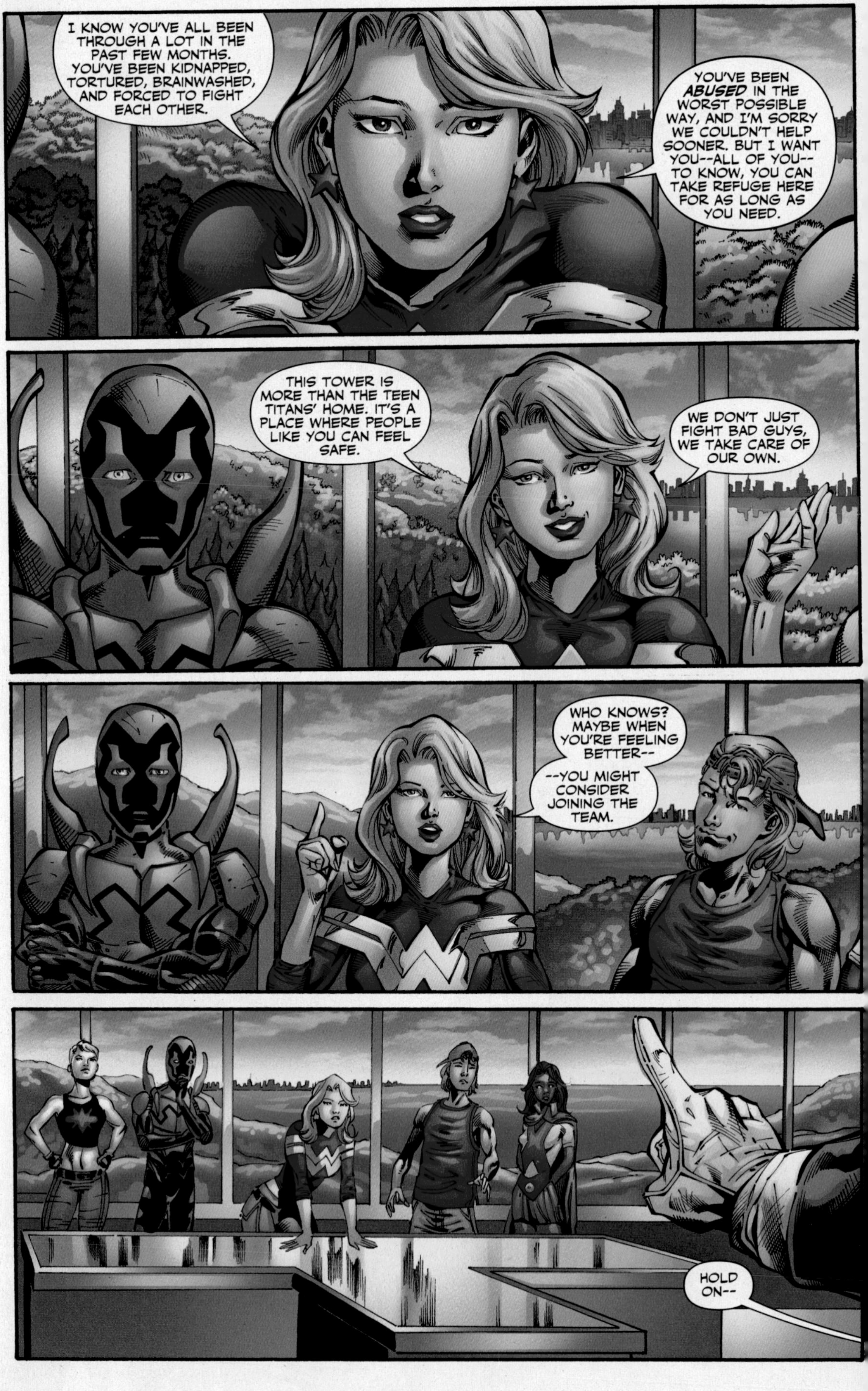
I KNOW YOU'VE ALL BEEN THROUGH A LOT IN THE PAST FEW MONTHS. YOU'VE BEEN KIDNAPPED, TORTURED, BRAINWASHED, AND FORCED TO FIGHT EACH OTHER.
YOU'VE BEEN *ABUSED* IN THE WORST POSSIBLE WAY, AND I'M SORRY WE COULDN'T HELP SOONER. BUT I WANT YOU--ALL OF YOU--TO KNOW, YOU CAN TAKE REFUGE HERE FOR AS LONG AS YOU NEED.
THIS TOWER IS MORE THAN THE TEEN TITANS' HOME. IT'S A PLACE WHERE PEOPLE LIKE YOU CAN FEEL SAFE.
WE DON'T JUST FIGHT BAD GUYS, WE TAKE CARE OF OUR OWN.
WHO KNOWS? MAYBE WHEN YOU'RE FEELING BETTER--
--YOU MIGHT CONSIDER JOINING THE TEAM.
HOLD ON--

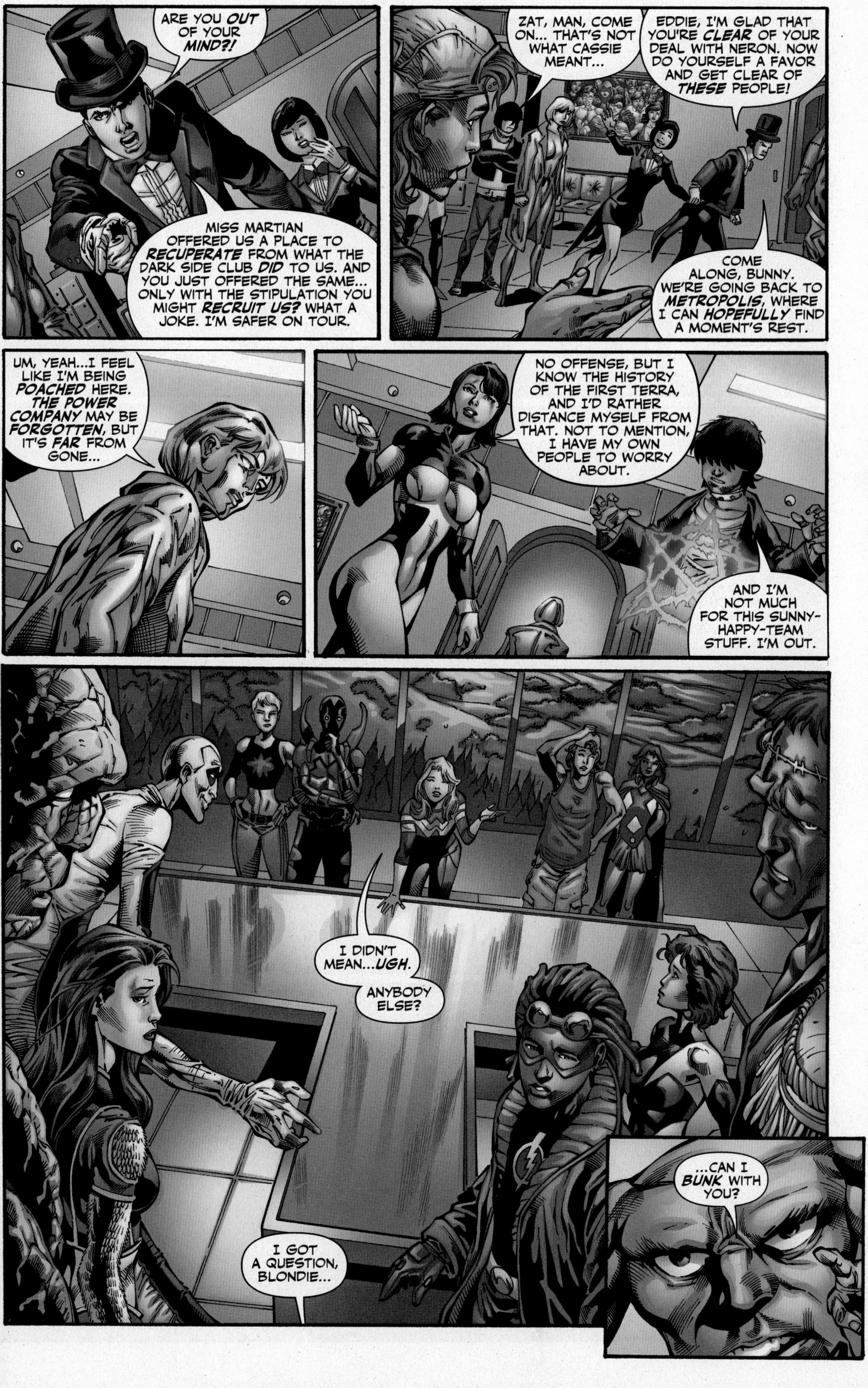
ARE YOU OUT OF YOUR MIND?!
MISS MARTIAN OFFERED US A PLACE TO RECUPERATE FROM WHAT THE DARK SIDE CLUB DID TO US. AND YOU JUST OFFERED THE SAME... ONLY WITH THE STIPULATION YOU MIGHT RECRUIT US? WHAT A JOKE. I'M SAFER ON TOUR.
ZAT, MAN, COME ON... THAT'S NOT WHAT CASSIE MEANT...
EDDIE, I'M GLAD THAT YOU'RE CLEAR OF YOUR DEAL WITH NERON. NOW DO YOURSELF A FAVOR AND GET CLEAR OF THESE PEOPLE!
COME ALONG, BUNNY. WE'RE GOING BACK TO METROPOLIS, WHERE I CAN HOPEFULLY FIND A MOMENT'S REST.
UM, YEAH...I FEEL LIKE I'M BEING POACHED HERE. THE POWER COMPANY MAY BE FORGOTTEN, BUT IT'S FAR FROM GONE...
NO OFFENSE, BUT I KNOW THE HISTORY OF THE FIRST TERRA, AND I'D RATHER DISTANCE MYSELF FROM THAT. NOT TO MENTION, I HAVE MY OWN PEOPLE TO WORRY ABOUT.
AND I'M NOT MUCH FOR THIS SUNNY-HAPPY-TEAM STUFF. I'M OUT.
I DIDN'T MEAN...UGH.
ANYBODY ELSE?
I GOT A QUESTION, BLONDIE...
...CAN I BUNK WITH YOU?

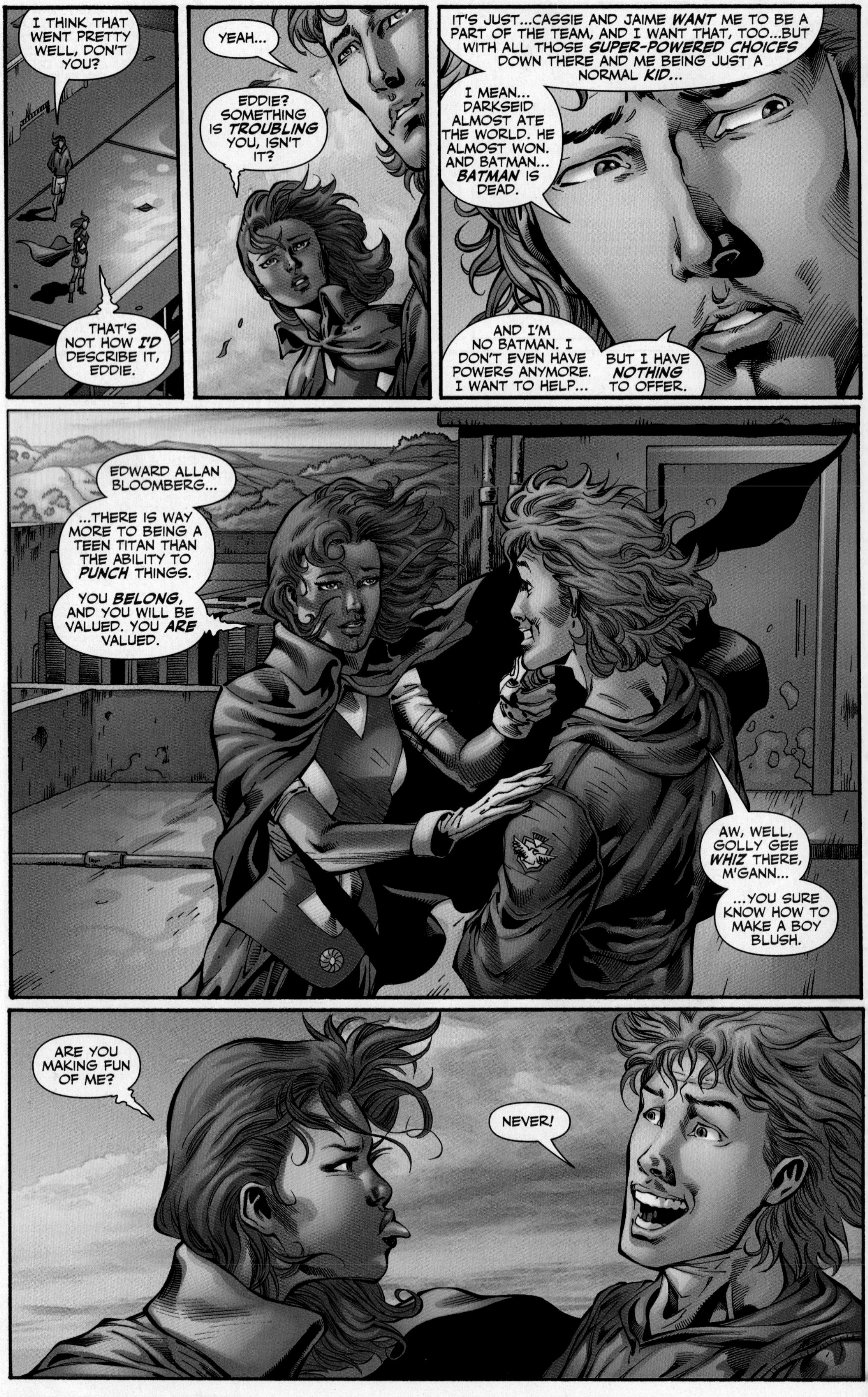
I THINK THAT WENT PRETTY WELL, DON'T YOU?
THAT'S NOT HOW I'D DESCRIBE IT, EDDIE.
YEAH...
EDDIE? SOMETHING IS TROUBLING YOU, ISN'T IT?
IT'S JUST...CASSIE AND JAIME WANT ME TO BE A PART OF THE TEAM, AND I WANT THAT, TOO...BUT WITH ALL THOSE SUPER-POWERED CHOICES DOWN THERE AND ME BEING JUST A NORMAL KID...
I MEAN... DARKSEID ALMOST ATE THE WORLD. HE ALMOST WON. AND BATMAN... BATMAN IS DEAD.
AND I'M NO BATMAN. I DON'T EVEN HAVE POWERS ANYMORE. I WANT TO HELP...
BUT I HAVE NOTHING TO OFFER.
EDWARD ALLAN BLOOMBERG...
...THERE IS WAY MORE TO BEING A TEEN TITAN THAN THE ABILITY TO PUNCH THINGS.
YOU BELONG, AND YOU WILL BE VALUED. YOU ARE VALUED.
AW, WELL, GOLLY GEE WHIZ THERE, M'GANN...
...YOU SURE KNOW HOW TO MAKE A BOY BLUSH.
ARE YOU MAKING FUN OF ME?
NEVER!

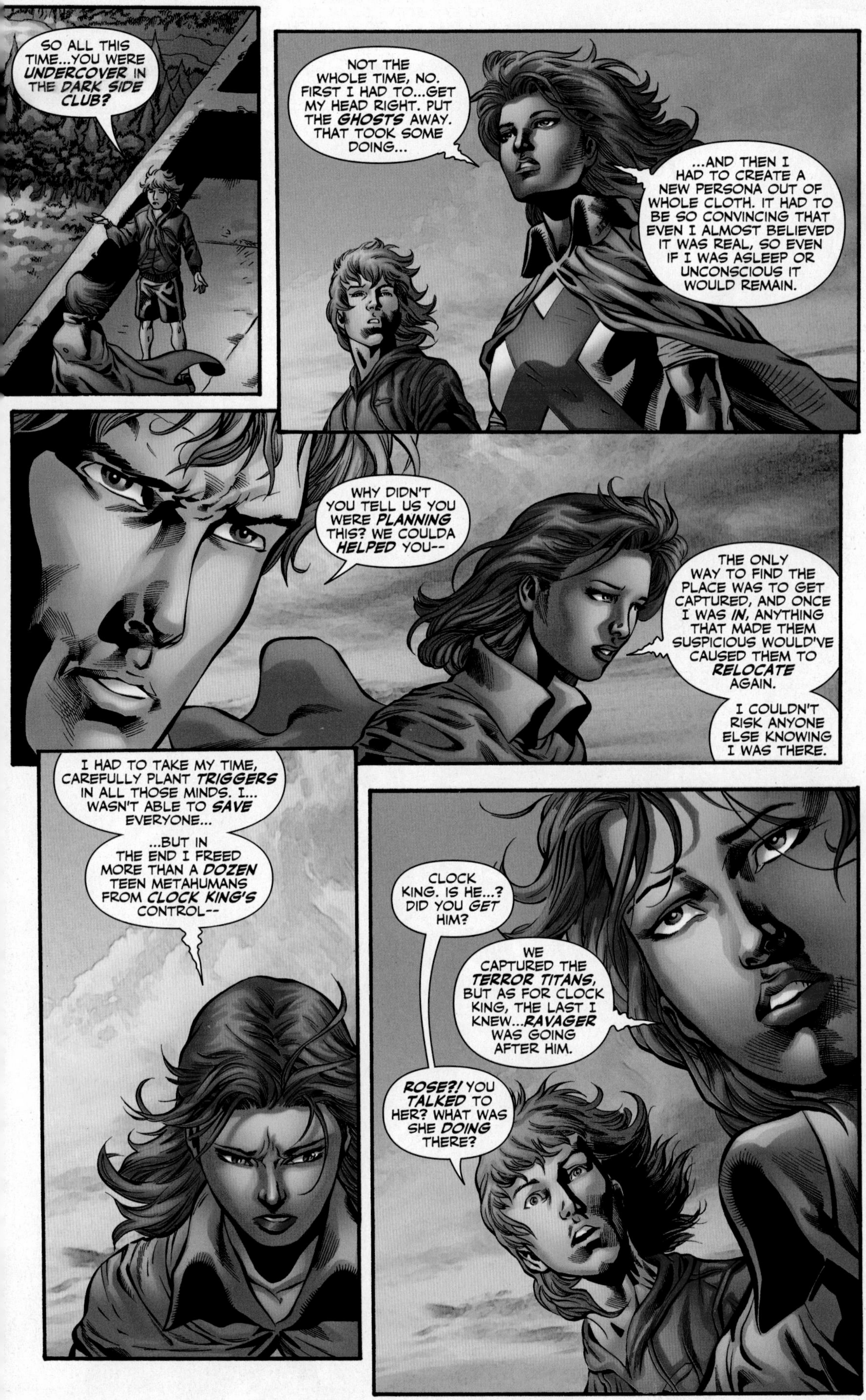

SO ALL THIS TIME...YOU WERE UNDERCOVER IN THE DARK SIDE CLUB?
NOT THE WHOLE TIME, NO. FIRST I HAD TO...GET MY HEAD RIGHT. PUT THE GHOSTS AWAY. THAT TOOK SOME DOING...
...AND THEN I HAD TO CREATE A NEW PERSONA OUT OF WHOLE CLOTH. IT HAD TO BE SO CONVINCING THAT EVEN I ALMOST BELIEVED IT WAS REAL, SO EVEN IF I WAS ASLEEP OR UNCONSCIOUS IT WOULD REMAIN.
WHY DIDN'T YOU TELL US YOU WERE PLANNING THIS? WE COULDA HELPED YOU--
THE ONLY WAY TO FIND THE PLACE WAS TO GET CAPTURED, AND ONCE I WAS IN, ANYTHING THAT MADE THEM SUSPICIOUS WOULD'VE CAUSED THEM TO RELOCATE AGAIN.
I COULDN'T RISK ANYONE ELSE KNOWING I WAS THERE.
I HAD TO TAKE MY TIME, CAREFULLY PLANT TRIGGERS IN ALL THOSE MINDS. I... WASN'T ABLE TO SAVE EVERYONE...
...BUT IN THE END I FREED MORE THAN A DOZEN TEEN METAHUMANS FROM CLOCK KING'S CONTROL--
CLOCK KING. IS HE...? DID YOU GET HIM?
WE CAPTURED THE TERROR TITANS, BUT AS FOR CLOCK KING, THE LAST I KNEW...RAVAGER WAS GOING AFTER HIM.
ROSE?! YOU TALKED TO HER? WHAT WAS SHE DOING THERE?

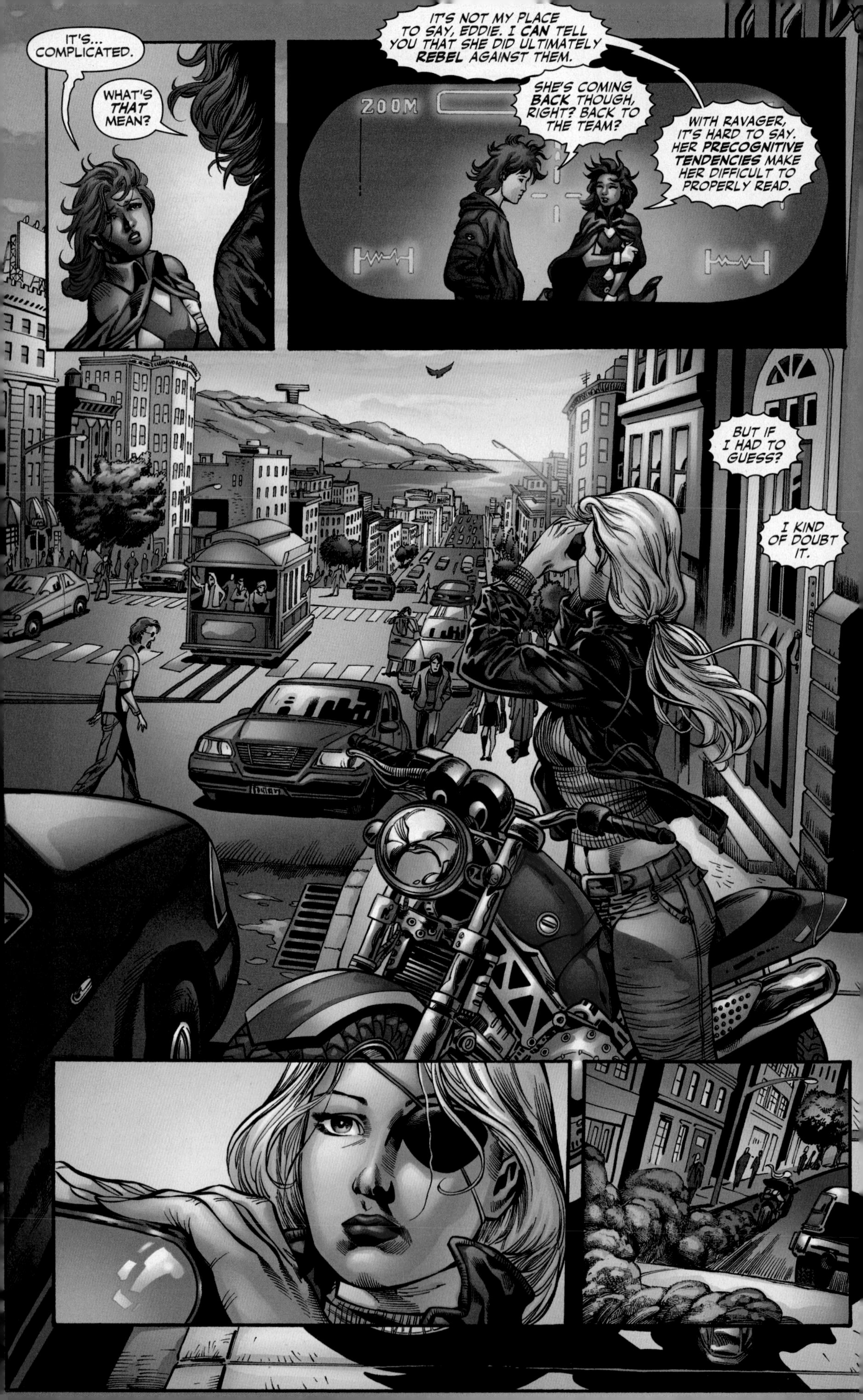
IT'S... COMPLICATED.
WHAT'S THAT MEAN?
IT'S NOT MY PLACE TO SAY, EDDIE. I CAN TELL YOU THAT SHE DID ULTIMATELY REBEL AGAINST THEM.
ZOOM
SHE'S COMING BACK THOUGH, RIGHT? BACK TO THE TEAM?
WITH RAVAGER, IT'S HARD TO SAY. HER PRECOGNITIVE TENDENCIES MAKE HER DIFFICULT TO PROPERLY READ.
BUT IF I HAD TO GUESS?
I KIND OF DOUBT IT.

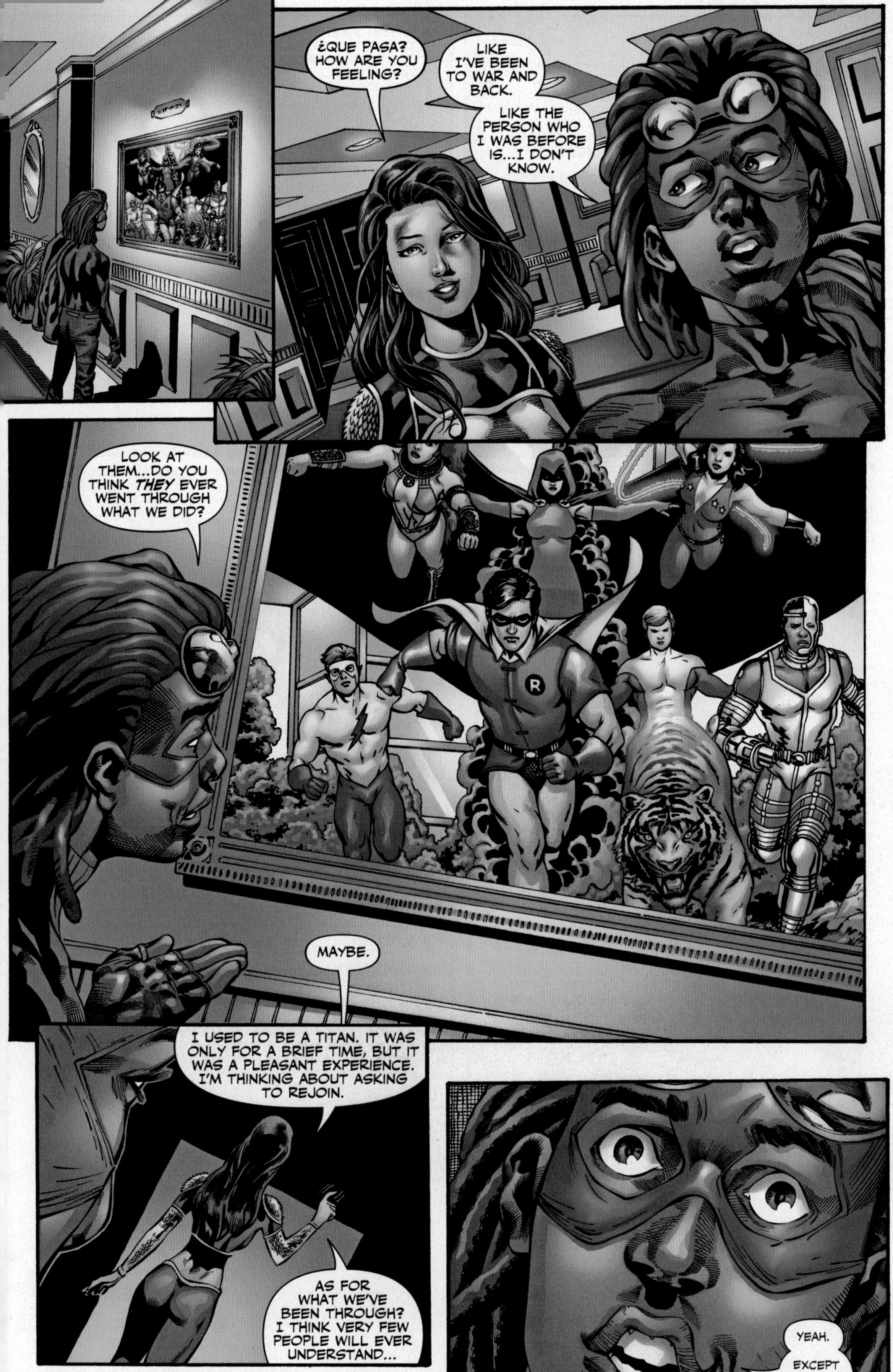

¿QUE PASA? HOW ARE YOU FEELING?
LIKE I'VE BEEN TO WAR AND BACK.
LIKE THE PERSON WHO I WAS BEFORE IS...I DON'T KNOW.
LOOK AT THEM...DO YOU THINK THEY EVER WENT THROUGH WHAT WE DID?
MAYBE.
I USED TO BE A TITAN. IT WAS ONLY FOR A BRIEF TIME, BUT IT WAS A PLEASANT EXPERIENCE. I'M THINKING ABOUT ASKING TO REJOIN.
AS FOR WHAT WE'VE BEEN THROUGH? I THINK VERY FEW PEOPLE WILL EVER UNDERSTAND...
YEAH.
EXCEPT US.

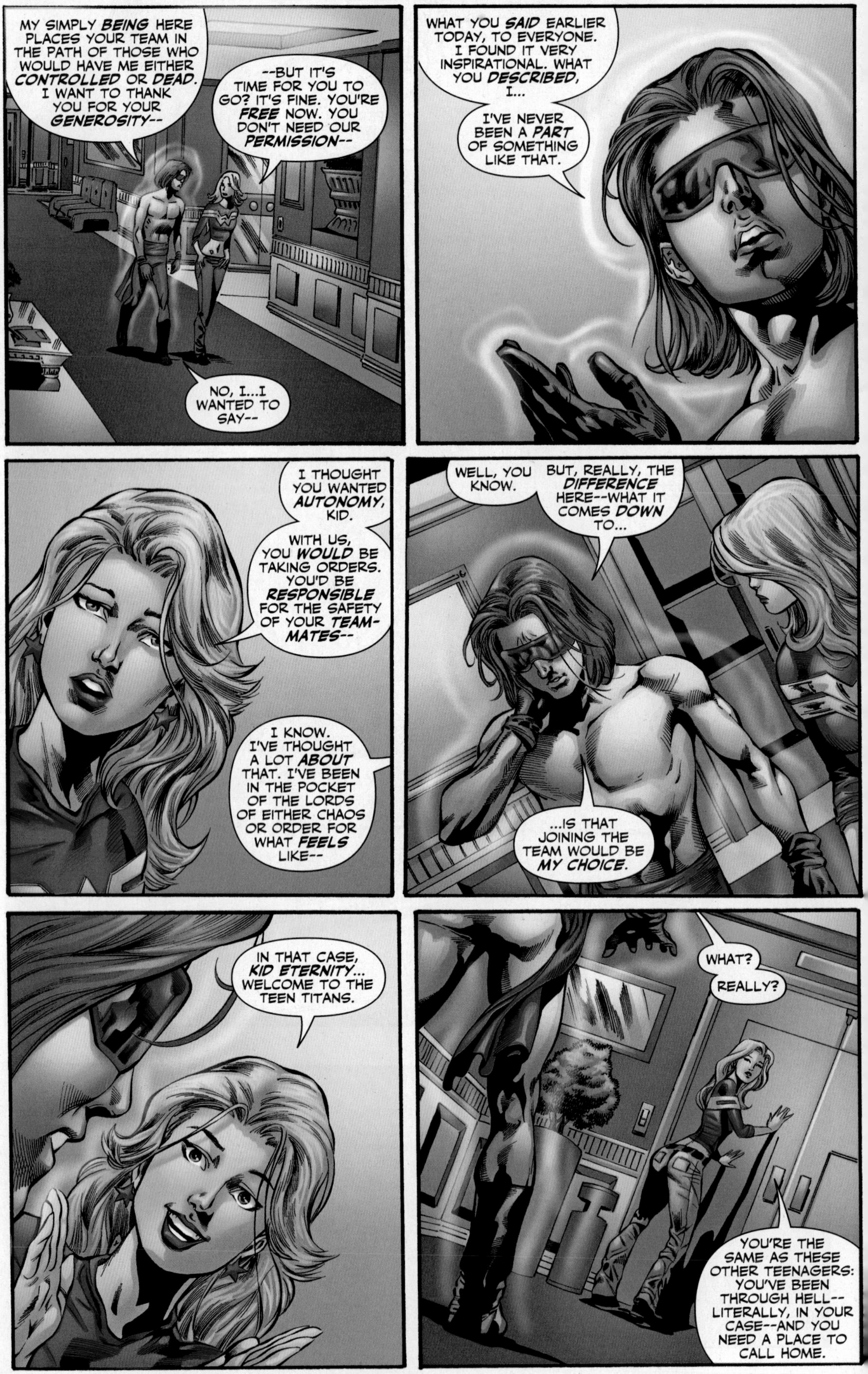
MY SIMPLY BEING HERE PLACES YOUR TEAM IN THE PATH OF THOSE WHO WOULD HAVE ME EITHER CONTROLLED OR DEAD. I WANT TO THANK YOU FOR YOUR GENEROSITY--
--BUT IT'S TIME FOR YOU TO GO? IT'S FINE. YOU'RE FREE NOW. YOU DON'T NEED OUR PERMISSION--
NO, I...I WANTED TO SAY--
WHAT YOU SAID EARLIER TODAY, TO EVERYONE. I FOUND IT VERY INSPIRATIONAL. WHAT YOU DESCRIBED, I...
I'VE NEVER BEEN A PART OF SOMETHING LIKE THAT.
I THOUGHT YOU WANTED AUTONOMY, KID.
WITH US, YOU WOULD BE TAKING ORDERS. YOU'D BE RESPONSIBLE FOR THE SAFETY OF YOUR TEAM-MATES--
I KNOW. I'VE THOUGHT A LOT ABOUT THAT. I'VE BEEN IN THE POCKET OF THE LORDS OF EITHER CHAOS OR ORDER FOR WHAT FEELS LIKE--
WELL, YOU KNOW.
BUT, REALLY, THE DIFFERENCE HERE--WHAT IT COMES DOWN TO...
...IS THAT JOINING THE TEAM WOULD BE MY CHOICE.
IN THAT CASE, KID ETERNITY... WELCOME TO THE TEEN TITANS.
WHAT?
REALLY?
YOU'RE THE SAME AS THESE OTHER TEENAGERS: YOU'VE BEEN THROUGH HELL--LITERALLY, IN YOUR CASE--AND YOU NEED A PLACE TO CALL HOME.

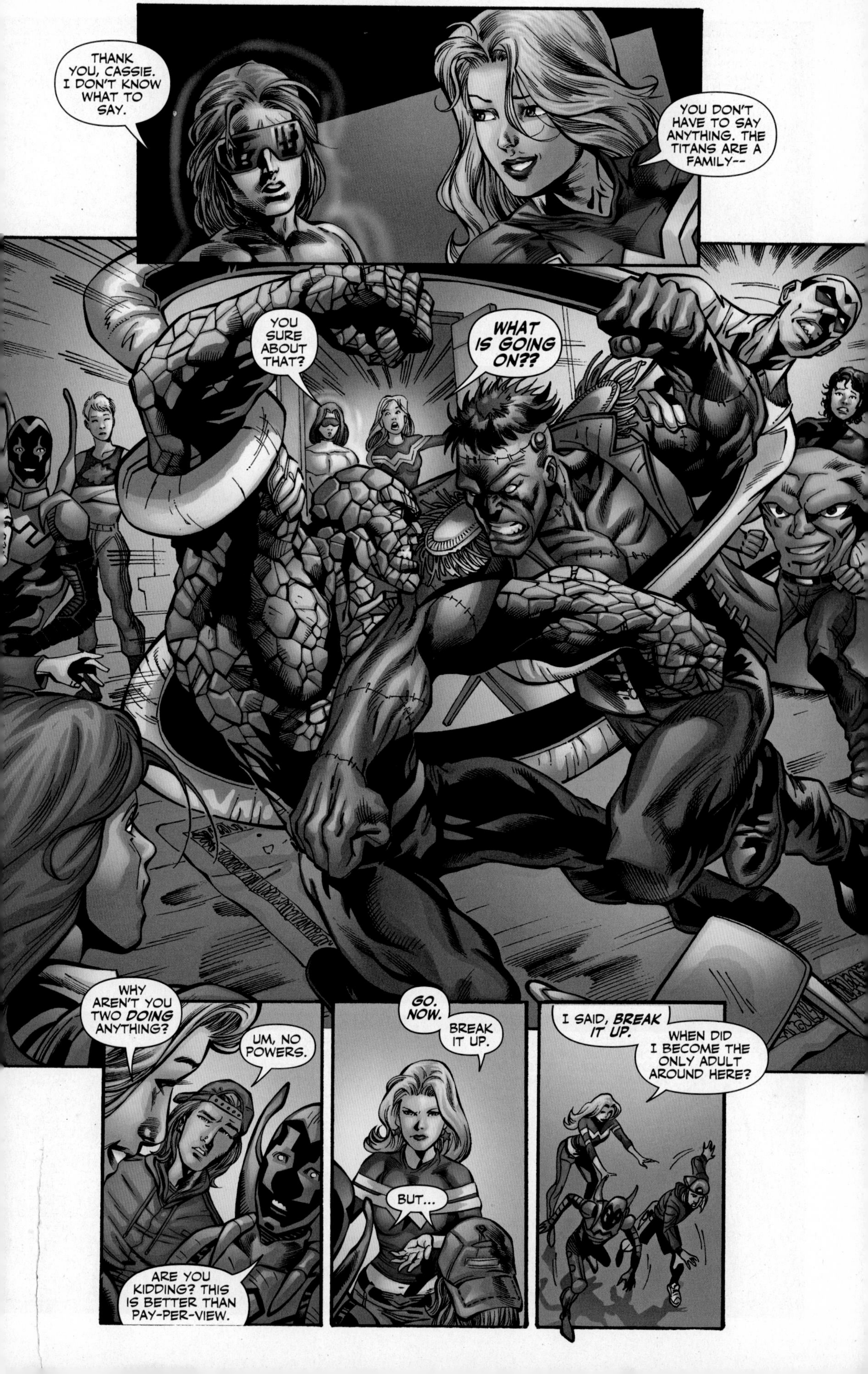
THANK YOU, CASSIE. I DON'T KNOW WHAT TO SAY.
YOU DON'T HAVE TO SAY ANYTHING. THE TITANS ARE A FAMILY--
YOU SURE ABOUT THAT?
WHAT IS GOING ON??
WHY AREN'T YOU TWO DOING ANYTHING?
UM, NO POWERS.
ARE YOU KIDDING? THIS IS BETTER THAN PAY-PER-VIEW.
GO. NOW.
BREAK IT UP.
BUT...
I SAID, BREAK IT UP.
WHEN DID I BECOME THE ONLY ADULT AROUND HERE?

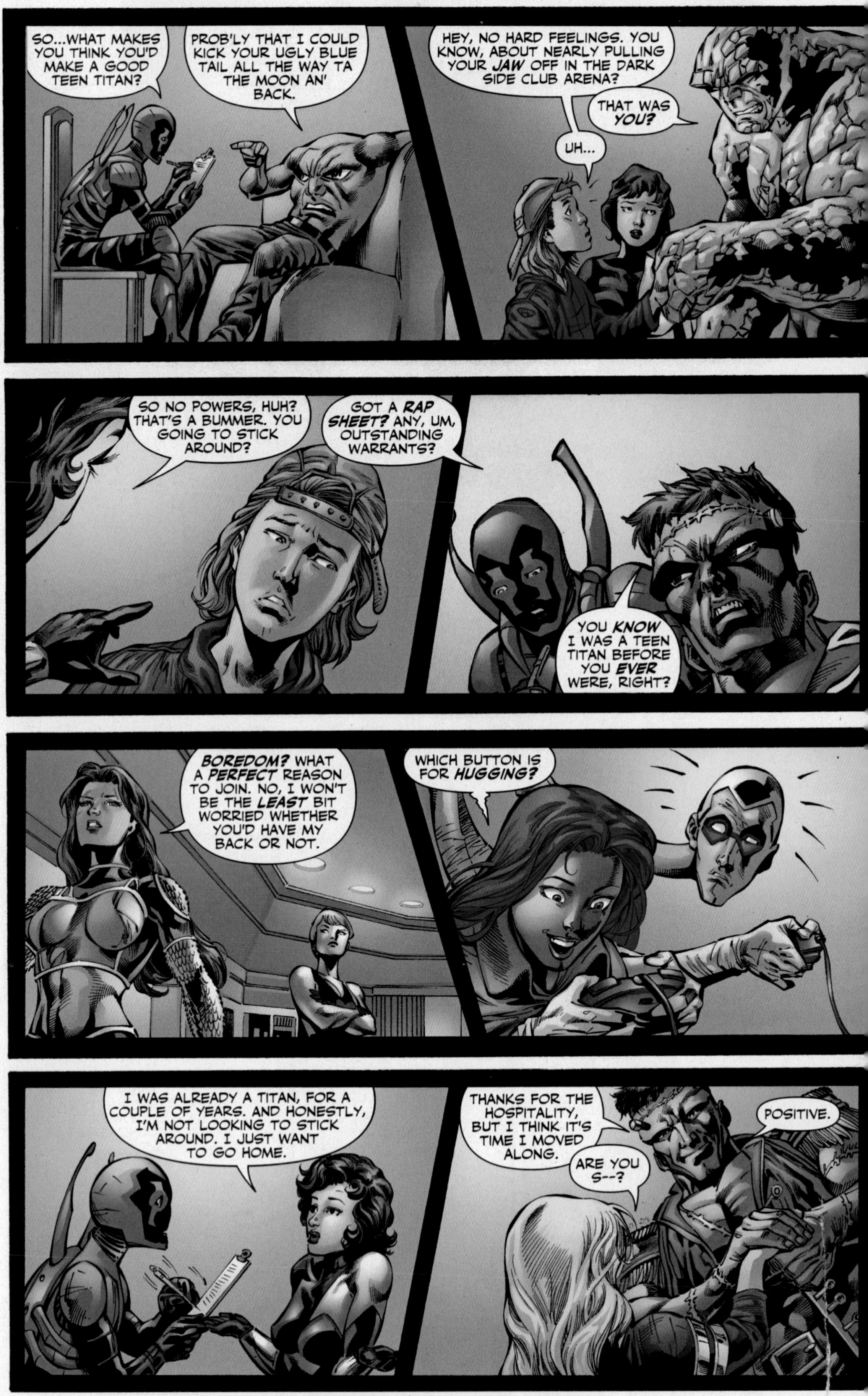
SO...WHAT MAKES YOU THINK YOU'D MAKE A GOOD TEEN TITAN?
PROB'LY THAT I COULD KICK YOUR UGLY BLUE TAIL ALL THE WAY TA THE MOON AN' BACK.
HEY, NO HARD FEELINGS. YOU KNOW, ABOUT NEARLY PULLING YOUR JAW OFF IN THE DARK SIDE CLUB ARENA?
UH...
THAT WAS YOU?
SO NO POWERS, HUH? THAT'S A BUMMER. YOU GOING TO STICK AROUND?
GOT A RAP SHEET? ANY, UM, OUTSTANDING WARRANTS?
YOU KNOW I WAS A TEEN TITAN BEFORE YOU EVER WERE, RIGHT?
BOREDOM? WHAT A PERFECT REASON TO JOIN. NO, I WON'T BE THE LEAST BIT WORRIED WHETHER YOU'D HAVE MY BACK OR NOT.
WHICH BUTTON IS FOR HUGGING?
I WAS ALREADY A TITAN, FOR A COUPLE OF YEARS. AND HONESTLY, I'M NOT LOOKING TO STICK AROUND. I JUST WANT TO GO HOME.
THANKS FOR THE HOSPITALITY, BUT I THINK IT'S TIME I MOVED ALONG.
ARE YOU S--?
POSITIVE.

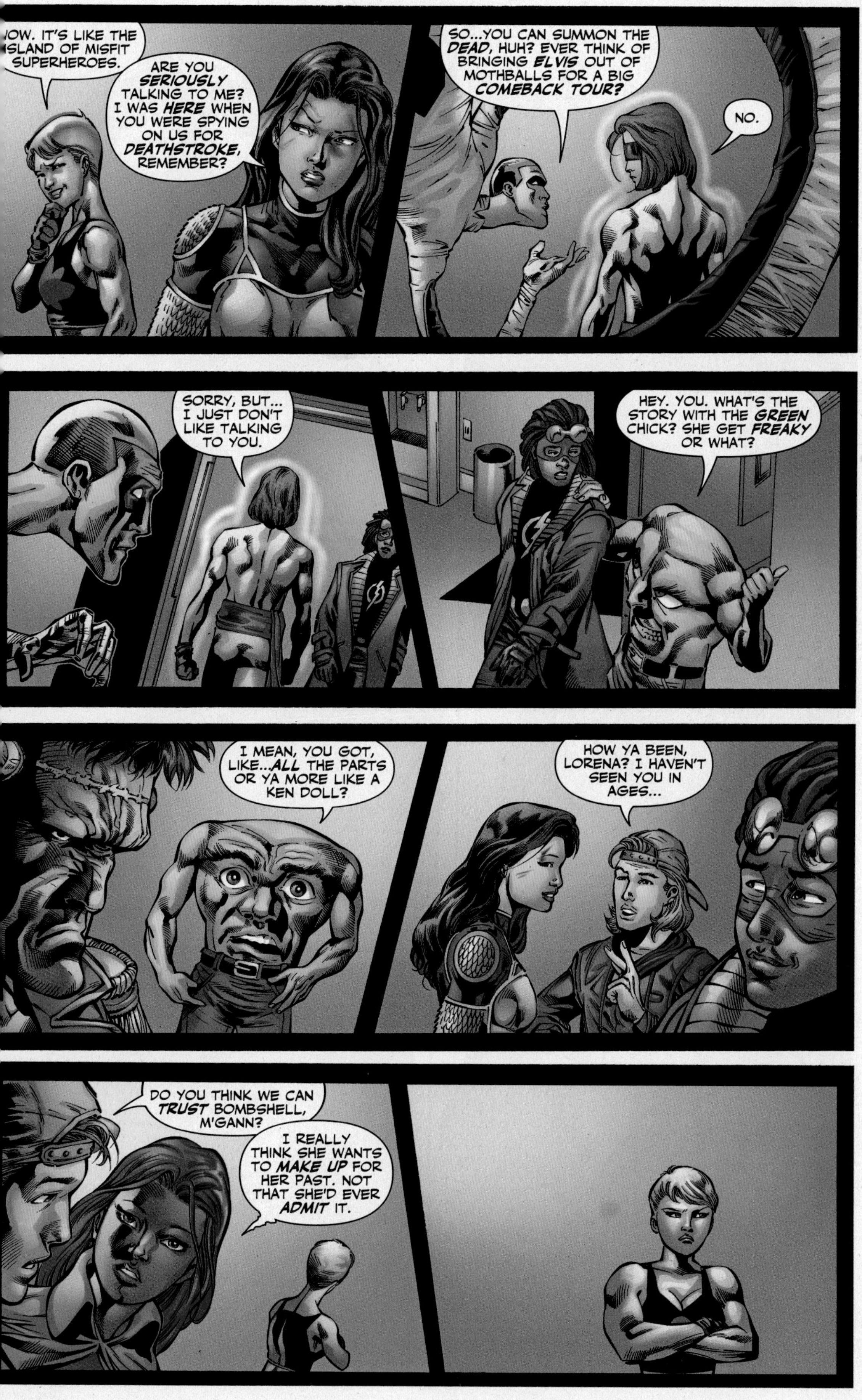
WOW. IT'S LIKE THE ISLAND OF MISFIT SUPERHEROES.
ARE YOU SERIOUSLY TALKING TO ME? I WAS HERE WHEN YOU WERE SPYING ON US FOR DEATHSTROKE, REMEMBER?
SO...YOU CAN SUMMON THE DEAD, HUH? EVER THINK OF BRINGING ELVIS OUT OF MOTHBALLS FOR A BIG COMEBACK TOUR?
NO.
SORRY, BUT... I JUST DON'T LIKE TALKING TO YOU.
HEY. YOU. WHAT'S THE STORY WITH THE GREEN CHICK? SHE GET FREAKY OR WHAT?
I MEAN, YOU GOT, LIKE...ALL THE PARTS OR YA MORE LIKE A KEN DOLL?
HOW YA BEEN, LORENA? I HAVEN'T SEEN YOU IN AGES...
DO YOU THINK WE CAN TRUST BOMBSHELL, M'GANN?
I REALLY THINK SHE WANTS TO MAKE UP FOR HER PAST. NOT THAT SHE'D EVER ADMIT IT.

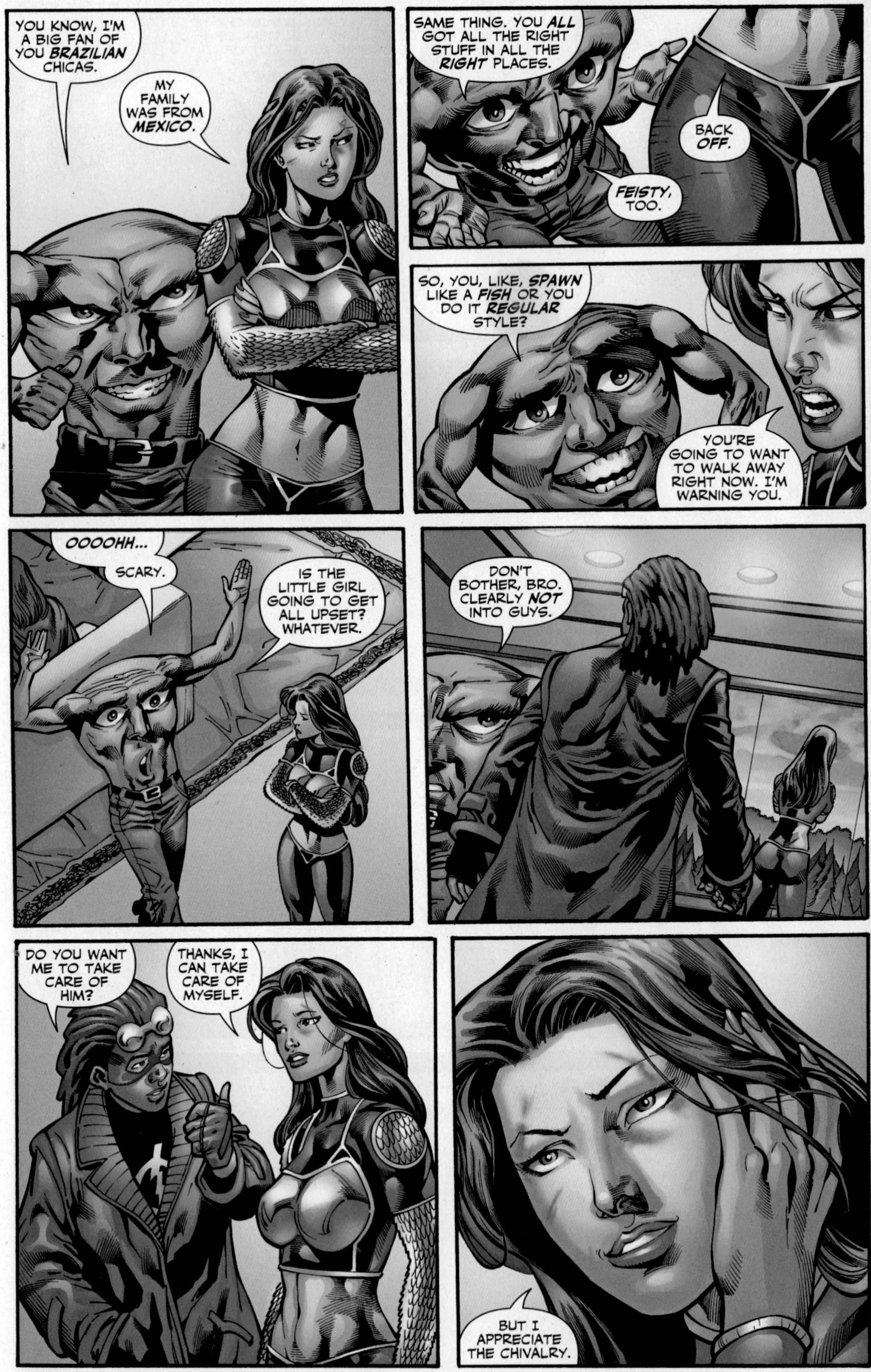
YOU KNOW, I'M A BIG FAN OF YOU BRAZILIAN CHICAS.
MY FAMILY WAS FROM MEXICO.
SAME THING. YOU ALL GOT ALL THE RIGHT STUFF IN ALL THE RIGHT PLACES.
BACK OFF.
FEISTY, TOO.
SO, YOU, LIKE, SPAWN LIKE A FISH OR YOU DO IT REGULAR STYLE?
YOU'RE GOING TO WANT TO WALK AWAY RIGHT NOW. I'M WARNING YOU.
OOOOHH...
SCARY.
IS THE LITTLE GIRL GOING TO GET ALL UPSET? WHATEVER.
DON'T BOTHER, BRO. CLEARLY NOT INTO GUYS.
DO YOU WANT ME TO TAKE CARE OF HIM?
THANKS, I CAN TAKE CARE OF MYSELF.
BUT I APPRECIATE THE CHIVALRY.

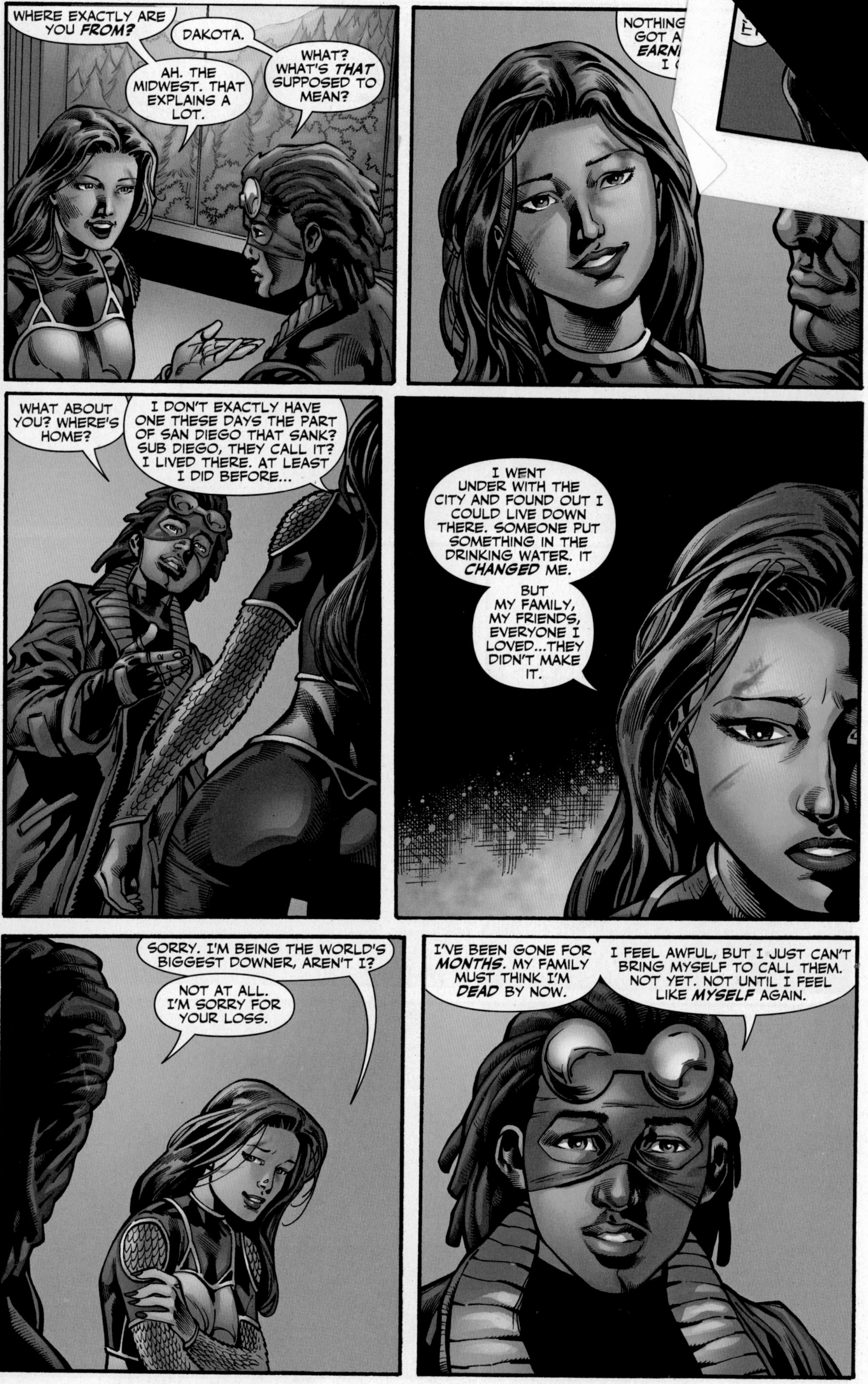
WHERE EXACTLY ARE YOU FROM?
DAKOTA.
AH. THE MIDWEST. THAT EXPLAINS A LOT.
WHAT? WHAT'S THAT SUPPOSED TO MEAN?
NOTHING
WHAT ABOUT YOU? WHERE'S HOME?
I DON'T EXACTLY HAVE ONE THESE DAYS THE PART OF SAN DIEGO THAT SANK? SUB DIEGO, THEY CALL IT? I LIVED THERE. AT LEAST I DID BEFORE...
I WENT UNDER WITH THE CITY AND FOUND OUT I COULD LIVE DOWN THERE. SOMEONE PUT SOMETHING IN THE DRINKING WATER. IT CHANGED ME.
BUT MY FAMILY, MY FRIENDS, EVERYONE I LOVED...THEY DIDN'T MAKE IT.
SORRY. I'M BEING THE WORLD'S BIGGEST DOWNER, AREN'T I?
NOT AT ALL. I'M SORRY FOR YOUR LOSS.
I'VE BEEN GONE FOR MONTHS. MY FAMILY MUST THINK I'M DEAD BY NOW.
I FEEL AWFUL, BUT I JUST CAN'T BRING MYSELF TO CALL THEM. NOT YET. NOT UNTIL I FEEL LIKE MYSELF AGAIN.

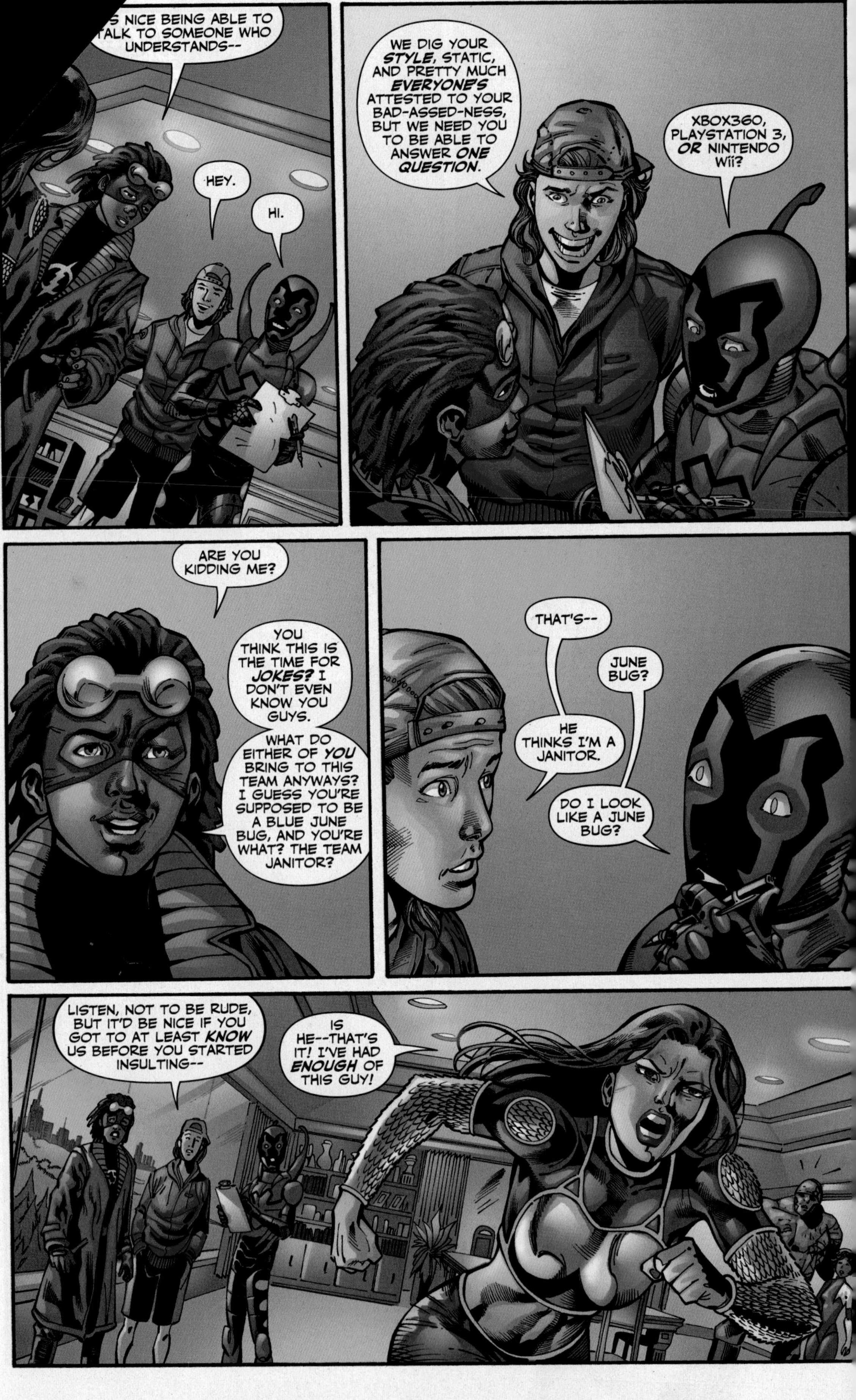
NICE BEING ABLE TO TALK TO SOMEONE WHO UNDERSTANDS--
HEY.
HI.
WE DIG YOUR STYLE, STATIC, AND PRETTY MUCH EVERYONE'S ATTESTED TO YOUR BAD-ASSED-NESS, BUT WE NEED YOU TO BE ABLE TO ANSWER ONE QUESTION.
XBOX360, PLAYSTATION 3, OR NINTENDO Wii?
ARE YOU KIDDING ME?
YOU THINK THIS IS THE TIME FOR JOKES? I DON'T EVEN KNOW YOU GUYS.
WHAT DO EITHER OF YOU BRING TO THIS TEAM ANYWAYS? I GUESS YOU'RE SUPPOSED TO BE A BLUE JUNE BUG, AND YOU'RE WHAT? THE TEAM JANITOR?
THAT'S--
JUNE BUG?
HE THINKS I'M A JANITOR.
DO I LOOK LIKE A JUNE BUG?
LISTEN, NOT TO BE RUDE, BUT IT'D BE NICE IF YOU GOT TO AT LEAST KNOW US BEFORE YOU STARTED INSULTING--
IS HE--THAT'S IT! I'VE HAD ENOUGH OF THIS GUY!

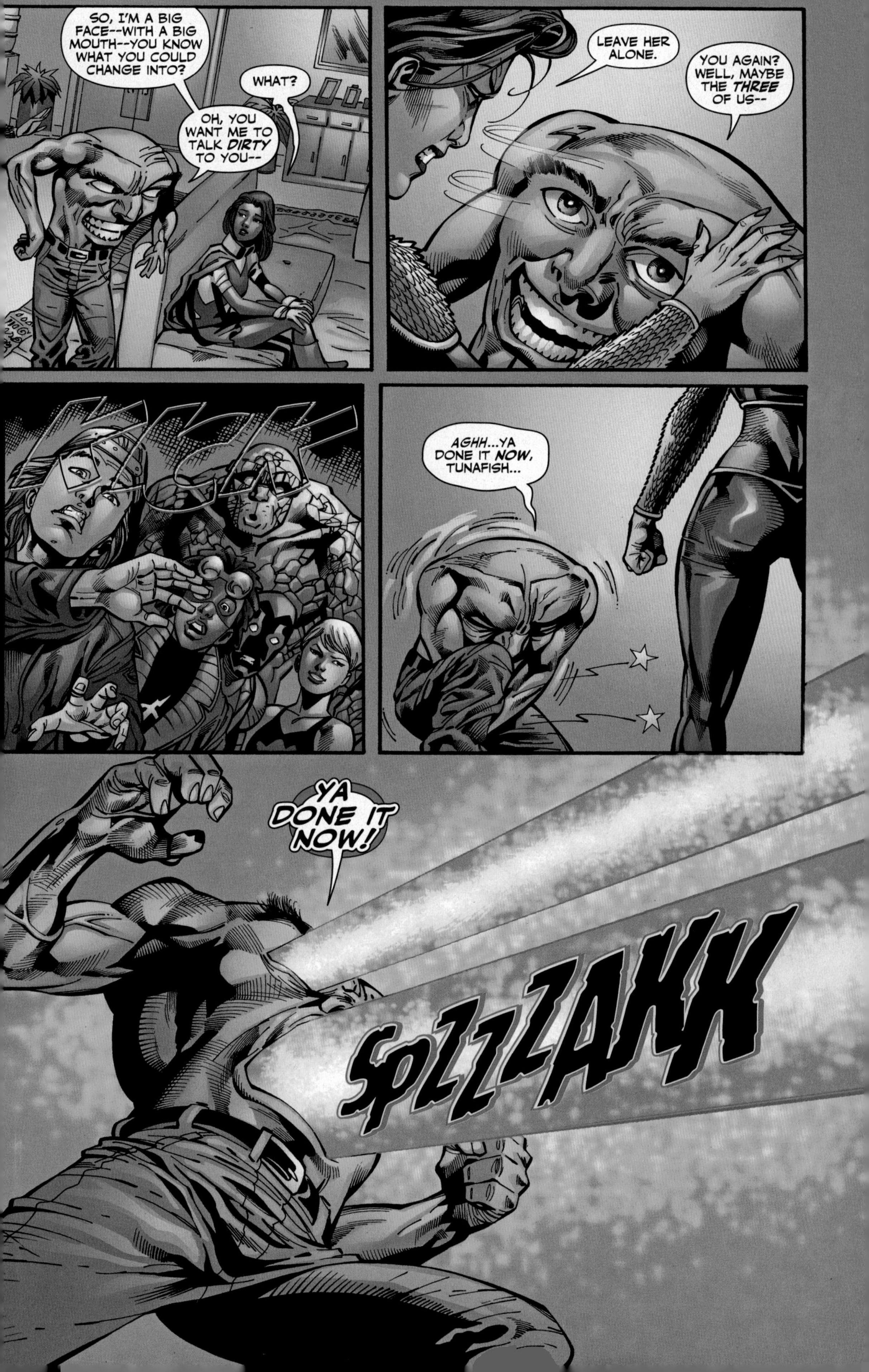
SO, I'M A BIG FACE--WITH A BIG MOUTH--YOU KNOW WHAT YOU COULD CHANGE INTO?
WHAT?
OH, YOU WANT ME TO TALK DIRTY TO YOU--
LEAVE HER ALONE.
YOU AGAIN? WELL, MAYBE THE THREE OF US--
AGHH...YA DONE IT NOW, TUNAFISH...
YA DONE IT NOW!
SPZZZAKK

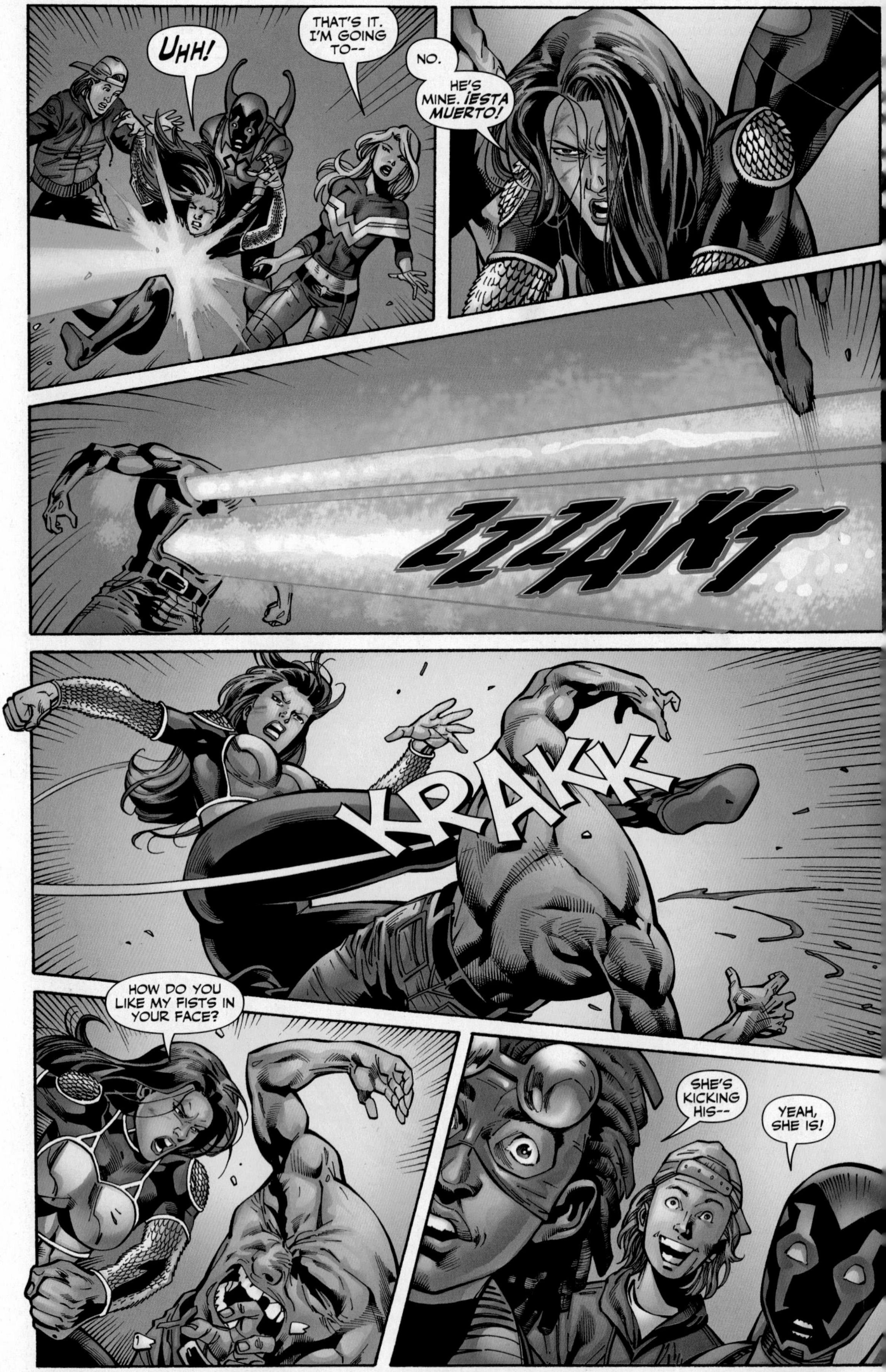
UHH!
THAT'S IT. I'M GOING TO--
NO.
HE'S MINE. ¡ESTA MUERTO!
ZZZAKT
KRAKK
HOW DO YOU LIKE MY FISTS IN YOUR FACE?
SHE'S KICKING HIS--
YEAH, SHE IS!

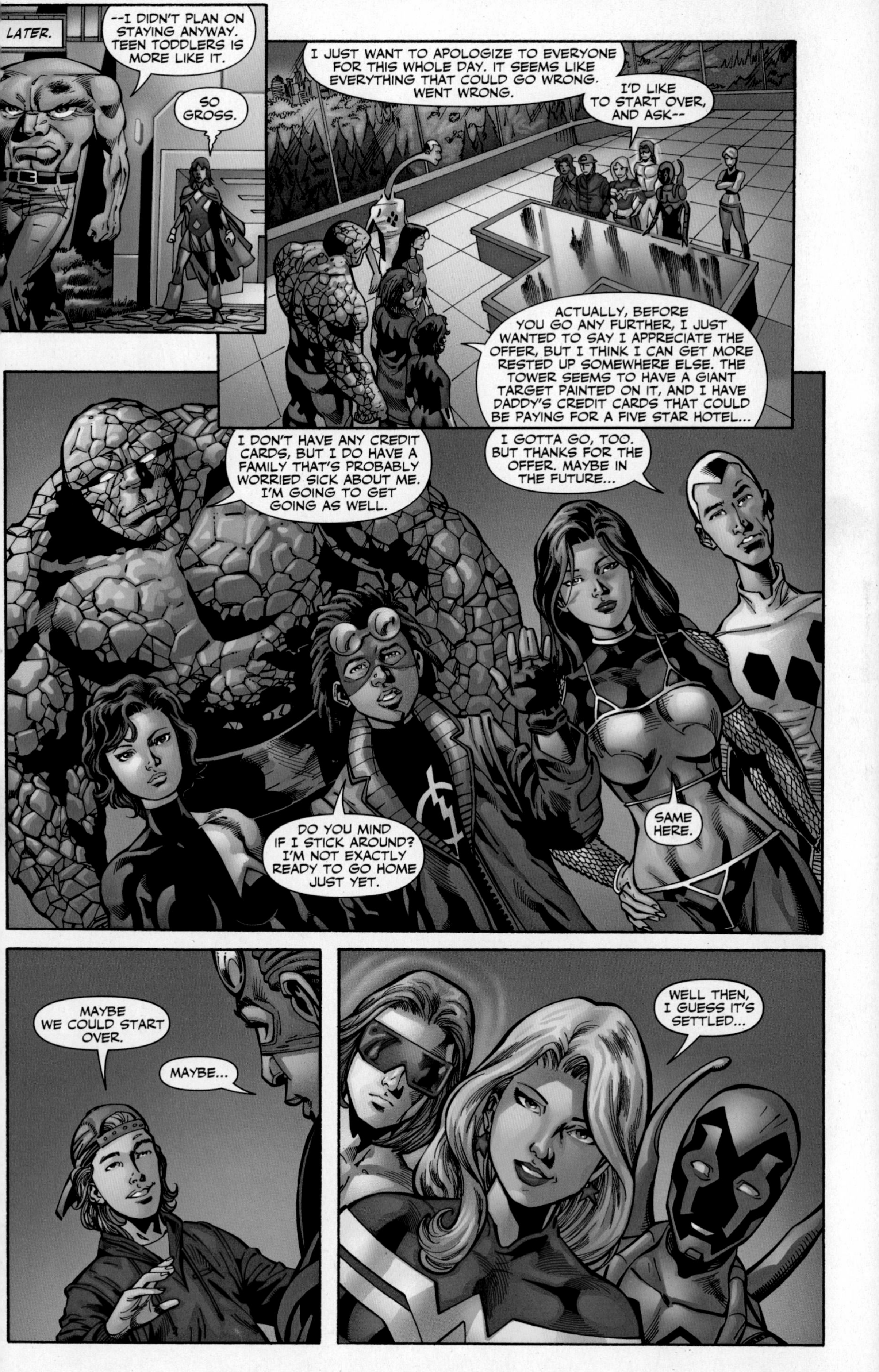

LATER.
--I DIDN'T PLAN ON STAYING ANYWAY. TEEN TODDLERS IS MORE LIKE IT.
SO GROSS.
I JUST WANT TO APOLOGIZE TO EVERYONE FOR THIS WHOLE DAY. IT SEEMS LIKE EVERYTHING THAT COULD GO WRONG. WENT WRONG.
I'D LIKE TO START OVER, AND ASK--
ACTUALLY, BEFORE YOU GO ANY FURTHER, I JUST WANTED TO SAY I APPRECIATE THE OFFER, BUT I THINK I CAN GET MORE RESTED UP SOMEWHERE ELSE. THE TOWER SEEMS TO HAVE A GIANT TARGET PAINTED ON IT, AND I HAVE DADDY'S CREDIT CARDS THAT COULD BE PAYING FOR A FIVE STAR HOTEL...
I DON'T HAVE ANY CREDIT CARDS, BUT I DO HAVE A FAMILY THAT'S PROBABLY WORRIED SICK ABOUT ME. I'M GOING TO GET GOING AS WELL.
I GOTTA GO, TOO. BUT THANKS FOR THE OFFER. MAYBE IN THE FUTURE...
DO YOU MIND IF I STICK AROUND? I'M NOT EXACTLY READY TO GO HOME JUST YET.
SAME HERE.
MAYBE WE COULD START OVER.
MAYBE...
WELL THEN, I GUESS IT'S SETTLED...

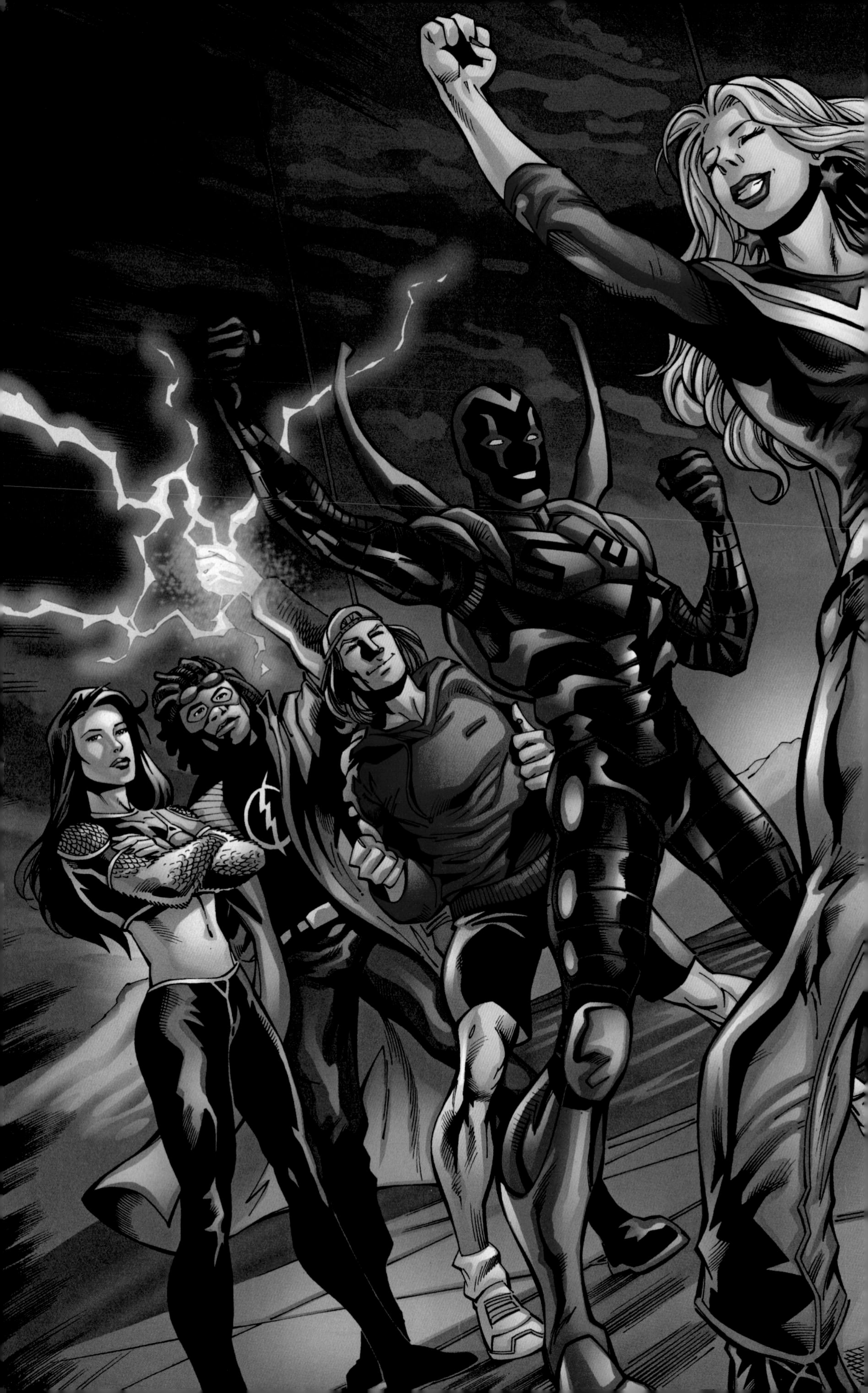

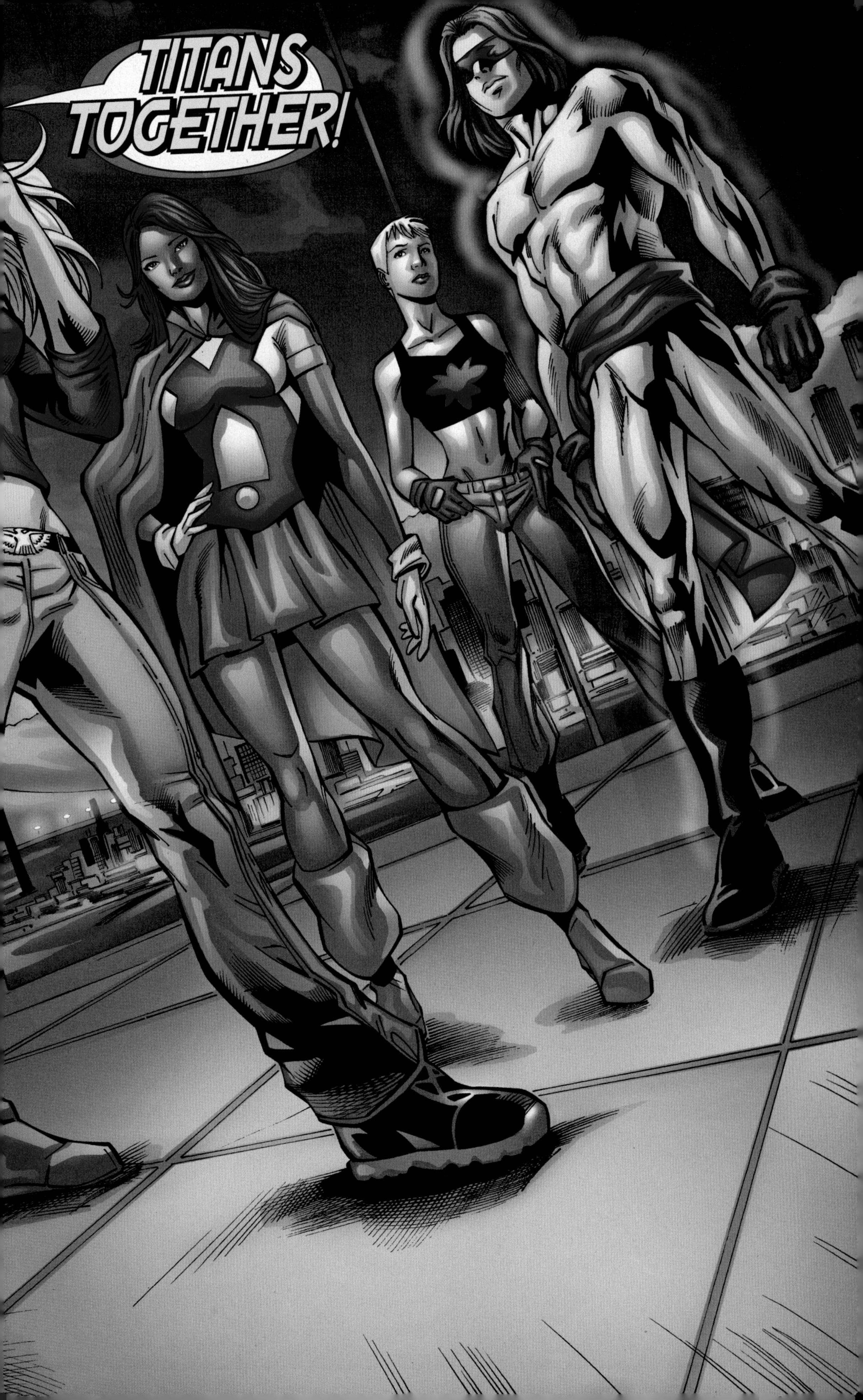
TITANS TOGETHER!

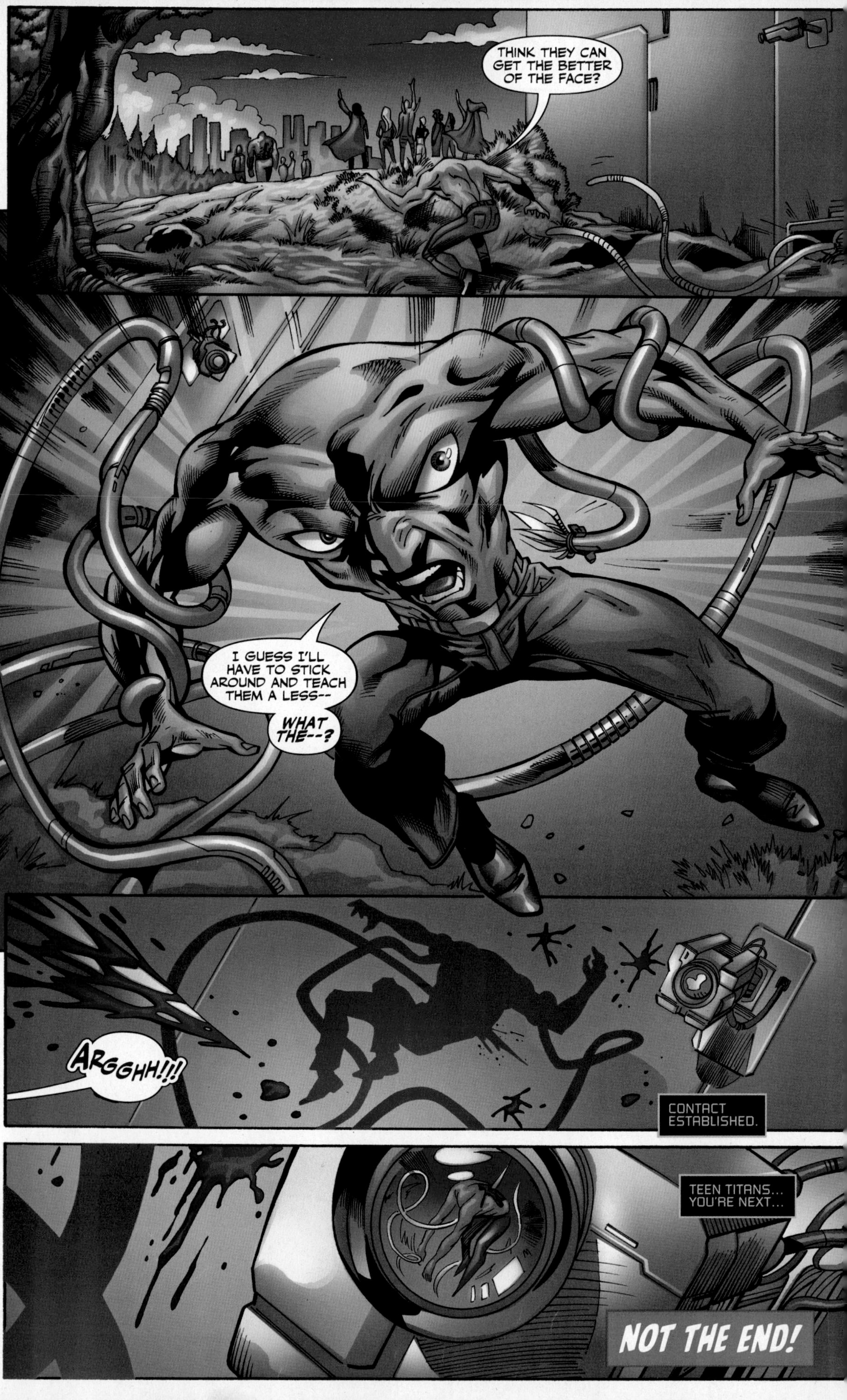
THINK THEY CAN GET THE BETTER OF THE FACE?
I GUESS I'LL HAVE TO STICK AROUND AND TEACH THEM A LESS--
WHAT THE--?
ARGGHH!!!
CONTACT ESTABLISHED.
TEEN TITANS... YOU'RE NEXT...
NOT THE END!

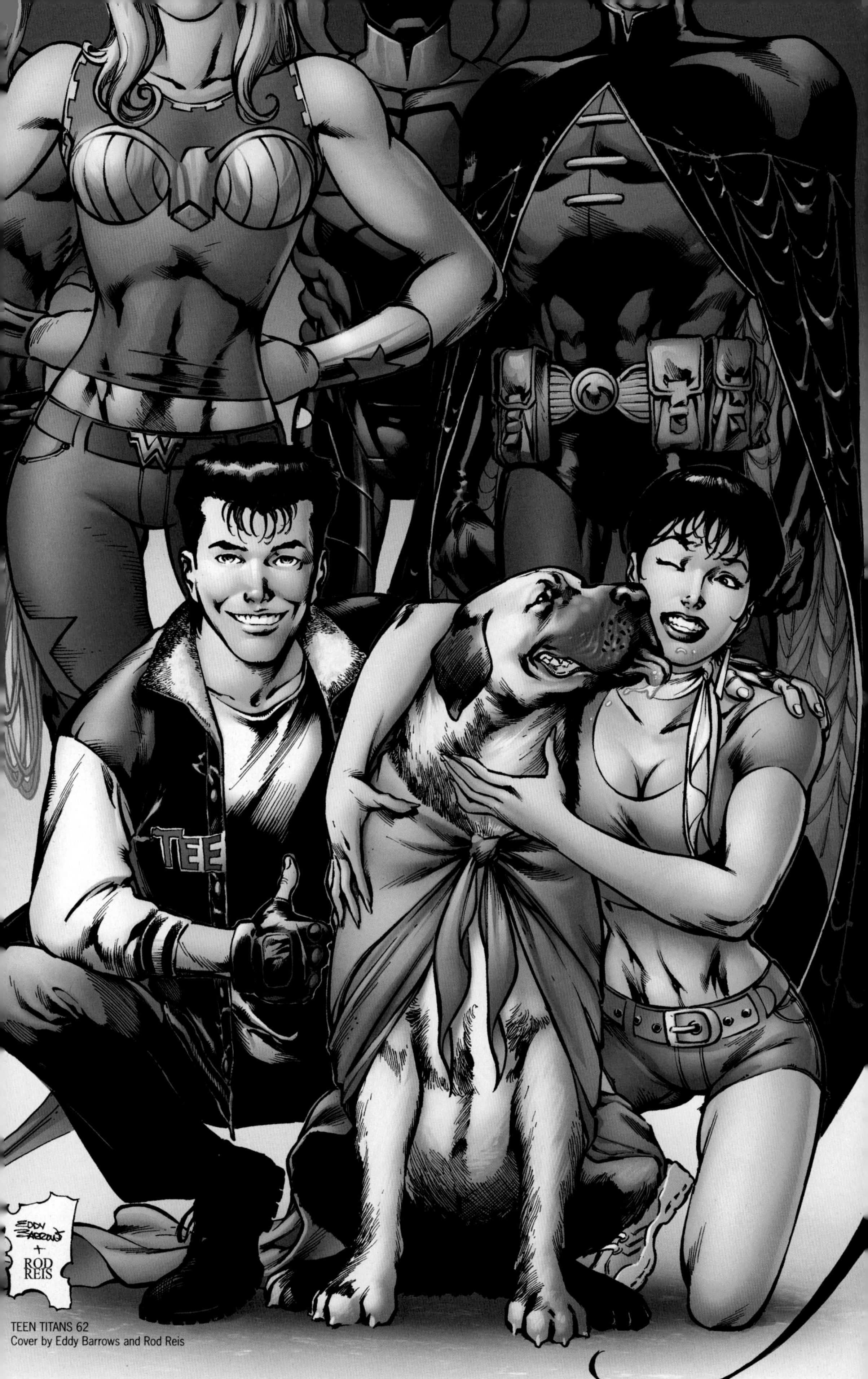
TEE
EDDY BARROWS
+
ROD REIS

TEEN TITANS 62
Cover by Eddy Barrows and Rod Reis

TEEN TITANS 63
Cover by Eddy Barrows, Ruy José and Rod Reis

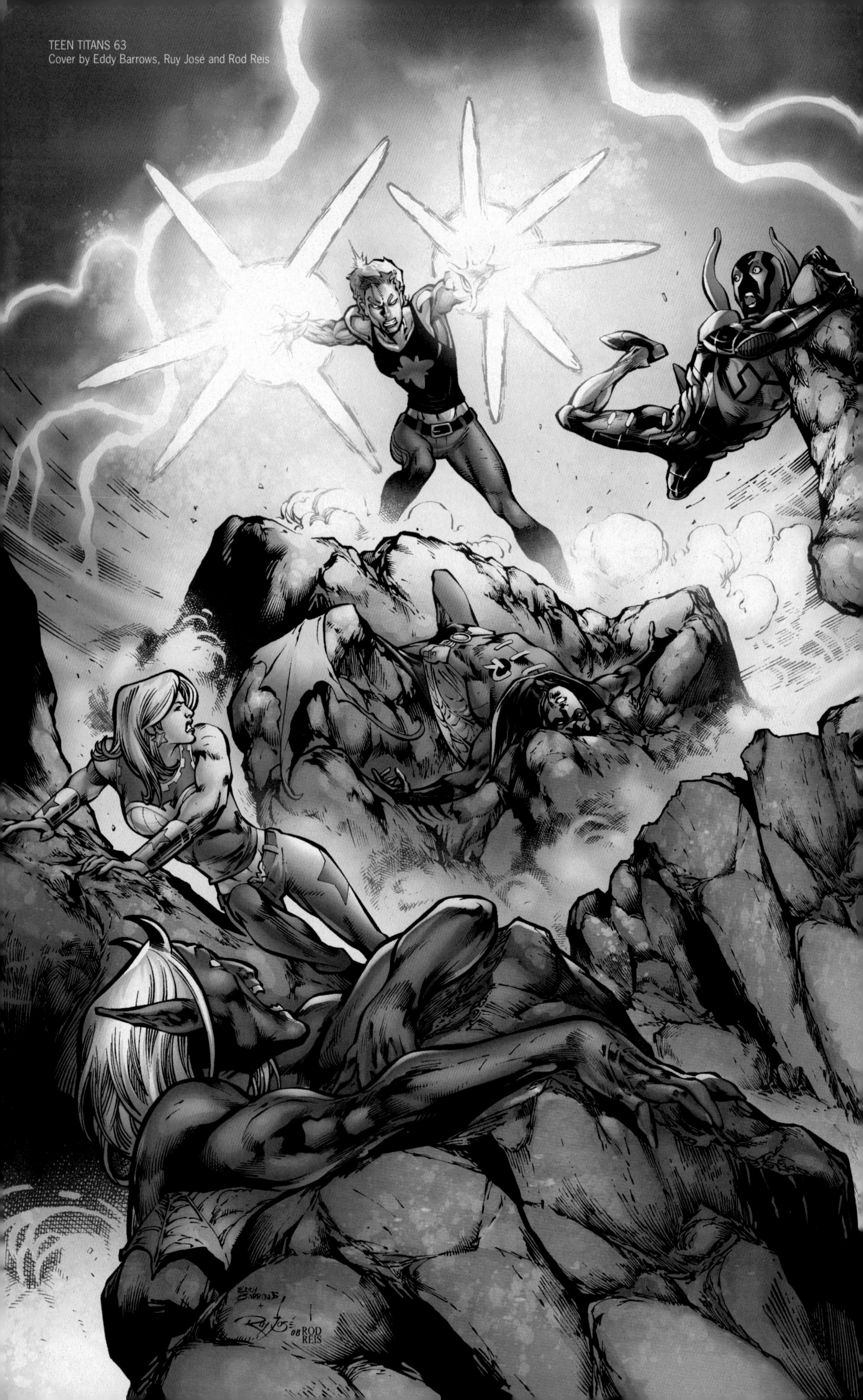

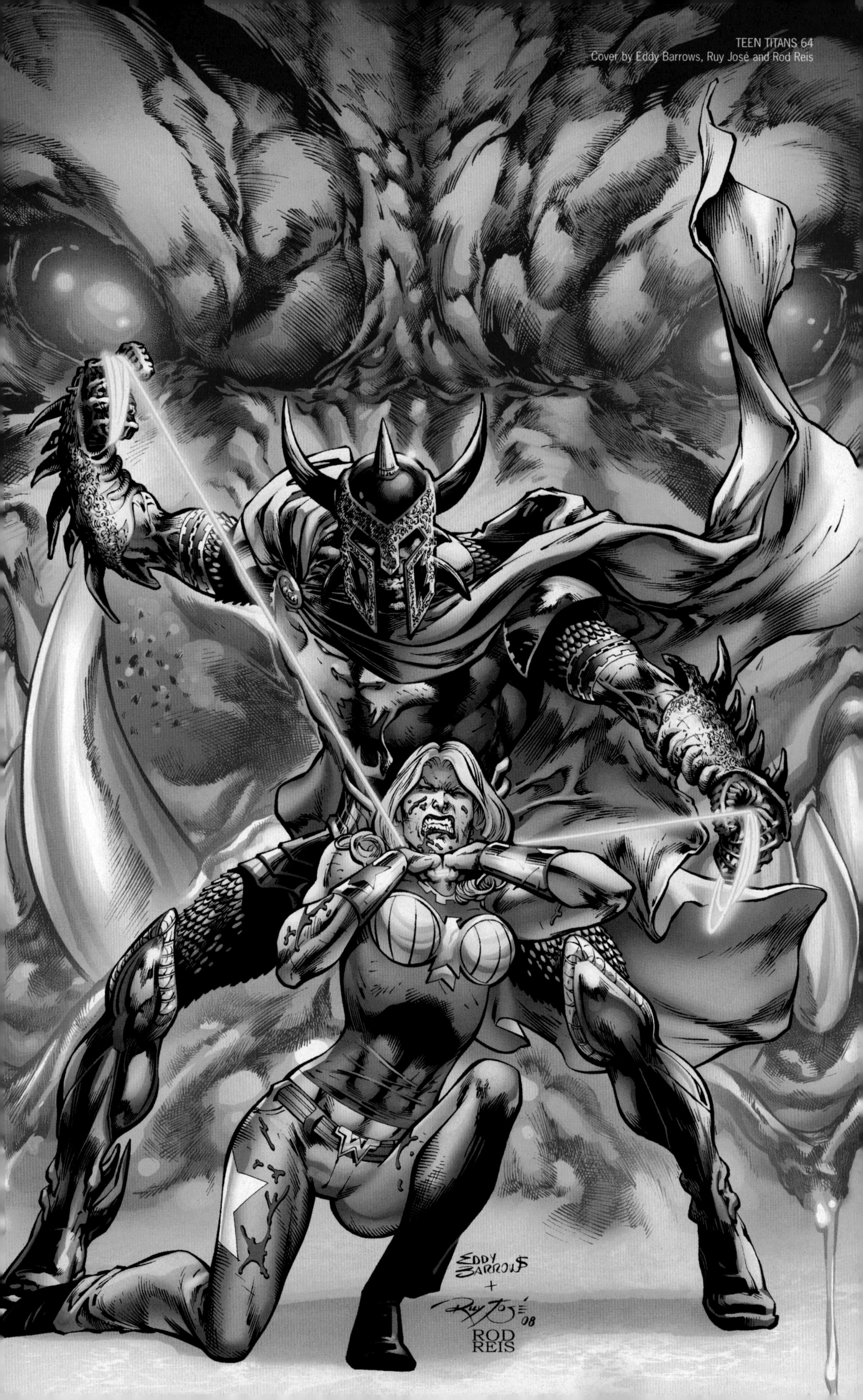

TEEN TITANS 64
Cover by Eddy Barrows, Ruy José and Rod Reis

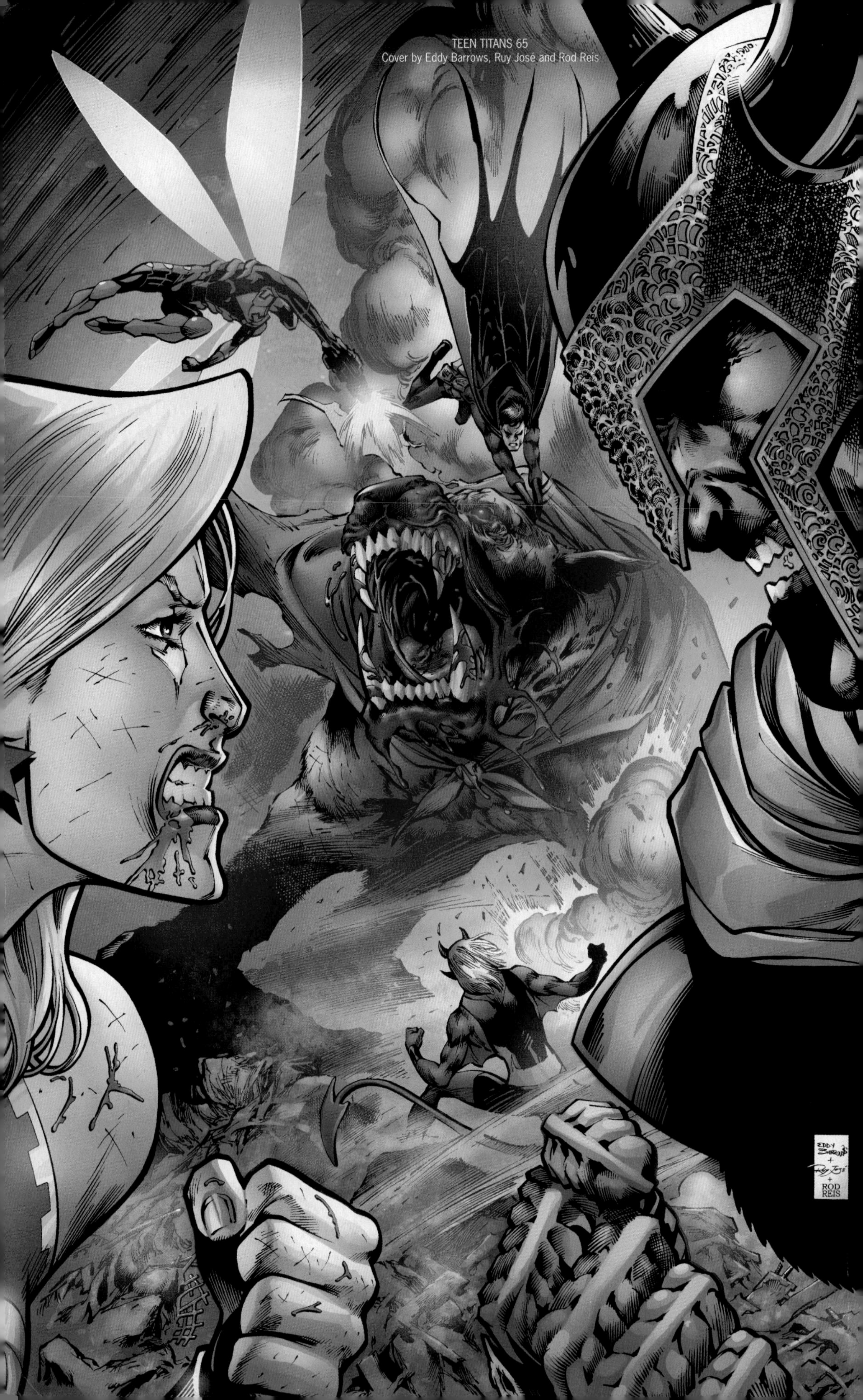

TEEN TITANS 65
Cover by Eddy Barrows, Ruy José and Rod Reis

TEEN TITANS 66
Cover by Eddy Barrows, Ruy José and Rod Reis

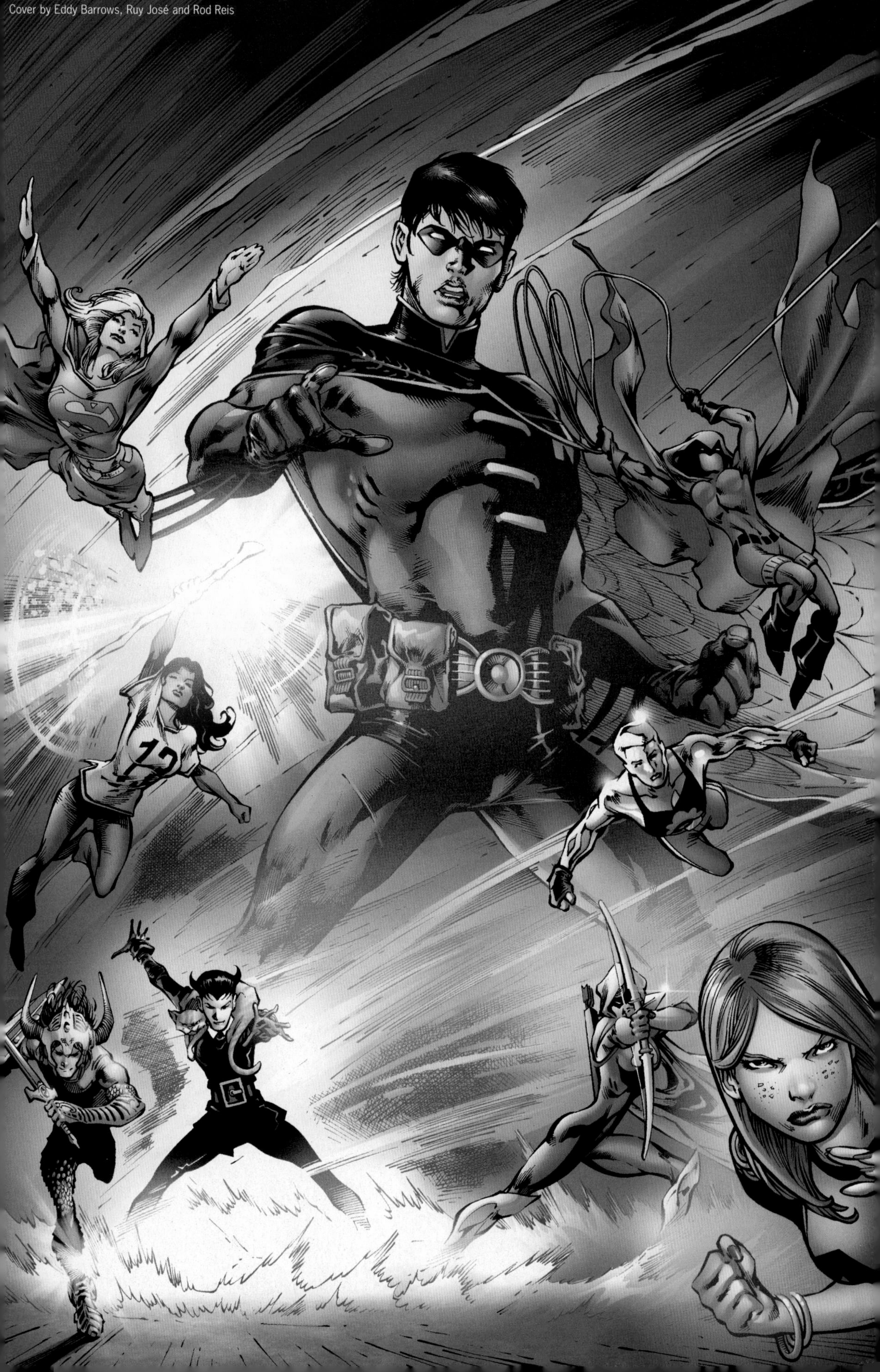

12

TEEN TITANS 67
Cover by Eddy Barrows, Ruy José and Rod Reis

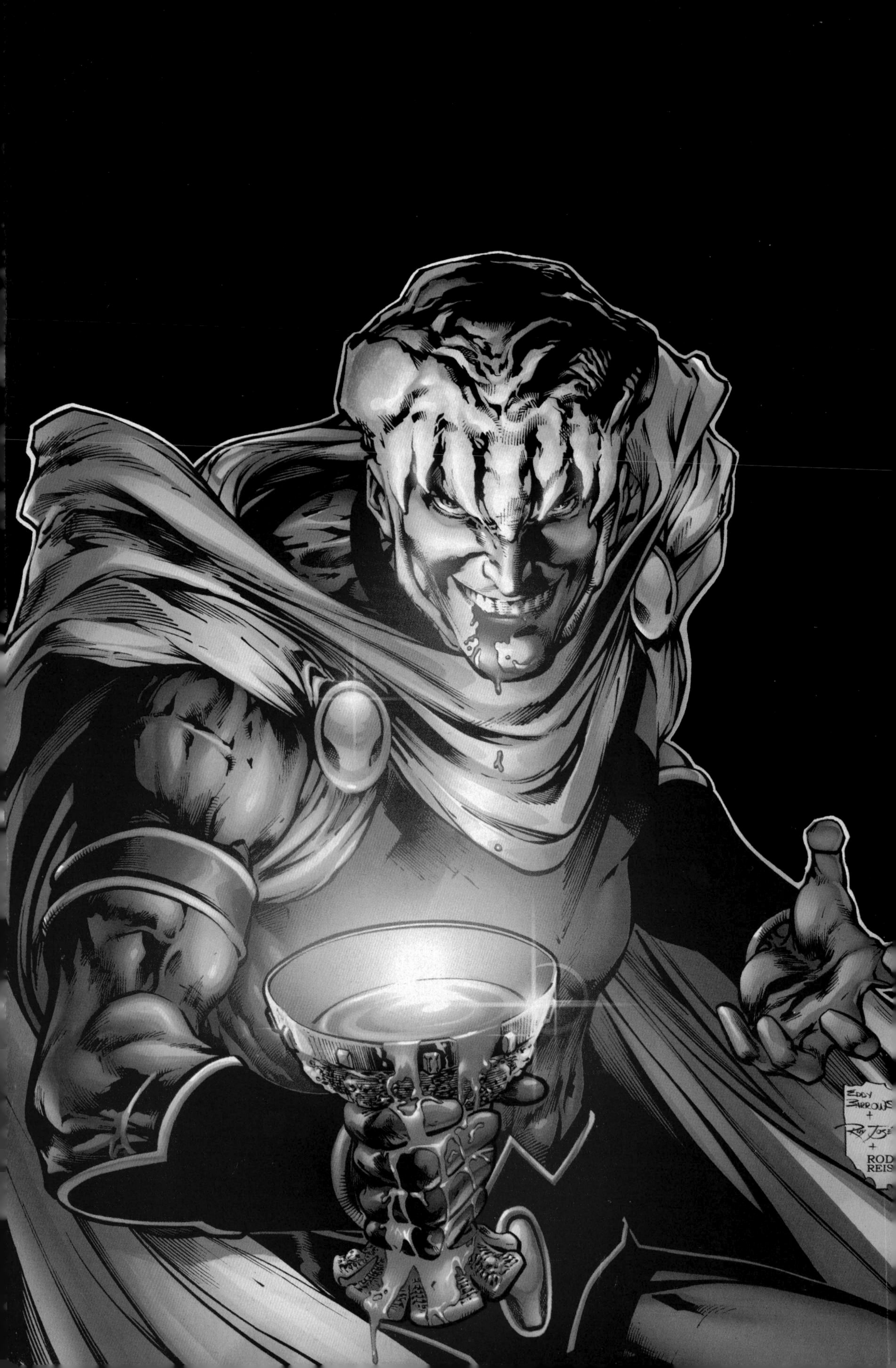
EDDY BARROWS + RUY JOSÉ + ROD REIS

TEEN TITANS 69
Cover by Eddy Barrows, Ruy José and Rod Reis

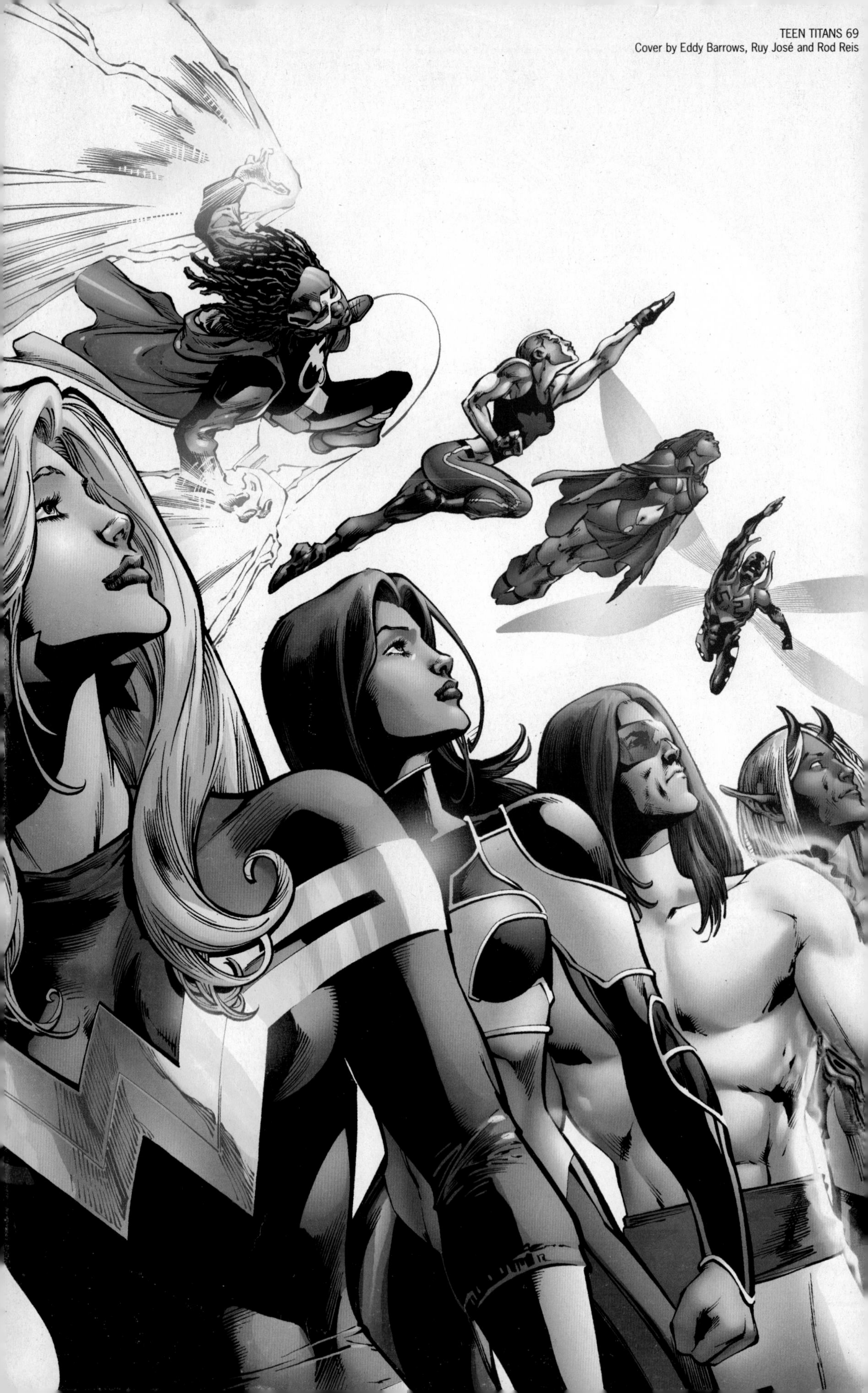